INTERWEAVEMENT
International Media Ethics and Rational Decision-Making

Mahmoud Eid

Custom Publishing

New York   Boston   San Francisco
London   Toronto   Sydney   Tokyo   Singapore   Madrid
Mexico City   Munich   Paris   Cape Town   Hong Kong   Montreal

Pearson
Custom Publishing
is a division of

www.pearsonhighered.com

ISBN 10: 0-555-03655-3
ISBN 13: 978-0-555-03655-6

Dedicated to the memory of

my father Abdel-Fattah Eid,

who taught me how to be responsible

Contents

IV. PROMISE

List of Figures

List of Tables

Introduction

In this book, I present a media decision-making model—the Crisis Decision-Making Model for Media Rational Responsibility, or $CD\_M^3\_R^2$— that helps media or communication decision-makers understand what *should be* done in the event of an international political crisis. The model contributes to the *effectiveness* and positive performance of media practitioners when covering international political crises by rendering their performance *rational* and *responsible*. To establish the foundation for the suggested model, I have created a new concept—*Interweavement*—drawing together four major theoretical frameworks: communication, mathematics, crisis management and decision-making. In studying these frameworks, the dynamic ideational architecture of *Interweavement* represents the interactions among them, illustrating the mutual relationships, and consequently demonstrating broad interactive relationships between communication and the other three fields.

The role of the transnational media is an important one in normal times; in times of conflict its importance increases significantly. War—the most extreme form of conflict—finds its most dangerous expression when rooted in international political crises. Thus, it is during these times that the transnational media perform its most valuable role. In the terminology of international relations theorists, conflicts and crises are games that are played by rational actors. And so, given the significance of the resulting consequences, the decisions made by actors in any conflict or crisis are crucial, and the decision-makers in these times bear great responsibility. Media decision-makers, like political decision-makers, hold this responsibility towards their societies, but the question must be asked, how *responsible* are they really during such times? Given that the media are usually involved in conflicts and crises, and especially when these take their worst forms, i.e., protracted and international, do they act as *rational* actors when covering developments and occurrences? Overall, I focus on the role and responsibility of the media *within* international political crises.

1

The functioning of communication in international political crises is a double-edged sword: it can work towards managing the crisis in a positive way, just as easily as it can exacerbate the situation. Although the blame should not be laid solely on the mass media, since they are influenced by the circumstances and situations in which they function, it is still necessary that they do whatever possible to function on the positive side of the sword. Thus, as long their decisions are well-made, they will work towards the de-escalation of the crisis; to help them do this, they will need to follow a careful decision-making process.

There is an insufficient understanding among media decision-makers about the rationality of conflicts and crises. This is not only evident in times of conflicts and crises, but also when dealing with situations where ethical principles are at the forefront. Telling the truth is one obvious example. It can happen that the media tell the truth as they know it, but what if what they know are in fact lies or distorted facts? The unavoidable end result is that they repeat, or tell, lies. Further, what about the concepts of the subjectivity of truths arising from the societal or contextual construction of it? As such, what might be considered ethical practices from one perspective can be considered quite the opposite from another. It would seem, therefore, that there must be a way to solve these dilemmas and make media conduct more responsible, no matter what side of the fence they are on.

A reasonable solution to the problems media personnel face of not adhering to ethical principles in given situations can be found using mathematics. In game theory, there is one type of a game called the Truth Game. Although it only focuses on the ethical principle of telling the truth, the same logic can be applied to other principles, especially since this ethical principle is fundamental to most dilemmas, including within it a group of other principles that are expressed in the various codes of ethics. The Truth Game, which is explained mathematically in this book, highlights the fact that telling the truth is a rational conduct that, in general, leads to an optimal outcome for the mass media in their relations with their audiences.

It can even be argued that the media can play an influential role with the government by being truthful. That is, if rationality leads the media to be truthful and abide by ethical principles, they will not rely blindly on announcements by government officials or military authorities in times of crises and conflicts. Rather, they will access various sources of information ensuring that the veracity of this information has been checked and verified before passing it on to the publics. If this adherence to the truth is followed, then audiences will trust that what the news media say is true. But, importantly, if they find that the news media say "the authorities are hiding facts" or that there is no access for the media to the information, then the audience will think that the government is doing something wrong, since if they were not, they would not be afraid of the media's scrutiny. Thus, denying the media access or lying to them will lead to negative attitudes about the authorities. That is, the credibility of the media that has been acquired by playing the Truth Game rationally and telling the truth to audiences gives them power over authorities, but their choice of not telling the truth, which is irrational according to the Truth Game, will make them lose credibility not only with their audiences, but also in their relations with the authorities.

The case study that is used to test the model of this book is the international political crisis between the United States and Iraq. It is argued here that the crisis between the American administration and the Iraqi regime started in 1990 in the era of the American president George H. W. Bush and the then Iraqi president Saddam Hussein. There was a pre-existing set of issues that led to the crisis' first conflict—the 1990/91 Gulf War, which understandably started as a result of the Iraqi invasion of Kuwait on August 2, 1990. The actual conflict (in the form of a war) began on January 17, 1991, and ended with the liberation of Kuwait on February 28, 1991. However, and according to the explanation that is presented here, the same crisis continued after this through less serious conflicts until a new cause emerged to re-escalate it—the attacks of September 11, 2001 (9/11), on the World Trade Centre towers in New York—which reactivated the political crisis between the two political systems, this time embodied by president George W. Bush, but with the same Iraqi regime. This reactivation resulted in the 2003 War on Iraq. The second phase of activation—the United States-Iraqi Crisis that evolved from American accusations that Iraq possessed Weapons of Mass Destruction (WMD)—and its latest consequence, i.e., the 2003 War on Iraq, is the focus of the discussion covered in this book. The dates of announcements, events, and developments found herein include the following: those which came about as a result of 9/11; those from the pre-war campaign; those from the fall of Baghdad on 9 April, 2003, when Iraq came under occupation following a largely one-sided war begun on 20 March, 2003; Bush's declaration of the end of major military operations in Iraq on 1 May 2003; the transfer of power on 28 June, 2004, when U.S. civil administrator Paul Bremer handed over sovereignty to Iyad Allawi's interim government of Iraq and left Iraq two days ahead of schedule; and finally the bringing of the former Iraqi president Saddam Hussein to court on 1 July, 2004 to face charges which include crimes against humanity and genocide that led to his execution on 30 December, 2006.

The wide range of the international media's audiences has been watching, hearing, and reading, from the fall of 2002 to the spring of 2004, about the War on Iraq. Audiences have repeatedly heard and read words such as game, play, winner, loser, tactic, trick, deception, offensive, and defensive, as well as expressions such as "that is what makes this war such a gamble," "have a trump card," "the other side of this coin," "if the dice of war roll unfavorably," and so on. They have even seen pictures of Iraqi officials on playing cards.

Does it mean that this was a game? If so, what kind of game was it? When did it start? Who were the players? Were they adequately warmed-up? What strategies were they using and for what goals? Most importantly, was the role of the media in this game *effective*? These questions are among those that the book attempts to answer in order to gain an understanding of the crisis situation and the function of mass media therein. As such, I have discussed and analyzed the involvement of communication and transnational media during the United States-Iraqi Crisis and the 2003 War on Iraq in terms of relevant and significant concepts, theories, and approaches.

In the first chapter of this book, I have looked at the emergence of communication research and the different approaches to the study of communication, as well as the complexity of communication and the many theories defining and/or investigating it, in order to position a particular view of communication. Then I have discussed the nature of work inside news-writing departments, the structural and institutional organization of these departments, the process of news-writing, the influence of politics and authorities on news-writing, and the mutual cooperation between mass media and government. I have also examined the nature of communication during times of international political crisis, recognizing that communication is a double-edged sword which can either escalate or de-escalate the crisis situation.

In Chapter 2, I have discussed the connection of crisis management and decision-making to communication and mass media practices. I have explained the centrality of the concept of decision-making, and described the political decision-making process. Further, I have discussed definitions of the crisis management and decision-making processes; illustrated the nature and the performance of decision-making process under conditions of uncertainty or stress; distinguished between crisis and routine decision-making; showed the difference between a rational and irrational resolution of the decision process; and drawn on theories and approaches of decision-making. I have conducted an analysis to outline the main distinguishing characteristics of crisis compared to other similar stress situations. In addition, I present a discussion of the principles, requirements, and strategies of successful crisis management.

Next, by adopting communication as a decision-making process and recognizing that media decision-makers are required to work rationally and responsibly, especially in times of crises and conflicts, I have examined both the rationality aspect and the responsibility aspect of this required performance in Chapter 3 and Chapter 4, respectively.

In Chapter 3, I have explained the intertwined relationship between mathematics and communication. Further, the consideration of rationality, drawn from mathematical theory, along with its behavioral decision theory dimension have been introduced as a major concept that could be used effectively in the communication field. This, in turn, paves the road to using game theory to theorize the performance of communication between adversaries in the United States-Iraqi Crisis. To show how mathematics is required for, and useful to, the discussions and themes of this book, I have demonstrated the importance of the use of mathematics in different fields as well as its contribution to knowledge overall, and shed some light on historical use of mathematics as a tool in the social sciences and particularly the field of communication studies. I have also discussed how useful mathematics has been in pursuing a wide range of research therein. Because of its major relevance to studying the United States-Iraqi Crisis, game theory has been adopted here, and I have explained its major uses and discussed its basic assumptions. As a key concept for the book, rationality has been also investigated and its definitions and concepts relevant to this book have been highlighted.

The main objective of Chapter 4 is to bring attention to the importance of ethical and responsible communication, and therefore it represents a confined picture of ethical conduct in terms of its principles, values, and rules. Then, by applying these concepts to the topic of the book, the discussion draws on different theories, branches, and meanings of ethics, as well as providing explanations of ethics and morality, presentations of types of ethics, and illustrations of various philosophers' perspectives on ethics. It also draws on social responsibility theory, explaining its core theme and, in evaluating its efficacy, presents the theory's basic recommendations for the media. Following this, through an examination of journalistic ethical principles and their significance, I have discussed the idea of *good* journalism, and investigated its models and the requirements for achieving it.

In Chapter 5, I have addressed critical issues regarding media ethics and responsibility through an analysis of the media codes of ethics, and research into the principles and fundamentals of journalistic practices. I have also discussed the debate surrounding a recent growing trend towards adopting a universal ethical standard for journalism, and presented general criticisms surrounding communication ethics.

In Chapter 6, I have presented the deeply-rooted crisis between the United States and Iraq, and analyzed the rationality of the political decision-makers involved therein. The overall clash of interests between the two opponents has been explained, as well as each side's strategic interests, regional and global goals, and the policies required to achieve these goals. Then, an understanding of the conflicts, or games, of the crisis on two levels has been presented, i.e., on a world-wide basis (or globally) and situationally. I have also explained the rationality of decision-making in the 2003 War on Iraq on the political level to see how both adversaries conducted their pre-game warm-up and made their strategic choices.

The following two chapters have been devoted to game-theorizing the conflicts of the crisis at stake, in order to discuss the rational role of mass media as key players similar to the political decision-makers. In Chapter 7, I have demonstrated the gaming of the 2003 War on Iraq, specifically studying the conflictual situations between the adversaries and actors involved based on game theory. In Chapter 8, the core argument is to show the media's involvement in the crisis at stake and to provide an analysis of their rational performance in the face of ethical principles throughout the conflictual situations. In addition, I have explained why journalists should be willing to engage in ethical journalistic practices even in times when conduct is frequently unethical.

In Chapter 9, I have called for the drawing together of four major theoretical frameworks—communication, mathematics, crisis management and decision-making—into a comprehensive body, to provide the foundation for the suggested theoretical model in this book. I have created a new concept—*Interweavement*—for analyzing these frameworks and representing interactions among the frameworks in a dynamic ideational architecture, illustrating the possible mutual relationships, and consequently presenting a broad interactive relationship between communication and the other three fields. As such, it has been a necessary step in this book to investigate the convergence of ethics and rational thinking in order to show how rational thinking and responsible conduct are two fundamental weights for the *effectiveness* of the suggested theoretical model in the last chapter of this book. In addition, and after distinguishing between the various models of decision-making in order to uncover the relevance of rational models to the topic of the book, and the significance of the expected-utility theory in the analysis of decisions in time of war, a group of roots of theoretical threads from the major frameworks have been synthesized in order to use them as inputs for structuring the model.

Finally, in Chapter 10, I have explained the components, tasks, and nature of the suggested model—The Crisis Decision-Making Model for

Media Rational Responsibility, or $CD\_M^3\_R^2$—that contributes to making the performance of the media decision-makers *effective*, as a result of being *rational* and *responsible*. I have introduced the simple form of the model first, followed by individual explanations of the main components, their internal tasks, and involved recommended actions, and finally demonstrated the extensive form of the model. In doing so, I acknowledge the fact that the model neither offers a one-size-fits-all solution, nor contains *all* potential variables within its structure. However, the model's flexibility allows for the inclusion of other variables. Nonetheless, the model can be attuned for a variety of circumstances or other approaches such as those stemming from the political economy of communication. Thus it is a versatile model for media decision-makers. I have also explained the *theoretical*, *prescriptive*, and *dynamic* nature of the model, which feeds from a theoretical basis—a group of synthesized roots of theoretical threads from the major fields, in an entire-exterior degree of interweavement, a newly created concept or ideational architecture of mutual theoretical interactions.

I.   PREMISE

CHAPTER 1

Communication and Decision-Making

The central objective of this first chapter is to show the connection of concepts, theories, and approaches of two major theoretical backgrounds—decision-making and crisis management—to communication and mass media practices. Decision-making is central to this book as it is intertwined in discussions about various themes. This chapter demonstrates that both communication in general and the news-writing process in particular fundamentally involve decision-making processes. In Chapter 3, decision-making is highlighted through the explanation of game theory and its applications in conflicts and crises. Later, in Chapters 9 and 10, the establishment of the book's model relies and draws on explanations of various decision-making models. Therefore, it is useful here to explore major decision-making theories and approaches, specifically focusing on their relevance to crises and conflict situations.

POSITIONING A VIEW OF COMMUNICATION

Communication is central to our experience. It is through communication that we learn who we are, and what the world around us is like. In large part, our identity as both individual personalities and as cultural beings is shaped through communication with other people. Through communication, we explore the world around us, and establish bonds, networks, and relationships with other people. Communication permits us to express our thoughts and feelings to others, and to satisfy our emotional and material needs. As we learn to communicate successfully, we begin to achieve some measure of control over events which affect us and others.

(Nolan, 1999: 33)

Communication is a word with a rich history, coming from "the Latin *communicare,* meaning to impart, share, or make common" (Peters (1999: 7). It entered the English language at some time during the 14th and 15th centuries. John Condon (1975: 97) discusses two concepts related to communication: paralanguage and meta-communication. He notes that paralanguage is the general name given to meaningful differences in tone of voice, inflection, rate, pitch, volume, and so forth. Meta-communication, on the other hand, refers to the vast range of nonverbal cues, such as facial expression, hair style, clothing, eye behavior, posture, distance between the people conversing, and gestures, etc., which send a variety of messages in any social setting.[1] Alternatively, Albert Mehrabian (1976: 99-103) calls meta-communication "communication without words," i.e., communication by facial expression, by tone of voice, by touch, and so on. He argues that, compared with facial and bodily means, words actually convey very little information. Facial expression, touching, gestures, self-manipulation, changes in body position, and head movements—all express a person's positive and negative attitudes, and many reflect status relationships as well.

More generally, Don Rogers (1976) asks, "How do I communicate with you?", and then goes on to describe the ways or forms in which one human being communicates with another: "I communicate through my art and science, through my pottery and politics, through my literature and religions, through my architecture and societies, through my music and economics, and my speech. Whatever I create is a way of communicating. Whatever I create extends me towards you" (256). Rogers argues that a human being communicates to the limits of body, mind, and spirit. As he eloquently declares, "I cannot speak of communication without me in it, because my communicating is me. Moreover, your communicating is you and our communicating is us. Communication does not and cannot exist independently of the people involved". For him, communication is a personal activity, which has reciprocal effects among those who communicate: "I shape my words, but my words also shape me." Like Descartes, who claimed that his ability to think was the only evidence of his existence, Rogers declares, "Because I communicate, I am" (257).

Like Littlejohn (2002), who notes the difficulty of defining communication and suggests that determining a single definition "has proved impossible and may not be very fruitful" (6), Lawrence Frey and his associates (1991: 27-35) admit that defining communication "is like trying to define the purpose of life itself" (27) due to the enormous number of interpretations and points of view. They describe definitions of communication as following two different approaches: information-based views and meaning-based views. The earliest definitions represented information-based views, which originated from the scientific study of how information could be transferred from one place to another. Later definitions represented a meaning-based view as they originated from the phenomenological study of how communication produces meaning and leads to developing effective interpersonal relationships. Communication was also perceived as a process of attributing meaning to people's actions and developing relationships between people. Frey and his associates define communication in this context as "the management of messages for the purpose of creating meaning," adding that it "occurs whenever a person attempts to send a message or whenever a person perceives and assigns meaning to behavior" (28). By this definition, they claim that communication captures and combines the key[2] characteristics of both the behavioral, information-based and the phenomenological, meaning-based perspectives. They also confirm that communication, as a complex and encompassing social process, is influenced by the context (the environment) in which it occurs. They define three important contextual aspects of communication: time, space, and level. The time when communication occurs and how people feel about the timing have a major effect on human interaction. The setting where it takes place inevitably affects the communication. If a person says the same thing to the same people, but in different situations and places, that communication will be different. Moreover, Frey et al. consider five basic levels[3] of human communication: intrapersonal, interpersonal, group, organizational, and societal communication.

In their 1949 *The Mathematical Theory of Communication*, Claude Shannon and Warren Weaver introduced a mechanical and mathematical model of communication that includes the following main elements: source, message, transmitter, signal, noise, received signal, receiver, and destination. Wilbur Schramm (1976: 11-12) thinks the essence of communication is getting the receiver and the sender "tuned" together for a particular message. As such, communication requires at least three elements: the source, the message, and the destination. When trying to build up the "commonness" with the intended receiver, the source encodes the message, i.e., puts the information or feeling s/he wants to share into a form that can be transmitted. In order to complete the act of communication, the message must be decoded. In contrast, Reilly and DiAngelo (1990: 129-130) oppose the idea that communication is what it appears to be. Instead, they argue that the significant base for understanding communication is not what is visible but rather what is hidden. For them, communication is not simply the transfer of information, which leads to action, nor a set of message giver, message and receiver. In that sense, communication begins with pre-set understandings, which make effective communication possible and probable. Therefore, form and message are secondary to pre-defined meanings or embedded culture, which pre-set communication among people and give meaning to the communicated messages. In other words, the hidden and symbolic elements give meaning to the visible communication.

Peters (1999: 64) distinguishes between meaning (content) and media (form), claiming that signs, like bodies, are "the containers of spirit." In this context, the main purpose of communication is to "move beyond, behind, or above sign-bodies to the immediate purity of meaning-minds." For communication to take place, Peters explains, it is crucial to achieve identity in spirit between individual minds by transmitting the spiritual content from one mind to another. To conclude his vision of communication, Peters stresses the uncertainty of the process:

> Communication is a risky adventure without guarantees. Any kind of effort to make linkage via signs is a gamble. . . . Meaning is an incomplete project, open-ended and subject to radical revision by later events. . . . At best, 'communication' is the name for those practices that compensate for the fact that we can never be each other.

> (1999: 267-268)

Recognizing the complexity of communication, James Wilson and Stan Wilson (2001) give both simple and complex definitions of communication and mass communication.[4] They first offer a simple definition of communication as "the process by which individuals share information, ideas, and attitudes" (7). They consider the key word here to be "share," which means "to give or receive a part of something or to enjoy or assume something in common." According to their complex definition, communication is "a process involving the sorting, selecting, and sharing of symbols to help a receiver elicit from his or her own mind a meaning similar to that in the mind of the communicator" (12). In their simple definition, mass communication consists of: "1) professional communicators shaping and sharing messages, then 2) transmitting them over great distances using technological devices called mass media to 3) influence large audiences" (13). In the complex form, it is "a process whereby professional communicators use technological devices to share messages over great distances to influence large audiences." Hiebert, Ungurait and Bohn's definition is similar:

> It is best to think of communication as a *process*. A process means a series of actions or operations, *always* in motion, directed toward a particular goal. Communication is not a static entity fixed in time

and space. It is a dynamic process used to transfer meaning, transmit social values, and share experiences.

(1974: 6)

The social sciences were developing in the early part of the 20th century, as Littlejohn (2002: 4-5) explains, and both sociology and social psychology were becoming leading fields in the study of communication. Indeed, the early part of the 20th century saw significant development in communication theory and research in the United States. The rise ofpragmatism and the success of the social sciences "helped legitimate the field of communication and media studies, reinforced its identity, and secured its position among the human and social sciences" (Hardt, 2001: 1). The growth of communication studies in America began with the work of the so-called founding fathers of the field including members of the Chicago School, and continued with that of Harold D. Lasswell (1902-1978), Paul F. Lazarsfeld (1901-1976), Kurt Lewin (1890-1947), Carl I. Hovland (1912-1961), Norbert Wiener (1894-1964), and Claude Shannon (1916-). Thus, most sociological research focused on the ways that communication affects individuals and communities, while social psychology studied the effects of movies on children, propaganda and persuasion, as well as group dynamics. Communication studies became even more important after World War II, when the social sciences became legitimate disciplines, and the interest in psychological and social processes increased, with both persuasion and decision-making in groups becoming central concerns among researchers and society in general. The study of communication took different approaches in Europe and the United States. While researchers in the United States tended to study communication quantitatively[5] to try to achieve objectivity, their Canadian and European peers were generally more interested in historical, cultural, and critical approaches. Littlejohn attributes the diversity of work in communication theory to the complexity of communication itself, noting that there can be no "best" theory, since each theory considers the many aspects and activities that comprise communication from a variety of different angles.

The fear of propaganda in the years surrounding World War I, which was increased by the sophistication of advertising and public relations, resulted in the emergence of communication research. Wilbur Schramm, a founder of the field of communication, identified Paul Lazarsfeld, along with Kurt Lewin, Harold Lasswell, and Carl Hovland, as the "founding fathers" of communication research in the United States. Schramm (1996: 125) suggests that they were united in their determination to explore the causes and effects of communication. Given that Schramm's view of communication research, according to Hanno Hardt (1992: 86), is "quantitative, rather than speculative" and that he sees "practitioners [as being] deeply interested in theory, but in the theory they can test," he considered the four founding fathers as behavioral researchers who were "trying to find out something about why humans behave as they do, and how communication can make it possible for them to live together more happily and productively."

If World War I encouraged the study of media effects in a general way, then World War II encouraged the study of international propaganda and of persuasion. Everett Rogers and William Hart (2002) explain that two important documents helped set the tone for future international communication research and policy after World War II. In the United States, the Hutchins Commission on Freedom of the Press published *Peoples Speaking to Peoples: A Report on International Mass Communication* (1946), which advocated that a laissez-faire, free flow of information across borders would lead to a better world: "What is needed in the field of international communication is the linking of all the habitable parts of the globe with abundant, cheap, significant, true information about the world from day to day, so that all men (and women) increasingly may have the opportunity to learn, know, and understand each other" (7). This view reflected how the high value of the First Amendment (freedom of the press) held by American journalists and by U.S. mass communication scholars of that day, extended to an international context. A similar idealism led to the League of Nations after World War I and the formation of the United Nations near the end of World War II. The United Nations Educational, Scientific and Cultural Organization (UNESCO) encouraged the free flow of information among nations. The 1946 UNESCO constitution, in its preamble, focused on the nations' determination to "develop and to increase the means of communication between their peoples and to employ these means for the purposes of mutual understanding and a truer and more perfect knowledge of each other's lives" (7). UNESCO encouraged free-flow policies through international conferences and other activities. Rogers and Hart (2002) define international communication as:

> the study of heterophilous mass-mediated communication between two or more countries with differing backgrounds. The communicating countries may differ ideologically, culturally, in level of economic development, and in language. The primary unit of analysis in [international communication] is the interaction of two or more societies/nations that are linked by mass media communication.
>
> (2002: 5)

Thussu (2000) explains that defining international communication as communication that occurs across international borders reflects the concern of government-to-government information exchanges, wherein a few powerful states dictate the communication agenda. Given that international communication in the contemporary world "encompasses political, economic, social, cultural and military concerns" and becomes "more widespread and multi-layered, . . . the need to study it has acquired an added urgency" (2).

Rogers and Hart (2002: 6-9) demonstrate that the focus of studying international communication in the early decades was on the flows of information between, and among, nations. Another major topic of study was propaganda, beginning with Harold Lasswell's analysis of propaganda in World War I, which assumed that no government could control the minds of people without using propaganda and therefore the mass media could move societies for good or ill. U.S. President Woodrow Wilson and scholars of that period such as Walter Lippmann advocated using the mass media for the betterment of all people. Rogers and Hart claim that the idealism of early international communication scholars concerning the media's role in improving the world continues to some extent today. They show that the field of international communication was conceptualized in the decade after World War II when the United States was involved in the Cold War with the Soviet Union. Behind the international communication paradigm was a pro-Western, anti-communist ideology and a favored research methodology. Central to the international communication paradigm were: 1) the free flow of information across national borders; 2) an idealistic view of bettering the world through mass media communication; and 3) the empirical, effects-oriented research methodologies pioneered by Harold Lasswell, Paul Lazarsfeld, and Carl Hovland. On the other hand, and influenced by Marxism and the Frankfurt School, critical communication scholars faulted the international communication effects-oriented research methodology for overlooking the ideological, economic, cultural, and historical contexts of international communication. In the present day, critical perspectives are acknowledged by international communication scholars and are often incorporated in contemporary international communication research.

Stevenson argues that international communication[6] as an area of study "has no identifiable substance, body of theory, or specific research methods, only geography" (1996: 181). He claims that this area of communication is diverse and unorganized. Besides embracing anything *foreign*, it includes the combination of *cross, inter,* and *comparative* linked to *cultural, national,* and *global* as found in books, journal articles, and conference papers. As a result, other than geographical regions, the available terms are confusing and ill-defined and do little to organize the area or guide its development. Stevenson suggests a simple three-dimensional definitional matrix that can serve as a starting point for defining international communication. He builds on William Paisley's 1984 two-dimensional matrix that locates communication as a field of study within the behavioral sciences. Paisley's first dimension "defined communication as one of the elementary behavior-defined disciplines such as cybernetics and systems analysis that served as elements of more general fields of study such as education (learning), economics (value), and political science (power)" (181-182). Paisley's second dimension "comprised disciplines defined by their units of analysis, ranging from atom and molecule (natural sciences) through cell and living subsystem (biological sciences) to individual, group, and culture (social sciences)" (182). By combining the two, a specific behavior (such as communication) is defined at a specific level (such as the individual). In sum, Paisley suggests that communication is a behavior that incorporates some more basic behaviors (such as feedback and systems maintenance) and is itself part of more general behaviors (such as learning, value, and power). It is studied at levels ranging from the whole planet as a single system to individual molecules or atoms. Responding to that, Stevenson suggests a third dimension to separate international communication from the more general field. This dimension includes four distinct categories: foreign, comparative, international or intercultural, and global. Foreign studies are single-country or single-culture studies, usually heavy on description and light on explanation. Comparison with other countries is usually implicit. Comparative studies contrast the communication behavior of individuals or institutions within one culture or nation with equivalent behavior in another. International and intercultural studies examine the flow of information and influences from one nation or culture to another. Global studies consider the planet as a single, unified system. The three dimensions together "form a cube whose sides define international communication in terms of (a) a focal variable that is some aspect of communication, (b) a unit of analysis that can range from the individual to the entire globe, and (c) the delineation of national or cultural boundaries that, in most studies, provide the basis of comparison or explanation" (182).

    Several topics are linked to the research undertaken in international communication, as McDowell (2002) explains, including more traditional subjects, such as studies of propaganda, the unbalanced flows of news and entertainment between countries, the dominance of Hollywood in world motion picture production and exhibition, and the factors underlying, and the implications of, the rise of the large digital delivery corporations (such as telecommunications, software, or online media companies). But more significantly, McDowell considers the role of the state in shaping national media, and the roles of intergovernmental organizations in shaping world media industries, flows, and uses. McDowell shows that "effects of the dominance of media corporations on individuals, cultures, and politics across national boundaries have been debated at different times, whether called cultural imperialism or transnational media" (295). Recently, he explains, new types of questions have also been considered, such as the rise of the transnational media firm, how transnational media can be situated within cultural, political and other contexts, and the use of new media in support of various goals including peace.

The focus of this book is on the international communication level of communication studies, specifically from the perspective that considers communication in general and international mass communication practices in particular as decision-making processes, concentrating on dealing with one of the most critical situations of stress, i.e., the international political crisis.

UNDERSTANDING COMMUNICATION DECISIONS

> [News-writing] is controlled, purposeful communication between the writer and the audience that is shaped and molded by the writer.
>
> (Dennis & Ismach, 1981: 108)

> The decisions by the [media] producer and his [sic] staff of what to include and what to reject control not only what the audience sees but also, to some extent, the direction of the future search for news.
>
> (Epstein, 1973: 182)

To investigate the relationship between communication and the process of decision-making, two areas of making decisions that are related to communication are distinguished here, with the main focus on the second: 1) political decision-making at the governmental level, and 2) news-writing decision-making within the media. Clearly, there is an essential need for an honest and open relationship[7] between the media and the government, especially during stress situations. The development of a clear and objective relationship requires significant time and effort on the part of both sides to eliminate professional and political obstacles and to explain rationale. Political leaders have to take particular care to develop a trusting relationship with the media. Some scholars, such as Shrivastava, propose the establishing of such a relationship before stress situations such as crisis: "News reporters are generally skeptical about organizational explanations of crisis events, and their suspicion level increases when explanations are provided by implicated organizations. It is therefore critical to establish a relationship with the media *before* the crisis" (1989: 111).

Robert Hackett (1991), in a discussion about the relevancy of the media to international peace and conflict, explains that media structure and content, and government policies pertaining to them, may work to maintain relations of inequality and antagonism between nations. He argues that "media themselves have become important subjects of international relations, both between governments and within international agencies . . . media may influence international relations of power and may themselves become a political issue. They may also less directly affect international peace by directing public attention and mobilizing support for or against the institutions and processes available for international conflict-resolution" (19-20).

The mass media intervene at a number of points in the political decision-making process during times of war and peace. According to Davison (1974: 15), the mass media help the government by carrying out five main duties which help to explain the significant relationship between the mass media and government.[8] This relationship can be extremely beneficial, it is argued here, if it is used with effective government cooperation. For their part, when setting their agenda for the public, the mass media have to take into account the political leaders' agenda. On their side, the government must clearly provide the mass media with the main elements of its agenda, the information most needed by the media, and substantial and significant items of political policy. The process of making ethical decisions in the communication environment, according to Wright (1996: 520), is easy if the facts and the choices are clear. The process is different when ambiguity prevails along with incomplete information, multiple points of view, and conflicting responsibilities.

There is also another duty for media personnel, in the context of media-government relations, which is important if that relationship is to serve democracy. Norman Solomon (2001) noticed that on January 19, 2001, after interviewing the new White House chief of staff, CNN's Judy Woodruff said "All right, Andy Card . . . we look forward to working with you, to covering your administration" (3). Solomon considers this a remarkable comment that passed without notice. He contends that if major news outlets were committed to independent journalism, Woodruff's statement on national television would have caused quite a media stir "as a sign of undue coziness with power brokers in Washington. Instead it was far from conspicuous" (3). He considers Woodruff's remark as a statement of fact because in a world of corporate-owned-and-controlled media, warm collaboration is routine and many reporters work closely with each new crew of top government officials. "Leading journalists and spinners in high places are accustomed to mutual reliance. That's good for their professional advancement. It doesn't, however, bode well for the public's right to know . . . democracy is only served when journalists keep searching for information that officials hide" (4).

Investigating decisions that are made under stress or tension can help to evaluate the performance of media institutions. An example of this is the performance of the Quebec Press Council[9] during the first half of 1980, when the government of Quebec asked its citizens to vote in a referendum that could have led to the secession of Quebec from Canada; the possible breakup of Canada was the gravest political crisis in Canadian history to that point. David Pritchard (2000*b*) analyzed the referendum-related decisions of the council. He chose this period because he believes that "periods of social and political tension are useful natural laboratories for studying institutions because the conditions of stress that accompany such periods tend to highlight flaws in the structures and/or operations of those institutions" (91). One of his analysis' questions was: "how coherent and defensible were the decisions that the press council made under conditions of stress?" (97). He recognized that

> At the time of the referendum, the QPC had no statement of principles to guide its decisions in individual cases. It had never adopted an ethics code. It had never organized and compiled the principles that could have been derived from the decisions it had made in several hundred cases since it began operating in 1973. In short, the press council had no set of established ethical principles to guide its decision-making.
>
> (2000*b*: 100)

As mentioned above, the second area of decision-making related to communication is that which is involved in the news-writing process within the media. In considering this area, it may be helpful to introduce a further explanation of communication here. Communication "involves" or, even, "is" a decision-making process. While this might be open to debate, nonetheless a few insights from this assertion can be illustrated here that support this statement. An analysis of both the original meaning of communication, as well as various definitions of it indicate that there is an inherent sense of "making" something; if the word "communicate" means "impart," "share," or "make common," one gets the sense of making something, e.g., mutual understanding, creating meanings, etc. This "something" can be considered a "desired outcome", i.e., a "decision"; that is, the whole communication process, whatever its components, can be considered a decision-making process. To grasp this, it is helpful to recall core concepts from the definitions of communication presented earlier in this chapter: the complicated nature of communication; the influencing of communication by contextual occurrences; communication as process (meaning a series of actions or operations) in which individuals do something (sharing information, ideas, attitudes, and experiences; sending and receiving messages; sorting, selecting, and sharing of symbols; transferring meaning; and transmitting social values), and the dynamic and goal-directed nature of this process.

As for mass communication, it is argued here that "bureaucratic decision theory", which is discussed later in this chapter, drops the assumption that the decision-maker is a unitary actor, and so can be applied to the mass media as a communication system. Each department and sub-department in a communication system develops its own preferred mode of functioning by working out an interpretation of its responsibilities and how they contribute to the national interest. The two components of the bureaucratic theory, a non-rational and a rational, can also be applied to the communication system. The non-rational component, which is a theory of consciousness, is reflected in the media personnel's attitudes, values, beliefs, and cognitive sensitivities that are reflected in their daily decisions, news-writing, production, etc. Also, like the application of the rational component of bureaucratic decision theory in politics, which aims at controlling any collective action for a public good through power, authority, and influence, the mass media have a rational component that stems from their unique and influential power.

Dennis and Ismach (1981: 108-113) argue that news-writing involves decision-making, as writers have to make decisions as they write. News-writing involves, in the simplest way, making compromises between one mode of expression and another, and deciding which facts are included in a story and which ones are not. But the process is not as simple as this form. Dennis and Ismach claim that "the writer, like it or not, becomes a ruthless decision-maker, sometimes discarding the very items that seemed essential only a few hours before and choosing the form and style that will most effectively present the information in the space allowed" (109). Generally, in writing a news story, a writer goes through seven distinct stages, each of which is full of decisions that must be made: 1) choosing a subject; 2) planning; 3) news gathering; 4) prewriting; 5) writing;

6) rewriting and polishing; and 7) getting feedback. Not surprisingly, these seven stages, which make up a kind of map of the reporter's work pattern, may vary greatly for different reporters. Decisions, whether simple or complex, and whether made by the writer, news sources, or editors, help shape news-writing and determine what the final product will look like. There are some reporters who concentrate much of their energy on planning; others who spend most of their time on newsgathering; and so on. In general, news-writing[10] requires decision-making in all of its stages. Dennis and Ismach explain that the real test of effective news-writing and reporting is addressed by two questions: "1) Does the story contain all the information readers need to understand the subject?" and "2) Does it present the information effectively?" (108). That is, they question two major issues related to news-writing—*actual information* and *high-quality written expression*—and consider them to be of equal concern for the competent reporter. Therefore, it becomes important to decide whether the news story presents sufficient information, and to recognize the criteria of good journalism and effective communication.

Considering these things in times of crisis better highlights the volume of decisions that need to be made in the context of news-writing. The nature of mass media intervention in stress situations in general, involves a series of decision-making processes. In addition to discussing the decision-making involved in news-writing, it may be useful to analyze some media guidelines[11] for covering one example of a stress event—acts of terrorism[12]. The following 12 major principles or cautions are the most frequently stated in media guidelines; all of them require decision-making. Media guidelines such as those explored in this chapter, suggest that news personnel, during a terrorist event, should do the following:

- Assign experienced staff members to the story.
- Approach the story with care and restraint.
- Report demands of the terrorist(s) after paraphrasing them, instead of presenting them directly.
- Cover the event in a thoughtful and conscientious manner.
- Maintain communication with authorities to seek guidance.
- Consult officials before making publishing decisions.
- Consider recommendations carefully and obey instructions by authorities.
- Avoid interfering in the duties of authorities.
- Do nothing to jeopardize lives.
- Avoid sensationalizing beyond the innate sensation of the story itself.

- Avoid providing a platform for the terrorist propaganda.
- Avoid using inflammatory catchwords or phrases, or reporting rumors.

Although there is much to say about these principles or cautions in terms of policies and ideologies, this chapter's discussion focuses on their practical nature, i.e., the processes of decision-making.

> There are *choices* [i.e., decisions] to be made. Think about it: The reporter has more information than she [or he] can use in the story; she [or he] must discard part of it. Some aspects of the remaining information will seem more important and more compelling than others, and thus deserve more emphasis. There are decisions [also] to be made about organizing the story—deciding what sequence the information should follow. And there are questions about rhetoric—the art of writing the story—such as deciding between and among particular words, phrases and sentences. Matters of style must be decided: Should the story be written in terse, spare language, should it be described in more detail? Should information from the meeting take the form of paraphrases or quotations? What combination of words and images will make the most compelling lead or first paragraph?
>
> (Dennis & Ismach, 1981: 107)

William Zinsser's 1998 book *On Writing Well: The Classic Guide To Writing Nonfiction* is considered a major source for nonfiction writers—hence over 900,000 copies of it have been sold to date.[13] In the introduction of *On Writing Well*, Zinsser says

> Writing isn't a skill that some people are born with and others aren't, like a gift for art or music. Writing is talking to someone else on paper. If you can think clearly, you can put what you think and what you know into writing.
>
> (1998: x)

It is significant here to highlight Zinsser's emphasis on thinking before writing. One of his new chapters to the latest edition, "The Tyranny of the Final Product", basically "advises writers not to visualize their completed article but to focus on all the prior decisions of selection, organization and tone that will eventually *let* them know what their piece is about" (xi). In various places in his book, writing decisions are emphasized and explained as an important part of the writing process. Zinsser demonstrates the many decisions a writer should make:

This has been a book about decisions—the countless successive decisions that go into every act of writing. Some of the decisions are big ('What should I write about?') and some are as small as the smallest word. But all of them are important . . . big decisions: [such as] matters of shape, structure, compression, focus and intention . . . little decisions [such as]: the hundreds of choices that go into organizing a long article. . . . The hardest decision about any article is how to begin it. The lead must grab the reader with a provocative idea and continue with each paragraph to hold him or her in a tight grip, gradually adding information . . . No less important than decisions about structure are decisions about individual words. . . . [Also a] crucial decision about a piece of writing is where to end it . . . [In sum,] . . . [decide] what you want to do. Then decide to do it. Then do it.

(1998: 265, 266, 270, 283, 285)

Digging deeper into the organizational structure of mass media where such decisions are made, as well as the nature of duties assigned to media personnel in various levels of management, sheds light on the significance of news-writing as a decision-making process. Bruce Garrison (1990: 32-35) explains that media companies, newspapers, magazines, and television and radio stations, produce a unique and highly perishable product. Garrison shows the newsroom as a unique place, whose organization is different from other places of work. In the standard newspaper newsroom and magazine office, activities are controlled by an editor. In a broadcast newsroom, a news director is in charge. As newsrooms get larger, the nature of leadership jobs becomes more specialized. Normally, the print media have several critical roles that are fulfilled in the organization of the newsroom. Reporters and photographers who gather information are directed by various desk editors, including copy editors who process information and graphics and layout editors who organize information for presentation. In a radio and television newsroom, reporters and photographers are directed by assignment editors, including tape editors who help process the raw audio and video as well as producers who are responsible for packaging each show. The newsroom is organized by positions and procedures that are set for efficiency in the flow of news in order to reduce the chance of error and overall cost, but simultaneously, to enhance speed in reporting. It is quite certain that the news business is not a *one-person* show, but requires a *team* to get each story to audiences. However, someone has to run the show. In a newspaper or magazine newsroom, it is an editor, while in a broadcast newsroom, the news director has final responsibility for the news operation. Editors and news directors report to publishers and general managers who may or may not get involved with the daily activities of journalism and decision-making in the newsroom because of the tradition of autonomy of the newsroom, and of news judgment as well as their involvement in so many other responsibilities.[14] Therefore, editors and news directors are to all intents and purposes in charge and are the final newsroom authority. They set policy, direction, and standards. Therefore, the quality of a news operation is attributed to the leadership of the editor and news director. They are responsible for the quality and completeness of the news product, but they also have to provide a product that will make money.

A more recent explanation than Garrison's is provided by Lorenz and Vivian (1996: 221-222). Newsroom managers in a typical newspaper and broadcasting station have three levels of management: top newsroom management, day-to-day newsroom managers, and news editors. At the higher level, the newspaper editor or radio or television news director deals with long-range planning and articulates the vision of the organization, as well as develops and manages the budget for the newsroom. At the middle level, the newspaper's managing editor or a television station's senior producer or assistant news director supervises the day-to-day operations. At the news editors' level, the news editor in a newspaper and the producer of each news program in a television station is a key position, whereas the person oversees the work of the copy desk, which is responsible for checking verifiable information, polishing copy and writing headlines, as well as laying-out the pages of the newspaper. Lorenz and Vivian also explain that the number of a newspaper's subeditors and their duties depends on the size of the community and the circulation of the newspaper. The larger the newspaper, the more sections or departments it has, and the more editors overseeing them. The size of a radio or television station's news staff depends on market size and the station's commitment to news.

As Hoffmann (2004) explains, people everywhere receive a wide-range of various media messages that convey information, but also values, norms, images, and so on that go into forming what he calls "mediated truths." By that term, he does not only mean that media companies are bringing the messages to audiences but also means that "the intended meaning of them has been carefully mediated, or determined, by those within the media industry" (75). Similarly, Nicholson (1997) explains that "most decisions of significance are taken by groups of people acting together. The members of a group will normally not have exactly the same view of the situation—they will differ in what they want and they will differ in their perceptions of the world" (52). Also, Epstein (1973) warns that "many of the producers' decisions are based mainly on personal preferences for one subject over another, or personal opinions that one story will be more interesting to the audience than another, and choices like these can only be explained in terms of the values of the individual producer" (183). Therefore, Dary (1973) suggests that the "news reporter's job is not to make news. It is to gather and organize in written form those facts that are newsworthy. The reporter is the middle man in the business of news dissemination" (41).

Examples of operational decision-making that is required in the news-writing process include choosing the structure of the news story and choosing the story's lead. There are various forms of structuring a news story such as the inverted pyramid, chronological presentation, and the climactic form. Lorenz and Vivian (1996: 94-96) illustrate the inverted pyramid as an upside-down triangle where the main news is located at the top; the chronological presentation in a vertical rectangular where the main news could occur anywhere; and the climactic form in a triangle where the main news is located at the end. They explain that the inverted pyramid serves readers and listeners who want the highlights right away. It lays out the main points at the beginning.[15] For those who want to know more, additional details follow later. In a chronological presentation the story would begin at the beginning and progress sequentially, presenting the most important element at whatever point it occurred. The climactic form is one that readers of mystery stories are used to, where the answer to *who-done-it?* is delayed until the very end.

Additionally, Garrison (1990) classifies approaches of structuring the news stories as inverted pyramid approach, chronological approach, essay approach, and hourglass approach. Garrison explains that inverted pyramid writing, the most frequently used, "gets its name from the inverted pyramid symbol representing the strengths of the story at the top, not at the bottom. . . . Writers seek to put the strongest information, that is, the most important, at the beginning of the story for the audience" (76). As for events that have a sequence of steps to explain, Garrison claims that "the chronological approach is still the best to use. Because chronological stories do not always offer the most important information first, most writers use chronological organization with a summary lead. This permits the most important information to go first, followed by a chronological structure to describe how events occurred" (79). Garrison claims that chronologies work well for crime, accidents, or other disaster stories", but they do not work well for speeches, meetings, or press conferences. Garrison notices that, of the three major approaches—inverted pyramid, chronological, and essay—essay writing is least used in news-writing. "Most often, essay organization is found in editorials, columns, or longer newspaper or magazine articles" (81). Essays begin with telling the audience the main thesis or point of view; in the middle, facts are presented to support the thesis; and then the ending provides a wrap up. Also, Garrison explains that one of the other ways to organize information in a news story is the hourglass approach, developed by Roy Peter Clark, past Dean of Faculty at the Poynter Institute in St. Petersburg, Florida. Clark considers this approach as alternative to the inverted pyramid because it "gives more flexibility for some types of news stories. The hourglass, shaped wide at the top and bottom, but narrow in the middle, represents strong parts of the story at the beginning and end with a transition or 'turn' at the midpoint of the story" (82). In addition, Garrison discusses three organizational approaches commonly used in broadcast news as a result of the special problems related to non-permanent, non-hardcopy journalism for television—chronological sequence, effect and cause sequence, and action-reaction sequence. The chronological sequence approach "has a longer-than-usual summary lead to set up and update audiences on the story" (86). In the effect and cause sequence, "broadcasters often emphasize the effect and then relate its cause because the effect is more significant than the cause" (86). The action-reaction sequence is similar to effect-cause stories, but "it is often used for issue-type stories that tell audiences of the action or issue and then give reactions from experts and others concerned" (86).

Choices of the news story leads also vary. David Dary (1973) explain that the news story lead serves to "summarize the story by answering the questions who, what, when, where, and often why and how". Leads also vary in their structure, length, and organization. Dary explains that a lead "may begin with the subject, a phrase, or a clause. It depends on the nature of the story and the writer's skill" (93). Dary shows that there are various types of news leads such as: anecdotal, personal, situation, as well as leads that begin with a question, epigram, or quotation. McKercher and Cumming (1998) explain two main approaches—hard leads and soft leads. For them, the hard lead "follows some very clear conventions. These dictate that the first paragraph should be short—not more than 35 words or so, often fewer than 20—summing up the central idea in simplest possible form. Almost always, the first paragraph has only one sentence . . . [and] in simple, declarative form. . . . Very often, the lead is simply a slight expansion of the headline, stated somewhat differently" (136). As for the soft lead, they explain that writers use it "when they have a broad, multifaceted story rather than a short, sharp development whose implications are immediately clear. In general, soft leads are associated with a more detailed or spacious approach to a topic than is possible in hard news-writing. . . . Soft leads signal to readers that the story is a complex one, deserving of their undivided attention. . . . Typically, the soft lead fastens on one small piece of action that symbolizes the larger theme. It might be called a 'specific-to-general' or 'problem-to-solution' or 'cause-to-effect' approach" (148).

THE CENTRALITY OF DECISION-MAKING

> The practice of communication by individuals and institutions is instrumental and goal-directed.
>
> (Mody & Lee, 2002: 381)

> A *decision* is a choice of action—of what to do or not do. Decisions are made to achieve goals, and they are based on beliefs about what actions will achieve the goals. . . . Decisions may concern small matters . . . or matters of enormous importance. . . . Decisions may be simple, involving only a single goal, two options, and strong beliefs about which option will best achieve the goal, or they may be complex, with many goals and options.
>
> (Baron, 2000: 6)

> Decision-making is fundamental to modern life in its individual, collective and corporate aspects.
>
> (Crozier & Ranyard, 1997: 5)

The high level of stress experienced during international crises makes the study of crisis decision-making very important for assessing the effects of that stress on policymakers, be they politicians or media personnel, and for determining whether or not the policymakers can think and act rationally under intense pressure. Svenson and Verplanken (1997: 40) explain that while decisions vary widely in importance for the decision-makers, reasons that increase their importance may be times when costs are involved, or when an outcome has far-reaching consequences. Lebow (1987*a*: 183-186) calls for a significant shift in our ways of thinking about international crisis and in the focus of contemporary research and planning for crisis management, and urges investigation into how to improve the quality of decision-making.

Crisis management during international crises faces two types of obstacles—one related to the nature of the crisis and the other to the decision-making process. The latter includes obstacles of misperception, insufficient information or simple errors of judgment, which can lead to decisions that diminish rather than enhance the possibilities for containing and defusing a crisis. Therefore, Williams (1976: 59) suggests that it is necessary to focus on the way decisions are made during a crisis and to address some of the problems that might obstruct effective and efficient decision-making.

Basically, the original meaning of the word "crisis" is "to decide", as Bokhari (1997) explains. To say that a person has made a decision, Eilon (1979: 135-136) suggests, may mean that 1) s/he has started a series of behavioral reactions in favor of something, or 2) s/he has made up his mind to do a certain action, which s/he has no doubt that s/he ought to do. But Eilon argues that perhaps the most common use of the term is this: "to make a decision" means 3) to make a judgment regarding what one ought to do in a certain situation after having deliberated on some alternative courses of action.

The process of crisis policymaking differs significantly from that of routine policymaking in that it is quickly elevated to the highest levels of government. Head, Short and McFarlane (1978), in their study of the influence of international crisis on policymaking, conclude (217-221) that an international crisis affords a U.S. president relatively more opportunity to make decisions and control implementation than periods of routine policymaking do. They explain that during non-crisis periods, key policymakers develop their objectives based on their individual and organizational backgrounds; during an international crisis, however, they agree quickly on national objectives and are less influenced by their bureaucratic positions. Head, Short and McFarlane suggest that crisis management procedures should be developed as an adjunct to the regular policy process. Comparing the two policy processes, they define seven[16] points of difference in terms of crisis policymaking. In sum, they conclude that, due to the increased opportunity for the president and his advisors to make decisions independent of bureaucratic constraints during a crisis, crisis decision-making tends to be accompanied by centralization, elevation, optimization, and lack of information.

Several scholars have attempted to develop better policy-relevant knowledge of foreign policy problems that must be dealt with by decision-makers. Alexander George (2003), for example, has joined this effort, but coupled it "with a sober view of the extent to which even high-quality scholarly studies and analysis can be expected to assure high-quality foreign policy" (259). George explains that although various political considerations and psychological factors frequently constrain the impact that objective analysis can have on the decisions of top-level policymakers, at least the availability of solid knowledge and objective policy analysis can reduce the negative impact such factors might have on decisions. George argues that the view of some scholars of policymaking which considers that the dominant criterion of good policy should be its analytic rationality, that is, identifying options likely to achieve policy objectives at acceptable levels of cost and risk, is, in fact, an "overintellectualized view of foreign policy" (259). Rather, George highlights the necessarily broader view and more complex concerns and interests that policymakers must take into account, and coins the term *political rationality*, which is juxtaposed to *analytic rationality*. He claims that although the impact of scholarly knowledge on political decision-making can be expected to be limited, it is still quite an essential contribution, because "scholarly knowledge can be only an input to, not a substitute for, competent, well-informed policy analysis of a specific problem conducted within the government. Policy analysts within and around the government have the difficult task of adapting available knowledge to the particular case on hand that top-level policymakers must address and decide" (260). Therefore, while scholars and policy analysts "must pre-occupy themselves with the task of identifying high-quality options that meet the criterion of analytical rationality, high-level decision-makers must exercise broader judgments that take account of a variety of additional considerations" (260).

There are two major approaches to the study of international crises in relation to decision-making: the *psychological* approach to crisis behavior, and the *rational choice* approach to crisis research. Ben Mor contends that despite the impressive research achievements in these areas, the results cannot give rise to a general theory. The psychological approach to crisis behavior is based on the assumption of crisis behavior, an assumption which employs actor-oriented definitions of crisis, which in turn are rooted in the perceptual perspective of decision-making theory. The psychological approach is concerned with the impact of two basic groups of factors on the performance of decision-makers: personality factors and situational variables.[17] The rational choice approach shares the common assumption that decision-makers are rational. The principle of rationality therefore directs and lends consistency to the theoretical expectations in these studies. To combine both approaches, Mor suggests a possible solution to the problem of integrating the psychological and rational choice perspectives, and develops a model of crisis behavior based on this conception (1993: 2-22).

Primarily, knowing what the decision is helps to introduce the process of decision-making as a whole. While many scholars have defined the term "decision"[18], the clearest definition in relation to the process of decision-making is Ofstad's. As Eilon (1979: 135-136) explains the fundamental elements of Ofstad's definition, the decision-maker has several options from which to choose, and that choice includes a comparison between those options and the evaluation of their outcomes. This explanation provides a sense of the process (including resolution and selection criteria) that the decision-maker goes through to reach a decision. To describe the decision-making process, Eilon (1979: 136) schematizes a model consisting of eight stages: information input, analysis, performance measure, model, strategies, prediction of outcomes, choice criteria, and resolution. He distinguishes between rational and irrational resolution in the decision-making process, and confirms that discussion of the decision-making process is confined to rational decisions. Consequently, every step described in the process is indispensable and the steps must proceed in the order specified. Rationality, he says, is best defined by "reference to the decision process itself: each time the final resolution deviates from what would be expected from following the process, then the resolution cannot be said to be rational" (1979: 143).

In this respect, George (2003) distinguishes between *effective* and *rational* decision-making. He explains that "decision-making is effective when the policymaker deals reasonably well with trade-offs between quality, support, and time and other resources", while rational decision-making "reflects the scholar's and the policy analyst's effort to come up with a high-quality policy without reference to these trade-offs or to various political considerations with which the policymaker must deal" (266). George notices the lack of theories of effective decision-making although also noting that scholars have provided a number of models of rational decision-making. Therefore, he calls for additional research and reflection to link analysis more closely to judgments that decision-makers are compelled to make.

Many theorists have investigated the decision-making process performance under conditions of stress or uncertainty.[19] As Robert Kahn (1991: 151) sees it, the decision-making process becomes more complicated when organizations are large and consist of numerous semiautonomous sub-units, and when the decisions to be made involve significant questions. The simple perspective relies on intuition as a tool. For example, Weston Agor (1986: 6-8) considers intuition[20] as a highly efficient way of knowing and claims that through practice we can learn to use our intuition to help make decisions successfully and reduce unnecessary delay in the process. He points to Carl Jung's research that showed that managers who become skilled in the use of their intuition tend to possess particular decision-making skills not normally possessed by others. These managers: see new possibilities in any given situation; have a sense or vision of what is coming in the future and how to response to it; are expert in generating new ideas and providing new solutions to old problems; and deal effectively with rapid change, crisis, and highly complex decision-making situations. As for when reliance on intuition is the most useful, managers claim it is in times of uncertainty and limitation of facts, among others. However, this chapter argues that given the fact that human beings make decisions every day, and that decisions may often be difficult or complex, there is an essential need for assistance in the decision-making process, especially in cases of conflicts and crises. Nicholson (1970: 162) asserts that conflict decisions "should be made on the basis of tested knowledge rather than of intuitive guesses." Indeed, decision theory provides this assistance for the real-life decision-making process.

Glenn Snyder and Paul Diesing (1977: 340-356) discuss three theories of the process of decision-making: "rational actor" theory, bounded rationality, and bureaucratic politics. Both the maximizing of expected utility or "rational actor" theory[21] and bounded rationality theory are called problem-solving theories because they deal with the intellectual process of tackling a problem, assuming that the decision-maker is a unitary actor. On the other hand, the bureaucratic politics theory drops this assumption and looks at the political processes occurring inside the decision-making unit. The "rational actor" or "maximizing" theory treats decision-making as a process of maximizing expected utility. The bounded rationality theory,[22] which goes back to John Dewey, drops two assumptions of the maximizing theory—homogeneous goods and perfect calculating ability. In doing this, it[23] gets closer to actual practice without losing theoretical simplicity. The "bureaucratic politics" theory drops the assumption that the decision-maker is a unitary actor. If the decision-maker is a government, within a political system, it is composed of a set of bureaus or departments or ministries with different responsibilities, resources, and information sources with variable influence within the government. Each department and sub-department develops its own preference function by working out an interpretation of its responsibilities and how they contribute to the national interest. The bureaucratic politics theory has two components, a non-rational and a rational. The non-rational component is a theory of consciousness, i.e., attitudes and where they come from. It states that the individual's values, beliefs, and cognitive sensitivities are mainly determined by his/her position in government. The rational component of the bureaucratic decision theory takes us to the heart of politics, which is concerned with public action and public good. In order to control or participate in controlling any collective action aimed at a public good, one needs power, authority, and influence. Politicians who wish to participate in public action are thus faced with the imperative of maintaining or increasing their power, authority, and influence.

To conclude, this first chapter has the important task of linking communication with decision-making, a central theme that I develop in this book. In the following chapter, we will look at the dependency of crisis management on communication and also investigate how communication can function as a double-edged sword in stress and conflict situations.

NOTES

1. Further, Don Fabun (1976: 118-121) demonstrates that time, color, and space and even silence itself, are like words and gestures: all communicate meaning. They can establish, maintain, and support a relationship or break it down. As long they exert a powerful influence on human interaction, he argues, they deserve attention along with the more obvious forms of communication. He claims that although the structure of our society is woven of spoken and visual symbols, people also communicate meaningfully in many non-verbal, non-symbolic ways. For instance, he argues that silence itself is a way of communication; that is, if someone says "Good morning," and we fail to respond, then we communicate something. For the language of time, he argues that if someone is "ahead of time," "on time," or "behind time," "or "early" or "late," then they express something in their culture. The way in which people use space is another way of communicating. Also, color "speaks" through its conscious and unconscious use, as do time and space.

2. The key combined elements include "messages and meanings," "communication acts and processes," "intentional and unintentional communication," "verbal and nonverbal message systems," "information and meaning," and "content and relationship dimensions."

3. Intrapersonal communication is an internal process that occurs within oneself through encoding (creating) messages, and decoding (interpreting) others' messages. Interpersonal communication takes place between two people, either face-to-face or through mediated forms, and is characterized by the mutual awareness of the individuality of the other. Group communication occurs among three or more people interacting in order to achieve commonly recognized goals, which are either task-oriented, such as a group making a decision within an organization, or "socioemotional," such as a family trip or a social gathering of friends. Organizational communication occurs within a particular social system composed of interdependent groups trying to achieve commonly recognized goals. It includes both formal and informal channels of communication and is also concerned with both internal (within an organization) and external (among members of various organizations) communication. As such, it is made possible by the prior three levels. The broadest level of communication, "societal," occurs within and between social systems composed of interdependent organizations trying to achieve commonly recognized goals. Therefore, it includes the four prior levels. It focuses on communication within a particular culture as well as different cultures. It has two forms: public and mass communication. While public communication occurs when

a small number of people address a larger group of people, mass communication occurs when a small number of people send messages to a large, unidentified, and diverse audience through specialized communication media.

4. For more definitions of communication and mass communication see: Trenholm (1995: 25-29 and 276-277).

5. Major scholars in the field of human communication have introduced and developed a number of approaches to studying the field, including persuasion, interpersonal communication, small group communication, intrapersonal communication, intercultural communication, organizational communication, and non-verbal communication. Major approaches and theories applied at that time include framing and priming, cognitive dissonance, spiral of silence, diffusion of innovations, gate-keeping, agenda-setting, cultivation, uses and gratifications, and knowledge gap.

6. Communication pioneer Wilbur Schramm founded communication research institutes and doctoral programs in communication at the University of Iowa, the University of Illinois, and Stanford University in the decade after World War II, and, by 1960, the academic study of communication was becoming well established in many U.S. universities. However, and after the emergence of international communication, anomalies in the dominant paradigm for international communication gradually appeared in the 1970s on two fronts. Herbert Schiller's books *Mass Communications and American Empire* (1969) and *Communication and Cultural Domination* (1976) strongly opposed the free-flow doctrine. Schiller, who was a critical communication scholar at the University of California, San Diego, argued that a laissez-faire policy on communication flows actually led to an asymmetrical flow. News and entertainment programming from Western nations dominated the media in Latin America, Africa, and Asia. Schiller (1969) introduced the concept of cultural (and media) imperialism, leading to investigations of how the media of one nation dominate other nations. Also, in the early 1970s, a growing number of the national leaders of developing countries recognized the imbalance and cultural imperialism in international communication flows. Developing nations called for a New World Information and Communication Order (NWICO). UNESCO modified its policy stance from the free flow of information, established in 1946, to a free *and balanced* flow of information in the 1970s. UNESCO appointed an eminent panel of communication scholars and media professionals to investigate the imbalance in world news flows. This panel published the MacBride report, *Many Voices, One World*, which called for a more balanced flow of information among nations. Several Western countries, however, objected, and the United States and Great Britain withdrew from UNESCO, in 1985 and 1986, respectively, in part because of the NWICO debate. This debate sparked considerable study by

international communication researchers in the late 1980s. Critical communication scholars led the charge for a new paradigm of international communication by critiquing the dominant international communication paradigm, beginning about 1970. They pointed to the documented imbalance in worldwide information flows and assisted in creating a Third World news agency through the Yugoslavian news agency TANJUG. The challenge by critical communication scholars to the Cold War paradigm for international communication trailed off in the 1990s, after the end of the Cold War in 1989. Scholarly interests in the international communication field shifted in an era of globalization, privatization, and informatization. Recent international communication studies focus particularly on the role of communication satellites, telecommunication, and the diffusion of the Internet, its consequences, and on the digital divide between developed and developing nations. (Rogers & Hart, 2002: 8-9).

7.   Having an honest and open relationship between the mass media and the government may help both sides to achieve their goals. For the government, hiding or distorting information given to the media may obstruct the performance of the media that could be helpful and more influential on the publics than the political or military actions in a crisis or conflict situation, while the opposite action may encourage the media to be more willing in serving the government to achieve their goals. For the media being in continuous relations and positive coordination with the government helps them acquire the government's trust, and consequently the high quality of information obtained helps them enhance their credibility and reach for their audiences, as ultimate goals.

8.   Firstly, they help to set the agenda for both the political leaders and the general public. Secondly, they provide these leaders with much of the information on which decisions are based. Thirdly, they influence the experts and elites, who in turn influence the decision-makers. Fourthly, they affect public opinion on specific issues and the public mood in general, thus limiting or expanding the alternatives that political leaders can realistically consider. Finally, they provide the channels through which governments must explain their policies in order to obtain the cooperation of the public.

9.   "The several North American press councils all are established and financed by the news industry for the purposes of receiving and resolving complaints about news media performance. Press councils have no legal power. Their authority depends upon public confidence in their fairness and impartiality" (Pritchard, 2000*b*: 90).

10.   For more about news making and managing the news, see Davis (2001: 150-157).

11.   There are four media guidelines for covering terrorism enclosed in the appendix (139-143) of the 1990 *Terrorism and the Media*, edited by Yonah

Alexander and Richard Latter. The media guidelines are those of CBS News Standards, *The Courier-Journal* and *The Louisville Times, The Sun-Times* and *Daily News* Standards for Coverage of Terrorism, and the United Press International.

12. The relationship between the media and terrorism is explained in detail through: Crelinsten (1989: 314-320), Steuter (1990: 258-275), Alger (1989: 128-131), Elmquist (1990: 74-80), Kelly (1989: 117-131), Picard (1990: 100-109), Finn (1990: 48-50), Protheroe (1990: 66-69), and Wittebols (1992: 267-269).

13. Now in its sixth edition, the book has been revised by Zinsser four times, to include points he is still discovering in his own work. The book grew out of a course in nonfiction writing that Zinsser started at Yale during the 1970s, where he taught based on his 13 years as a writer and editor for the *New York Herald Tribune* and an even longer career as a writer of nonfiction articles and books.

14. Publishers and general managers rarely are involved in the day-to-day activities and decision-making in the newsroom, except occasionally in very small operations. They are coordinators and planners for all the various divisions and the products of their publications and stations. Publishers have responsibility for the news, production, circulation, business, advertising, promotion, and other departments. Some publishers supervise more than one publication—a.m. and p.m. newspapers, a Sunday magazine, an electronic news service, and so on. General managers have responsibility for directing news, sales, production, engineering, business, promotion, public affairs, and other departments. Many general managers supervise more than one operation especially where combined AM-FM radio and television stations are housed under one roof. (Garrison, 1990 and Lorenz & Vivian, 1996).

15. Stein (1985) explains that the inverted pyramid style serves two main purposes: "It allows the reader to quickly grasp the essential part of the story, and it permits swift and efficient editing of copy. . . When an editor cuts a story, it is usually from the bottom up so as not to break up the continuity and allow the basic facts to remain" (60).

16. Crisis policy planning involves 1) heightened consciousness of threat and risk among the media and the public; 2) greater opportunity for presidential determination of a national policy priority; 3) focused attention of many high-level officials for an unusual length of time; 4) tendency towards high-level involvement in normally low-level functions; 5) heightened uncertainty about the details of the crisis; 6) increased difficulty in the evaluation of options, and of interdepartmental and intergovernmental coordination and consultation; and 7) higher probability of miscalculation

due to the limited information available and reduced time for analysis and evaluation.

17. Personality factors include individual personality structures, belief systems, and related images. Situational variables refer to environmental changes and their relation to individual motivation and cognitive performance, and examine organizational roles and their impact on the preferences of decision-makers and their ability to process information.

18. According to Moskowitz and Wright (1979: 4), there are three types of decisions: decisions under certainty (facts are known) versus uncertainty; static decisions (decisions made once) versus dynamic decisions (sequence of interrelated decisions are made); and decisions where the opponent is nature or a thinking (rational) opponent. For any decisions, there are five constituent elements: a decision-making unit, a set of possible actions that may be taken to solve the decision problem, a set of possible states that may occur, a set of consequences associated with each possible action and state that may occur, and the relationship between the consequences and values of the decision-making unit.

19. According to Scanlon (1999: 30), Russell Dynes classifies organizations that respond to emergencies in four ways: regular, expanding, extending and emergency. Scanlon concluded that those typologies fit the 1998 ice storm that left about one-fifth of Canadians without power. (In January 1998, a series of ice storms in Eastern Canada and some neighboring U.S. states led to a build-up of ice that was so heavy that trees, telephone and power poles, and even steel transmission towers came down. In some areas, the total ice accumulation was more than 100 millimeters, five times the historic high.) However, in this case, the "emergent" groups were formed from inside rather than outside the established response structure and, consequently, there was none of the expected conflict between existing and emergent organizations. Scanlon suggests that the lesson for planners is that if they adapt rapidly to changing circumstances and are ready to sponsor or include emergent groups in their existing structure they can reduce or eliminate conflict.

20. There are two different types of intuition: immature intuition and mature intuition. Each type is differentiated by the level of expertise of the individual in a specific subject area. Immature intuition is most available when an individual is a beginner in a given knowledge domain, where his/her analytical knowledge of the subject does not interfere with the ability to make unique insights. Mature intuition is more rare and is most available when an individual is an expert in the subject area with well-developed relevant knowledge (Baylor, 2001: 237).

21. Three primary assumptions underlie this theory: 1) There is a single, homogeneous, good utility that is present in all actually desired ends, and an

increased amount of any end brings with it an increased amount of utility, at a steadily diminishing rate; 2) There is a set of well-defined and mutually exclusive alternatives, one of which the decision-maker must choose; 3) The decision-maker is able to estimate the outcome and calculate the expected value of each alternative. Two additional fundamental assumptions of this theory are infinite calculating ability and omniscience— two essential abilities needed to calculate the outcome of an infinite set of alternatives and the expected value of each outcome.

22. The bounded rationality theory, according to Snyder and Diesing (1977: 347), focuses directly on a central point: crisis decision-making is a search for a strategy that will correct the intolerable situation, that is, a strategy that will preserve or achieve all endangered goods at an acceptable level. It is a search for an acceptable strategy, not a best strategy.

23. Assumptions of this tradition are, first, the heterogeneity of goods, i.e., an inability to compare the value of two different alternative goods because achieving one means sacrificing the other, e.g., peace and national security; second, the whole set of available alternatives is not given at the start of decision-making as new alternatives may turn up from time to time or may be constructed by modifying old ones; third, even for the known alternatives, one is not able to calculate the probability of their achieving specific goods, except very crudely. Obviously, bounded rationality and maximizing theories are compatible as they can be combined in two opposite ways, by taking one theory, maximizing, as basic and the other, bounded rationality, as supplementary. In this way, decision-making is considered as a process of finding the best alternative, which promises to achieve most of various desired goods. However, it is sometimes difficult and perhaps even impossible to find the absolutely best alternative. It is impossible to consider all alternatives, but a decision-maker may consider those two or three that appear most obvious, reasonable, or promising.

CHAPTER 2

Communication and Crisis Management

In this second chapter I demonstrate that communication is an essential requirement to the field of crisis management. To this end, it is necessary to understand and distinguish the crisis situation from other similar stress situations in order to deal with it effectively. Additionally, it is necessary to recognize the ultimate goal of the crisis management process. In this chapter, I also introduce the concept of communication functioning as a double-edge sword in stress situations—in that it can escalate a situation or facilitate its resolution.

CHARACTERIZING THE CRISIS SITUATION

Crisis, as the most extreme of all stress situations, holds the highest degree of attention of most, if not all, diversified individuals, groups, systems, and countries, especially if it occurs on a transnational level—known as the *international crisis*. The political crisis is considered the most dangerous type of crisis since it may lead to internal conflict or series of conflicts on the national level, or may lead to a war, or perhaps several wars, on the international level. Therefore, the *international political crisis* deserves the highest degree of attention. Conflict is the most similar stress situation to crisis in terms of characteristics and, in the same way, the *international protracted conflict* is the worst kind of conflict.

The term "crisis" has been identified, conceptualized, and classified in various ways. Crisis is a situation that happens on various levels—organizational, national, regional, or international. It also happens in various fields or systems—social, economic, political, environmental, and so on. Specifically, the main concern here is the political dimension, and still more specifically, the international. The significance of the international crisis results from its less frequent occurrence and more consequent dangers, as well as its crucial location between peace and war. Given the high level of stress present in an international crisis, the study of crisis decision-making is important in assessing the effects of that stress on policymakers, whether politicians or media workers; and in determining whether or not the players can think or act rationally under such extreme pressure.

Scholars have presented many definitions of the term "crisis," and each one, or group of definitions, follows one or more approaches. I explore the definition of crisis according to six different approaches: 1) characteristics; 2) the system; 3) decision-making; 4) the middle way between the system and decision-making; 5) conflict; and 6) the process of management. The word "crisis" itself, as Bokhari (1997: 3) tells us, "is derived from Greek and means 'to decide.' . . . In its present usage it means a decisive point which changes the course of events." Using the first approach, the characteristics of crisis, Rosenthal, Hart and Charles define crisis as "a serious threat to the basic structures or the fundamental values and norms of a social system, which—under time pressure and highly uncertain circumstances—necessitates making critical decisions" (1989: 10).[1]

Conflict is the situation most similar to crisis. There is actually a sequential relationship among situations of conflict, crisis, and war. When conflict causes damage to the basic structure of a system it becomes a crisis, which may be escalated into a war. In Bokhari's (1997) words, "A conflict draws attention only when it reaches a point at which it becomes disruptive to the system. At that point it is no longer a conflict, but a crisis" (8-9). I argue that two major distinctions between conflict and crisis are the life cycle and the way of termination. The crisis has a life cycle but conflict does not. Bokhari (1997:8-9) describes crisis as an aberration on the continuum of a conflict, like sickness in the life of an individual. While remaining part of a conflict, a crisis is still a distinct phenomenon and has its own dynamics. In terms of the termination of both situations, Bokhari contends that crises are more challenging, as by nature they are more amenable to management. Conflicts, on the other hand, are a more stubborn phenomenon and are, therefore, less susceptible to management. For that reason, I defend the idea that crisis management and conflict resolution are always possible, while crisis resolution and conflict management are not. That is, the life cycle of crisis resists resolution at its various stages but is open to management that de-escalates or calms it down, while conflict that does not have a life cycle can be resolved as by nature there is no place for management. In other words, crisis stays longer in different statuses during its life cycle's stages, during which crisis is willing to management rather than resolution because the latter cannot stop its life cycle while the former can. In conflict, on the other hand, resolution can stop the situation whether after a short or long time, but management has nothing to do given the nature of the developments of the situation.

However, the distinction between crisis management and conflict resolution[2] is easier to make than that between each one and its related terms. That is, the distinction between conflict resolution and related terms such as peacekeeping, conflict negotiation, conciliation, etc., and the distinction between crisis management and related terms such as deterrence in crisis, management by crisis, etc., is more difficult to clarify than the distinction between conflict resolution and crisis management.[3]

Crisis researchers classify the many types of crises according to nine different factors: 1) the political-historical genesis of crisis; 2) the systemic-structuralist view and locale in the system; 3) the inner working and basic mechanism of the crisis; 4) actors' perceptions about the likelihood of violence; 5) the foreseeability and extent of preparation; 6) the extent of volition involved in producing the crisis; 7) the object of the basic threat; 8) the domain of threat; and 9) the origins of threat. Others discuss six types of crises, which are classified on the basis of foreseeability and extent of preparation, and the extent of volition involved in producing the crisis. These six types are: 1) the unimaginable crisis; 2) the neglected crisis; 3) the quasi-unavoidable crisis; 4) the compulsive crisis; 5) the wanted crisis; and 6) the willful crisis.[4]

It can be argued here that the characteristics of crisis information are influenced by, and thus similar to, the characteristics of crisis. As Rosenthal, Hart and Charles describe crisis information, "It is threatening, it is frightening, it is unfamiliar, it is new, it is surprising, and it has 'never been heard of before'" (1989: 19). Therefore, crisis information must be dealt with in a different way, which is also influenced by the characteristics of crisis, i.e., response should be fast, accurate, obvious, and so on. In crisis situations, there is a considerable increase in the volume and speed of upward and downward communications: time-spending procedures are set aside, and high-level officials communicate directly with low-ranking bureaucrats. Also, decision-makers tend to give priority to the source of information rather than its content, and they are inclined to depend on trusted, well-liked sources.

In the decision-making approach of crisis definitions, referring to Mor (1993: 3), psychological theories of crisis view and define crisis in subjective terms, namely as a phenomenon whose existence depends on the perceptions of decision-makers. He considers Hermann's *situational cube*, which consists of three dimensions—threat, decision time, and awareness—

in which one could locate various situations facing decision-makers. For Hermann a crisis situation was distinct in that it ranked high on all three dimensions: a crisis is a situation that 1) threatens high-priority goals of the decision-making unit, 2) restricts the amount of time available for response before the decision is transformed, and 3) surprises the members of the decision-making unit by its occurrence.

I argue that the most important approach to defining crisis, among the six approaches mentioned here, is the characteristics approach. In contrast to the other approaches, which may be considered misleading as they are partly comparable, in some instances, to crisis and other situations[5] in terms of the types or ways of confronting the opponent, the characteristics' approach goes directly to the main distinguishing and determining attributes of the situation. An analysis in the form of a comparative summary of the distinct characteristics of crisis and similar situations and the connections among them has been prepared here in *Table 1* in order to show their similarities and differences and to help avoid misapprehension in dealing with them.

With the main focus on the crisis situation, the analysis divides the characteristics into four groups[6]: 1) the unique and distinguishable characteristics of the crisis; 2) the characteristics common to similar situations; 3) the probable characteristics of crisis, which may or may not occur in specific cases; and 4) the characteristics inapplicable to crisis. On the basis of this analysis, I propose a concluding definition of crisis, which takes into account only the unique characteristics of the crisis situation. Crisis may be defined as a situation of sudden threat of destruction to the basics of a system combined with uncertainty as to the unfolding of events. It has a life cycle that begins instantly and grows quickly towards maturity that may or may not be managed, but may not be resolved. The only consequence of its mismanagement is destruction, i.e., war, in the case of an international political crisis. Effective management leads to the de-escalation or inactivation of the crisis, but not the end, until the emergence of new cause(s) reactivates or at least partly implicates the old, to constitute a new and different crisis.

A situation defined in this way relies solely on successful management. The purpose of crisis management is to resolve a dangerous confrontation without fighting, and with vital interests preserved. It attempts to maintain control over events, not allowing them to escalate. Communication, among other factors, is a basic principle of crisis management as previously discussed. The maintenance of communication among adversaries through open, direct, and clear channels is one dimension of management.

Table 1: **A Distinction Guideline for Characteristics of Crisis and Similar Stress Situations**

Characteristics	Problem	Accident	Disaster	Terrorism	Conflict	Crisis	War
Threat to/Disruptive of system's basics	□	□	□	□	□	■	□
Uncertainty	□	□	□	‖	□	■	□
Has a life cycle	□	□	□	□	□	■	□
Manageable	□	□	□	■	□	■	□
Tension	‖	‖	‖	■	■	■	■
Stress	‖	‖	■	■	■	■	■
Disputes	□	□	□	‖	■	■	■
Need critical/crucial decision	□	□	□	■	■	■	■
Opposition/confrontation	□	□	□	■	■	■	■
Obstacles	‖	‖	‖	■	■	■	■
Surprise/sudden	□	■	■	■	□	■	□
Inconsistency	□	□	□	‖	■	■	‖
Time pressure	□	‖	■	‖	□	■	‖
Need rational decision(s)	‖	‖	‖	‖	■	■	■
Damaging	□	■	■	■	‖	‖	■
Governmental fault	□	■	■	‖	‖	‖	‖
Dissatisfaction	■	□	□	‖	‖	‖	‖
Military force	□	□	□	‖	‖	‖	■
Violence	□	□	□	‖	‖	‖	■
Capability for resolution	■	□	□	‖	■	□	□
Escalation	□	‖	‖	‖	■	□	■
Failure of intelligence/judgm.	□	‖	■	‖	□	□	□
Frustration	□	□	□	‖	■	□	■
Has solution(s)	■	□	□	‖	‖	□	‖
Inevitable	□	□	□	□	■	□	□
Scarce resources	□	□	□	‖	■	□	□
Struggle	□	□	□	‖	■	□	■

■ Applicable   ‖ Probably in/applicable   □ Inapplicable

THE SIGNIFICANCE OF CRISIS MANAGEMENT

Although preventing and avoiding crisis is better than managing it, when a crisis occurs, crisis management is the best way to proceed. Crisis prevention and crisis avoidance are preferred more, but used less. As long as crisis occurs suddenly or quickly, as is its nature, the likelihood of preventing or avoiding it is less than that of managing it. Garthoff asserts the importance of crisis management because he believes that political efforts to resolve disputes peacefully are not always successful. As a result, he states, "We must be prepared to deal with and defuse any crises that may occur. This includes the need to de-escalate crises, and still more any armed hostilities that might break out" (1989: 154). Thus, crisis management is considered extremely important, especially when the crisis involves the possibility of the use of military force or the eruption of nuclear war. The purpose of crisis management is to resolve a dangerous confrontation without fighting, and with vital interests preserved. This usually involves allowing for some flexibility. The importance of crisis management in the resolution of the 1962 Cuban Missile Crisis was reflected in the rather presumptuous announcement made by then Secretary of Defense Robert McNamara some months after the event: "Today there is no longer any such thing as strategy; there is only crisis management"[7].

Crisis management, according to Clutterbuck (1993: 7-8), is a term that came into general use after the 1962 Cuban Missile Crisis, when the Kennedy administration successfully handled a dangerous situation without going to war. The 1962 Cuban Missile Crisis[8] demonstrated the importance of using diplomatic options rather than military force. In 1962, the United States and the Soviet Union were on the edge of nuclear war between the 22nd of October, when President Kennedy announced a "quarantine" on Soviet ships carrying weapons to Cuba, and the 28th of October, when the Soviet Union announced that it would remove some 42 medium- and 24 to 32 intermediate-range ballistic missiles it had placed in Cuba, in return for a U.S. pledge not to invade Cuba in the future or undermine its communist regime and certain assurances regarding the removal of U.S. Jupiter missiles from Turkey. The 1962 Cuban Missile Crisis, the most dangerous crisis of the Cold War, provides a case study of how John Kennedy and Nikita Khrushchev, in a war-threatening confrontation, used careful crisis management approaches to reach a peaceful end. The management of this crisis was proclaimed in the United States as a great victory, and scholars of international relations studied the incident in order to learn lessons about crisis management.

Many scholars in the field of crisis studies have defined the concept of crisis management. Yet the term itself has not been as thoroughly examined as its individual parts—crisis and management. The first part of this term, "crisis," has been extensively defined through many different approaches as previously illustrated. The second part, "management," is defined by the Oxford Dictionary as "control," which is central to Williams' view:[9] "The attempt to maintain control over events and not allow them to get out of hand or develop a logic and momentum of their own is one of the major tasks of the 'crisis-managers'" (1976: 30). I consider Williams' definition of crisis management as the most apt articulation to date:

> Crisis management is concerned on the one hand with the procedures for controlling and regulating a crisis so that it does not get out of hand and lead to war, and on the other with ensuring that the crisis is resolved on a satisfactory basis in which the vital interests of the state are secured and protected. The second aspect will almost invariably necessitate vigorous actions carrying substantial risks. One task of crisis management, therefore, is to temper these risks, to keep them as low and as controllable as possible, while the other is to ensure that the coercive diplomacy and risk-taking tactics are as effective as possible in gaining concessions from the adversary and maintaining one's own position relatively intact.
>
> (1976:30)

Discussions about crisis management refer to an agreement on basic principles that was expressed for the first time during the 1962 Cuban Missile Crisis. I acknowledge Richardson's (1988: 18-22) classification of these principles into seven agreed-upon principles of crisis management: the decision-making process, the implementation of policy, the limitation of objectives, maintaining flexible options, time pressure, perception of the adversary, and communication. Alternatively, Neuhold (1978: 4-15) determines five major principles of crisis management: limitation of objectives, gradual application and localization of armed force, face-saving on both sides, the maintenance of communication with the adversary, and consideration of the precedent effect of crisis behavior.

There are a number of specific requirements for successful crisis management. George (1991a: 23-25) distinguishes between two types: political and operational requirements. Policymakers must be sensitive to these requirements in managing a crisis that may escalate into war. Because crisis management tends to be highly context-dependent, not all of these requirements are equally important in any given crisis. There are two political requirements for crisis management: limitation of the objectives pursued in the crisis, and limitation of the means employed to further those objectives. The possibility of terminating diplomatic confrontations successfully without war may depend on whether one or both sides have carefully limited their crisis objectives. From earlier studies of past crises, seven operational requirements have been identified: political control over the military options; the slowing down of military movements to enhance diplomatic communications in assessing the situation; coordination between military movements and diplomatic actions; consistency between military threats and limited diplomatic objectives; avoidance of the military threats to give the impression of resorting to war; the diplomatic-military tendency to negotiation rather than military solution; and diplomatic proposals and military providence to the adversary with the opportunity of achieving his interests.[10]

Crisis management involves various strategies.[11] As noted above, George (1991c: 378) explains that optimal strategy for crisis management is extremely context-dependent. He argues that although most crises share some characteristics, the precise configuration of each crisis varies in ways that have different implications for the selection of an appropriate strategy. Consequently, there is no single dominant strategy that is equally suitable for managing every crisis. Instead, strategy needs to be carefully formulated and sometimes carefully adapted to meet the distinctive configuration of the crisis. George introduces two major kinds of crisis management strategies: offensive and defensive. The five offensive crisis management strategies (379-383) are: 1) blackmail; 2) limited probe; 3) controlled pressure; 4) *fait accompli*; and 5) slow attrition.[12] On the other hand, the seven defensive crisis management strategies (383-392) are: coercive diplomacy; limited escalation of involvement to establish ground rules more favorable to the defender, plus efforts to deter an escalatory response by the opponent; tit-for-tat reprisals without escalation, plus deterrence of escalation by the opponent; accepting a "test of capabilities" within the restrictive ground rules chosen by the opponent that initially appear disadvantageous to the defender; drawing the line; conveying commitment and resolve to avoid miscalculation by the challenger; and time-buying actions and proposals that provide an opportunity to explore a negotiated settlement of the crisis that might satisfy some of the challenger's demands.

THE FUNCTIONING OF COMMUNICATION AS DOUBLE-EDGED SWORD IN SEVERE STRESS SITUATIONS

As indicated earlier, the significance of the decision-making process increases in times and situations of high stress. Crisis and its consequent conflicts (most dangerously wars) are situations of the highest level of stress on decision-makers. Communication in general, and mass media in particular, can work towards the benefit of resolving the conflict and managing the crisis situation just as easily as it can work towards the exact opposite, hence the labeling of communication as a double-edged sword.

Communication, according to Williams (1976), can help to define the structure of a crisis so that both sides accurately perceive the relative values of the interests at stake: "Communication helps to establish the 'rules' of the game in a confrontation, so that the adversaries share common assumptions about the kinds of actions that are legitimate and those that are tacitly, if not formally, prohibited. . . . Communication may minimize the likelihood of miscalculation" (182). The importance of communication "moves", as Williams notes, was recognized by the superpowers during the 1962 Cuban Missile Crisis as an essential part of the bargaining process, and as an acceptable and valid substitute for some high-risk techniques. Both powers have acknowledged the relevance of communication as an aid to understanding and compromise. For example, the Hotline, formally called the Direct Communications Link, was created to link Washington and Moscow.

The 1962 Cuban Missile Crisis offers a good example of how the superpowers, for the first time in history, were successful in managing a crisis. Contrary to what was understood about communication during crisis, the lesson most frequently drawn from the 1962 Cuban Missile Crisis was the need to maintain open lines of communication with the adversary, i.e., the essential need for more open channels of communication between adversaries, not the reverse. "At moments of greatest tension, although communication was relatively close, compared with many earlier crises, policymakers on both sides perceived a need for a more direct channel" (Richardson, 1988: 22). George (1988: 82-83) agrees, with considerable justification, with the often stated assessment that the United States and the Soviet Union could have reduced the risk of confrontations through timely clarification and communication of their interests in particular areas and situations. Systematic examination of the history of U.S.-Soviet relations from this standpoint, he argues, shows that there are many episodes in which they failed to do so. Some of these failures might be attributed to oversight, human error, and/or technical communication difficulties of a kind that could have been rather easily avoided or improved upon in the future. Other failures to define and communicate one's interests effectively and successfully cannot be so easily explained and are rooted in causes that cannot be so readily eliminated. One root cause pertains to *difficulties of diplomatic signaling and communication*—i.e., a failure to convey what one's interests and intentions are in a timely, clear manner that is comprehensible and credible to the opponent and a failure of the recipient to attend properly to serious communications directed towards him/her and to interpret them correctly.[13]

A significant problem of miscommunication that occurs during stress situations is the usage of language that is not interpreted or understood in the way it was meant. For example, in 9/11, usage, interpretation, and understanding of language by the mass media proved to be highly significant factors. Another problem is that people often do not depend on formal or official communication during a crisis situation; consequently, the dependence on informal communication increases.

> Official warnings do not necessarily have high credibility. In fact, people generally tend not to rely solely on official communications. They check local media for their reading of the situation, they talk to neighbors, they call friends and relatives. Official warning agencies often fail to take into account the role of these informal networks.
>
> (Rosenthal, Hart & Bezuyen, 1998: 3)

Research indicates that communication is influenced by the circumstances and situations in which it is used, to the extent that it may be studied through different perspectives—sociological, psychological, environmental, political, and so on—during the situation. When the situation is a crisis and the circumstances are threat, distortion of basics, uncertainty, tension, stress, surprise, and disputes, it is highly expected that communication will be used in various forms. On the basis of his analysis of the activities of scholars, governments, media practitioners, and individual citizens in the field of international communication over the past half century, Mowlana (1984*a*: 27-28) introduces four basic approaches that have characterized international communication. In the first approach, *the idealistic-humanistic approach*, the communication process is seen as a means of bringing nations and peoples together and as a power to assist international organizations in providing their services to the world community. This approach strives toward increasing understanding among nations and peoples and toward the attainment of world peace. The second approach, sometimes called *political proselytization*, sees international communication as propaganda, ideological confrontation, advertising, and the creation of myths and clichés. These are usually one-way communications, and all require central organizing authorities of some kind. Thus they are imbued with a certain authoritarian, totalitarian character that makes the manipulation of human beings possible. The third approach, which is becoming increasingly visible, is to view information in the international context as economic power. Here its operation is more subtle, the message more subliminal. Overtly respectable international development projects, technology transfer, and business, marketing, and trade ventures have been characterized by this approach, and have usually resulted in the domination of weaker, peripheral nations. The modernization of less-developed countries has in fact resulted in their conversion to Western ways and has made them more amenable to control by Western power centers. The fourth approach to international communication is to view information as political power. Information in the form of news and data is treated as a neutral, value-free commodity. A study of international media, the wire services, literature, cinema, and television programs reveals a concentration of the means of production in very few countries. When information is conveyed from one country to another, the culture of the source is also conveyed, and this may not always be in the best interests of the recipient.

It is assumed here that these four approaches and most forms of communication may be involved when talking about crisis. The communication of crisis, in some cases, aims at achieving peace among adversaries. In the idealistic sense, it tries to promote understanding among nations, governments, or individuals in order to manage the crisis and reach some kind of settlement. It is also expected that each adversary will use one-way communication as propaganda during a crisis to manipulate and ideologically confront the other side's claims. Furthermore, using information as economic power sometimes helps to exert pressure on the weak party or parties in a crisis to implement the desired action or decision. Finally, using information as political power through forms of mass media is one of the most significant and indispensable ways of communicating among participants in a crisis. In addition, the existing technologies of communications are used extensively to manage or resolve crises and conflicts: "Communications technologies of one sort or another have always been important in the management of international conflict" (Dordick, 1984: 40). Therefore, when looking at a crisis situation this discussion does not exclude any form of communication.

During a crisis situation, it is argued here, the indicator of good or bad usage of communication is the degree to which it affects the escalation or de-escalation of the situation. On their part, the media either decrease tensions and violence or they fuel rumors and provoke the public to further conflict. Depending on the nature of the crisis, there may be an escalating situation that erupts into a war, or a de-escalating situation that reaches management. In doing so, the media decision-makers should adhere to the objective truth.

> De-escalation is seen essentially as the reverse of the process of escalation. Therefore, if escalation is defined in a simple manner— for example, as the 'controlled and specified application of sanctions in a fashion of increasing magnitude over time'—then de-escalation is defined as the same process but with a *decreasing* magnitude over time.
>
> (Fisher, 1990: 170)

The midpoint between peaceful conflict resolution or crisis management and escalated-crisis situations is a critical one, which is reflected in the processes through which various mediators, including the media, interfere to either help reach peaceful conflict resolution or influence events towards escalated crisis. Given their serious role, mass media can either help overcome the state of uncertainty, misunderstanding, and miscalculation, which prevail in a crisis situation or provoke violence. As such, the mass media can either "contribute toward a favorable mood for conflict resolution when they avoid a tone of crisis" (Davison, 1974: 47), or escalate the situation by using a tone of crisis while moving the public toward an unfavorable mood leading to an escalation of the crisis. However, crisis communication usually faces several impediments. As Rosenthal et al (1989: 464-465) explain, the importance of time is especially significant when communication arrangements are complex and multi-layered. Under this condition the processing and distribution of messages and crisis communications can suffer. Also, when tensions grow, communication between the opposing parties is reduced. This allows for separate circuits of information and image formation to develop, impeding instead of facilitating tension reduction and conflict resolution. For their part, the mass media face obstacles in effectively performing their decision-making processes during crises. The crisis decision-making process, in general, occurs under conditions of high tension and extreme pressure. In turn, this, in addition to other important factors[14], may negatively affect the functioning of the mass media.

When communication is well used as one of the strategies to effect de-escalation during a crisis situation, it becomes an essential factor in helping adversaries to reach management. In contrast to Mowlana's four approaches discussed above, some perspectives consider less communication to be better in some cases. Others hold that, in order to assess the impact of communication, this field of communication should be combined with a sociological perspective. Coser (1984) claims that "open channels of communication, while they may indeed enhance human understanding in specific circumstances, may not invariably accomplish this" (25). Thus he does not see communication as a general cure-all for human dilemmas. Some circumstances, he believes, need less rather than more communication. In assessing communication impacts, Coser argues, sociologists are interested in recognizing the answer to four questions: "(1) Under what circumstances can communication serve useful functions, and under what circumstances is it likely to be counterproductive? (2) What are the structural circumstances that limit the impact and effect of communication? (3) What purpose does such limitation serve? (4) Who is benefited and who suffers harm?" (25). He contends that when such questions are addressed, the sociology of communication becomes a significant area of research, and communication is no longer regarded as a "panacea."

Although the mass media typically participate in the de-escalation of crisis and conflict situations for the benefit of society, they sometimes contribute to the exacerbation of situations. The interference of mass media in the crisis decision-making process is a dangerous function. It is important to control that interference in order to avoid any harmful effects. In general, the crisis decision-making process occurs under conditions of high tension and extreme pressure.

> There is generally a shortage of information about the causes of the crisis, its short- and long-term health consequences, and remedial actions. Simultaneously, decision-makers are under great pressure to provide this information to minimize damages. Under these circumstances, the failure to communicate effectively further exacerbates an already bad situation.
>
> (Shrivastava, 1989: 111)

In addition to these circumstances, other important factors may negatively affect the functioning of the mass media. While the pressures on media people and the circumstances of crisis situations influence the performance of the mass media in general, the individual responses of media people vary considerably. As Simmons (1998) suggests, "No two people doing the same thing will react in the same manner to the same kind of pressure under the same set of circumstances" (159). This variance itself is another factor that may contribute to the exacerbation of the crisis situation.

> The situation of journalists in extreme predicaments, wars, famines, natural disasters, is unusual. However much journalists ritualize their response to it—the jokes, the drink, the media-bared routines in the face of death, the deadlines—there is always an appalling gap between journalists' own front-line experiences and the places in which their reporting is received: in comfortable, remote homes.
>
> (Seaton, 1999: 57)

Evidence of the involvement of the mass media in exacerbating crisis is so widespread that "in many nations, political leaders and government officials have periodically denounced the press and electronic media for their alleged roles in creating conflict" (Arno, 1984*a*: 3). Therefore, much attention should be paid to the nature and dynamics of the role of the mass media during crisis and conflict situations.

The mass media intervention in conflicts is similar also to their intervention in crises. The conflict situation, which usually involves two major conflicting adversaries, depends heavily on certain kinds of mediators for resolution. Intervention by these mediators is a process sometimes called negotiation. It may also be referred to as mediation, arbitration, or adjudication, for instance, in cases of escalated or international conflict and in conflicts of historical or economic rights. "Most conflicts that are settled peacefully are resolved as the result of some kind of negotiation, mediation, arbitration, or adjudication" (Davison, 1974: 40). In this respect, there are various types of mediators, including the mass media, which represent the third party. Arno contends that,

> in many cases, a third party profits from the conflict of two others, and this is especially true of news organizations. Were it not for such conflict, in fact, they would not even exist. Newspapers or television stations could serve other purposes, such as education, national integration, or entertainment. In order to function as news media, they need the conflict of others.
>
> (1984*b*: 234)

This benefit that accrues to the mass media does not mean that its function of providing news is its most important one, but serves only as an example of the benefit acquired as a result of interfering or playing the role of the third party within conflict situations. From other perspectives the argument is made that "the proper role for the mass media, when international disputes are being negotiated, mediated, or adjudicated, would be to remain silent—to refrain from interfering" (Davison, 1974: 40). Silencing the media during conflict, I argue, would not be beneficial, for it would likely result in the loss of credibility of and public confidence in the mass media as a result of their not being informative. Rather, a favorable alternative would be the active contribution of the mass media "toward the success of negotiations by helping to ensure that each side is truly familiar with the other's position" (Ibid: 41). In this way, the mass media execute one of their most important functions as well as contribute to the success of the negotiation. The content of media during conflict situations exerts a two-sided influence on the situation. It "does not merely reflect the level of conflict in the society but has a functional relationship to it: it either intensifies or diminishes it" (Arno, 1984a: 3-4). Conflict can reach the most dangerous and destructive stage if it is escalated or gets out of control. As an essential part of the process of resolving the conflict, the mass media play their role effectively when controlling[15] the content so as to be helpful in de-escalating the situation. When the mass media, including press, radio, and television, supply information to an extended audience, they help to contain and resolve problems in the community that may lead to conflict situations. The media directly affect public opinion. For example, as Dordick (1984) points out, "The national broadcasting station has become an early target of every revolutionary as a means to inform the citizens of his presence and his progress and also to initiate a resolution of the conflict" (40-41). Illustrating the role of the mass media during conflict, which I refer to as a good-bad, two-sided role (double-edged sword), Mowlana (1984b) states: "Perhaps the greatest potential contribution of mass communication to peaceful conflict resolution is in the media's ability to influence the *moods* of government, elites, and the public. It is ironic that the trait of the media that perhaps has done the greatest damage also has the potential for doing the greatest good" (94-95).[16]

To conclude, this chapter has looked at communication from the angle of decision-making. Understanding communication as a decision-making process allows communication to meet with theories of crisis management and mathematics on the central ground of decision-making. The communication studied here is the one between or among countries with different backgrounds, ideologies, cultures, and so on. Among the several areas of researching international communication, my main concern in this book is the involvement of transnational news media of such countries in international political crisis. The definition of crisis presented in this chapter illustrates the necessity for successful management because the opposite results in negative developments. The requirements for successful crisis management and its strategies discussed here reflect a major fact—mediators in the management of crises, including the mass media practitioners and theorists, should seriously examine the media decision-making process, especially in stress situations.

It is, therefore, argued in this book that the media decision-making process must be effective. I argue that effectiveness relies on two major dimensions—*rationality* and *responsibility*. When the mass media are used rationally and responsibly as an important means to effect the de-escalation of a crisis, they become key players in helping the opponents to manage it. Because of the shortage of comprehensive, dynamic, and contingent models, it has been difficult for the participants in a complex conflict or crisis situation to structure the problem systematically and to access the possible means for management. To work towards this end, the following chapters are structured to cover these dimensions. Chapter 3 focuses on the rationality dimension, and Chapter 4 on the responsibility dimension. Both dimensions are applied in Chapters 7 and 8 as a precursor to constructing the basis of the book's model in Chapter 9 and then discussing the model itself in Chapter 10.

NOTES

1. Michael Brecher's definition is similar: "[Crisis] is a situation with three necessary and sufficient conditions derived from a change in a state's external or internal environments. All three are perceptions held by the highest level decision-makers of the actor concerned: *a threat to basic values*, along with the awareness of *finite time for response* to the external value threat, and a *high probability of involvement in military hostilities*" (Bokhari, 1997: 6). Nicholson's definition is also similar: "First, a crisis situation is one of great uncertainty, where the possibility of a really disastrous conclusion to the crisis is quite large. . . . [T]he second defining characteristic is that the crisis involves an abnormal degree of pressure on the decision makers in that it is carried on over a relatively short period of time" (1970: 103-104).

2. For definitions of, and approaches to, conflict resolution, its emergence, its basic assumptions and principles, and its intervention models see: Laue (1987: 18), Wedge (1987: 280-281), Schellenberg (1996: 9-15, 213), Friedman (1999: 47), Burton (1993: 55-61), and Abu-Nimer (1999: 11-28).

3. Terms and processes related to conflict resolution are, for instance, adjudication, arbitration, coercion, conciliation, reconciliation, peacekeeping, intervention, mediation, negotiation, and alternative dispute resolution (ADR). For explanations, see: Clutterbuck (1993: 223), Colosi (1987: 92-94), Dean (1987: 215), Dotson (1987: 160), Gaughan (1987: 107-108), Pruitt (1987: 62), Schellenberg (1996: 133-134, 143, 171, 182, 195-196), Scimecca (1991: 29; and 1993: 211-218), Dupont and Guy-Olivier (1991: 40-56), and Whittaker (1999: 1-6). Important issues related to the concept of crisis management include the process of management itself, management by crisis, crisis mismanagement, deterrence in crisis, and stability in crisis—all concepts which often appear in discussions about the process of controlling crisis. For explanations, see: Rosenthal et al. (1989: 471), MacGillivray and Winham (1988: 91), and Bouchard (1991: 15).

4. First, Rosenthal et al. call the totally unexpected, unplanned, and unwanted crisis the *unimaginable* crisis. Second, a crisis that falls within the scope of imagination and is unwanted, yet within the range of social and political expectation, is called the *neglected* crisis. The third type of crisis relates to situations that achieve the same risk level as the neglected crisis, is equally unwanted, but is subject to more or less serious planning; this is the domain of unacceptable risks. A crisis that occurs as a result of the unpredictability of specific place and time is termed the *quasi-unavoidable* crisis. The fourth type describes a situation where, in spite of their good intentions, the relevant actors seem to be doing their utmost to produce a full-fledged crisis. The more effort they make to avert the crisis, the more inevitable it becomes. This is called the *compulsive* crisis. The fifth type of crisis, the *wanted* crisis, is distinguished by a volitional impulse: some actors want it to happen and come to the arena with a straightforward plan to create as many complications and critical circumstances as possible, and to dismiss attempts for crisis management. The sixth type, the *willful* crisis, describes social conflict that leads to confrontation, where the main parties involved all seem to compete in using escalatory devices (1989: 446-447).

5. For definitions of these similar situations see: Nicholson (1970: 2-3), Deutsch (1982: 15-16), Fraser and Hipel (1984: 5), Netanyahu (1986: 200), Laue (1987: 17), Wilkinson (1990: 26-27), Shiels (1991: 3), Schellenberg (1996: 8-9), Bokhari (1997: 10-11), Rosenthal, Hart and Bezuyen (1998: 5), Starr (1999: 3), Azar (1999: 32), and Friedman (1999: 38).

6. The unique and distinguishable characteristics of the crisis are threat to the basics of the system, uncertainty, having a life cycle, and the capability for management. As well, there are some characteristics common to similar situations. Tension is a characteristic of terrorism, conflict, crisis, and war. It is sometimes a characteristic of problem, accident, and disaster. Stress is involved in situations of disaster, terrorism, conflict, crisis, and war, as well as it can happen in problem and accident. There are only three mutual

characteristics among conflict, crisis, and war: disputes, confrontation or opposition, and the need for critical or crucial decisions. Surprise is a mutual characteristic of crisis, terrorism, disaster, and accident. Inconsistency occurs in crisis and conflict. Working under time pressure is a mutual characteristic of crisis, disaster, and probably accident. The probable characteristics of crisis, which may or may not happen in specific cases, are the fault of government, dissatisfaction, damage, violence, and the use of military force. Ultimately, the characteristics that are not applicable to the crisis are capability for resolution, escalation, failure of intelligence, frustration, scarce resources, struggle, and unpredictability.

7. This statement is frequently referred to in studies of crisis management.

8. For information about the 1962 Cuban Missile Crisis, including: the anatomy of the crisis; assessment of the crisis managers' actions and the crisis management approaches of their advisory systems; the deception and power of the crisis; the U.S. strategy formulation process; Kennedy's adherence to the operational requirements of crisis management; Kennedy's bargaining strategy and tactics; Kennedy's limitation of objectives and means; Kennedy's motivations, objectives, and strategy; Kennedy's problem—how to demonstrate resolution without triggering war; U.S. warnings and Soviet responses; Khrushchev's bargaining strategy and tactics; Khrushchev's missed opportunity; Khrushchev's motivations, objectives, and strategy; Krushchev's gamble; the abortive U.N. initiatives; the lessons learned; and the crisis as a bargaining contest, see: Grattan (2004: 55-67), Pious (2001: 81-84), Clutterbuck (1993: 106-111, 243), George (1991*d*: 223-241), Nathanson (1991: 94), Garthoff (1989: 155), Lebow (1987*a*: 182-183), Lebow (1987*b*: 17-20), Brams (1985: 55-59), and Lebow (1983: 431-439) as well as Bertrand Russell's work, including *Unarmed Victory* (1963).

9. Like Williams, many researchers use the word "control" to express the process of managing crisis. For example, Laurence Martin states, "Crisis management is no more than a phrase to describe the aim of remaining as much in control of events as possible" (Williams, 1976: 30).

10. Also, Cimbala (1999: 121-123) discusses four requirements for successful crisis management: communications transparency; the reduction of time pressure on policymakers; the ability of each side to offer the other a safety valve or a face-saving exit from a predicament that has escalated beyond its original expectations; the ability of each side to maintain an accurate perception of the other's intentions and military capabilities. Crisis management requires "reasonably high capabilities to acquire, manage, and process data rationally in accordance with effective theories about how the world works" (Pious, 2001: 92), and along with game playing, as explained in Chapter 5, requires "effective control over the pieces on the board" (Ibid: 93).

11. In the 1962 Cuban Missile Crisis, Robert Grattan (2004) explains that there was a parallel between the crisis discussions and strategic management thought. Grattan suggests three levels of strategy for the U.S. position in the crisis and illustrates them horizontally in a figure. In the upper line, Grattan situates the grand strategy, which he considers it equal to corporate strategy. In the middle line, the crisis strategy is equalized to the business strategy. And in the bottom line, the input from Defense Department, State Department, CIA, and ambassadors are equalized to functional strategy. Grattan explains that "the grand strategy, the U.S. position in the world and the strategy for its maintenance, were not directly affected by the crisis, but it did provide the context for the crisis strategy" (61). He also explains that the result of the work that was done in the State Department was fed upwards through their representatives on the Executive Committee. That is, "the strategy process is not wholly linear, up or down, but continues to iterate around the levels until an acceptable result, and consensus, is reached (that is, satisficing)" (61).

12. The challenger uses blackmail strategy to generate a crisis from which s/he hopes to benefit. Limited reversible probe strategy means that the challenger attempts to deal with the policy dilemma of crisis management by initiating a probing action that begins the process of bringing about a favorable change in the status quo but, in the interest of avoiding unwanted escalation, does so by means of an action that can be quickly and easily called off. Using the strategy of controlled pressure, the challenger contrives small actions that exert pressure against continuation of the status quo that the defender finds difficult to counter, either because he does not possess appropriate capabilities or options for doing so. The *fait accompli* strategy describes a situation where the challenger is confident that the adversary is not committed to defending the position under dispute, then decides that quick, decisive action is not only the most efficient way to change the status quo but is also risk-free insofar as the likelihood of unwanted escalation is concerned. A highly motivated but relatively weak actor can adopt a guerrilla or terrorist form of attrition strategy in an effort to wear out a stronger adversary.

13. Other lessons can be learned by examining the unsophisticated attempts of the superpowers, Britain and France in this case, at crisis management in the Suez Crisis of 1956. Since then, as Jönsson (1991: 184) notes, the importance of signaling has gradually been recognized, and the superpowers have learned to back their words by deeds. Their repertoire of signaling instruments has progressively increased, and the ability of each side to signal its own intentions and to understand the other's signals has gradually improved.

14. Journalists, for instance, cannot report news that their media organizations will not consider publishing or broadcasting. These organizations consider

news as a commodity, which is supposed to at least cover the cost of reaching the audience as well as provide a little profit: "The forces of media economics, audience wishes, deadlines, and accepted journalistic work routines imply that media performance is unlikely to improve dramatically in coverage of future crises" (Maher & Chiasson, 1995: 222).

15. The suggested model in Chapter 7 provides some measures to explain how the media decision-makers can control, or manage, the media content in a way that enhance their performance.

16. Davison (1974) also uses the term *mood* when talking about the influence of the mass media on the midpoint between peaceful conflict resolution and escalated crisis that may erupt into a war.

CHAPTER 3

Communication and Mathematics

The central purpose of this chapter is to highlight the intertwined relationship between mathematics and communication. Additionally I introduce the consideration of rationality, which is drawn from mathematical theory, along with its behavioral decision theory dimension, as a major concept which can be used effectively in the communication field. This, in turn, facilitates the use of mathematical theories, and game theory in particular, to theorize the performance of communication between adversaries in a conflict situation. A deeper appreciation of game theory also helps us understand how rational thinking can be useful for decision-makers, especially in times of conflicts and crises.

MATHEMATICS REQUIRED

Mathematically you can cook up anything. You can imagine any sort of situation and represent it by a mathematical model. The problem becomes that of finding something in the real world to fit the model. . . . There was a man who liked to fix things around the house, but the only tools he could use were a screwdriver and a file. When he saw a screw that wasn't tight, he tightened it with his screwdriver. Finally there were no more screws to tighten. But he saw some protruding nails. So he took his file and made grooves in the caps of the nails. Then he took his screwdriver and screwed them in. To paraphrase Marshall McLuhan's famous remark, 'The medium is the message,' the mathematician could well say, 'The tool is the theory.'

(Anatol Rapoport, cited in Weintraub, 1985: 35)

Although the preceding quote refers to his belief that sophisticated mathematical tools bias economic discourse, the mathematical biologist Anatol Rapoport brings our attention to one dimension of the relationship between mathematics and communication by paraphrasing Marshall McLuhan's famous remark. Considering a form of communication as a tool that reflects a calculated theory is an assumption of the possibility of using mathematical tools to reflect communication content. The form of communication can work as a mathematical tool if the message or the communication content seeks objectives similar to those of a particular mathematical theory. In other words, if the content of communication is to achieve specific goals in a situation that is, or can be, mathematically theorized, media of communication can help achieve these ends if they work in a fashion similar to mathematical tools.

Among the many different answers that have been given to the question *what is mathematics?* throughout history is the definition given by the French mathematician Henri Poincaré. Anna Sfard (2002) finds Poincaré's definition particularly useful: "mathematics is the science of calling different things the same name" (145). She argues that this deceptively simple statement, if interpreted in a way not necessarily intended by Poincaré himself, can be seen as a forerunner of the *communicational* vision of mathematics. She sees that mathematics is a kind of discourse or a way of communicating. The issue of *naming* in Poincaré's definition implies that mathematics is, in principle, a discursive activity, which is a special way of communicating. Sfard opposes the claim that *thinking* rather than *communicating* should be given prominence in the definition by arguing that thinking is already included in the term *communication*. Undeniably, according to the basic tenet of the communicational framework, she argues, thinking can be regarded as a special case of communicative activity (145-146).

Poincaré's definition and the discussion surrounding it, as well as Rapoport's claim highlight the significance of drawing on mathematics when studying communication. The latter can benefit from the mathematical theory in the pursuit of some of its goals; at the very least its goals will be better performed through the use of mathematics. Drawing on the literature concerning mathematical theory, this chapter will now explain the broad sense of mathematics, first tracing the historical use of mathematics as a required tool in the social sciences, and then distinguishing two basic concepts: 1) doing mathematics and employing mathematical methods, and 2) analyzing the criticism of the use of mathematics in the social sciences.

In searching for best answer to his question "what is mathematics about?", Michael Dummett considers the so-called "logicist" thesis, given by

Gottlob Frege and sustained by Russell and Whitehead, to be a brilliant answer:

> [M]athematics is not about *anything in particular:* it consists, rather, of the systematic construction of complex deductive arguments. Deductive reasoning is capable of eliciting, from comparatively meager premises and by routes far from [the] immediately obvious, a wealth of often surprising consequences; in mathematics, such routes are explored and the means of deriving those consequences are stored for future use in the form of propositions. Mathematical theorems, on this account, embody deductive subroutines which, once discovered, can be repeatedly used in a variety of contexts.
>
> (Dummett, 2002: 21)

Dummett argues that the "logicist" thesis simultaneously explains various puzzling features of mathematics. The thesis explains the methodology of mathematics, which relies on deductive proof; it explains the high-ranking qualification mathematics demands for an assertion; it explains the generality of mathematics; it explains our impression of the necessity of mathematical truths; and it explains why mathematics has such manifold applications.

Returning to Immanuel Kant's influential formulation of a theory of knowledge, which includes a philosophy of mathematics, Vladimir Tasic (2001: 10-13) explains that Kant's philosophy can be seen as an attempt to investigate the somewhat unclear connection between reason and experience: "Concepts without experiences are empty; experiences without concepts cannot constitute knowledge" (10). Therefore, Tasic says that an explanation of how mathematical knowledge is possible requires something more than just having the intuitions of space and time; it requires our ability to know that mathematical concepts correspond to possible experiences. Tasic (45-46) also draws from Brouwer to compare mathematical knowledge to language. He explains that Brouwer sees mathematical knowledge as always an active determinant, the work of the "creative subject"; i.e., mathematics is a process of creation. For Brouwer, mathematics is an act of will, of creation, while language is at best a flawed vehicle for the transmission of that will: "Linguistic edifices, sequences of sentences that follow one another according to the laws of logic . . . have nothing to do with mathematics, which is outside of this edifice" (46).

> Empirical knowledge which is applicable to man . . . [which] we may still term "human sciences" . . . has a relation to mathematics:

like any other domain of knowledge, these sciences may, in certain
conditions, make use of mathematics as a tool; some of their
procedures and a certain number of their results can be formalized.

(Foucault, 1994: 349)

The most important lesson that history teaches us about the role of
mathematics in the modern social sciences at the dawn of their
existence is that the social sciences require the use of mathematics
and could not exist without them.

(Senn, 2000: 271)

Mathematics has historically been a key tool of the social sciences.
Peter Senn (2000) traces the use of mathematics from the late pre-modern
period of the development of the social sciences up to about 1800. To
understand the relationship of the pre-modern social sciences to mathematics,
Senn establishes the broad sense in which the term "mathematics" is used:
"Mathematics refers both to the use of numbers and as a method of
reasoning. It also denotes statistics and statistical methods. The term . . .
covers the use of mathematical logic and methods" (272). He discusses the
history of mathematics in the late 1700s, concluding that it has its own
history that "is not congruent with that of the other sciences" (274). He
focuses on only one aspect of the history of mathematics—its availability to,
and application by, social theorists to social problems.

It is quite striking that Senn distinguishes two basic concepts: "doing
mathematics" and "employing mathematical methods." Doing mathematics
means performing a mathematical operation, while employing mathematical
methods refers to how problems are formulated and handled. Both these
common uses of the term "mathematics" include "statistics," a term which he
defines as "a body of methods for handling numerical data or for making
decisions about numerical data either in the face of uncertainty or when a
multiplicity of causes are involved" (275). He argues that the dominant force
driving the use of mathematics in the development of social thought was the
desire to provide answers to social problems. In the pre-modern period, the
users of mathematics knew they required data and mathematical tools to
describe the problems that interested them and to imagine and devise rational
policies. However, not all social thinkers used mathematics. There are several
possible reasons why the mathematics available was not used: 1) lack of
knowledge about the mathematics available; 2) some who knew the requisite
mathematics could not see any use for it in tackling the studies that interested
them; and 3) some did not use it for philosophical or ideological reasons
(283-284).

Criticisms of the use of mathematics in the social sciences can be categorized as two main types—philosophical and technical. According to Senn, philosophical criticism argues that some of the subjects of social science should not or cannot be studied mathematically. The aim here is to define, to restrict, or to eliminate the use of mathematics in the social sciences. Technical criticism accepts the use of mathematics and is concerned with how it is used. It is concerned with errors of logic, mathematical mistakes, the sizes of databases, the kind of mathematics appropriate for a given problem, and so on. This kind of criticism improves the quality of mathematical work in the social sciences (290-291).

However, these criticisms had no significant long-term effect on the continuing growth of the use of mathematics in the social sciences. Senn looks at this in terms of one of the canons of modern science: "Scientists must be able to use any tools they see fit for their problem. Their peers will judge the results and, in the long run, accept or reject them" (290). Also, he shows that the conception of "mathematics as a language" is a source of misunderstanding about the use of mathematics in the social sciences. The confusion can be clarified through six points of comparison. First, while language is spoken, mathematics cannot be; except for elementary formulations mathematics must be written in order to communicate its reasoning. Thus, while a human being typically learns at least one language very early on, s/he does not learn mathematics in the same way. Second, the mandatory conditions of strict deductive proof from admitted assumptions in the case of mathematics do not exist for language. Third, and most significantly, while languages can be translated, both literally and figuratively, mathematics, in general, cannot be translated into any other written or spoken language. Fourth, while mathematics requires an axiomatic structure and written symbols for effective communication and understanding, language does not. Fifth, while mathematics is a consciously constructed system of concepts, language is not. Finally, while mathematics is a method of reasoning, language uses words through which reasoning takes place (290-291).

THE INTERTWINEMENT OF MATHEMATICS AND COMMUNICATION

History shows that mathematics has been intimately associated with, indeed is intrinsic to, the arts, religions, technology, sciences, economics and politics of modern civilization. Every philosophical proposal since antiquity has strongly relied on a discussion of the nature of mathematics. As has been said so frequently,

mathematics is the real basis of Western thought. . . . It is
undeniable that mathematics is well integrated into the
technological, industrial, military, economic and political systems
of the present world. . . . We may say that mathematics is intrinsic
to today's culture.

(D'Ambrosio, 2001: 327)

Major scholars and philosophers have connected mathematics to
knowledge and social sciences in general and communication in particular.
For instance, Michel Foucault (1994) discusses two fields of sciences: *a
priori* sciences and *a posteriori* sciences. He explains that the field of *a priori*
sciences is "pure formal sciences, deductive sciences based on logic and
mathematics," while the domain of *a posteriori* sciences is "empirical
sciences, which employ the deductive forms only in fragments and in strictly
localized regions" (246). He gives historical examples of the use of
mathematics as a tool in human sciences: in politics, Condorcet was able to
apply the calculation of probabilities to politics; in psychology, contemporary
psychologists make use of information theory in order to understand the
phenomena of learning (349).

Randall Collins (1998) claims that it took many generations of
continuous intellectual inquiry to recognize that the objects mathematicians
investigate are "intellectual operations". The men who effected the
mathematical revolution, Collins explains, were Cardan, Tartaglia, Viète,
Descartes, Fermat, Brahe, Kepler, Napier, Gilbert, Stevin, and Snel (571). He
suggests that the mathematical revolution is a fourth link in the chain of
successive innovations that began with astronomy, followed by medical
physiology and chemistry (559). The chief dynamic of scientific discovery,
Collins argues, is new technology or equipment rather than theory; for
example, he says, the great scientific advances of the 1600s began with
Galileo's use of the telescope to discover new phenomena in astronomy.
Meanwhile, mathematics as an alternative route to rapid-discovery science is
another key to the scientific revolution (538). While Collins accepts that the
two routes may coincide—"many aspects of the scientific revolution of the
1600s and 1700s were carried out not only by experiment but also by
formulating quantitative principles for the results" (538)—he also argues that
they were not identical: "Traditional mathematical science, such as
astronomy among the Greeks, Chinese, or Indians, does not have the
characteristics of consensus and rapid discovery which are central to modern
science" (538).

Although, by around 1780, the widespread belief among leading
mathematicians was that "mathematics had exhausted itself, that there was

little left to discover" (679), the following century "was the most flamboyant in the history of the field, proliferating new areas and opening the realms of abstract higher mathematics. The sudden expansion of creativity arose from shifts in the social bases of mathematics" (679). Most importantly, Collins concludes that mathematics and intellectual operations are internalized in communication. "Since thinking is internalized from communication within a social network, mathematics is the investigation of the pure, countless properties of thought as internalized operations of communication per se" (848). He argues that mathematicians have discovered the pure reflexiveness of intellectual operations and that a self-conscious meta-mathematics becomes a mathematically inspired philosophy (848). Building on his argument that mathematics has a social reality[1] since it is inevitably a discourse within a social community, Collins considers how numbers are like other symbols that structure human discourse. He shows that the universality of numbers does not come from any character of the objects to which they are applied, but instead from their universal use (865-868).

In the political sciences, mathematical models first became popular in the 1950s when statistics came into common usage. Johnson (1989) explains that there are two major mathematical approaches: political economy and systems modeling. According to the political economy, or "rational choice" approach, individuals in a political system are rational actors and social outcomes result from the interaction of these individuals within the constraints imposed by social institutions. This approach calls for research on legislative relations, international alliances and war, and interest groups and presidential power. "Game theory is the mode of investigation, which unifies these studies" (397). In sociology, Boudon (1974) states "one of the essential functions of mathematics—perhaps *the* essential function . . . is *clarification*" (11); that is, "mathematics is brought in to *clarify* a particular problem, a particular concept, a particular research procedure" (13).

For social scientists, the use of mathematics for analyzing data[2] through such functions as correlation coefficients and tests of significance, is relatively well known: "The social scientist finds it necessary to develop some competence in statistical reasoning for data analysis, as well as using elementary skills in quantitative measurement" (Schellenberg, 1996: 105). As a widely noticeable example in the social sciences and communication research, Paul Lazarsfeld's mathematical knowledge effectively helped him to analyze the behavioral data gathered in human action studies. His extensive experience codifying empirical research methods led him to create a professional school of social research. Lazarsfeld, in relation to other European philosophers and social scientists, called himself "a 'European positivist' who had been influenced by Ernest Mach, Henri Poincaré and Albert Einstein, and who felt intellectually close to members of the Vienna Circle" [3] (Hardt, 1992: 99).

Lazarsfeld (1954b) noted the increased interest in the role of mathematical thinking in the social sciences. He saw two sources of that increased interest: "The success of mathematics in the natural sciences is a lure for the younger social sciences, and the prestige and charm of mathematical work a temptation for many of its practitioners . . . In addition, sociologists and social psychologists have increasingly felt the need for a more rigid and precise language" (3). In his 1966 study with Neil Henry, Lazarsfeld pointed out the increased use of mathematical applications in two areas of the social sciences: economics and psychology. Economists have long worked with mathematical formulations of their theories, and psychologists also have used mathematical tools in certain aspects of their work, especially in the development of tests and in psychophysics (3). Lazarsfeld did much to codify empirical research methods: "Lazarsfeld's prime concern with methodology was embodied in a series of projects for *codification* of social research methods, by which he meant the documentation of examples accompanied by logical analysis" (Barton, 2001: 260).

Norbert Wiener, one of America's most famous mathematicians, advanced communication study in several important ways. His cybernetic theory has been used in a broad range of interdisciplinary applications including international communication. As Rogers (1994: 386) explains, cybernetics, the theory of self-regulating systems, which rests on the concept of *feedback*, also contributed directly to the rise of systems theory in the 1960s.

To illustrate communication as a social science, Littlejohn (2002: 11) explains, "Communication involves understanding how people behave in creating, exchanging, and interpreting messages. Consequently, communication inquiry combines both scientific and humanistic methods." John Durham Peters (1999) argues that the notion of communication theory[4] that emerged in the 1940s "meant a mathematical theory of signal processing" (9-10). He discusses the issue of the distance between speaker and listener, or sender and receiver, raising Kierkegaard's idea of "making the recipient self-active," thus placing the burden of interpreting the message on the shoulders of the audience (52).

Significantly, Martin Shubik (1954) argues that without mathematics, researchers analyzing a social phenomenon or problem, which involves multiple factors, could not carry out the analysis without facing substantial difficulty because verbal discussion of the phenomenon would become so complex as to be almost unmanageable. But once the problem is mathematically formulated, little trouble is encountered in re-computing for adjusted conditions. Shubik confirms that mathematics has been used in the social sciences for a long time. The role of mathematics in any study is to provide a language by means of which investigation of phenomena can be carried further than would be possible without the introduction of symbols (1-2). For example, Shubik notes that the major use of game theory as a mathematical theory in the social sciences is to provide researchers with a tool for examining and formalizing the concepts of information and communication (11).

THE RELEVANCE OF GAME THEORY

> Social situations involve the interaction of individuals; to study and understand social situations, we need a theory that explains how individuals' decisions are interrelated and how those decisions result in outcomes. Game theory is one such theory. . . . [It] provides a way to formalize social structures and examine the effects of structure on individual decisions. . . . Game theory can model economic, political, [5] or more general social situations.
>
> (Morrow, 1994: 1-2)

> As a branch of mathematics, game theory is an intellectual edifice of assumptions and theorems, to be judged by standards of deductive logic. Like all of mathematics, game theory is a tautology whose conclusions are true because they are contained in the premises.
>
> (Flanagan, 1998: 164)

Emphasizing the use of game theory in social science, Heap and Varoufakis, in the introduction to their 1995 book *Game Theory: A Critical Introduction*, write, "Game theory is everywhere these days. . . . [I]t is spreading like a bushfire through the social sciences" (1). They also quote from two prominent game theorists, Robert Aumann and Oliver Hart, who explain its popularity as follows:

> Game Theory may be viewed as a sort of umbrella or 'unified field' theory for the rational side of social science. . . . [It] does not use different, ad hoc constructs. . . . [I]t develops methodologies that apply in principle to all interactive situations.

Heap and Varoufakis (1995) claim that this view is widely held not only among practitioners of game theory but even among apparently disinterested parties. They quote, for example, Jon Elster, a well-known social theorist with very diverse interests: "If one accepts that interaction is the essence of social life, then . . . game theory provides solid microfoundations[6] for the study of social structure and social change" (1).

James Morrow (1994) claims that to study and understand social situations, we need a theory that explains how individuals' decisions are interrelated and how those decisions result in outcomes. That theory, he says (1), is game theory. Classical decision theory, which is based on utility theory, has been applied in many fields; for example, in economics it is used to study interest conflicts in the market. Of all the social sciences, economics has become the most mathematically oriented. However, theorists in many other social sciences, e.g., political science and sociology, have also increasingly used mathematical thinking in their theories, most focusing on social conflict. Game theory stands as the most common area of application of mathematics to the social sciences.

In 1944, game theory came to prominence for the first time with the publication of John von Neumann and Oscar Morgenstern's *The Theory of Games and Economic Behaviour*. In this text, the authors provided a firm mathematical foundation for game theory and revived the concept of utility theory.[7] Morrow (1994: 16) explains that game theory is based on utility theory, which is closely tied to probability theory. As with probability theory, the rigorous analysis of gambling problems drove the early development of utility theory. Utility theory is a "simple mathematical theory for representing decisions," in which it is assumed that actors are faced with choices from a set of available actions. Each available action provides a probability of producing each possible outcome. Utility is a measure of an actor's preferences for the outcomes. It reflects the actor's willingness to take risks to achieve desired outcomes and avoid undesirable outcomes. To calculate an expected utility for an action, the utility of each possible outcome is multiplied by the probability that it will occur if the action is chosen, and then summed up across all possible outcomes.

Tracing the origin of the theory of probability, a branch of pure mathematics, Harald Cramér (1955) illustrates that it developed from very humble beginnings—gambling.[8] In current games of chance involving dice, cards, a roulette wheel, etc., every single performance of the game must lead to one of a definite number of possible outcomes, but we cannot predict whether, for example, at the next toss, the coin will fall as heads or tails. Cramér illustrates that this very impossibility of prediction constitutes the *randomness,* the element of uncertainty and chance in the game. The focus is on the calculation of the numbers "a" and "c" of favorable and possible cases in various actual games. As soon as these numbers were known for a given game, their ratio $p = \dfrac{a}{c}$ was defined (11-12). This ratio gradually came to be known as the *probability*. Eventually this led to the famous classical definition[9] of probability (13):

> The probability of the occurrence of a given event is equal to the ratio between the number of cases which are favorable to this event, and the total number of possible cases, provided that all these cases are mutually symmetric.

Game theory is a branch of pure mathematics, as Michael Nicholson (1970) explains: "From a particular set of mathematical postulates, a rich, interesting and sometimes surprising set of mathematical conclusions were derived. It is this mathematical structure which is, strictly speaking, the theory of games" (51-52). Fundamentally, according to Nicholson, game theory is prescriptive and not descriptive. It recommends a rational course of action and then describes the consequences of such conduct. It tells us what would happen if the recommended behavior rules are followed.[10] On the other hand, a descriptive theory describes what people actually do, whether the action is wise or foolish. It is a description of the world as it is, not as it might be if certain forms of behavior were adopted. Edwards (1967: 48) offers a simple clarification of the concept of game theory in his description of a game of tic-tac-toe. He says that although we know at any moment in the game what the moves available to our opponent are, we do not know which one s/he will choose. Certainly, the choice will not, in general, be completely random; s/he will make a move that is designed to increase her/his chance of winning and diminish ours. Consequently, the situation is one of uncertainty rather than risk.

While there are many important uses for game theory, the most important are the applications to conflicts and crises. In general, according to Schellenberg (1996: 112), game theory rests on some basic assumptions[11] regarding the way the interests of different individuals may be related to each other, which can be analyzed mathematically: 1) games always involve two or more players, each with an opportunity to choose between alternatives; 2) each available alternative is fully known to each player; 3) all possible outcomes that might occur to any player may be expressed in terms of numerical measures of utility; and 4) each player will make those choices that will provide the maximum expected utility.

To explain some of the basic concepts of game theory, Nicholson (1970) considers a simple form, which still preserves the characteristics of a game, one of a class or type called zero-sum games[12], by which is meant that "whatever one player wins, the other loses so that the total benefit of the two players is zero[13]—hence the name" (53). In explaining the rules of the zero sum game[14] and its functions, Nicholson uses basic terms of any given game, such as pay-off matrix, mixed strategy, minimax strategy, saddle point, and so on. As for non-zero sum games, two very simple games of this type have played an essential role in the analysis of conflicts—Prisoners' Dilemma and Chicken games. Another classification for game theory, in addition to zero-sum (pure conflict) or non-zero-sum (cooperation)[15] is based on the number of persons, groups, or nations involved: two-person games and *multi-* or *n-*person games. Most of the work on game theory has been devoted to two-person games, situations with just two parties, and game theory has been especially successful in its analysis of situations of pure conflict, or zero-sum games.

Within the formal representations of games, according to Eichberger (1993: 1-2), game theory studies the behavior of rational players in interaction with other rational players. Non-cooperative game theory has been applied to politics, international crises, and international organizations. Essentially, there are three ways to represent a social interaction as a game. The first is the extensive form, which details the various stages of the interaction, the conditions under which a player has to move, the information an agent holds at different stages, and the motivation of agents. The second is the strategic form or normal form, where one notes the possible strategies of each agent together with the payoff that results from the strategy choices of the agents. The third is the characteristic function form or coalitional form, which describes social interactions where binding agreements can be made and enforced.

RATIONALITY IN MATHEMATICS AND DECISION-MAKING

Given the fact that game theory is often used as a synonym for mathematical decision theory, it may be wrongly understood that the game theory approach to decision-making offers only a mathematical dimension. However, as long as the decision-makers or game players are human beings, behavioral theory is also involved. The notion of rationality, which exists in both behavioral decision theory and mathematical decision theory, provides a suitable link between both. Rationality is a key concept in this book because it has two major aspects. First, rationality is a core assumption in game theory, and second, it is used in the proposed model found in Chapter 10 as the other fundamental component needed to maintain balance, whether in opposition to, or in support of, with ethics.

Explaining the distinction between behavioral decision theory and mathematical decision theory, Lee (1971: 15-16) notes that behavioral decision theory is largely concerned with the hypothesis of general rationality, and is particularly concerned with human behavior in relation to decisions. In this context, the distinction between *normative* and *descriptive* decision theory must be noted. Normative decision theory concerns the choices that a rational person *should* make in a given situation, regardless of the choices that real people *actually* make. Descriptive theory concerns the choices real people actually make, regardless of the choices they should make. In practice, the distinction between normative and descriptive theories often becomes unclear. In any case, the hypothesis of general rationality states that people *do* make the decisions they *should* make. If this is the case, normative and descriptive theories merge into one.

Generally speaking, there is a common comparison between what Nicholson (1997) terms "rational people" and "feeling people". Sometimes, rationality is held to be a cold and arid characteristic and a *rational person* something of a cold fish, Nicholson argues. That is, rational people are unfavorably juxtaposed with feeling people. A resulting question, from Nicholson, is: If we build a society with rational people, are we not in danger of building a soulless society? However, Nicholson provides two answers, one of defence and one of positive advocacy, in order to highlight more favorably rational people for the sake of more *effectiveness*:

> The defence is that 'feeling' and 'rationality' are not contradictory. While it might seem rather arid to refer to being in love with someone as merely reflecting a preference, even a passionate preference, the inadequacy of the formulation is not owing to its being wrong, but to its missing out important things. The rational view of preferences does not claim to be a comprehensive account of preferences, but merely a partial account and useful within its context. I advocate rationality by arguing that, if we take decisions rationally, in general they are more likely to be effective. This might sound rather prosaic, but even the most passionate lovers who live in different towns will find their love more effectively consummated if they make effective plans for meeting and first study the road map or appropriate time-tables before seeking each other's company. If I want to be an effective decision maker, then I shall also be a rational decision maker. If I am affected by a decision, and my interests and preferences coincide with a decision

maker, then I shall hope for someone who is rational in their
decision making. This is of particular importance for political
decisions.

(1997: 52)

In their 2000 *Elements of Reason: Cognition, Choice, and the
Bounds of Rationality*, Lupia, Mccubbins and Popkin try to create a new
understanding of how people reason. Their goal stems from the fact that a
primary objective of social science is to explain *why people do what they do*.
They (1-3) see that one of the great difficulties inherent in crafting such
explanations is that we cannot observe the thoughts that precede a choice,
and consequently, social scientific explanations of individual behavior must
be based on assumptions about the relationship between thinking and
choosing. By applying these insights to politics, they argue that many
scholarly approaches to the study of politics rely on controversial
assumptions about the relationship between thinking and choosing. One of
these approaches to the study of politics operates on the premise that people
are rational. Although rational choice theories are rarely vague in their
assumptions about how people think, they are controversial because some of
the applications are perceived to rely on unrealistic assumptions. Further, the
term *rationality* means different things to different people. As a result, when
people argue about the role of rationality in the study of politics, they argue
about very different concepts.

Lupia, Mccubbins and Popkin (3-8) use the controversy about
rational choice theories to demonstrate that more careful attention to reason
can help scholars to craft better explanations of why people do what they do.
What is meant by rationality is fundamental for them; however this is
confronted by the absence of consensus on the meaning of the term
rationality, even within economics—the discipline with which rational
choice explanations are most frequently associated. If there was a consensus
on the constitution of a scientifically useful definition of rationality, it would
solve many of the problems caused by the multiplicity of the existing
meanings. For example, a consensus that rationality is wealth-maximizing
behavior, or that a behavior is rational only if it is the same one that an
omniscient calculator would choose, would help determine whether
rationality is a useful basis for social scientific explanation. Ironically
enough, they claim that the present condition of the term *rationality* is that it
has multiple personalities. Therefore, they suggest distilling the many
definitions of rationality into one that is sensible empirically and widely
applicable, avoiding much of the confusion associated with the concept, and
crafting better explanations of why people do what they do. They argue that

there is at least one issue on which these many definitions of rationality agree. The issue is that people have reasons for the choices they make. That is, regardless of people's genetics or socialization, if they are able to make choices, then reasons will precede these choices. Consequently, they conclude that "a rational choice is one that is based on reasons, irrespective of what these reasons may be" (7). To support their definition, they claim that if the collective social scientific goal is to explain why people do what they do, then our task is to understand the reasons for the choices they make. They argue that whether we agree with these reasons or not, whether these reasons make sense to us or not, and whether we use the term *rationality* to describe the process by which these reasons are formed or not, is irrelevant. For them, if social scientists desire improved explanations of why people do what they do, then they must introduce greater clarity about the properties of human reason into their analyses.[16]

Rational behavior, a basic assumption in game theory, can mean many things in our everyday languages including reasonable, thoughtful, wise, just, or sane behavior or action. However, for game theory scholars, rational behavior has a more focused and centered meaning than the broad or common meanings of the term rationality. Given that game theory assumes rational behavior, Morrow, for instance, in answering the question *what is meant by rationality?* in game theory, defines rational behavior as "anything from reasonable, thoughtful, or reflective behavior to wise, just, or sane actions" (1994: 17).[17] Morrow describes it as follows:

> [R]ational behavior means choosing the best means to gain a predetermined set of ends. It is an evaluation of the consistency of choices and not of the thought process, of implementation of fixed goals and not of the morality of those goals. . . . Rational behavior is goal directed; actors are trying to create more desired outcomes rather than less desired outcomes.
>
> (1994: 17)

As such, rational behavior in game theory is goal-directed towards *more* desired outcomes rather than *less* desired outcomes. When the assumptions of utility theory are reviewed, the relationship between utility theory and rationality becomes apparent. Von Neumann and Morgenstern, as Eilon notes, place great emphasis on the need for quantitative measurements in economics. After discussing their proposed axioms, they state that their purpose is "to find the mathematically complete principles which define 'rational behavior' for the participants in a social economy, and to derive from them the general characteristics of that behavior" (1979: 158). As explained above, game theory also requires the assumption of rationality. In discussing the rational-choice approach, Morrow (1994: 7-8) explains that in game theory it is assumed that people have goals and that they attempt to realize those goals through their actions. The focus here is on how individuals' attempts to achieve their goals are constrained by one another's actions and the structure of the game. Therefore, Morrow considers four distinctive elements of the rational choice approach assumed by rational choice[18] theorists: first, people have goals which they attempt to achieve; second, people have some freedom of choice; third, individuals choose actions that they believe will help them achieve their goals; and, finally, models simplify and abstract reality.

For decision-making, Wayne Lee (1971) clarifies the meaning of the concept of "rationality" used in decision theory, including some of the problems with its usage. He (7-9) opposes some of the connotations of the term, including the following ideas: a rational person is one who understands his/her own motivations and does not get angry or "carried away" by emotion, and, in the economic context, is one whose decisions are most favorable for producing profits; secondly, the rational individual has special abilities (reasoning, logic, scientific method, etc.) that are not enjoyed by others. On the contrary, Lee confirms that, in decision theory, a rational person is one who, when confronted with a decision situation, makes the choice (decision) that is best for him/her. This best decision is called a rational or optimal decision.

It is argued that rationality in decision-making is a desirable but elusive goal. Hybel (1993: 11) claims that realization of rationality in decision-making does not guarantee success, given that in a world where decisions are made without complete information, leaders sometimes opt for the wrong alternative, regardless of how rational they are. However, Hybel acknowledges that if rationality is no panacea, it does distinctly reduce the room for error. In addition, rationality facilitates: 1) the depiction of a problem's nature; 2) the collection of information; 3) the isolation and ranking of values; 4) the identification of possible alternatives; 5) the calculation of the costs and benefits the implementation of each alternative could elicit; and 6) the selection of the best option and the monitoring of its effectiveness.

Analyzing the notion of rational decision-making, Williams (1976: 60) claims that it presents severe problems for the observer of public policymaking. These problems stem from, first, its being an area of analysis where description and prescription merge, often unnoticeably; and second, the considerable disagreement about the meaning of rationality. Generally, rationality[19] is interpreted as the application of reason to solving problems, and sometimes as part of an attempt to elaborate the precise procedures involved in rational decision-making. These problems result in a lack of consensus about the requirements that have to be fulfilled if decision-making is to be judged rational. Not surprisingly, Williams (1976: 61-64) explains that models of rational decision-making diverge considerably in both form and content. He analyzes the three existing models—comprehensive rationality, limited or bounded rationality, and incremental additions model—then introduces a fourth one, the model of strategic rationality. In the context of foreign policy decision-making, Williams suggests that constructing the model of strategic rationality is helpful as it incorporates a very modest notion of rational behavior. The basic assumptions of Williams' model are highly relevant to the media decision-making process that was discussed in Chapter 1. The basic assumptions underlying the strategic model in terms of foreign policy are as follows: first, foreign policy is guided by a "controlling intelligence," a monolithic decision-making body capable of making clear its major values and objectives and pursuing them in a careful and systematic manner. Second, the constituent members of this decision-making body are politicians and officials endowed with a strong sense of responsibility and concerned primarily with protecting and advancing the interests of their state in a competitive and highly dangerous environment. Third, policymakers consider very carefully the probable responses of other states. Fourth, if the responsible decision-makers feel that a particular response is necessary or required, they do not allow themselves to be deflected from the preferred alternative by irrelevant pressures. Political convenience is less important than what is strategically desirable, as politicians act in harmony with reasoned and logical calculation rather than non-rational domestic pressures.

Even under conflict, rational decision-making is different from other situations. For example, Nicholson (1997: 47) explains that rational decision-making under conflict, where the actions of other calculating actors affect the outcome, is different from decision-making where the outcome depends on some inanimate feature of the situation, such as the weather. In conflict, decision taking involves *strategic decision-making* where what actor A does affects actor B, whose actions similarly affect actor A. Accordingly, in deciding what to do, actor A must not only take into account what his/her rival will do, but analyzes what actor B will do in terms of what s/he thinks actor A will do. Actor B likewise is wondering what actor A will do in formulating his/her own actions. Nothing similar occurs in *non-strategic decision-making*, also called *parametric decision-making*, as the parameters are fixed and not affected by any thoughts about actions of actor A. Therefore, it will rain or not rain independently of whether or not actor A takes out her/his umbrella, because the weather is not trying to trick actor A.

Rational choice theory, according to Nicholson (1996), is not a set of principles embedded in stone, but an approach to social behavior that is adaptable and developing. The conception of human beings as pursuing goals is central to this approach. In this sense, Nicholson argues, it can best be seen as a scientific research program rather than a static body of theory. Indeed, it has been suggested that the forms of interactions which are the province of *game theory* would be better called *drama theory* in that this is a more appropriate metaphor. Whether or not this is a useful terminological device, to view the rational choice approach as a developing research program is more fruitful than seeing it as a static theory. The case of crisis decision-making illustrates this. Decision-makers may pursue their goals as they perceive them at the time in a perfectly efficient manner but come to regret it later. That is, the goals and preferences of the decision-takers became momentarily warped by the stress of the crisis. Nicholson concludes that whether rational choice theory will eventually prove to be a progressive research program in either the social sciences in general or international relations in particular will only be able to be asserted with confidence after further exploration. So far, it seems to be doing well and at the very least, the contributions to certain aspects of strategic thinking have been fruitful. He claims that international relations theorists have a research program which straddles the social sciences, with international relations as a prominent feature, and which looks at the moment to be a progressive one (165-168).

When using rational choice theory as an explanatory theory, Nicholson (1996: 157-158) illustrates that *rationality* means the efficient pursuit of consistent goals. Nicholson claims that it is an entirely proper concept as far as the explanation of behavior is concerned, as the explanation should be separated from its evaluation. However, he criticizes this restricted concept of rationality, which is most commonly known as *instrumental rationality*, and considers it an unfortunate use of the word *rationality*, as well as one which can lead to confusion and misunderstanding of the whole field of rational choice theory; he suggests these might be better called *goal-directed theories*. If we are not careful to remember the limited sense in which we use the term rationality, the concept of instrumental rationality can lead to some curiously apparent paradoxes. For example, there is a debate over whether dictators, such as Napoleon, Stalin, and Hitler, were rational or not, at least in this sense of instrumental rationality. Some argue, Nicholson explains, that Hitler had a long-range plan that might have defied the principles of broad rationality, but nonetheless it was a coherent scheme. The implementation of the plan was instrumentally rational until the later part of the war when its chances of success became slim. Hitler as a short-term opportunist, like other leaders, was guided by a general plan only in the vaguest way, again like any other leader. However, he could still have been instrumentally rational except inasmuch as he allowed his racial policies to influence his behavior. In a similar way, Saddam Hussein, I argue, can be regarded as having been instrumentally rational, although unlucky. He gambled on the quite plausible hypothesis that Iran would be defeated quickly, in the early 1980s, but the gamble failed, and similarly he gambled that nothing would be done when he invaded Kuwait, on August 2, 1990, but again the gamble failed. Both were arguably good bets from Iraq's self-interested perspective and hence instrumentally rational.

To conclude, this chapter discusses the first of the two major dimensions that constitute the balance required in the model proposed in this book, that is, the rational dimension. The second dimension—the responsible side—is explained in Chapter 4. Together with the rationality of mathematics and decision-making, ethics and social responsibility are included in the model that I present in this book in order to maintain balance and to function as safety valves in the process of managing the United States-Iraqi Crisis and its latest development the 2003 War on Iraq. That is, the actors involved should work not only towards individually desired utilities, but also for the social good.

NOTES

1. Regarding mathematics and reality, Schellenberg (1996: 108) explains how Lewis Richardson's mathematical model fits well with events in the real world. Richardson tested his mathematical model for fit against actual patterns of international relations, specifically, the arms race that preceded World War I. He concluded that the model was a workable one: although a gross simplification of reality, it mirrored the dynamics of the real world sufficiently well that it could be used to make reasonable predictions.

2. For example, Lazarsfeld dealt with the application of a mathematical model to one problem of measurement in the social sciences. He (1954a: 349-350) used a measurement, which he called "the procedure of itemized tests," that consists of making a number of qualitative observations on a person, and then attributing to him/her a "measure" of some kind by which s/he can be compared with other persons who have also undergone the test. He assumed that all items of observation are of a dichotomous nature. He focused on

answering the question of how such sets of qualitative observations are translated into measurement. For him, the purpose of latent structure analysis is to provide mathematical models by which the various uses of itemized tests can be related to each other, mainly to bring out the assumptions which are implicit in that type of measurement. Lazarsfeld's main claim in that study was that "latent structure analysis puts practices and discussions in the measurement field into reasonable axiomatic form, and that its axioms permit algebraic operations which lead to hitherto unobserved relationships and suggest more precise meanings of the notion of measurement in the social sciences" (350).

3. This was one of approximately fifteen circles that organized European thought during the eleven generations from 1600 to 1965 that Collins discusses (1998: 531). He explains that "the Vienna Circle . . . was the personal seminar conducted by Schlick from 1924 to 1936; as the movement grew, it became formalized through the leadership of Neurath with its manifesto in 1929 and its own journal, *Erkenntnis,* in 1930" (1998: 1016).

4. In 1948, Claude Shannon's information theory, or "mathematical theory of communication," had an impact on many scientific fields. Essentially it provided the basic paradigm for communication study: "It shaped the directions taken by the field of human communication, determined many of its main concepts, and contributed toward the closer intellectual integration of this field that arose from diverse multidisciplinary roots" (Rogers, 1994: 411). Shannon defined the main elements involved in communication as source, message, transmitter, signal, noise, received signal, receiver, and destination. Definitions of these elements in addition to other terms related to the mathematical theory of communication, such as signal, bit, noise, redundant, channel, channel capacity, information superhighway, etc., are provided by Baran and Davis (2000: 195-197).

5. In his 1998 book *Game Theory and Canadian Politics*, Flanagan has proceeded on the assumption that "game-theoretic models can represent the real world of Canadian politics in an enlightening way" (164). He explains that game theory portrays rational actors in the hunt for maximizing their own self-interest, and also that politics is driven to a large extent by the pursuit of self-interest. Therefore, he claims, "Game theory has the potential to highlight the threads of self-interest in the fabric of politics and the designs in which they are woven" (164).

6. For further explanation of the micro-foundations function of game theory, see Flanagan (1998: 5) who illustrates that within the rational-choice research paradigm, game theory most often plays the role of providing micro-foundations; that is, game theory is used to "create a decision-making model of a simplified situation thought to capture the essential features of the larger problem under analysis."

7. Von Neumann and Morgenstern proposed two basic assumptions. First, the basic framework for deriving measures of utility comes from the question "What do we prefer?" when faced with a choice. Second, individuals have a basic consistency in the way they make their preferences known. They ended with a theory that can provide interval measures of utility. Their derivation of utility measures depends on a basic tool, which is the idea of a lottery. They conceived the lottery as combining percentages of success with different objects of our preference, i.e., we might conceive of being given the option of choosing between; a) $50 for certain; or, b) a 50-50 chance of winning either $100 or nothing (Schellenberg, 1996: 110-111). For more explanations of von Neumann and Morgenstern's *Theory of Games and Economic Behavior* see: Wald (1954: 33-41), Edwards (1967: 48-55), and Eilon (1979: 157-158).

8. Cramér explains that, in the French society of the 1650s, gambling was a popular and fashionable habit that was not very restricted by law. At that time, the need was felt for a rational method for calculating the chances of gamblers in various complicated games with cards, dice, etc. A passionate gambler, the chevalier De Mere, consulted the famous mathematician and philosopher Blaise Pascal in Paris on some questions connected with certain games of chance, and this gave rise to a correspondence between Pascal and some of his mathematical friends, especially Pierre Fermat in Toulouse. This correspondence outlines the origin of modern probability theory (1955: 11-12).

9. According to this definition, the probability of throwing heads in one toss with a coin is $\frac{1}{2}$, the probability of obtaining a 6 in 1 throw with an ordinary die is $\frac{1}{6}$, the probability of drawing a heart from an ordinary set of 52 cards is $\frac{13}{52} = \frac{1}{4}$, etc.

10. From a psychological point of view, Heap and Varoufakis (1995) explain that Festinger's 1957 cognitive dissonance theory proposes a model where reason works to "rationalize" action rather than guide it (17-18). In fact, the concept of cognitive dissonance is a communication theory adopted from social psychology. Situations in which individuals get into decision-making process are among others that much of the research on cognitive dissonance has concentrated on, as dissonance is likely to result. A basic principle of this theory of cognitive dissonance is that the psychological conflict that results from holding two or more inconsistent cognitive elements produces stress and pressure on individuals to change the situation by reducing it and avoiding any additional dissonance. This relationship between dissonance and the need to reduce it can be represented in a positive regression line, i.e., the greater the dissonance, the greater the need to reduce it.

11. Heap and Varoufakis (1995), sketching the philosophical moorings of game theory, discuss three key assumptions: 1) agents are instrumentally rational; 2) they have common knowledge of this rationality; and 3) they know the rules of the game (2-3).

12. A constant-sum game is strategically equivalent to a zero-sum game, and some writers use the two terms almost interchangeably.

13. Morrow (1994: 75, 316) represents the "zero-sum game" mathematically in the following summation notation as a way to simplify writing large sums:

$$\text{A game is "zero-sum" } \underline{\text{iff}}: \sum_{i=1}^{n} M_i = 0.$$

That is, <u>if and only if</u> the sum of the payoffs to all players equals zero. A capital sigma Σ denotes a sum. Each term in the summation is indexed, typically by i, and the first and last terms of the summation are given by the bounds of the sum placed below and above the summation sign respectively.

14. For detailed illustration of the "zero-sum game", see Michael Nicholson's (1970: 53-59) explanations, terms, and expressions as he is considered a pioneer scholar in the field of international relations and conflict analysis. In addition, his work is among the most frequently quoted in research studies about game theory.

15. The main assumption of the theory of cooperative games is that players are able to make binding agreements. On the other hand, the theory of non-cooperative games is not based on the presence of an external enforcer of agreements (Siebe, 1991: 182). For more explanations of the zero-sum games see: Eichberger (1993: 41-42), Schellenberg (1996: 113), Colman (1995: 53-54, 186), Edwards (1967: 53), and Lee (1971: 281-286). As for non-zero-sum games, see: Schellenberg (1996: 114), Colman (1995: 161), and Edwards (1967: 53).

16. Examples of the contemporary definitions of the term *rationality* are presented by Lupia, Mccubbins and Popkin (2000: 5-6) as follows: 1) A decision is only rational if it is supported by the best reasons and achieves the best possible outcome in terms of all the goals. 2) Rational choice theory holds that choices among relevant goods involve comparing goods against each other to make correct choices dictated by preference schedules. 3) A basic assumption of positive economics is that people are rational in the sense that they have an objective and pursue it in a reasonably consistent fashion. People are assumed to strive toward the goal of making themselves as happy as they can, given their limited resources. 4) Consumers always strive to obtain the greatest possible satisfaction from spending their incomes, and businessmen always try to make the biggest profits they can. 5) As far as economics is concerned, a utility

function can assign as much or more utility to giving away goods as to consuming them. Rationality is independent from selfishness. 6) A rational agent is simply one who obeys certain axioms, and that is the end of it. 7) A key economic assumption is that individuals, in making choices, rationally select alternatives they perceive to be in their best interests. This reliance on *rational self-interest* should not be viewed as blind materialism, pure selfishness, or greed. 8) Rational choice involves three optimizing operations: the action that is chosen must be optimal, given the desires and beliefs of the agent; the beliefs must be optimal, given the information available to the agent; and the amount of resources allocated to the acquisition of information must be optimal. 9) Virtually all human behavior is rational. People usually have reasons for what they do, and if asked, can explain what these reasons are.

17. Game theory, moreover, belongs to a family of methodologies variously known as rational choice, public choice, social choice, and collective choice. In game theory, players are assumed to be rational actors armed with ordinal or cardinal utility functions. Strategies are the choices that the players can make within the rules of the game. A strategy is a complete set of choices from beginning to end of the game. A solution is the set of payoffs arising from the strategies that rational players would choose under the rules of the game. Game theory depicts rational actors seeking to maximize their own self-interest (Flanagan, 1998: 3-5, 20, 164).

18. Flanagan (1998: 5) explains that rational choice sees human beings as decision-makers who are facing a continuous series of choices between alternatives: "Each decision-maker has what is known in the jargon of economics as a utility function. A function in mathematics is a relationship between variables, as in the equation $y = x + 2$, which states that for any value of variable x, variable y will be 2 units larger. A utility function is a statement of the relationship between the alternatives in the choice set and the preferences in the mind of the decision-maker."

19. The definition of "rationalism" in philosophy is "a philosophy based on the notion that individuals can derive knowledge of the world around them through the use of reason and that such knowledge reveals a larger system," whereas "reason" in numerous philosophies is defined as "the ability to think and reflect in the consideration of any problem" (Leslie, 2000: 319).

II. PRACTICE

CHAPTER 4

Communication Ethics

and Media Responsibility

Media decision-makers, in times of crisis and conflict, are expected to work rationally and responsibly. In this chapter, I build on this discussion by examining the responsible side of this expected performance. This follows the investigation into the rational side, which was the concern of Chapter 3. My main objective in this chapter is to bring attention to the importance of ethical and responsible communication in a general sense, and also the specific importance in the face of international political crises and conflicts—the most dangerous circumstances of our world. Concentrating on the crisis at hand, the discussion here draws on theories, branches, and meanings of ethics. There are explanations of ethics and morality, presentations of types of ethics, and illustrations of various philosophers' perspectives on ethics. Furthermore, the chapter examines journalistic ethical principles and shows their significance. It also draws on social responsibility theory, explaining its core theme and, in evaluating its power, presents its basic recommendations for the media. The topic of ethics is further investigated to build a strong philosophical base for the examination of ethical media practices. This fourth chapter concludes with an investigation of *good* journalism, a discussion of its models and what is required for it to be achieved.

ETHICAL COMMUNICATION REQUIRED

Communication cannot be effective without being ethical and socially responsible.

Donald Wright—(1996: 521)

Rights and duties are inseparable. But the human being is inclined
to claim rights without mentioning the duties coupled with them,
especially nowadays, especially in the West. Well, media ethics is
mainly concerned with duties. It posits that freedom and
responsibility go hand-in-hand.

Claude-Jean Bertrand—(2002: 29)

Ethics are remote from me . . . I do not break my head very much
about good and evil, but I have found little that is "good" about
human beings on the whole. In my experience most of them are
trash, no matter whether they publicly subscribe to this or that
ethical doctrine or to none at all. . . . If we are to talk of ethics, I
subscribe to a high ideal from which most of the human beings I
have come across depart most lamentably.

Sigmund Freud—(cited in Meissner, 2003: 5)

Ethics and responsibility are key fundamentals to the effective
performance of communication. For mass media, rights should be connected
to duties. As a guide for its workers (including media owners, managers,
editors, and journalists), journalism, as most other professions, has codes of
ethics. However, it is often difficult to find workers in the field who adhere
to, or are obliged to adhere to, these codes. Media personnel's responsibility
to the common good of society has proved largely inadequate and deficient.
Reasons vary from simple to complex and justifications go further to the
extreme of the philosophical perspective that suspects the very possibility of
the existence of ethics. But given the necessity for seeing ethical conduct that
helps improve communication, which stems from the important and
potentially dangerous role of communication in society, most significant in
times of international crises, it becomes necessary to investigate the
characteristics of ethical and responsible communication. Discussing the
theories, branches, meaning, relation to morality, and various philosophical
perspectives on ethics, provides the required background for investigating the
concept of "communication ethics," while also demonstrating its conceptual
complexity. Media codes of ethics attempt to clarify this and, indeed, are
useful and necessary while greatly benefiting the common good of society.
Journalistic codes of ethics attempt to instill moral balance to the interests of
the journalist, the public, and media organizations. Significantly, the
requirements of media ethics are more valid during war, given the great
effects of the consequences. This is evident by looking at examples of the
media coverage during the 2003 War on Iraq which demonstrate the use of
unethical journalistic practices such as misleading the public through

manipulation, a lack of objectivity and truthfulness, and imbalance in coverage.

The word ethics, Leslie (2000: 16-18) explains, comes from the Greek "ethos," which means "character." Individual ethical behavior is governed by one's character, as well as by the values one assigns to various activities or aspects of one's life. Although there are many complex definitions of ethics, Leslie offers the following as the simplest and most straightforward: "Ethics are moral principles for living and making decisions" (16). A term closely related to ethics is "morality," which is derived, Leslie explains, from the Latin "moralis," meaning "customs and manners." As seen, morality often involves issues reaching beyond the individual to the larger social group. Therefore, he considers the key factor for successful ethical decision-making to be the development of a set of moral beliefs that serve not only the individual but also the society.

There are three branches of ethics as presented in the work of Louis Day (2000: 4-5): metaethics, normative ethics, and applied ethics. He explains that "metaethics" is concerned with the study of the nature or characteristics of ethics. It examines the meaning of abstract terms such as "good," "right," "justice," and "fairness" and attempts to identify those values that are the best "moral" values. It also provides the broad foundation for ethical decision-making. On the other hand, "normative ethics" is concerned with developing general theories, rules, and principles of moral conduct, i.e., the principles that are the ethical markers of any civilized society. The logical next step is the task of "applied ethics," which is the use of the insights derived from metaethics and the general principles and rules of normative ethics, in addressing specific ethical issues and concrete cases.

Although ethics and morality, as Markel (2001: 28-29) points out, are synonyms in popular usage—both mean the study of right and wrong—for most philosophers they are quite dissimilar. While morality refers to a society's set of beliefs and customs concerning proper conduct, ethics pertains to the individual's thinking and conduct in matters of right and wrong. Moreover, Markel continues, "the central distinguishing characteristic of thinking about ethics is that it is rational" (31). He explains that effective thinking about ethics entails making claims that are supported by clear, valid reasoning and suitable evidence, and acknowledges the ethicist Manuel Velasquez's (1998) definition of three important aspects of effective thinking about ethics: 1) the argument must be structured logically; 2) the evidence used in support of the claims must be accurate, relevant to the context, and comprehensive; and 3) the ethical principles used in the argument must be applied consistently.[1]

Inevitably, defining ethics leads to an investigation into its various incarnations. For the present purposes, the question is whether there are ethical theories guiding the field of mass communication. According to Donald Wright (1996: 524-526), there are. He divides them into two types: classical ethical theory and moral reasoning theories. Of classical ethical theory, he writes:

> The study of ethics began in ancient Greece with Socrates (c. 470-399 BC), who claimed virtue could be identified and practiced. His disciple, Plato (c. 428-348 BC), advocated moral conduct even in situations when responsible behavior might run counter to societal norms. Plato's student, Aristotle (384-322 BC), argued that moral virtue often required tough choices.
>
> (1996: 524)

For Wright, classical ethical theory views ethical obligation in two different ways—teleological and deontological. "*Teleological ethics* underscores the consequences of an act or decision, whereas *deontological ethics* emphasizes the nature of an act or decision" (525). As for moral reasoning theories, Wright explains that they are based on the shared values of wisdom, justice, and freedom. He defines four requirements that must be met before ethical judgments can be made[2]: First, society must reach an agreement on its standards of moral conduct; second, these standards should be based on reason and experience; third, a system of ethics should seek justice; and finally, an ethical system should be based on freedom of choice.

The broad scholarly discipline of "ethics" falls under the study of philosophy and contains many perspectives, subcategories, and approaches. It refers to the principles of "right conduct" or doing "the right thing". In general, the need to consider the ethical component of a decision becomes practically relevant when we consciously confront a choice or decision and know that our action will have a potentially harmful impact on another person or persons. For media professionals, there is an overriding ethical responsibility to serve their audiences by imparting information—a form of communication. As such, ethical dilemmas they confront can be categorized under the larger umbrella of "communication ethics". Ethical communication, as an overarching principle, however, is complex to determine. Philosophers over the centuries have analyzed, from numerous perspectives, what kinds of communication are either ethical or unethical. Richard Johannesen, in his lucid and comprehensive 2001 textbook *Ethics in Human Communication*, has identified and categorized eight broad "perspectives"[3] that philosophers and observers have taken over the years when examining communication ethics and elucidating their own principles and ethical stances: political, human nature, dialogical, situational, religious, utilitarian, legalistic, and feminist. (Berkman & Shumway, 2003: 5-6).

Similarly, Lorenz and Vivian (1996: 550-551) explain that four sets of ethical theories developed by philosophers stand out as bases for "correct" behavior: Golden Mean, Categorical Imperative, Utilitarianism, and Golden Rule. The Golden Mean, formulated by Aristotle who lived in Greece in the fourth century B.C., requires that when there are extreme positions in a situation, one seeks a middle ground. The Categorical Imperative, formulated by the 18th century German philosopher Immanuel Kant, is a theory claiming that people should behave only as they wish everyone else to behave. One is bound by duty to do what is right in every instance, unconditionally (or categorically). Utilitarianism, developed by a late-18th and early-19th century Englishman, Jeremy Bentham, and later refined by John Stuart Mill, would have the discerning of what is right pertain to what will give the greatest good to the greatest number of people. For ethical behavior in any situation, one must balance right and wrong and act in a way that results in more good than evil. "The Judeo-Christian ethic, or the so-called Golden Rule, calls on people to do unto others as you would have them do unto you" (550). To apply these ethical theories to the field of communication, journalists, according to the Golden Mean, are caught between the extremes of publishing or broadcasting everything they know about an issue, situation, or event and publishing or broadcasting nothing. Obviously, they choose the Golden Mean and develop stories that are appropriate to the medium, the outlet, the editor, and the audience. If they were to follow the Categorical Imperative they would be required, for one, to always tell the truth without exception. Also, according to the Golden Rule, journalists would seldom print anything regarding individuals that would be considered negative. It would clearly be foolish and contrary to good journalistic practice to say "I would not want my name printed in the paper if I were arrested for driving under the influence of alcohol, therefore I will not report that the mayor was picked up for drunken driving" (551). It is clear that these perspectives often cannot be applied to communication at face value, however the Golden Rule, for instance, can find its way into the practical work of journalists, by interpreting it as a requirement to treat other people fairly.

Linked to the core idea of the rational component of the bureaucratic decision theory, discussed in Chapter 1, that calls for needs of power, authority, and influence in order to control or participate in controlling any collective action aimed at a public good, communication, according to Thomassen (1992: 142), consists of managing power over others' lives and one's own life. That is, with every action or decision, one, consciously or unconsciously, affects others' happiness and unhappiness and contributes to the development of their life and fate. Ethics proves its necessity through the fact that the management of this power is abused and disrespected to an incredible extent. Also, the ethical justification of an action has a double nature: the universal element dictates that all parties should be regarded equally, while the individual element calls for the objective consideration of each individual, and thereby to each person's individual identity and actual state. Therefore, it is in the nature of ethics that reasons for action become composite phenomena as various relationships of both a general and an individual nature must permeate throughout.

Media codes of ethics, as Gordon (1999a: 61-62) argues, are useful and necessary to the media and to society. They serve an important purpose by setting standards against which conduct can be measured and evaluated—an important service for both the media and society. On one hand, within the media, codes ensure that standards are set internally, rather than having the courts or the legislatures take on this responsibility. They can provide an ideal standard by which the industry can evaluate its own performance and against which individual practitioners can measure their own values and performance. They can act as the conscience of the professional. For both the whole media industry and individuals within it, codes can help keep attention directed toward principles that are particularly important as guidelines for appropriate behavior. In effect, because ethics deals with normative behavior as well as philosophy, codes of ethics can be a major factor in helping to establish those norms, especially if they provoke discussion as to their content and the expression of such in words. On the other hand, in society as a whole, codes may provide reasonable standards and guidelines that help the public discuss, debate, and measure the media's performance. In this respect, if the codes are realistic, they can help to protect the mass media and media practitioners from unrealistic expectations, demands, and criticism. At the same time, they can help the public express reasonable demands to, and criticism of, the media when warranted. In this way, codes can help make the mass media more accountable to their various publics.

Political scholar Miklos Sukosd believes the legal and professional requirements of media ethics are valid even during war. Therefore, to remain authentic, media in a country that is at war cannot uncritically shift towards war propaganda. The Hungarian News Agency asked the expert to comment on how the Iraq war appeared in the American and British media. Sukosd suggested that an objective approach, impartiality, and a certain distancing from the events must always characterize democratic media. Contrary to this, the major American television networks and local channels were undeniably in favor of the war. He noted that this implies major tension within democratic countries from the point of view of upholding authenticity, while it is an everyday phenomenon in a dictatorship as was the case in Iraq. Sukosd advised that experts of the Arab world should have been able to speak about the events in the region and the events leading up to the war in the various programs, and viewers could have been warned they were watching censored pictures during American news reports (Iraq War: Political scholar..., 2003, April 2).

From Sukosd's advice, two relevant examples emerge—the production of news photography and balance of coverage—as useful in the examination of the media coverage of the 2003 War on Iraq.

There is a great deal of ethical questioning surrounding the production of news photography and whether or not photojournalists deceive viewers. As Warburton (1998: 129-131) explains, photographs have the potential to be misleading about what is going on.[4] Therefore, it is part of the picture editor's job to select images that are as unambiguous as possible or at least not misleading on significant issues. The conventions surrounding the use of news photographs include the toleration of minor deceptions in order to produce a legible image. Although it is usually acceptable to adjust contrasts, to burn in important details, and to crop out extraneous details, these conventions do not tolerate any maneuver that distorts the viewer's appreciation of the relationship between the photograph and its main subject. It is a matter of professional integrity for photojournalists to abide by these conventions. The responsibilities of the photojournalist must include to avoid deceiving the public about how images were made.

> Any discussion of "manipulated" photography must begin with the recognition that photography itself is an inherent manipulation—a manipulation of light, a process with many steps and stages, all subject to the biases and interpretations of the photographer, printer, editor, or viewer. Photography is not absolute "reality." It is not unqualified "truth." It is not purely "objective." It was never any of those things, and it has been subject to distortion since its inception.
>
> (Wheeler, 2002: 3)

Similar to constitutions and laws that seek to balance individual freedoms and the common good, journalistic codes of ethics, Wheeler (2002: 75) argues, attempt to balance in a moral way the interests of the journalist, the public, and media organizations. Although these interests[5] may seem mutually supportive, given that the journalist and his/her institution seek to serve the public, and the public wants to be served, they actually often conflict.[6] Wheeler illustrates with examples: in a desire to get the story, a journalist may want to interview a private citizen who does not want to be interviewed; in telling the story, a journalist may embarrass someone who does not deserve to be embarrassed; to inform the public, a newspaper may run a photo of a burn victim that disturbs some readers, or a photo of a nudist that offends some readers; or, to inform the public about the progress of a crime investigation, the journalist might publish facts that enable guilty parties to escape detection.

Responsible journalists, Wheeler (2002: 76) confirms, have long subscribed to a code of practice designed to protect the integrity of visual journalism. That code was captured in the National Press Photographers Association's (NPPA) 1990 statement of principle:

> As journalists we believe the guiding principle of our profession is accuracy; therefore, we believe it is wrong to alter the content of a photograph in any way that deceives the public . . . altering the editorial content of a photograph, in any degree, is a breach of the ethical standards recognized by the NPPA.

The labeling of a photo as "ethical" or "unethical" is not uncommon to hear, yet it is possible for a photo to actually be unethical? Wheeler (2002: 102) clarifies that there is an agreement that while words can be used in unethical ways, words themselves are ethically neutral; accordingly, photographs are not any different. He explains that the decisions journalists make about how they compose, set up, process, or use a photo can be ethical or unethical, appropriate or inappropriate. Their judgment in making these decisions can be good or bad. But like a word, a given photo is itself ethically neutral. Consequently, sound ethical judgments must address not only the content or even the manipulation of a photo but also what might be called its larger meaning.

This view of "neutral" word or photo can be argued here by drawing on Roland Barthes' perspective. Barthes (1991) explains that "the press photograph is a message" (3). He demonstrates that connotation, "i.e., the imposition of a second meaning upon the photographic message proper, is elaborated at different levels of photographic production (selection, technical treatment, cropping, layout)" (9).

> We saw that the code of connotation was in all likelihood neither "neutral" nor "artificial" but historical, or, if it be preferred, "cultural." Its signs are gestures, attitudes, expressions, colors, or effects, endowed with certain meanings by virtue of the practice of a certain society: the link between signifier and signified remains, if not unmotivated, at least entirely historical . . . Thanks to its

> code of connotation the reading of the photograph is thus always
> historical; it depends on the reader's "knowledge". . . . Nothing
> tells us that the photograph contains "neutral" parts, or at least it
> may be that complete insignificance in the photograph is quite
> exceptional.
>
> (Barthes, in Sontag, 1982: 206-207)

Although there is a contradiction of "neutrality" of photos in both Barthes' and Wheeler's perspectives, Wheeler acknowledges that a photo can mean different things to different people or even different things to one person at different times or in different contexts. But in attempting to distinguish unethical alterations from the kinds of posing and enhancements accepted throughout photography's history, Wheeler reminds us that "a photo is not merely an image bound within a frame but rather one element of a process that begins in the mind of the photographer and ends in the mind of the viewer" (2002: 103).

On March 31, 2003, an altered picture was published on the front page of one of the most respected U.S. daily newspapers and the leading newspaper in the country's second largest city. This altered war photo led *The Los Angeles Times* to fire its staff photographer working in Iraq, who had been with the paper since 1998. He had admitted to electronically manipulating a picture showing a British soldier directing Iraqi civilians to take cover from a firefight, a practice strictly forbidden under of code of journalistic ethics and in violation of the paper's policy. The paper published a statement stating, "After publication, it was noticed that several civilians in the background appear twice. . . The photographer, Brian Walski, reached by telephone in southern Iraq, acknowledged that he had used his computer to combine elements of two photographs, taken moments apart, in order to improve the composition". The photographer appeared to take the image of the soldier motioning the Iraqi civilians to keep down and combine it with a similar shot taken seconds apart in which the soldier is no longer motioning, but an Iraqi carrying a baby is in the centre of the picture looking towards the camera. (LA Times sacks..., 2003, April 2).

Balance is another example that can determine the degree to which the coverage of the crisis was ethical. Michael Parks, director of the School of Journalism at the Annenberg School for Communication, said that journalists should maintain a balanced view of the war in Iraq and should avoid using words such as "us" and "them." He also said ABC producers should tell anchor Ted Koppel that America, not ABC, is at war with Iraq. News organizations such as ABC and Fox News often report as if they are the ones who are at war. Journalists should not forsake ethics in the name of competition. (News outlets..., 2003, March 31).

The *BBC* reported an official's announcement on Zimbabwean radio on March 25th, 2003, that the parading of captured prisoners of war and dead people from the ongoing war in Iraq by British and American media stations was "barbaric". The Minister of State for Information and Publicity in the office of the president and cabinet, Jonathan Moyo, says it is even more barbaric and shocking that the networks are bringing into the full glare of television how the U.S. and Britain are conducting war. Minister Moyo added that international television networks have not only shocked the Iraqis but the rest of humankind by showing how their nations are conducting the killings. Also, Permanent Secretary for Information and Publicity in the office of the president and cabinet, George Charamba, said the coverage of the war on Iraq has raised questions relating to media ethics surrounding *balance* in reporting (most importantly), the employment of media technology around Baghdad, the independence of and autonomy of journalists, as well as the selective protection of combatants and freedom of expression. (Zimbabwe: Official terms..., 2003, March 25).

The Australian government logged 68 complaints against reports on the "AM" program, the flagship current affairs show of the Australian Broadcasting Corporation (ABC), alleging anti-American bias. Communications Minister Richard Alston accused the ABC's Washington correspondent, John Shovelan, of this for a story on U.S. President George W. Bush and another on the Pentagon. Australia's public radio broadcaster conceded that Shovelan's report on April 9, 2003, about the Pentagon was sarcastic in tone and excessive but denied government allegations that its coverage of the conflict was anti-American. Shovelan introduced the story with: "Oh the civility of this U.S. military. The daily Pentagon briefing begins with an illustration of its mercy and kindness." The ABC said the comment was "mocking in its manner and judgment". Also, the ABC concluded the report by stating that the sensitivities of Bush could have been better expressed. Shovelan said in his introduction on March 22, 2003: "White House spokesman Ari Fleischer said the President hadn't watched the opening of the air offensive on television, an indication of just how sensitive he is to launching a massive bombing campaign in an area so heavily populated." The ABC's investigative report found that Fleischer had acknowledged Bush's sensitivity to launching the strike. But it said, "to link that sensitivity with the President having not watched television because he was sensitive about civilian casualties is speculative." Senator Alston was not convinced by the findings and is considering whether to ask the broadcasting watchdog to review his complaint. He said "I remain concerned that AM program's coverage of the Iraq conflict did not meet the journalistic standards that one would expect from a national broadcaster that is fully committed to accuracy and impartiality". However, the ABC's managing director, Russell Balding, said that the findings vindicated AM and its staff. He considers that the ABC's war coverage "was second to none", and that "Overall I believe our coverage of the conflict was balanced and delivered in a professional manner upholding the standards of objective journalism." (Australian radio admits..., 2003, July 21; Marriner, 2003, July 22; and Crabb, 2003, May 28).

MEDIA RESPONSIBILITY IN THEORY AND PRACTICE

[S]ocial responsibility is the preferred system for the news media to function under in our society . . . the news media must be socially responsible for selfish reasons . . . the media must be a credible source of information. To be credible, they must be socially responsible, and social responsibility includes adherence to strict ethical standards . . . and dedication to disclosing the truth about all institutions, including one's own. . . . There are also times when the media make mistakes. Social responsibility means admitting mistakes and, if necessary, offering an apology for them.

(Wilson & Wilson, 2001: 421)

Journalism is a profession with unique privileges and obligations. Journalists can claim their goal is to seek and communicate truths about the world on behalf of the common good. The information or news that journalists seek and communicate serves to inform persons, allowing them to make good decisions.

(Callahan, 2003: 3)

Media social responsibility is very relevant and significant for the development of communication. Discussing the rise of social responsibility theory, its core theme, tracing this notion's entrance into the consciousness of media practitioners, examining its definitions, balancing it with freedom, and exploring the psychological aspect of it, illustrates how the theme of media responsibility is conceptualized theoretically before examining how it is practically conducted. Furthermore, the discussion encompasses the power of the media and media accountability, which are closely related to media responsibility. For instance, given their essential role in times of crises and conflicts, the media's involvement in War on Iraq can be examined. War correspondents have contributed to major developments of the media, and consequently, often paid the price of being front-line journalists. The significant role of the media during wars requires that they act with a sense of responsibility; when the coverage of the United States-Iraqi Crisis and its latest development, the 2003 War on Iraq, is examined in this light, it can be seen that the media failed to act responsibly.

Perhaps the most important event affecting journalistic ethics during the period of the rise of social responsibility was the formation of the nine-member Commission on the Freedom of the Press by Robert M. Hutchins in 1944. Hutchins, president of the University of Chicago, was asked by *Time* editor-in-chief Henry R. Luce to evaluate press freedom in light of the powerful media systems that had developed after the end of World War I. This coincided with a surge of media criticism, attacking the norm of an obsessively objective press that devalued the importance of intervention, social reform, and creativity. The Hutchins Commission report, *A Free and Responsible Press,* published in 1947, provided a framework for discussing media ethics during the next several decades. It emphasized the need for: 1) truthful accounts within a proper context; 2) public forums to solicit feedback and criticism; 3) representation for the various cultural groups within society; 4) a focus on social goals and values; and 5) public access to knowledge and information. (Keeler, Brown & Tarpley, 2002: 51).

The social responsibility theory is included here due to its relevance and significance in the development of recommendations and directions for the functioning of mass media in society. Fred Siebert, Theodore Peterson, and Wilbur Schramm, in trying to answer their own questions about why the press is as it is (1956: 1-2) and why the media of mass communication appear in widely different forms in different countries, attributed these differences in part to what people do in different places and what their experience leads them to want to read or watch. Their core thesis explaining the reasons behind these differences is that the media reflect the system of social control whereby the relations of individuals and institutions are adjusted. They believe that "an understanding of these aspects of society is basic to any systematic understanding of the press" (2). Looking at the social systems in which the media function, through the basic beliefs and assumptions which the society holds—the nature of the individual, the nature of society and the state, the relation of the individual to the state, and the nature of knowledge and truth—they analyzed the philosophical and political rationales or theories which lie behind the different kinds of media. They discussed four basic theories of the media of mass communication—Authoritarian, Libertarian, Soviet Communist, and Social Responsibility[7]—considering the last two as merely developments and modifications of the first two, and explained (1956: 3-4) their development through several centuries. In later decades, they suggested, a growing wave of criticism was directed towards the media[8]; there was a tendency to examine the performance of the media of mass communication and find fault with it. The media were accused of wielding enormous power in politics and economics, resisting social change, paying more attention to the superficial and sensational rather than the significant, endangering public morals, invading the privacy of individuals, and so on. Social responsibility theory looks at how the media should perform to fulfill their social function.

The core theme of social responsibility theory arises from the dividing line between authoritarian or communist societies and libertarian society. The theory imposes a burden on media practitioners and increases the need for testing the mass media as responsible instruments of a diverse society.[9] The strengths and weaknesses of social responsibility theory are summarized by Baran and Davis (2000: 110) as follows. Its strengths are that it values media and audience responsibility, limits government intrusion in media operations, allows reasonable government control of media, values diversity and pluralism, aids the "powerless," appeals to the best instincts of media practitioners and audiences, and is consistent with U.S. legal tradition. Its weaknesses are that it is overly optimistic about the media's and an individual's willingness to accept responsibility, underestimates the power of profit motivation and competition, and legitimizes the status quo.

Elizabeth Hindman (1997: 49-50) has examined how the United States Supreme Court has defined media responsibility[10] over a sixty-five-year period (1931-1996) by focusing on media functions and on significant canons of ethical journalism appearing in case decisions. She found that the Court has valued the political and educational functions and defined press responsibility primarily in terms of *truth telling* and *stewardship*. The two functions of the media provided both concrete and abstract illustrations of the Court's conceptions of media responsibility. The Court did not permit the media to misrepresent willfully factual information if that misrepresentation harmed an individual. Also, the justices frowned upon inaccurate information of any kind, though they grudgingly accepted its inevitability in the performance of the media's educational and political functions. As for stewardship, which encompassed much of what the justices saw as appropriate behavior by the media, the Court meant that the media would both exhibit a general responsibility and guard their rights and the rights of others. Like other institutions and individuals, the media must maintain a minimum level of responsibility to others in order for society to function.

In their *Power Without Responsibility*, Curran and Seaton conclude with a suggestion that a rapidly changing industry needs to be guided. The mass media, which daily intrude into our lives in ever more sophisticated ways, need to be themselves the subject of continual public surveillance. . . . It is important that we begin to think more radically about the media, for the press and broadcasting exercise a massive power, but it is more than ever a power without responsibility.

(1997: 4)

In making their case for freedom of the press and the responsibility that freedom entails, Rivers and Schramm (1969: 53) cite George Bernard Shaw: "Liberty means responsibility. That is why most men dread it." They argue that the greatest danger in trying to combine freedom and responsibility is that the mass media may lose sight of their basic responsibility, which is to remain free in the face of international forces, government, domestic power groups, individuals, and even restricting influences within the media (53-54). They address some issues that should be handled carefully as part of the mass media's responsibility, such as accuracy of information, pictures, and headlines, objectivity, and interpretation.[11] For example, they disagree with the widely accepted aphorism that "pictures don't lie," pointing out that some pictures tell the truth, some tell part of the truth, some mislead, and some lie terribly (132-155). Furthermore, regarding objectivity and interpretation, they agree with the most widely understood standard of truth and fairness in journalism that news reports must be clearly separated from commentary.[12]

Did you know that, if you drop a frog into boiling water, it will leap out immediately? But, if you place it in a bowl of cold water and then heat it up gradually, it will stay there until it is cooked.

(Porter, 1996: 13)

William Porter presents this peculiar fact as a metaphor for the impact and power of the media on society, claiming that it can only be understood in the context of the gradual warm-up. He argues that the impact has not been dramatic from day to day, but has certainly been dramatic between 30 years ago and the present.

The power of the media stems from a dependence on them for information and entertainment in conjunction with their multiple functions in society. Studies of media effects have demonstrated the enormous influence[13] of mass media on audiences' attitudes, opinions, and behaviors.[14] With the complexity of societies, speed of events, and enormous diversity of information and news, along with the limited ability of audiences to follow up on information provided, the media have the power to formulate our understanding of the world. Analyzing the functions of mass communication, Rivers and Schramm (1969: 14-15) explain that the media help us to watch the horizon, much as the ancient messengers once did, to correlate our response to the challenges and opportunities which appear on the horizon, to reach consensus on social actions, and to transmit the culture of our society to new members. Many other scholars have examined the political power of the media.[15] In sum, it is argued here that the exclusive power in the hands of the mass media,[16] which is not found in any other social institution, authority, or social system, rather than being subjected to calls for its limitation,[17] should be called upon to serve a rational and responsible social purpose.

> [N]ews media exist, in part, to check government claims against reality. But when reporters don't bother to look for answers beyond the press conference, they can turn an official fiction into a documented "fact."
>
> (Pein, 2003, May/June)

Another dimension of the media's power relies on the relationship between media and government.[18] Richard Davis (2001: 1-8), looking at the relations between the media and American politics,[19] claims that the role of the press has become a major source of discussion and controversy in recent years, and that the influence of the media is much more pervasive now than it was three decades ago. In general, Americans perceive the media as extremely powerful. Davis acknowledges the political reliance on the news media: "If the governed rely on the news media as a credible and accessible source of information, those who govern also depend on the press, both in electoral politics and in the process of governance" (3). The increasing political power of the media has made it essential for presidential candidates to develop new skills and strategies. "A press secretary for one presidential candidate estimated that his candidate spent more than one-third of each day in direct contact with the press" (4). Davis observes that a fundamental source of tension between the news media and politics has developed in recent American political history: first, because of the increased reliance of both citizenry and government on the press as a primary "communications bridge" or linking mechanism; and second, because the increasingly divergent imperatives of press and politicians have resulted in a more autonomous position for the press, out from under traditional political controls.[20] For him (95), what really distinguishes the American politics/media system from almost every other system is the freedom of the press from political control, extensive private ownership, and the minor part that political leaders have in determining the media's role.[21]

In his 2000 *Holding the Media Accountable: Citizens, Ethics, and the Law,* David Pritchard, referring to the fact that much of what people know about the world beyond their own experience comes from the mass media whose content directly and indirectly influences what they believe, what they think about, and how they act, presents eleven studies of how citizens and media organizations deal with conflict. He (2000*a*: 1-2) explains that the term "media accountability", which is frequently used but rarely defined, is surrounded by some confusion. Some scholars think of media accountability in terms of news credibility, others see it in terms of legal[22] obligations and prohibitions, and still others discuss media accountability without defining it at all. Plaisance (2000) argues that the concept is inadequately defined, and often restricted to a one-dimensional interpretation. By most definitions, accountability is "a measurement of performance; it is understood nearly exclusively in relation to what it is measuring" (260). Plaisance (257-258) suggests that media accountability be more broadly understood as a dynamic of interaction between a given medium and the value sets of individuals or groups receiving media messages. In communication literature, accountability is routinely referred to as a static entity and measured by the presence or absence of what could be called indicators of fallibility corrections, feedback outlets, ombudsmen, and so forth. However, accountability must be understood as a fluid dynamic of interaction.

Pritchard defines it as follows: "Media accountability is the process by which media organizations may be expected or obliged to render an account of their activities to their constituents" (2000*a*: 2). Although many agree that the media should follow ethical standards, there is still no consensus on what those standards are. Pritchard (2000*c*: 187-188) looks at how, in the absence of significant value systems, many news organizations have adopted codes of ethics or instituted ombudsman to enhance accountability. However, surveys show that journalists' actual views of ethics are sharply different from what is found in their news organizations' codes of ethics. Most journalists seem to be fairly insensitive to ethical concerns and fairly superficial in their thinking about them. That journalists pay scant attention to codes of ethics may be related to the fact that such codes are often intended more as tools of public relations—as attempts to persuade the public that the media are ethical—than as meaningful guides for media conduct. Also, significant media criticism focuses on questions of media ethics and accountability. Moreover, news industry groups in some regions of North America have established news councils[23]; bodies designed to serve as more or less voluntary, informal ethical courts.

Given the fact that media responsibility begins with and highly depends on individuals (e.g., journalists), it might be useful to consider the concept of responsibility from a psychological perspective.

> From a psychoanalytic perspective, there is little incompatibility between subjective and objective responsibility. . . . [W]hen analysts address responsibility they are usually thinking of subjective responsibility. This, of course, diverges from the concerns of courtrooms and legal philosophy, where the focus is on objective responsibility, conformity, or deviance from social norms and standards, and the evaluation of culpability . . . [S]ubjective responsibility . . . accords primacy to man as the initiator of acts instead of man as an object acted upon. It recognizes the reality of choice, freedom, consciousness, motivation, and the capacity to control the consequences of purposeful action. . . . Objective responsibility is a matter of the responsibility man encounters as an object rather than as a subject, that is, as an object responding to the impersonal influences impinging on him. These may take the form of internal processes, more-or-less physiologically derived, that impinge upon his subjectivity, or from outside the body, usually in the form of social conventions or sanctions. There is a range of socially acceptable behavior and rules that we are normally expected to observe. When the conduct is deviant or the rules broken, we blame the deviant, but we consider him primarily as an object and generally disregard his subjectivity. Objective responsibility is concerned with culpability and irresponsibility, the stuff of social judgment and legal accountability.
>
> (Meissner, 2003: 199-201)

Meissner also explains (196-197) Thomas Szasz's three modes of responsibility—descriptive, prescriptive, and ascriptive. In the descriptive mode, responsibility connotes a connection of cause-and-effect and implies nothing ethical. For instance, the sun is responsible for a shadow. In the prescriptive mode, however, responsibility conveys a more-or-less negative note and an implied note of command to change an undesirable situation or to prevent its recurrence. For example, cigarette smoking is responsible for the incidence of lung cancer, implying that smokers should put an end to this habit. The ascriptive mode takes a further step toward the ethical by ascribing an ethical dimension to an action or other causal connection. Szasz's example is the statement "John killed James." The first question is whether he did it or not; if the answer is affirmative, the question becomes "Is he guilty or innocent?" The law undertakes to evaluate the facts and circumstances of the case in order to determine responsibility, that is, guilt or innocence. Responsibility is often associated with guilt. If the act is correctly attributed to John, then he is descriptively responsible, but if the accusation is false, then he is not. Thus, Szasz's argument is that any charge of responsibility is open to four possibilities: 1) the charge is true descriptively and ascriptively—John did it and is guilty as charged; 2) the charge is descriptively true but ascriptively false—John did it but it was an accident; 3) the charge is descriptively false and ascriptively true—he did not do it but was framed or convicted even though innocent; and 4) the charge is both descriptively and ascriptively false—he did not do it and the jury verdict was not guilty. Meissner claims that persons experience a sense of responsibility for actions they have decided on and chosen, exactly as they correspondingly hold others responsible for their choices and actions. This relatively mature and autonomous ego with its capacities for effective choice and self-determination is the basis for a sense of responsibility.

The psychological perspective can also serve to link responsibility as discussed in this chapter to the process of decision-making discussed in Chapter 1. Decision and responsibility, according to Meissner (2003: 200), are paired in the sense that making a decision leads to action, the effects and consequences of which the agent is responsible. The responsibility falls to the agent as source of the action, but the further issue arises as to the degree to which the agent accepts and feels a sense of responsibility. The decision process, for Meissner, is responsive to motivational factors—the needs, wishes, and desires of appetitive experience—and is guided by the balance of motivational influences on the decision in question. However, the gain of motivational satisfaction must be balanced against the effects and consequences of the action and the associated demand for responsible acceptance. For an external observer, the decision-making agent carries the weight of responsibility for the action and its effects, but this does not necessarily connote that the subject experiences or accepts that responsibility—one can be objectively responsible while subjectively not.

In times of crises, the work of the mass media is becoming increasingly essential in the actual development of events. In the 2003 War on Iraq, the U.S. mass media's influence was key to achieving the objectives of U.S. foreign policy. To destroy the major part of the Iraqi centre of gravity—Saddam Hussein's regime—and consequently achieve the goals of a pre-emptive U.S. strategy in the war, as explained in Chapter 6, it was very important to use psychological war techniques through the mass media. The actions and reactions, offences and defenses that the mass media of both parties were practicing in the war led many observers to call it the "war of media".

In this context, it can be useful to consider the argument that Manuel Torres (2002: 245-246) makes that American war correspondence has reflected the major developments of the American press ever since its beginnings. In many occasions, war has accelerated such developments. Consider the following examples: first, war correspondents have always pushed for speeding up the reporting and delivery of news; second, the effectiveness of war correspondents has motivated the government and military to increase their censorship of war news; and thirdly, the war correspondent has risen as one of the most important members of the American press, although the job is still dangerous.

However, war correspondents pay a price. In fact, journalists in Iraq, whether embedded with coalition forces or holed up under the eye of Iraqi authorities in Baghdad, faced an immense challenge reporting on a difficult war that has singularly failed to stay on message. Journalist Phil Smucker once told CNN in an interview as battle raged around him in southern Iraq "We're about 100 miles (160 kilometres) south on the main highway. It's an unfinished highway. It goes between the Tigris and Euphrates River in the direction of Baghdad." That dispatch was enough to see the *Christian Science Monitor* reporter escorted to the Kuwaiti border by U.S. forces and "expelled" for endangering a military unit by being too specific. For journalists working outside the control of the U.S. and British militaries or the Iraqi authorities and the conditions they set in exchange for special access, expulsion is the least of their worries. Since the U.S.-led war in Iraq was launched on March 20, 2003, veteran British ITN television news correspondent Terry Lloyd is believed to have been killed in southern Iraq, apparently after coming under fire from coalition forces as he tried to cross the front lines independently. Lloyd's French cameraman Fred Nerac and Lebanese interpreter Hussein Osman were declared missing. Australian freelance cameraman Paul Moran was killed in a suicide car bombing in northern Iraq while covering U.S. air strikes against an alleged terrorist organization. In an apparent accident not linked to military action, Gaby Rado of Britain's Channel 4 News fell from the roof of a hotel in the Kurdish-controlled area of northern Iraq. A cameraman of the Qatar-based Arabic-language Al-Jazeera television news network reported missing was picked up by U.S. forces outside Basra and detained and interrogated for about 14 hours before being released. In Basra, a reporter for Al-Jazeera, the sole media outlet with a crew inside the southern Iraqi city, said the television team came under fire as they tried to film food warehouses being shelled by British tanks. Seven relieved Italian newspaper journalists who were reported missing turned up in Baghdad after being arrested in Basra when they asked Iraqi policemen for directions (Phillips, 2003, March 31).

The significance of the role of the media during wars requires a sense of responsibility. In effect, during the coverage of War on Iraq, "U.S. and Iraqi media policies have more in common than the leaders of either country would care to admit" (Erlich, 2003: 20). The following examples examine media responsibility during the coverage of the United States-Iraqi Crisis and its progeny, the 2003 War on Iraq.

Abunimah and Masri (2002) observed that media coverage of Iraq in the United States and United Kingdom twelve years after the beginning of the 1990/91 Gulf War overwhelmingly ignored the devastating effect of United Nations sanctions and bombing on civilians, provided skewed reporting of major issues, such as weapons inspections, and focused almost exclusively on the opinions of those aligned with U.S. policy. They analyzed the media coverage of Iraq focusing on two periods of Iraq coverage—the week of December 15-22, 1998, during which the United States and Britain staged a major attack on Iraq, launching approximately 400 cruise missiles and 600 bombs, and the period from August 1, 1999, until October 1, 1999, which covered both the August 12 publication of a major UNICEF (United Nations Children's Fund, formerly United Nations International Children's Emergency Fund) report on the effects of sanctions and the visit later that month of a delegation of congressional staffers to Iraq. They (102-111) categorized six major tendencies in the media coverage of Iraq—calling them the six deadly media sins—that observers and activists should look out for, beyond the obvious problem of presenting false information and the general tendency of the media to neglect serious, in-depth analysis of events: 1) ignoring or downplaying the effects of U.N. sanctions on the Iraqi people; 2) ignoring or discrediting reports of civilian victims from bombing; 3) personifying Iraq as Saddam Hussein; 4) speaking with the voice of the government; 5) creating an artificial "balance" in coverage; and 6) using a narrow selection of "experts".

They made many clear observations of specific incidents of media organizations in the context of these deadly sins while covering news coming out of Iraq. For example, there was a manipulation in the coverage of the 1999 UNICEF report—the first comprehensive, countrywide survey since 1991 of child and maternal mortality in Iraq. The *Washington Post* editorial "The Suffering of Children," stated:

> Saddam Hussein is not the first to use the suffering of children as an instrument of war, but he is surely distinctive in his manipulation of the suffering of his country's own children. His

evident purpose in exploiting Iraq's most vulnerable citizens is to advance his campaign against the embargo imposed by the United Nations for his invasion of Kuwait nearly 10 years ago. In this way, he has sacrificed his nation's future in this grisly effort.

(2002: 104)

The editorial, Abunimah and Masri explain, condemns Iraqi delays in ordering nutritional supplements for children, without mentioning the U.S. and British delays in approving urgently needed humanitarian imports. While expressing outrage at the "suffering of children," the *Post* neglects to mention UNICEF's most staggering estimate: 500,000 additional children would have lived had the declining child mortality rates in pre-sanctions Iraq continued. Also, they observe that a *Los Angeles Times* article leaves one with the impression that the United States, not Iraq, is the principal victim of sanctions policy and politics. The article stated:

[T]he Clinton administration must decide over the next month whether to do battle with some of its own allies to keep alive a policy aimed at undoing the regime of Iraqi president Saddam Hussein—or compromise in ways that might help a leader who was once compared to Adolf Hitler stay in power.

(2002: 104)

In addition, Abunimah and Masri (104-105) observed that omissions and half-truths are another method used to shift blame for the sanctions policy onto Iraqi shoulders. A *New York Times* article titled "Children's Death Rates Rising in Iraqi Lands, UNICEF Reports," only briefly mentioned the 1999 UNICEF report. The rest of the article was filled with unsubstantiated allegations and deceitful statements. In one sentence alone, the reporter presents three demonstrably false statements: "From the beginning of sanctions, President Hussein has been permitted to import food and medicines free of restrictions, but with oil sales blocked, he chose to spend what money was available on lavish palaces and construction projects." First, stating "from the beginning of sanctions" falsely implies that the sanctions themselves did not in effect limit food and medicine imports. Second, the Iraqi government was not allowed to import food and medicines "free of restrictions." The U.N. Security Council sanctions committee in New York could arbitrarily reject submitted contracts, as did so frequently. Third, the Iraqi government did not have any "money available" from the oil-for-food deal; all the money is held in a U.N.-managed escrow account, and transactions are approved by the U.N. Security Council. Additionally, approximately 25 percent of the oil-for-food money was reserved to pay reparations.

While a few of the journalists included in Abunimah and Masri's (2002: 106) investigation reported the truth, the majority did not. The *Atlanta Journal Constitution* reported, without providing any countervailing perspective, the views of "defense experts" that claimed "with shrewd use of the news media . . . the Iraqi president has tightly controlled the world's view of the nightly pounding by American and British missiles. . . . Through such public relations offensives the Iraqi leader has placed blame for the suffering of the Iraqi people on Americans." Also, a *Los Angeles Times* article stated that "the administration's extreme reluctance to risk civilian casualties is very evident." While the government's efforts to suppress or discredit reports of such victims were evident, the *Times* did not offer any evidence for its claim, except assertions from the Pentagon.

In their 2003 *Target Iraq: What the News Media Didn't Tell You*, editors Norman Solomon and Reese Erlich present examples of the disputes between American reporters and editors when covering the 2003 War on Iraq and more importantly, show how most American journalists blindly follow U.S. policy. Erlich (2003: 12) presents Bert as an example, a political moderate highly critical of Hussein's government, but feeling pressured by his much more conservative editors. Bert said "Whenever I propose stories showing the impact of sanctions on ordinary Iraqis, the editors call it 'old news'" (12). He wondered why the editors never tire of reworking old stories about corruption and repression in Iraq. Consequently, Bert has internalized his editors' preferences and generally files stories he knows they will like. The alternative is to write stories that will either never get published or come out buried in the back pages. Moreover, the problem goes beyond disputes between reporters and editors. Most journalists who get coveted foreign assignments already accept the assumptions of empire. Erlich says "I didn't meet a single foreign reporter in Iraq who disagreed with the notion that the U.S. and Britain have the right to overthrow the Iraqi government by force" (12). Rather, Erlich explains that they disagreed only about timing, whether the action should be unilateral, and whether a long-term occupation is practical. Ironically, Erlich further illustrates this issue by saying "When I raise the issue of sovereignty in casual conversation with my fellow scribes, they look as if I've arrived from Mars" (13). They argued that of course the U.S. had the right to overthrow Saddam Hussein because he had weapons of mass destruction and might have been a future threat to other countries. The implicit assumption is that the U.S.—as the world's sole superpower—has the right to make this decision and must take responsibility to remove unfriendly dictatorships and install friendly ones. The only question for them is whether or not sanctions or invasion are the most effective means to this end.

The invasion of Iraq by the so-called "coalition forces", composed basically of American and British troops, is radically altering the way the media are covering war. After this, media coverage of an international conflict will never be the same again. The media have been practically conscripted into the fight, and more than 500 journalists have been "embedded" in military units. One advantage is that the journalists gained a "ringside view" of the fighting and so could provide fresh, detailed, on-the-spot reports to their readers and viewers. The disadvantages, however, outweigh the advantage. The greatest disadvantage is that freedom of the press suffers because the reporting of the "embedded journalists" is limited by the coverage restrictions meant to "guide" them. Reporting is expectedly biased in favor of the U.S. military because journalists are living with the troops. It is difficult to be unfriendly to, or critical of, people with whom one is figuratively in bed with. Tim Blackmore, professor of media studies at the University of Western Ontario, said that from embedded journalists "we can only expect the Stockholm syndrome where those who are supposed to be innocent witnesses become perpetrators, joining with those about whom they are supposed to be objective". (Philippine daily cites. . ., 2003, April 8).

The following comments and involvements in war by journalists seriously puts into question the extent to which these journalists can be considered "responsible".

The BBC's Kate Adie, who happily wore a military uniform, commented: "I'm not just a reporter reporting independently, I'm actually with the army" (Keeble, 2001: 101). *Boston Herald* correspondent Jules Crittenden, who covered the Iraq War as an embedded journalist and whose blunt prose deals in absolutes—good vs. evil—in his writing for the *Poynter Institute*, admitted that while the unit he was following was on patrol outside one of Saddam's palaces, he aided in the killing of Iraqis. The piece detailed the event. There is a dichotomy of roles that Crittenden seems to have difficulty understanding: reporter vs. participant. To his critics, he had this to say: "I'm sure there are some people who will question my ethics, my objectivity, etc. I'll keep the argument short. Screw them, they weren't there. But they are welcome to join me next time if they care to test their professionalism." Crittenden's admission that he assisted in the killing of three human beings does much more than raise questions about his professionalism. War correspondents are civilians, afforded specific protection under the Fourth Geneva Convention. By picking up a weapon or assisting in the fighting, not only do they strip themselves of that protection, they also put every other journalist covering the war in jeopardy by blurring the line separating reporters from combatants. (Maher, 2003, May/June).

Aspects of "Good" Journalism

> Good journalism aims at discovering and promoting the audience's
> understanding of an event via truth-promoting methods. This is,
> indeed, why impartiality is important. For a journalist must aim to
> be impartial in his considered judgments as to the appropriate
> assessment of particular events, agents' intentions, why they came
> about and their actual or potential significance. A failure of
> impartiality in journalism is a failure to respect one of the methods
> required in order to fulfil the goal of journalism: getting at the truth
> of the matter. Conversely, bad journalism is truth-indifferent and
> fails to respect truth-promoting practices. . . . Honesty, discipline
> and impartiality are required to be a good journalist.
>
>   (Kieran, 1998: 34-35)

Journalistic performance, like in other professions, can be considered
good or *bad* from various perspectives. Discussing the meaning and
indications of both descriptions, the models of good practice, and the
requirements of achieving good journalism, is to pinpoint the major
journalistic principles and cornerstones that contribute to the achievement of
good journalism. These include truth telling, accuracy, fairness, balance,
verification, and maintaining context. In examining some of these principles
in the coverage of either the first consequence of the United States-Iraqi
Crisis, the 1990/91 Gulf War, or its latest consequence, the 2003 War on Iraq,
the picture appears unsatisfactory for those who are peace seekers, or would
seek a resolution to the conflict.

There are different means of informing the public about their
concerns and interests, Kieran argues, which justifies in some ways why the
craft of journalism is akin to an art rather than a science. However, like
science, journalism as a practice aims at truth, and it is relative to this
fundamental aim that news reports be classified as good or bad. That is, the
more journalism goes towards truthful coverage the closer it gets to good
practice, and vice versa.

Richard Keeble (2001: 124) presents significant questions regarding
what journalism should be and how journalists are to react in the face of the
vastness and complexities of the ethical dilemmas presented by the modern
media: "What precisely is good journalism? What are the models for 'good'
practice? How can the bad, the ugly and the unacceptable be eliminated?" He
argues that journalists often focus on skills when describing a "good

journalist". In consequence, "having a nose for a story", being able to take reliable notes and handle computer technology confidently, and writing accurately and colorfully are amongst the attributes commonly stressed. However, Keeble claims that most journalists, if pressed to identify the strictly ethical aspects of "good journalism", are likely to display ambivalent and contradictory attitudes.

To clarify this issue Keeble identifies (130-132) a few prominent positions: 1) fairness and accuracy; 2) social responsibility and the public interest; 3) the promotion of pluralism: media as the mirror of society, 4) codes of conduct/practice, and 5) the need for training. He explains that there is a strong ethical commitment among many journalists towards fairness in reporting and accuracy, the values that are stressed in codes of conduct throughout the world. The social responsibility theory, discussed earlier, has been recently updated by many American journalists through the promotion of the concept of civic journalism.[24] Journalists have increasingly opted to drop their detachment and deliberately intervene in the political process to increase knowledge and encourage participation. While it is usually acknowledged that the media operate according to the demands of a profit-oriented economy, it is still stressed that the market can function benignly, not simply in the interests of shareholders but of all the people, given the notion that journalists ultimately have a social responsibility to work in the interests of the public. Keeble considers that the media are crucial in promoting political and cultural pluralism, together with the view that the media bear the responsibility of reflecting society in its complexity: with as many legal viewpoints as possible covered, and different perspectives acknowledged. He explains that "professionalism" is usually linked to the promotion of codes of conduct. Thus, individual journalists unite with others to acknowledge common standards of behavior with various practices recognized as being the best to which they should all aspire. In effect, journalistic codes of ethics serve to create something like a collective conscience for the profession of journalism. The need for training to impart standards is linked to the notion of professionalism.

Although most people agree that journalists must tell the truth, Kovach and Rosenstiel (2001: 37) argue, people are confused about what the *truth* means. Kovach and Rosenstiel illustrate that, when asked what values they consider paramount, 100 percent of journalists interviewed for a survey by the Pew Research Center for the People and the Press and the Committee of Concerned Journalists answered "getting the facts right." Journalists significantly point to truth as a primary mission as well, and that the desire that information be truthful is elemental.

Gordon (1999*b*: 73-74) argues that truth telling is a first principle in journalism, to the point where if choices must be made, truth must be given primacy over any other ethical concerns. Gordon reminds us with a quote from Walter Lippmann's 1922 *Public Opinion*, that the "function of news is to signalize an event, the function of truth is to bring to light the hidden facts, to set them into relation with each other, and make a picture of reality ..." (73). Telling the truth as fully as possible, for Gordon, should be a "first principle" for journalists and public relations practitioners, in the spirit of Kant's categorical imperative.

Joe Roidt of the *Charleston Gazette* reported on February 11, 2003, that the media left the public misinformed on the war with Iraq. Roidt argues that since President Bush inaugurated the confrontation with Iraq with his "axis of evil" reference in January 2003, the U.S. news media has evidenced a troubling propensity to miss the forest for the trees. This is unfortunate because it leaves the American public ill-informed about the course of action its government is contemplating and the potential consequences it entails. For one, the media misrepresented the inspections process. Since November 18, 2002, when U.N. weapons inspectors touched down in Iraq, media coverage has been similarly truncated. Roidt explains that the news media focused narrowly on the inspections themselves as well as on the inaccurate notion of deadlines. Moreover, the media failed terribly to provide sufficient coverage and analysis of the phenomenal changes in the national security policy of the United States.

Truth telling, according to Hindman (1997: 35-36), is key to both the U.S. Supreme Court's view of media responsibility and the media's view of their own role in U.S. society. Telling the truth—that is, representing various views as fairly and accurately as possible—about society is seen as a primary responsibility of the media, one about which the Court has thought carefully. For the Court, journalists should tell the truth, for that is part of their responsibility of enlightening the public. Also, telling the truth can mean more than just reciting accurate factual information; it can mean presenting various perspectives, which taken together represent a "larger" truth about, or picture of, society. Although the justices, Hindman explains (41), never agreed on an overall theory of media responsibility with regard to truth telling, they have articulated various conceptions of responsibility: act with reasonable care, provide discussion on public issues, and present information fairly and from a variety of perspectives. In addition, the only definition the entire Court agreed to over time was the media responsibility not to lie knowingly.

John Kittross (1999: 81-85) argues that truth and objectivity are not adequate standards for the news media and calls for accuracy and fairness: "Don't we need to be *fair* as well as truthful, *accurate* as well as objective?"

(81). He suggests that journalists must meet these two other standards, interwoven with, but distinct from, truth and objectivity, with fairness being more important. In the context of explaining how accuracy is important, Kittross refers to false accuracy in Darryl Huff's 1954 *How to Lie with Statistics*. For example, to say that 33.33% of the female students, at a specific university in a specific year, married members of the faculty may be true, but it may mean that there were only three women in the student body that year, and one cannot generalize from that year to another. Also, other fallacies or errors that are technically accurate but actually false abound in journalism, as they do in scholarly or commercial research. The researcher distinguishes between validity (something measures what we say it does), reliability (repeated measurements of the same phenomenon have the same result), and precision. Kittross argues that journalists often tend to ignore these distinctions and are concerned only with a somewhat ambiguous concept of accuracy. Kittross warns that this can be serious: "Without carefully defined standards, it is unlikely that high quality will be achieved" (85). Moreover, if a reporter is accurate, but does not give the whole story, the overall effect is one of inaccuracy.

As for fairness, Kittross (1999: 86-87) claims that, to a certain extent, we can think of fairness in terms of what *not* to air or publish. He asks "Should a mass murderer have as much attention as the victims?" (87). He gives an example by asking: "During the Gulf War, should the ruler of Iraq automatically have rated 'equal time' or 'equal space' with the combined leadership of the coalition arrayed against him? Was the situation different in 1998? Should a spokesperson for an unpopular view or other controversial position . . . automatically have exactly the same attention from the media as those on the other side?" (87) and so on. Kittross defines fairness as follows:

> Fairness is the act of keeping an open mind, of suspending individual judgment until enough information is available so that judgments or decisions can validly be made. It is impartiality, but not ignorance. The media are not merely a conduit; they have the responsibility to assess the validity or truth of the information they disseminate. Of particular importance is the need to provide sufficient valid and reliable information that will allow readers, listeners, and viewers to reach their own conclusions.
>
> (1999: 86)

Harris and Spark (1997: 224-229) stress fairness and accuracy and claim that both give journalism honesty. They claim that these elements also promote the credibility and authority of newspapers and, therefore, help defend journalists against their critics. However, they argue that fairness and accuracy are not everything, but there is a great deal of concern for accountability. They explain that journalists are accountable to their editors who bear the legal responsibility for what is published, as well as having accountability to their readers for the accuracy of their reporting and the fairness of their conduct.

> In mid-March [2003], *Washington Post* reporter Jonathan Weisman made a startling confession on media columnist Jim Romenesko's Web site. Weisman acknowledged that he changed a quote in a story about R. Glenn Hubbard, President Bush's departing economic adviser, after receiving pressure from the White House. He admitted that the switch violated journalistic ethics, but he also said reporters need to "reconsider the way we cover the White House."
>
> (Jones, 2003: 39)

Accuracy, for Kovach and Rosenstiel (2001: 43), is the foundation upon which everything else builds: context, interpretation, debate, and all of public communication. If the foundation is faulty, everything else is flawed. One of the risks of the new proliferation of outlets, talk programs, and interpretative reporting is that it has left verification behind. A debate between opponents arguing with false figures or purely on prejudice fails to inform. It only inflames. It takes the society nowhere. However, mere accuracy can be a kind of distortion all its own. The 1947 Hutchins Commission warned about the dangers of publishing accounts that are "factually correct but substantially untrue." Consequently, "It is no longer enough to report *the fact* truthfully. It is now necessary to report *the truth about the fact*." Kovach and Rosenstiel bring to the surface two tests of truth according to philosophers: correspondence and coherence. For journalism, these roughly translate into getting the facts straight and making sense of the facts. Coherence must be the ultimate test of journalistic truth.

Although Kovach and Rosenstiel (2001: 46-48) acknowledge that the two most common substitutes for truthfulness that some journalists have suggested over the years are fairness and balance, they argue that both fairness and balance, under scrutiny, become inadequate. Fairness is too abstract and, eventually, more subjective than truth. Fair to whom? How do we test fairness? As for truthfulness, for all its difficulties, it can at least be tested. Also, balance is too subjective because balancing a story by being fair to both sides may not be fair to the truth, if both sides do not in fact have equal weight. Alternatively, Kovach and Rosenstiel suggest, the media needs to concentrate on *synthesis* and *verification*: sift out the rumor, innuendo, the insignificant and the spin, and concentrate on what is true and important about a story. Rather than expand the time they spend sorting through information themselves people need sources they can go to that will tell them what is true and significant. They need an answer to the question: "What here can I believe?" Then, the role of the media becomes working to answer the question: "Where is the good stuff?" Verification and synthesis become the backbone of the new gatekeeper role of the journalist.

In his 2003 article "Balance and context: Maintaining media ethics", Deni Elliott (16-17) claims that the most pressing issue for American journalism is one reflected in the coverage of the United States-Iraqi Crisis. For him, the most important job of journalism in democratic countries is to provide information that allows citizens to engage in fully informed self-governance. Accordingly, American journalists and news managers must figure out how journalism can best accomplish that goal in an increasingly global environment. He suggests that news reporting in the 21st century requires independence, investigative skills, and a keen ability to look where others are not pointing. Elliott considers balance and context as requisite for comprehensive reporting and maintaining ethics. However, he gives examples of reporting from January to March 2003, to illustrate how news media have failed to report stories in a timely fashion and how they have demonstrated the lack of balance and context. As one example, while the American press and U.S. citizens had become familiar with antiwar sentiments in the U.S. and around the world by mid-March, knowing how to report these expressions lagged far behind the worldwide antiwar effort. Most notably, during the first half of February, nothing appeared in the nation's press on the plans for the international week of antiwar resistance that concluded on February 15 and 16 with millions of people around the globe demonstrating against a potential war in Iraq. Wire-service photos of that weekend's antiwar demonstrations contained, which many U.S. newspapers ran, a picture that showed two demonstrators with American flags printed on one half of their faces and death masks on the other. The implication of such photos, Elliott explains, is that these clownish extremists fairly represented the millions of protestors. Such pictures of extremists, which were also popular in illustrating antiwar protests during the 1990/91 Gulf War, minimized the importance of the protest.

For Elliott, "balance" and "context" refer to the journalistic attempt to help readers and viewers create meaning. Journalists "balance" claims made by one source of information with other legitimate but competing claims. They also provide "context" for a story when they let their audience know more facts than those selectively provided by a source. However, reporting on U.S.-governmental perspectives has been decidedly without balance. For instance, in contrast to the coverage of representatives of countries that opposed U.S. action in Iraq, statements made by Secretary of State Colin Powell before the U.N. Security Council were consistently treated by U.S. news media as facts. When journalists report what was "said" they imply the truth of the statement, whereas "claimed" or "alleged" signal a need for external verification. Columnists and news reporters consistently offered claims that should have been used to balance governmental statements at the time that they were initially reported. Robert Sheer, a regular opinion writer for the *Los Angeles Times,* dissected Powell's February 5 presentation: "The main evidence presented by the secretary of state was a satellite photo of a forlorn outpost, allegedly linked to Hussein and Al-Qaeda and which Powell claims is in the business of producing chemical weapons" (18). Scheer pointed out that the camp was outside of the part of Iraq controlled by Hussein, and inside the area patrolled by U.S. and British warplanes, information clearly available to reporters, yet seldom included in U.S. media reports. Another example of news media repeating governmental rhetoric rather than reporting on it is the use of the "axis of evil," a phrase developed by the Bush administration to provide a link between the September 11, 2001 (9/11) terrorist attacks and Iraq. The speech writer's assignment, in his words, was to further the World War II analogy already begun by the administration in describing the attacks as "another Pearl Harbor" and "to extrapolate from the Sept. 11 terrorist attacks to make a case for 'going after' Iraq" (20). From his speech for the State of the Union address, Bush said, and news media repeated that "a lesson taken from Sept. 11 was that the United States of America will not permit the world's most dangerous regimes to threaten us with the world's most destructive weapons" (20). To strengthen the analogy with the Axis powers in World War II, two other bad actors were required to lump in with Iraq. Iran and North Korea fit the bill. "Axis of evil" is no longer used by the administration due to the increasing effort needed since August to explain how North Korea and Iraq are different from each other and how the provocative actions of the former necessitate a diplomatic response while the less provocative actions of the latter necessitate a military response. Once the administration dropped the phrase, it disappeared from the journalists' lexicon as well, with no explanation of how or why. (2003: 18-20).[25]

In the context of the debate around "where did all the Iraqi weapons go?", it emerged that the media clearly overlooked a key story before the war. Seth Ackerman (2003*b*, May/June) explains that the media seemed surprised by the U.S. military's failure, as of this writing, to find any hidden chemical or biological weapons in Iraq. Ackerman argues that this is because they virtually ignored a critical story that was lost in a flood of stories about the dangers of a chemically armed Saddam Hussein. Weeks before the war began on March 3, 2003, *Newsweek*'s John Barry published an account of a secret U.N. transcript recording the 1995 interview between U.N. weapons inspectors and Iraq's highest-ranking defector, former weapons chief Lt. Gen. Hussein Kamel. The story of Kamel's defection had been used by reporters, pundits, and high-ranking U.S. foreign policymakers for many years to prove that Iraq amassed vast stockpiles of dangerous weapons. But in the transcript obtained by *Newsweek*, Ackerman explains, Kamel added a crucial qualifier: "All weapons—biological, chemical, missile, nuclear, were destroyed . . . after the Gulf War, Iraq destroyed all its chemical and biological weapons stocks and the missiles to deliver them. . . . The weapons were eliminated secretly in the summer of 1991 . . . in order to hide their existence from inspectors, and in hopes of someday resuming production after inspections had finished." Ackerman adds that when *Newsweek*'s story appeared, during the height of the U.N. Security Council debate over weapons inspections, CIA spokesperson Bill Harlow angrily denied it, and told *Reuters* on February 24, 2003: "It is incorrect, bogus, wrong, untrue." The media helped the U.S. officials to make use of Kamel's story to support their position. The media focused on Powell's presentation on February 5, 2003, to the U.N. Security Council: "It took years for Iraq to finally admit that it had produced four tons of the deadly nerve agent, VX. . . . A single drop of VX on the skin will kill in minutes. Four tons. The admission only came out after inspectors collected documentation as a result of the defection of Hussein Kamel, Saddam Hussein's late son-in-law." Also they acknowledged the warning by Vice President Dick Cheney on August 27, 2003 that inspectors would be unable to find Iraq's weapons: Kamel's story "should serve as a reminder to all that we often learned more as the result of defections than we learned from the inspection regime itself." Deputy National Security Advisor Stephen Hadley wrote in the *Chicago Tribune* on February 16, 2003, that "because of information provided by Iraqi defector and former head of Iraq's weapons of mass destruction programs, Lt. Gen. Hussein Kamel, the regime had to admit in detail how it cheated on its nuclear non-proliferation commitments." Also, the media treated Kamel as an authority on Iraq's weapons. In the four months prior to *Newsweek*'s story, the defector was cited four times on the *New York Times* op-ed page in support of claims about Iraq's weapons programs, but never noting his assertions about the elimination of these weapons.

Seth Ackerman (2003a, July/August) gives examples of newspapers' coverage that follow American claims about WMDs without, in general, questioning them. Ackerman argues that by the time the war against Iraq began, much of the media had been conditioned to believe, almost as an article of faith, that Saddam Hussein's Iraq was bulging with chemical and biological weapons, despite years of U.N. inspections. Reporters dispensed with the formality of applying modifiers like "alleged" or "suspected" to Iraq's supposed unconventional weapon stocks. Instead, *NBC Nightly News* on January 27, 2003, wondered "what precise threat Iraq and its weapons of mass destruction pose to America". The *Washington Post* on the same day wrote matter-of-factly of Washington's plans for a confrontation "over Iraq's banned weapons programs". Also, *Time* on February 3, 2003, referred to debates over whether Saddam Hussein was "making a good-faith effort to disarm Iraq's weapons of mass destruction". All of this came despite repeated reminders from the chief U.N. weapons inspector that it was his job to determine if Iraq was hiding weapons, and that it should not simply be assumed that Iraq was doing so.

However, there are also examples of a responsible coverage. Oliver Moore of *The Globe and Mail*, for instance, wrote on December 6, 2002, that the Iraqi Ambassador to the United Nations said that his government was tired of repeating "again and again" that it was not breaking any U.N. resolutions. Moore quoted Mohammed al-Douri who said:

> Everything has been destroyed and we have no intention to do that again . . . Iraq is clean of any kind mass destruction offences. . . . We did provide all confirmation they need. . . . Inspectors are now in Europe, we are co-operating with them, they have the full access anywhere in Iraq. If Americans have this evidence, they have to tell the inspectors. . . . We are saying they will find nothing.

Leonard Sussman (1995: 76-77) offers seven ethical concerns which can be used to set a standard for journalism to serve as an educative force for peace. First, it should be understood by government officials and the public that journalists in a free society should not be directed to do or not do anything, except abide by traditional libel laws and the society's code of good taste. Second, freedom from such governmental strictures or penalties does not reduce the responsibility of the journalist, it increases that responsibility. The journalist, including owner, editor and reporter, becomes a free agent of the whole society. Third, the responsibility of the journalist relates directly to the ingrained commitment of each journalist to a voluntarily adopted code of the individual journalist ethics and practices. Fourth, it should be understood, each journalist who addresses the public by floating ideas has a responsibility that extends beyond higher television ratings. They should consider the impact of their words on possible actions to follow. Fifth, accuracy and balance are high and commendable standards, and more realistic than professing objectivity. Sixth, moves toward international problem-solving, peacekeeping, arms reduction, and/or conversion to peaceful pursuits should be sought out and featured. The implications of peaceful realignments of nations are relevant themes for investigative reporters. Finally, the ethical implication is clear: peace is a vital human subject, and needs as much continuing attention in the mass media as sections on other aspects of life.[26]

I would like to conclude this chapter, by reiterating its objective, which is to explore the responsibility side of how media decision-makers are expected to work. This discussion built on the preceding chapter, which looked at the first of the two major that constitute the balance required in the proposed model—the rational side. In the next chapter we move to a discussion of crucial issues regarding media ethics, specifically a thorough analysis of international media codes of ethics and fundamentals of journalistic practices.

NOTES

1. Markel (32-34) sheds light on the "theory of blameworthiness," which reflects a group of general philosophical principles about the circumstances under which a person should or should not be held accountable for performing a wrong action or for failing to perform a right action. The concept of "blameworthiness," however, is not black and white. There are four mitigating factors that decrease a person's or organization's blameworthiness: uncertainty, difficulty, involvement, and seriousness. Thus, blameworthiness can be alleviated if a person or organization is: 1) uncertain whether an action is wrong because the facts are unclear or because the relationship between the facts and the relevant ethical standard is unclear; 2) under some pressure that makes doing the right thing difficult; 3) part of a team that together performs a wrong action; and/or 4) committed to carrying out a minor, not a major, transgression.

2. Ethical decisions, according to Day (2000: 5), are always made within a specific "context," which includes the political, social, and cultural climate. He argues that although the context does not necessarily determine the outcome of an ethical judgment, it exerts an influence that cannot be ignored.

3. "Political perspectives" look at the communication relevant and important in the realm of the public and society at large. "Human nature perspectives" look at what kinds of communication serve to enhance human attributes and do not dehumanize. Specific approaches here include looking at human rational capacities and symbol-using capability, the moral imperative of Immanuel Kant, the use of language, epistemological approaches, value judgments, use of rhetoric, and an ethics grounded in the field of evolutionary psychology. "Dialogical perspectives" look specifically at the attitudes that people have toward each other and the characteristics important to those who focus on creating a dialogue. Key components of this perspective are authenticity, inclusion, confirmation, presentness, spirit of mutual equality, and a supportive climate. "Situational perspectives" look at the particular type of communication case by case in order to make a judgment on the ethicality of that specific communication. "Religious perspectives" look at communication ethics from the principles of a religion and its fundamental religious texts. As examples, there is the Christian ethic, which stems from human reflection of God's image; the Confucian emphasis on facts and logic; the Taoist values of empathy and insight; Buddhist principles; and the Muslim emphasis on God's law over human-made ones. "Utilitarian perspectives" evaluate the consequence of an action or behavior as the ultimate test and does so by looking at factors like usefulness, pleasure, and happiness for the greatest number. Johannesen notes that this perspective is usually combined with one of the other major perspectives. "Legalistic perspectives" generally take the view that if an action is illegal, it is unethical; and if something is not illegal, it would therefore be considered ethical. As for "feminist perspectives", they typically look closely at issues related to balance of power, domination, and subordination. They look at relationships in a web and focus less on the individual as an atomic unit. (Berkman & Shumway, 2003: 5-6).

4. That is, there are many factors which accompany photographs that can mislead the viewers such as context, comment, etc. For instance, de-contextualizing the central object in a photo can either increase or decrease its importance, or the caption can add interpretations that might not be evident by only looking at the photo.

5. As examples, the interests of journalists include: advancing their status, salaries, or careers; contributing to the efforts of their colleagues; and serving the public. The interests of the public include: a desire to be well informed regarding different aspects of life and news at the local, regional, national and international levels. The interests of media organizations include: informing the public and making a profit.

6. Consideration of journalists' own perspective(s) on ethical issues raises questions about potential conflicts even between journalists as: 1) seekers

of truth and servants of the market; 2) citizens and employees; and 3) professionals and workers (Harcup, 2002: 101).

7. For more about these, including an in-depth analysis of social responsibility theory, see: Baran and Davis (2000: 104-110), Hiebert, Ungurait and Bohn (1974: 18-19), Rivers and Schramm (1969: 45-52), and Peterson (1956: 73-96).

8. The Commission on Freedom of the Press, according to Rivers and Schramm (1969: 47-48), formed the most intense body of criticism in the late 1940s. They presented what Theodore Peterson summarized as the general themes of the criticism of all the media.

9. As Rivers and Schramm explain (1969: 50-52), the difference is that responsibility in the monolithic communist society is delimited and enforced, but in the pluralistic libertarian society it is never so neat. Responsibility in the pluralistic society allows for diversity of views and opinions, while this is unimaginable in the authoritarian society. For Rivers and Schramm, social responsibility is defined by groups of various publishers and journalists, is certainly relative, and is sometimes nebulous. So, it is clear here that if social responsibility were defined by the government, it would be some sort of authoritarian system. What really distinguishes the libertarian society from the authoritarian society is the diversity of views of responsible performance by different journalists. However, the performance of the media is targeted by rational people who can distinguish truth from deception.

10. Wilbur Schramm looks at media responsibility as a shared one. In answering the question, "Who is responsible for the quality of mass communication?" he (1966: 348-361) asserts that responsibility should be shared by the media themselves, the government, and the public. Considering the responsibility of the public, Schramm calls upon the public as far as possible to make itself an alert and discriminating audience. For more on media responsibility, see Hermon (1990: 37-41), and Rivers and Schramm (1969: 238-242).

11. Another issue is credibility. As Charles Self (1996: 421-422) argues, each person believes some sources of information more than others, values some institutional sources more than others. He illustrates how communication scholars have explored the role of source credibility in persuasive messages. About half a century ago, communication scholars began the scientific study of credibility, an endeavor which is inherently tied to interpersonal and persuasion research.

12. There are other more general problems. Marshall McLuhan and Harold Innis are examples of Canadian philosophers and critics of communication who argue that there are some differences when we look at the world through the mass media. For example, as Severin and Tankard (1988: 315)

recount, when McLuhan said that the content of mass communication does not matter, this bothered many communication theorists and people working in mass communication. However, what McLuhan meant was that the important effects of the medium come from its form, not its content. Baran and Davis (2000: 286) tell how political economist Harold Innis traced the way Canadian elites used various technologies, including the railroad and telegraph, to extend their control across the continent. He expressed a deep distrust of centralized power, and believed that newer forms of communication technology would make even greater centralization inevitable. He referred to this centralized control as the inherent bias of communication.

13. However, the mass media are not the only components, determinants, or motivators in changing, modifying, and creating attitudes, opinions, and behaviors in the social world. There are many others: "Mass-media information works within a tightly bounded framework of other influences" (Morrison & Tumber, 1988: 348). Most prominently during events of stress and tension, the information provided by the mass media in general—and television, the most influential, in particular—is not separated from the individual's previous knowledge, values, traditions, beliefs, and experiences in their recognition and understanding of the meanings of events.

14. For example, Lazarsfeld's contribution to the field of communication research became more concentrated in 1937 when he launched the Princeton Radio Project to examine the influence of radio broadcasting on listeners. This project had three important results, as Barton (2001: 251-252) explains: 1) it established the field of mass communication research; 2) it discovered psychological and social mechanisms theoretically generalizable beyond the field of radio-listening behavior; and 3) it disclosed the inadequacy of simple cross-sectional surveys to answer questions on the effects of media exposure. Lazarsfeld used the data of commercial consumer studies, public opinion polling, and radio audience surveys as "the raw material for the new field of communication and opinion research" (Chaffee & Rogers, 1997: 54).

15. For example, Raju, Jagadeswari, and Dissanayake (1984: 106) define six main functions of the mass media in society: 1) informing the people about public affairs; 2) creating awareness and reinforcing the opinions and attitudes of the audience; 3) presenting alternative views and approaches to problems and interpreting events, constructing a cohesive framework and position towards them; 4) providing open public forums for discussion of the implications of a given event; 5) mobilizing historical and contemporary evidence in order to support a particular position or oppose it; 6) informing the public, through providing insights, enabling them to make judgments on given issues in given situations.

16. What could be more dangerous than a recognized public authority that controls information and awareness; affects opinions and attitudes; imposes interpretations of events, views and explanations; leads discussions of opposition or support; and, finally, directs public attention to specific judgments?

17. The most significant limitation for the mass media, according to Raju, Jagadeswari, and Dissanayake (1984: 106), is to operate within the context of laws and traditions that reflect the values of equity, justice, and fairness.

18. The nature of media-government relations in the United States, Alger (1989: 154-158) explains, includes the definition of five basic functions performed by the media for presidents, Congress, and the other governmental institutions: 1) to tell the public about how the Presidency itself is being conducted by the incumbent, and about the Presidency and processes of the government as a whole; 2) to provide a means by which the President (and other officials) can communicate directly with the public; 3) to provide a channel for the President to communicate with other officials, and vice versa; 4) to provide communication through the media of political feedback from other political actors and from the general public; and 5) to transmit to the President and other officials information about events and developments. For more, see: Thrall (2000), Soderlund and Lee (1999), Schiller (1986), Levine (1981), and Chittick (1970).

19. The decision-making process procedures inside governments, for instance, face various biases from many organizations, including pressure groups, political parties, organized groups, the mass media, and so on. Pocklington (1985: 396-400) explains the significant influence of the mass media on the governmental decision-making process.

20. Moreover, Davison (1974: 18) argues that the mass media influence governmental decisions indirectly through elite groups—those groups inside and outside the government that share in the process of policy initiation and formulation although they do not make the final decisions.

21. In analyzing the role of mass media in the shaping of American public policy and democracy, Davis (2001: 305-306) discusses how the press serves as an observer in society, recording events, statements, and policy decisions. He explains three other roles of the press that Bernard Cohen has described: that of observer, participant, and catalyst. As observer, the press observes and reports the events of the policymaking process. As participant, the press serves as representative for the public, government watchdog or critic, advocate of certain policy positions, and actual policymaker. But as a catalyst, through news content, the press impels issues to the forefront and affects the public's agenda and reaction to those issues. Most importantly, Alger (1989: 183-184) draws attention to significant findings of a study regarding the impact of the media on policy,

explaining the two most notable types of impact. First, substantial news coverage speeds up the decision-making process; and second, substantial coverage, especially if it is negative coverage of administrative actions, tends to push decision-making up the bureaucracy to higher levels, even to the White House.

22. To explore the connection between ethical responsibility and legal rights, Paul Voakes (2000) conducted a survey of 1,037 journalists and in-depth interviews with 22 others, and found out that there are three models of the relation of law and ethics: (1) a Separate Realms model, (2) a Correspondence model, and (3) a new "Responsibility Model" in which the law is considered in problematic situations but only as one of several considerations in what is essentially an ethical decision.

23. In his research article of 1991—"The role of press councils in a system of media accountability: The case of Quebec," David Pritchard analyzes the Quebec Press Council as a mechanism for media accountability and traces its effectiveness as a forum for complaints about media ethics. He assumed that the conceptual muddle could not be clarified without careful exploration of how mechanisms of media accountability actually function. His article offers a brief overview of the North American experience with press councils, and explores how one of them—the Quebec Press Council— functions as a mechanism of media accountability. His article demonstrates that press councils can provide the kind of justice most libel plaintiffs say they would like, are quicker and cheaper than courts, and accept complaints from a broader range of "plaintiffs" about a broader range of problems. Most importantly, he concludes that although press councils cannot impose fines or send people to prison, the survey suggests that what most complainers want is not to punish media, but rather a fair review of press performance.

24. The idea of civic journalism is based on the media desire to enhance news stories by letting citizens discuss public policy issues, and define their problems and suggest solutions through using the various kinds of media— broadcasting, print, the Internet, etc. It holds a sense of responsibility towards better life in the community.

25. Elliott (2003: 20) suggests two major jobs for American news media. The first is to refrain from being journalistic cheerleaders. News organizations became flag-waving, banner-rippling, nationalistic voices during the 1990/91 Gulf War and in the wake of 9/11. In both cases, the journalists' nationalistic rhetoric became more vehement as the public-approval rating for military intervention soared, which resulted in higher public approval both for the action and for the media. News media need to break out of the government-citizen approval spiral to provide opportunities for alternative

voices, no matter how quiet or few. The second is to convince citizens and government that providing a public forum for discussion and alternative views is not disloyal. News organizations need to provide context for statements and stories, especially those made by the U.S. administration. Contextualized reporting includes letting citizens hear the voices of our government's enemies, as well as critics of governmental policy from within and from outside of the country. The purpose of providing alternatives is not to lessen the effect of governmental messages, but rather to open those messages to broad examination and understanding. Support for governmental perspective, if warranted, will be stronger when citizens can understand that view in light of opposing alternatives.

26. In addition, there are ten commandments of peace journalism. First, never reduce the parties in human conflicts to two. Second, identify the views and interests of all parties to human conflicts. There is no single truth; there are many truths. Third, do not be hostage to one source, particularly those of governments that control sources of information. Fourth, develop a good sense of skepticism. Fifth, give voice to the oppressed and peacemakers to represent and empower them. Sixth, seek peaceful solutions to conflict problems, but never fall prey to panaceas. Seventh, your representation of conflict problems can become part of the problem if it exacerbates dualisms and hatreds. Eighth, your representation of conflict problems can become part of the solution if it employs the creative tensions in any human conflict to seek common ground and nonviolent solutions. Ninth, always exercise the professional media ethics of accuracy, veracity, fairness, and respect for human rights and dignity. Tenth, transcend your own ethnic, national, or ideological biases to see and represent the parties to human conflicts fairly and accurately. (Tehranian, 2002: 80-81).

Media Codes of Ethics

This chapter addresses important issues regarding media ethics and responsibility through an analysis of the media codes of ethics, and research into the principles and fundamentals of journalistic practices. I also discuss the debate surrounding the recent emerging trend towards adopting a universal ethical standard for journalism. Chapter 5 then concludes with an investigation into general criticisms surrounding communication ethics.

ANALYSIS OF EXISTING MEDIA CODES OF ETHICS

Ethics (a word that appears both in singular and plural constructions) presupposes a human being's awareness of right and wrong, and evaluates human conduct as reflective of moral values. More specifically, ethics refers to a discipline, theory, or other system that seeks to provide moral guidelines by integrating or balancing personal values with institutional or community obligations. The goal of ethics, then, is to improve society as well as the individual. In their most concrete expressions, ethical standards are spelled out in codes and lists of rules. These codes and lists reflect general principles, which in turn may be rooted in multiple sources such as the teachings of social and political philosophers, legal documents such as the First Amendment to the U.S. Constitution, and religious dictates such as the Golden Rule and the Ten Commandments.

(Wheeler, 2002: 70)

Analysis of the existing journalistic codes of ethics results in the exploration of a wide umbrella of responsibility, which is linked to accountability, and also contains a range of principles, many values, and a tremendous number of rules. However, the analysis sees the appropriateness of grouping the most significant and relevant under six major principles: independence, truth, accuracy, fairness, integrity, and serving the public interest.

Most nations and regions of the world possess media codes of ethics. Codes are diversely called a code of honor, of conduct, of practice or (in Latin countries) of "deontology." They are also called canons of journalism, a charter of journalists, a statement of principles, a declaration of the duties and rights of journalists, etc. The drafters of a code realize that what they write is not a sacred text to which they would expect every journalist to adhere, but instead a guide which can only become operational if the journalist is endowed with a moral sense. As in any organized craft, the code of ethics aims at eliminating people who have dishonest and criminal intents. It informs the public about its rules of conduct, consequently increasing its credibility, insures the loyalty of its patrons and the loyalty of its advertisers, the source of its prosperity. The code generates solidarity within the group and preserves the prestige of the profession. Those who adopt the code give themselves an ideal and they strive to reinforce the moral conscience of every professional by making clear the values and principles unanimously recognized by the profession. The code can provide a feeling of security, of collective strength. The code aims at avoiding state intervention. Also, professionals acquire protection against an employer who might ask them to act contrary to the public interest as they can argue that such behavior would cause them to be rejected by their peers. Codes issued by a government are nothing but executive orders, but true codes include the following: national, adopted by one or several professional associations; international; or those issued by associations of media owners or by unions or again by associations of news people. Some codes concern only one medium, some are specific to a publication, or to a broadcasting network. A code of professional ethics should normally be conceived by the professionals themselves. That is why some professionals refuse to take into account the regulations prescribed by employers for their employees. (Bertrand, 2002: 41-43).[1]

The literature on journalistic ethics, though relatively recent, is growing rapidly (Harcup, 2002: 101). The benefits of codes of ethics are illustrated by David Gordon (1999*a*: 63), who confirms their usefulness and necessity for the mass media and society. He demonstrates that codes of ethics not only help to protect the public from unethical performance and the media from unreasonable public demands, but also provide a reference point that can be invoked to protect media workers from internal pressures that could force them to violate their own consciences. In addition, codes can provide a context for media practitioners to discuss and reflect on their responsibilities and obligations. Catherine McKercher and Carman Cumming (1998: 383-386), in their discussion of an ethical consensus among Canadian journalists, draw up a list of principles that journalists have endorsed, which include the following: admit error; protect your sources; do not under any circumstances distort, fabricate or plagiarize; do not accept favors; do not let anybody else make your news judgments; stay away from the group as much as you can; be reluctant to suppress news; do not lie, steal or misrepresent yourself; and so on.[2]

When reviewing codes of ethics of various associations, it becomes clear that, although each one is different, the basic principles and ethical standards are quite similar. Basically codes provide a group of overriding guiding ethical principles as well as a listing of specific ethical rules and guidelines. Berkman and Shumway (2003: 24) found that the codes of ethics of major media organizations have many principles in common. Examples of these principles include informing and serving the public interest, seeking the truth, avoiding conflicts of interest, being fair, being accurate, treating subjects of stories with decency and compassion, keeping editorial separate from advertising, and helping protect free speech. Similarly, Lorenz and Vivian (1996: 549-550) also confirm that a careful reading of the codes will show that the organizations share many values, such as truth, accuracy, fairness, and responsibility to the public, objectivity, honesty, impartiality, respect for others, and condemnation of conflicts of interest.

This chapter analyzes eleven major codes of ethics representing a wide range of national, regional, and international media associations; they are those most frequently quoted and investigated in the scholarship of media ethics, which cover a variety of media, as well as most prominent figures and pioneers in establishing guiding codes for journalistic ethical conduct. The selected codes, listed alphabetically, are:

- American Society of Newspaper Editors (ASNE): Statement of Principles[3]
- Associated Press Managing Editors (APME): Code of Ethics[4]
- Federation of Arab Journalists (FAJ): Code of Ethics[5]
- Gannett Newspaper Division (GND): Principles of Ethical Conduct for Newsrooms[6]
- International Declaration of the Rights and Obligations of Journalists (IDROJ)[7]
- National Press Photographers Association (NPPA): Code of Ethics[8]

- Radio-Television News Directors Association (RTNDA): Code of Ethics and Professional Conduct[9]
- The British Press Complaints Commission (BPCC): Code of Practice[10]
- The Code of Professional Conduct of the Russian Journalist (CPCRJ) [11]
- The Society of Professional Journalists/Sigma Delta Chi (SPJ/SDX): Code of Ethics[12]
- Third World Code from India (TWCI): Norms of Journalistic Conduct[13]

In general, the analysis shows that *responsibility* is the core theme and larger umbrella of most, if not all, codes of ethics under which fall most other principles and values of journalistic conduct. Codes acknowledge that the journalist's responsibility towards the public exceeds any other responsibility, particularly towards employers and authorities. Journalism should serve the general welfare by informing the people and enabling them to make judgments on the issues of the time. It should serve as a constructive critic of all segments of society, reasonably reflect in staffing and coverage, diverse constituencies, vigorously expose wrongdoing, duplicity or misuse of public or private power, and advocate needed reform and innovation in the public interest.

Indeed, the American Society of Newspaper Editors sets "responsibility" at the head of its *Statement of Principles* (currently) or *Code of Ethics or Canons of Journalism* (previously),[14] followed by "freedom of the press," "independence," "sincerity, truthfulness, accuracy," "impartiality," "fair play," and "decency." Addressing responsibility, the *Statement of Principles* states:

> The primary purpose of gathering and distributing news and opinion is to serve the general welfare by informing the people and enabling them to make judgments on the issues of the time. Newspapermen and women who abuse the power of their professional role for selfish motives or unworthy purposes are faithless to that public trust. The American press was made free not just to inform or just to serve as a forum for debate but also to bring an independent scrutiny to bear on the forces of power in the society, including the conduct of official power at all levels of government.

Linked to the theme of media responsibility is the concept of media accountability which figures prominently in the codes of ethics. Bertrand

(2002: 52-53) explains the concept of media accountability, i.e., the media professional is accountable first to her/himself. S/he should not betray her/his convictions, and must refuse any assignment contrary to ethics. S/he is also accountable towards her/his employer. A journalist must respect the law, must not publicize the internal affairs of her/his company, or in any other way hurt its reputation. Neither her/his private life, political commitments, nor huge honoraria for outside jobs should generate suspicion of a conflict of interest. A journalist is mainly responsible towards the four following groups: 1) peers; 2) sources; 3) people involved in the news; and 4) media users. Journalists should not discredit the profession and must fight for journalistic rights, against all censorship, and for access to information, public and private. They must behave fraternally towards other journalists and must help colleagues in trouble, especially foreign correspondents. Journalists should respect embargoes on news releases; should be careful about the accuracy of reported words; should not distort a statement by quoting it out of context, or summarizing a long declaration. Journalists should not cast charges, even true, if they do not serve the public welfare. If someone is accused or criticized, that person must be given the opportunity to respond. They should not mention any characteristic of a person, such as gender, name, nationality, religion, ethnic group, caste, language, political orientation, job, address, sexual preference, mental or physical handicap, if is not relevant. In general, unless the public interest is at stake, the right to inform must never be exerted in a way that may harm individuals or groups, physically, morally, intellectually, culturally, or economically. In no case should a professional cause loss or injury to consumers. In addition to these responsibilities, media have duties towards the community where they operate. They must: not offend the moral conscience of the public; identify the needs of all groups and serve them; look after the interests of the public instead of satisfying its curiosity; publish nothing that can severely harm the family institution; not sing the praises of jungle law; fight against injustice and speak on behalf of the under-privileged; improve cooperation between peoples; not speculate on fear; not cultivate immorality, indecency or vulgarity; not encourage the lower instincts, like greed or violence; and not glorify war, violence or crime.

The codes analyzed here suggest a wide range of general principles and a number of detailed practices that can guide the work of either the whole profession (journalism), a specific medium, or media, or journalists. In most cases, codes spell out the principles and detailed practices in the form of dos and don'ts, and sometimes combine general principles and/or individual practices together as either interrelated ones or a mix of both. It is recognizable in analyzing the codes that they differ in situating specific practices under the general principles. Therefore, only the general principles have been categorized and constituted in the analysis according to the most relevant and adopted. For the sake of clarity, the following categorization lists a selection of major and prevalent principles and individually points out major statements of guidance under each principle. The six prevalent principles, as illustrated in *Table 2*, are: independence, truth, accuracy, fairness, integrity[15], and serving the public interest. However, within these general principles there are others which intervene in relation to these such as objectivity, balance, and maintaining context.

Table 2: **Major Prevalent Principles and Relevant Selected Rules in the Journalistic Codes of Ethics**

Independence	Truth
⇒ Accept nothing of value from news sources or others outside the profession.	⇒ Avoid misleading re-enactments or staged news events.
⇒ Avoid impropriety or the appearance of impropriety and any conflict of interest or the appearance of conflict.	⇒ Avoid stereotyping by race, gender, age, religion, ethnicity, geography, sexual orientation, disability, physical appearance or social status.
⇒ Avoid working for the people or institutions they cover.	⇒ Be honest in the way of gathering, reporting and presenting news.
⇒ Be free of improper obligations to news sources, newsmakers and advertisers.	⇒ Be persistent in the pursuit of the whole story.
⇒ Be vigilant against all who would exploit the press for selfish purposes.	⇒ Clearly disclose the origin of information and label all material provided by outsiders.
⇒ Defend the rights of the free press.	⇒ Do not misstate identities or intentions.
⇒ Determine news content solely through editorial judgment and not as the result of outside influence.	⇒ Diligently seek out subjects of news stories to give them the opportunity to respond to allegations of wrongdoing.
⇒ Eliminate inappropriate influence on content.	⇒ Continuously seek the truth. Do not lie or fabricate.
⇒ Gather and report news without fear or favor, and vigorously resist undue influence from any outside forces, including advertisers, sources, story subjects, powerful individuals, and interest groups.	⇒ Do not manipulate, alter, or distort the content of news photographs, images, sounds, or videos in any way that is misleading.
⇒ Remain free of improper obligations to news sources, newsmakers and advertisers that may compromise the credibility of news.	⇒ Hold factual information in opinion columns and editorials to the same standards of accuracy as news stories.

⇒ Remain free of improper obligations to outside interests, investments or business relationships that may compromise the credibility of news.

⇒ Resist any self-interest or peer pressure that might erode journalistic duty and service to the public.

⇒ Resist those who would seek to buy or politically influence news content or who would seek to intimidate those who gather and disseminate the news.

⇒ Identify sources whenever feasible. Use as sources only people who are in a position to know.

⇒ Report the news accurately, thoroughly and in context.

⇒ Seek to gain sufficient understanding of the communities, individuals and stories covered to provide an informed account of activities.

Accuracy

⇒ Be aware that information attributed to a source may not be factually correct.

⇒ Correct promptly and prominently significant errors of fact and errors of omission.

⇒ Consider using "accuracy checks" as an affirmative way to search out errors and monitor accuracy. (Accuracy checks are a process by which published stories are sent to sources or experts asking for comment on accuracy, fairness or other aspects.)

⇒ Be especially careful with technical terms, statistics, mathematical computations, crowd estimates and poll results.

⇒ Distinguish clearly between comment, conjecture and fact.

⇒ Do not stretch beyond the facts of the story.

Fairness

⇒ Exercise special care when children are involved in a story and give children greater privacy protection than adults.

⇒ Give the earliest opportunity to persons publicly accused to respond.

⇒ Give voice to the voiceless; official and unofficial sources of information can be equally valid.

⇒ Observe the common standards of decency and stand accountable to the public for the fairness of their news reports.

⇒ Present a diversity of expressions, opinions, and ideas in context.

⇒ Present analytical reporting based on professional perspective, not personal bias.

⇒ Do not guess at facts or spellings. Do not make assumptions.

⇒ Take special care to understand the facts and context of the story.

⇒ Use care in writing headlines.

⇒ Respect the rights of people involved in the news. Respect the right to a fair trial.

⇒ Strive to include all sides relevant to a story and not take sides in news coverage.

⇒ Treat all subjects of news coverage with dignity, respect and compassion.

Integrity

⇒ Deal honestly with readers and newsmakers.

⇒ Do not intrude upon or invade the privacy of an individual unless outweighed by genuine overriding public interest, i.e., do not be prurient or exhibit morbid curiosity.

⇒ An apology must be published whenever appropriate.

⇒ Do not plagiarize words or images.

⇒ Eschew suggestive guilt, do not name or identify the family or relatives or associates of a person convicted or accused of a crime, when they are totally innocent and a reference to them is not relevant to the matter reported.

⇒ Treat sources, subjects and colleagues as human beings deserving of respect.

⇒ Keep promises.

⇒ Obey the law.

⇒ Provide a forum for the exchange of comment and criticism.

Serving the Public Interest

⇒ Any commitment other than service to the public undermines trust and credibility.

⇒ Provide a full range of information to enable the public to make enlightened decisions.

⇒ Be a vigilant watchdog of government and institutions that affect the public.

⇒ Provide a public forum for diverse people and views.

⇒ Provide the news and information that people need to function as effective citizens.

⇒ Reflect and encourage understanding of the diverse segments of the community.

⇒ Seek solutions and expose problems and wrongdoing.

⇒ Seek to promote understanding of complex issues.

⇒ Be constantly alert to see that the public's business is conducted in public.

TOWARDS A UNIVERSAL CODE OF JOURNALISTIC ETHICS

> Journalism is a practice and profession dedicated to truth and the common good. It is now recognized as inevitably a moral enterprise, and I think there is a universal ethical standard for journalism that applies cross-culturally and will apply in the future. The universality of ethical standards of journalism exists because ethics and morality are a universal human enterprise based on the discovery of universal moral truths by human beings with a common human nature always and everywhere.
>
> (Callahan, 2003: 11)

There is a recent growing trend among ethical communication theorists towards the creation of a universal ethical standard for journalism. Advocates of this trend investigate the possibility and desirability of it in 21st century journalism. They examine the circumstances of its required existence, its main principles, values, requisites and considerations, and its conditions of application. However, there are inevitably some critics of this trend.

In defending the possibility of a universal ethical standard for journalism, Callahan (13-14) explains that morality and ethics are not arbitrarily imposed on human groups, but instead they grow out of the bonds, and thus cooperation is necessary in order to survive and flourish. That is, the individual discovers universal moral truths rather than constructs them. Moreover, Callahan considers ethics and morality as rational discoveries of rational beings emotionally bonded to others. Callahan claims that today there is a growing movement toward a global ethics that is based on the formulation in the United Nations Declaration of Rights. She believes that globalization can speed up this global ethics movement. For her, science operates as a universal enterprise and thus so can movements toward a universal system of ethics. In a comparison, she suggests that scientists can hold to their common ethical codes of practice, and interestingly sees the codes of journalistic ethics as being similar.

Is a universal code of ethics possible in the world of journalism of the 21st century? If so, is it desirable? Roberto Herrscher (2002) claims that ethical challenges for journalists will become increasingly global as long as the worlds of economics, politics, culture, and communications face growing waves of globalization. He presents a set of considerations and specific rules applicable to codes of ethics for professional journalists. Herrscher advocates a universal code of journalistic ethics but points out problems and warns against dangers that have made the application of such codes difficult in the past. He suggests that a universal code should consider the voluntary nature of such an endeavor, the cultural and economic differences in various journalistic traditions, and the problem of producing solutions acceptable to all involved.

When wondering, "What can we expect of a code that has no judges, police, or prisons to enforce it?", Herrscher (278) has assumed that for a journalistic code to be accepted, recognized as valid, and followed, it must take into consideration the general ideas and concepts of ethics that are actually prevalent within the journalistic world (journalists, owners, and managers) and the real conditions under which collection and presentation of news takes place in today's newsrooms. Herrscher (279-282) proposes eight principles[16], which might be included in a universal code of ethics, especially for journalists as subjects of rights and obligations. The principles are related to: 1) truth; 2) completeness; 3) conflict of interests; 4) freedom, independence, and self-esteem; 5) honesty; 6) respect of privacy and honor; 7) treatment of ethnic groups, sexes, minorities, religious and sexual persuasions, and other groups; and 8) importance and relevance.

In calling it "A Code for all Seasons", Herrscher (288) justifies that, in times of war, disaster, and so on, the media will usually suspend their role as watchdog or their quest for objectivity and do what they believe is required: participate in the national or social sentiment, lead, soothe, inspire, exult, shout, or cry. In such moments, when so many media owners, editors, and reporters abuse the standards of their daily work, it may be more important than ever to stick to solid ethical principles. The public is listening with special attention and tend to respond with actions to what they read and hear. An ethical code is designed to stay valid under all circumstances. He thinks it is important to discuss the possibility of a code for all seasons in the face of politicians, social leaders, and even journalists who change their ethical standards according to the moment.

Although Herrscher (288) believes that the discussion of a universal code of ethics is a necessity, given the power and influence of journalism and its capacity to shape ideas, values, metaphors, and myths in the social minds of almost all of the world's communities today, he still does not know if a universal code of journalistic ethics is possible. However, he concludes, provided that cultural, political, social, and economic differences are acknowledged, it can do as much good as a universal declaration of human rights. Human rights are still violated, but without the declaration the world would be much worse off. Throughout the world there are examples of positive developments due to the adoption of codes of ethics by individual media, regional or national associations of journalists, or groupings of media owners. Open discussion of a possible code is already in itself an important step. For him, the challenge is significant since many aspects have to be taken into consideration, but as the power and effect of mass media grow, the need for a journalistic code of ethics is seen as more useful and important than ever.

In support also for a universal code, Richard Keeble (2001: 14) argues that there are 12 values which are evident in journalistic codes throughout the world: 1) fairness; 2) the separation of fact and opinion; 3) the need for accuracy linked with the responsibility to correct errors; 4) the condemnation of deliberate distortion and suppression of information; 5) maintaining confidentiality of sources; 6) upholding journalists' responsibility to guard citizens' right to freedom of expression; 7) recognizing a duty to defend the dignity and independence of the profession; 8) protecting people's right to privacy; 9) respecting and seeking after truth; 10) struggling against censorship; 11) avoiding discrimination on grounds of race, sexual orientation, gender, language, religion or political opinions; and 12) avoiding conflicts of interests (particularly political and financial journalists/editors holding shares in companies they report on).

Significantly, Herb Strentz (2002: 267-274) argues that if a quest for universal ethical standards in journalism is to be productive, it becomes necessary to be able to articulate an overarching set of universal ethical standards that can be applied across cultures, ethical schools of thought, and professions. Strentz offers four likely universal standards that are relevant to journalism, suggesting that universal journalism standards can also be identified: 1) use restraint: violence should never be the first resort in conflict resolution; 2) know thyself: self-deception—lying to oneself—is not a healthy practice for an individual or for a society; 3) respect others: do not abuse one's authority or stewardship; and 4) be accountable: one bears responsibility for the consequences of one's actions. He confesses that these and other standards will not be panaceas for the ethical dilemmas journalists often face, but nevertheless they provide the anchors needed for decision-making.[17]

Moreover, Kai Hafez (2002: 225) compares journalistic codes from Europe and the Islamic world in order to revisit the widespread assumption of a deep divide between Western and Oriental philosophies of journalism. Hafez's analysis shows that there is a broad intercultural consensus that standards of truth and objectivity should be central values of journalism. Hafez concludes that despite existing differences between Western and Middle Eastern/Islamic journalism ethics, formal journalism ethics have seen a sphere of growing universalization over the last decades.

CRITICISM AND DEBATE OF ETHICAL CONDUCT

> Ethical inquiry is crucial for all media workers. . . . It encourages
> journalists to examine their basic moral and political principles;
> their responsibilities and rights; their relationship to their employer
> and audience; their ultimate goals. Self-criticism and the
> questioning approach are always required.
>
> (Keeble, 2001: 1)

There are widespread fears about the intentions of professional journalists and their media organizations in the way they interpret ethical conduct. Also, there are critics for the codes of ethics in terms of conceptualization, perception, understanding, influence, and application. There is significant controversy among media practitioners regarding the ethical codes of conduct. Moreover, some criticize the trend of a universal code of ethics.

In the rising mass communication milieu, with its potential for virtually infinite numbers of communication channels throughout the world, Dean Kruckeberg (1995: 84) expects that professional journalists within their respective press systems will be part of a highly libertarian, or free press system, which will be virtually impossible to regulate. In an era of electronically inexpensive and pervasive media on a global scale, pluralism will be ensured—and undoubtedly so will a massive diffusion of power in controlling news and information. He claims that professional journalists and their media organizations will be as ethical as they want to be according to what *they* perceive to be ethics and ethical conduct.

Critics of codes, Keeble (2001: 13) explains, claim that few journalists are aware of the content of codes, particularly when they are constantly being changed: the original U.K. Press Complaints Commission's code of 1991, for instance, has been amended 16 times. Journalists regard codes of ethics from various perspectives. Some journalists see codes of ethics as vehicles of professionalisation, as a means of professional education, as instruments of consciousness-raising, and as deliberate attempts by journalists to regulate the media and ward off legislation restricting their activities. A contrasting response stresses the role of codes as mere rhetorical devices to preserve special privileges such as access to the powerful and to camouflage hypocrisy. Some even argue that codes inherently restrict press freedom by encouraging certain patterns of behavior and condemning others, while some suggest that, regardless, the media are more effectively regulated by the market.

David Pritchard (2000*c*: 188) confirms that research has been unable to demonstrate that codes of ethics have any noticeable influence on the behavior of journalists. In cases where some news organizations may be deemed more ethical than others, codes of ethics are not the reason for the difference. Surveys show, according to Pritchard, that journalists' actual views of ethics are sharply different from what is found in their news organizations' codes of ethics. He claims that journalists and other media personnel may have ethical sensibilities, but they do not factor them into their routine work in any coherent fashion.

There is a great controversy among media practitioners regarding codes of ethical conduct. Although most media practitioners agree that ethical norms are important in their fields, Day (2000: 45) explains, formal codes of conduct are still controversial. Day illustrates the debate of both perspectives of proponents and opponents. On the one hand, proponents of such codes argue that a written statement of principles is the only way to avoid leaving moral judgments to individual interpretations and that if ethical values are important enough to espouse publicly, they should be codified. In addition, codes provide employees with a written notice of what is expected of them. On the other, opponents of such codes view them as a form of self-censorship, a retreat from the independence and autonomy necessary for a free and robust mass communication enterprise. Also, the critics argue, such codes must necessarily be general and vague and consequently are incapable of confronting the fine nuances of the ethical skirmishes that occur under specific circumstances. Moreover, there is a fear that formal codes of conduct will be used against the media in legal battles as evidence that employees have behaved carelessly in violating their own standards of ethical deportment. Above all, opponents contend that codes are nothing more than statements of ideals and are conveniently ignored in the competitive environment of the marketplace. Day claims that codes are of two kinds: professional and institutional. They serve the dual purposes of establishing the common ground on which members of a profession stand, as well as serving a public relations' function of letting the public know that the organization is serious about ethics.

Despite an increasing concern with media ethics, Kieran (1997: 1) illustrates that there are many who remain skeptical about the very idea. Most normative research presumes that the media ought to be ethical in their professional conduct, and as a result concentrate on journalistic codes, guidelines, and ideals of media responsibility. However, there are arguments suggesting that the entire aim of media ethics is fundamentally mistaken. Kieran explains that its very notion appears paradoxical. For example, many professional journalists in Britain often greet the suggestion that they ought to be ethically sensitive with sneers of disdain. After all, how could journalists possibly hope to get at stories that matter, or stories that the public wants to know about, if they have to be entirely honest in their investigations or clearly respect the feelings, wishes, and privacy of the subjects of their reports? Moreover, the public generally tends to presume that journalists are ultimately concerned with only what sells.

Some scholars, such as Sawant (2003: 16), call for the need for press or media councils that can work cooperatively with the press or media to assure responsibility. Sawant claims that global forces make it important for the mass media to explore the virtues inherent in media accountability systems, such as press councils.

Claude-Jean Bertrand (2002: 152-153) warns that overestimating ethics would be just as dangerous as underestimating it. Bertrand claims that, in today's world, after the collapse of the communist bloc, the main threat to the freedom and quality of media consists in the frantic exploitation of communication channels by giant profit-oriented firms. Bertrand asserts that no one should dream that their greed could be curbed by ethics. So, Bertrand suggests, there will always be a need for laws and regulations for many purposes: first, to ensure a level playing field for all media; second, to restrain the natural trend of commercial firms towards concentration, maximum profit, and ensuing neglect of public service; and lastly, because a journalist is not responsible alone for all that goes right or wrong in the media. Bertrand ironically questions, "Is it not absurd to think that the media would be rid of their flaws if only their personnel became ethical?" (153).

Gordon (1999a: 63) argues that codes of ethics cannot be universal in their application, given human ingenuity in creating unique dilemmas. However, Gordon still sees that even though codes cannot possibly be tailored to every situation where media ethics issues arise, they certainly can be useful in dealing with general concerns that face most practitioners in a given medium. Gordon argues that a written code may provide ideal standards of excellence to strive for. Although codes of ethics will never provide complete solutions to the problems of the news media, they, even if imperfect, can be useful in pointing the way to self-improvement in the media and greater accountability to the public. When codes work well, Gordon claims (67), they can focus attention on key issues and help make those concerns part of the media's general decision-making process.

To conclude, the problem that actually leads to unethical conduct by journalists or media organizations does not stem from a lack or shortage of codes of conduct or ethical guidelines. As illustrated in this chapter, there are plenty of ethical guiding principles, values, practices, and rules that media personnel can benefit or learn from, to the extent to which a general look at the codes gives the impression that if journalists followed them, it would be rare to hear of the word "unethical" in any discussion regarding the performance of mass media. Though codes of ethics are usually made public, creating the impression that journalists and media associations are greatly aware of such principles and must adhere to them, most examinations of journalism in practice give the opposite impression.

The problem does not even exist in the application of such codes: *what* journalists and media organization do or even *how*. It should be stated clearly here that, along with those who have been considered unethical, there are several journalists and media organizations' practices and performances that have been described as *ethical*. To be sure, *who* performs ethically or unethically is not the issue, given the fact that it is not unusual for the same medium or journalist to be attributed to both adjectives in different situations or periods. Can it therefore be a matter of *where* or *when*? Unsurprisingly, these examples are similarly unrevealing. For a same situation, such as the 2003 War on Iraq, at the same stage of development, world audiences can witness both ethical and unethical media practices not only among the nations, but also within one nation, one organization, or even by one reporter.

The problem exists in the *why*. No matter what it is that is ethical or unethical and *how*, no matter *who* is behind it or *where* or *when* it occurs, the specific journalistic practice is still under investigation: *Why* does journalistic coverage or practice take an *unethical* path? If it can be accepted, exceptionally for the sake of responding to resistance, that, given the assumption that they all should be aware of codes of their conduct, journalists or media organizations never *intentionally* commit unethical practices, then it might be apt to rephrase the question in the following way: *Why* does journalistic coverage or practice take an *ethical* path? If some media practitioners or theorists can easily defend unethical practices in specific situations through various reasons,[18] it follows that it is difficult for them to guarantee ethical conduct in *similar* situations. Chapters 7 and 8, which discuss and analyze conflictual situations among adversaries and actors involved in the 2003 War on Iraq according to game theory, provide one solution, certainly not a panacea, but at least an encouragement to motivate journalistic practices towards ethical conduct during situations where conduct is frequently unethical.

If the answer to the question *why* is "for the benefit of the journalist that will result in the benefit of the medium, which in turn will result in the benefit or common good of society", then journalists, editors, managers, and owners are unlikely to resist and may agree to the solution that Chapter 8 suggests. The suggestion calls for them to follow the majority of the key principles of codes of ethics, as a key condition for achieving the goal of benefiting all parties, in times of international crises. Chapter 8 justifies this practice, explaining how truth telling, accuracy, and other major principles of codes of ethics are fundamental in achieving *goodness* and peacefully managing an international crisis or winning a game. Motivation towards ethical conduct, where otherwise the tendency may be to opt for another path, would stem from a desire for achieving beneficial consequences. In addition, this contributes to the debate surrounding the ambiguity of "ethical and unethical, but from whose perspective?" For example, journalists will recognize that telling the truth, whatever it is, or whoever is favored by its content, will lead to their benefit or at least better consequences at the end of the day.

But before arriving at this discussion in Chapter 8, I have examined the rationality aspect of the required effective performance of media decision-makers in Chapter 3, through the explanation of the intertwined relationship between mathematics and communication, and the consideration of rationality that could be used effectively in the communication field. Game theory is adopted as relevant to studying the United States-Iraqi Crisis, which is presented in the next chapter, along with an analysis of the rationality of the political decision-makers involved therein. Moreover, Chapter 8's investigation into the media games of War on Iraq, in order to show the media's involvement in the crisis at stake and to provide an analysis of their rational performance in the face of ethical principles, is preceded in Chapter 7 by a discussion of the gaming of the 2003 War on Iraq, specifically studying the conflict between the adversaries and actors involved based on game theory.

To conclude, we will return to our focus of this chapter—characteristics of and debates surrounding international media codes of ethics—when we look at the solution that is presented in Chapter 8. Before this, however, we will examine our case study, by investigating the deeply-rooted crisis between the United States and Iraq.

NOTES

1. Also, Wheeler (2002: 75-76) shows that various groups of associations have established codes of conduct that counsel journalists to serve the public; tell the truth; report the news with accuracy and objectivity; question the

government; respect the privacy of individuals; protect the confidentiality of sources; avoid plagiarism; avoid stereotypes of race, gender, age, or ethnicity; and publish corrections to errors.

2. In his research article of 2002, "Responsibility and ethics in the Canadian media: Some basic concerns," Raphael Cohen-Almagor analyzes some of the troubling issues in Canadian media ethics, based on in-depth interviews with more than 50 experts on Canadian media. He discussed guidelines for placing limitations on media coverage thought necessary for the protection of individual privacy.

3. ASNE's "Statement of Principles" was originally adopted in 1922 as the "Canons of Journalism". The document was revised and renamed "Statement of Principles" on October 23rd, 1975. Published on August 20th, 1996; Last Updated on August 28th, 2002. For the full text, see for example: (Berkman & Shumway, 2003: 321-323), (Englehardt & Barney, 2002: 259-261), (Day, 1997: 423-424), and (Dennis & Ismach, 1981: 369-370). As "Canons of Journalism", see for example: (Dennis & Ismach, 1981: 367-368), (Cassata & Asante, 1979: 259-261), (Rivers & Schramm, 1969: 253-255), and (Gross, 1966: 405-406).

4. APME's Code of Ethics was revised and adopted in 1995; last updated on February 17th, 1999. For the full text, see for example: (Berkman & Shumway, 2003: 323-325) and (Englehardt & Barney, 2002: 262-264).

5. FAJ's Code of Ethics was adopted by the Third Conference of the Federation of Arab Journalists in April 1972, in Baghdad. For the full text, see for example: (Nordenstreng & Topuz, 1989: 273-274).

6. GND published its Principles of Ethical Conduct for Newsrooms in July 1999. For the full text, see for example: (Berkman & Shumway, 2003: 333-341) and (Englehardt & Barney, 2002: 264-273).

7. IDROJ was approved in 1971 by representatives of the journalists' unions of six countries of the European Community, in Munich (Germany). For the full text, see for example: (Bertrand, 2002: 79-81).

8. NPPA's Code of Ethics was published and last updated on October 26th, 1999. For the full text, see for example: (Berkman & Shumway, 2003: 327-328) and (Englehardt & Barney, 2002: 288-290).

9. RTNDA's Code of Ethics and Professional Conduct was adopted at RTNDA2000 in Minneapolis on September 14th, 2000; and last updated on December 9th, 2002. For the full text, see for example: (Berkman & Shumway, 2003: 329-332), (Englehardt & Barney, 2002: 273-277), and (Day, 1997: 425).

10. The BPCC's Code of Practice was adopted in 1994 and revised in 1997. For the full text, see for example: (Bertrand, 2002: 81-86) and (Harris & Spark, 1997: 239-244).

11. The CPCRJ was adopted by the Congress of Russian Journalists on June 23rd, 1994 in Moscow. For the full text, see for example: (Bertrand, 2002: 86-89).

12. SPJ/SDX's first Code of Ethics was borrowed from the American Society of Newspaper Editors in 1926. In 1973, Sigma Delta Chi wrote its own code, which was revised in 1984 and 1987. The present version of the Society of Professional Journalists' Code of Ethics was adopted in September 1996. For the full text, see for example: (Haas, 2003: 35-38), (Berkman & Shumway, 2003: 12-15), (Englehardt & Barney, 2002: 290-293), (Day, 1997: 421-422), and (Dennis & Ismach, 1981: 370-372).

13. TWCI's Norms of Journalistic Conduct was adopted in 1992 and revised in 1996. For the full text, see for example: (Bertrand, 2002: 89-101).

14. See for example: (Berkman & Shumway, 2003: 321-323), (Englehardt & Barney, 2002: 259-261), (Day, 1997: 423-424), (Dennis & Ismach, 1981: 369-370), (Dennis & Ismach, 1981: 367-368), (Cassata & Asante, 1979: 259-261), (Rivers & Schramm, 1969: 253-255), and (Gross, 1966: 405-406).

15. "Professional integrity is the cornerstone to a journalist's credibility", states the preamble of the Society of Professional Journalists' code of ethics. According to the code, integrity is accomplished by: 1) being "honest, fair and courageous in gathering, reporting and interpreting information"; 2) minimizing harm by treating "sources, subjects and colleagues as human beings deserving respect"; 3) acting independently by being "free of obligation to any interest other than the public's right to know"; and 4) being "accountable to readers, listeners, viewers and each other" (Keeler, Brown & Tarpley, 2002: 44).

16. Herrscher places the powerful dictum "to tell the truth, all the truth, and nothing but the truth" (280) at the core of a Universal Code of Journalistic Ethics. He believes that the information must be complete and considers a half truth to be in part a lie. Journalists may select arguments, quotes, and material that fit well with their general hypothesis, ignoring what does not. Journalists cannot have personal interest in the causes, businesses, or parties of their sources. For him, a universal code of journalistic ethics should push journalists and media to build relationships in which the integrity, independence, and professional criteria of the journalist and the interest of the public in receiving an impartial account are respected. He argues that the publics have a right to know how the information was collected and why the medium or the journalist in question considers it important and relevant in cases in which absence of that information leaves the story

incomplete. Also, private people have a right to demand and obtain privacy for their private lives, and even public figures have a right to privacy in a more limited sphere. Moreover, Herrscher stresses that for journalists, all people are equal. Finally, he suggests that a code of ethics should discuss the definition of news and the way in which each medium and each society defines it. As a result, a journalistic profession serving its society and presenting what happens in its midst with accuracy and completeness should not leave important and relevant events or developments untreated. It is certainly up to each society to discuss which issues are important.

17.   Neither the words "violence" nor "violent" are found in the news-oriented codes of the ASNE or the SPJ, yet news reporting historically and theoretically has instrumental value among those seeking nonviolent resolution of social conflicts. Journalists often pride themselves on matters of integrity and self-awareness, and critics routinely are told that no profession is as introspective. In such declarations, journalists usually have reference to their endless conversations about how a news story was or was not covered or should have been covered. However, Strentz argues that to "know thyself" and to avoid "self-deception" require more than being candid about one's mistakes. In addition, he reminds us that principles of respect and stewardship are inherent in ethical relations and articulated in the Golden Rule teachings of Confucius, Christ, and others. The Kantian maxim that we treat people as ends, not as objects or means is also relevant here. Finally, Strentz acknowledges the five concepts of the Commission on the Freedom of the Press (1947) which hold that the press should be accountable for providing: 1) a truthful, comprehensive, and intelligent account of the day's events in a context that gives them meaning; 2) a forum for the exchange of comment and criticism; 3) the projection of a representative picture of the constituent groups in the society; 4) the presentation and clarification of the goals and values of the society; and 5) full access to the day's intelligence. (Strentz, 2002: 267-274).

18.   There is a wide range of journalistic fundamental ideals that have been debated and defined, especially by American journalists, and inserted in professional codes of ethics since the beginning of the 20th century. However, Keeler, Brown and Tarpley (2002: 44) argue, since the colonial era, both those who have created and consumed journalistic fare have struggled with ethical issues related to the profession. Their concerns have been influenced by prevalent political, economic, social, religious, and technological conditions characterizing the specific historical era in which they lived.

III.   PRAXIS

CHAPTER 6

The Rationality of the

United States-Iraqi Crisis

This chapter introduces the deeply-rooted crisis between the United States and Iraq. To this end, I analyze the rationality of the political decision-makers and explain the overall clash of interests between the two opponents—the Saddam Regime and the Bush Administration, while also discussing each side's strategic interests, regional and global goals, and the policies that were required to achieve these goals. The rationality of the 2003 War on Iraq decision-making on the political level is explained in detail, in order to see how both adversaries conducted their pre-game warm-up and made their strategic choices. As such, this chapter lays the foundation for Chapter 7, which discusses the gaming of the 2003 War on Iraq, specifically studying the conflict between the adversaries and actors involved based on game theory.

UNDERSTANDING THE UNITED STATES-IRAQI CRISIS

The one thing that is certain about the Gulf area is that it will continue to be of central importance to international affairs in the coming decade. It is likely that the focus on the Gulf will involve several crises and one or more war. To a large extent, the 'war' arising from the 11 September 2001 terrorist attacks on the United States was generated by Gulf politics. Indeed, bin Laden cited as the direct reason for his revolt the presence of U.S. forces in Saudi Arabia from 1991 on.

(Rubin, 2002: 20)

It is argued here that the two wars, the 1990/91 Gulf War and the 2003 War on Iraq[1], were launched as a result of an underlying crisis between

149

the United States and Iraq. This crisis, which can be classified under the category of international political crises, was not successfully managed. This mismanagement resulted in the on-going and unresolved conflicts and wars between the parties. This supports the argument explained in Chapter 2 that crises can be managed, but not resolved. When conflicts reach resolutions or wars stop, this does not mean that a crisis no longer exists. Rather, the crisis persists throughout the rise and ebb of conflicts and wars.

The American policy regarding Iraq in the 1990s was described as narrow realism by many scholars such as Kaplan and Kristol (2003). The first Bush and the Clinton administrations opted for a combination of incomplete military operations and diplomatic accommodation. Rather than press hard for a change of regime, something that was done later by George W. Bush, George H. W. Bush halted the U.S. war against Iraq prematurely and the Clinton administration avoided confronting the moral and strategic challenge presented by Saddam, hoping that a policy of containment would suffice to keep Saddam boxed in. But on the broader question of how to use American power in the world, George W. Bush, after 9/11, embraced an alternative which he calls "a distinctly American internationalism," a philosophy that seeks to combine the most successful elements of realism and liberalism. This worldview was not created by the Bush administration; rather, examples of it are evident in American history. Presidents from Theodore Roosevelt and Harry Truman to John F. Kennedy and Ronald Reagan put into practice the tenets of a distinctly American internationalism, marrying American power with American ideals. American internationalism follows from "American exceptionalism", a belief in the uniqueness and the virtue of the American political system that offers the United States as a model for the world. In late September 2002, the White House published "The National Security Strategy of the United States", a document that codified the three principles President Bush had spelled out at West Point in June 2002: preemption, regime change and American leadership. Some claim that the publication of this document inaugurated a new era, a shift in perception about America's global role comparable to the advent of the containment doctrine a half-century earlier. It transformed the war from a police action designed to round up the perpetrators of 9/11, into a campaign to uproot tyranny and export democracy. It also transformed the tenets of a distinctly American internationalism into the official policy of the U.S. government. Regime change, as a tenet of the Bush Doctrine, is the recognition that the United States cannot really coexist peacefully with governments that seek to develop weapons of mass destruction, threaten their neighbors and brutalize their own citizens. The Bush Doctrine reserves the right to bring about—

whether through diplomatic or military means—the demise of these regimes. (Kaplan & Kristol, 2003: 37, 63-64, 74, 95).

The liberation of Kuwait on February 28, 1991, and the end of the Gulf War was, according to Byman (2000: 493), only the beginning of a series of conflicts. Following this event, the United States and its allies repeatedly used limited force against Iraq, maintained tight sanctions, conducted intrusive inspections of Iraq's weapons of mass destruction (WMDs) and missile programs, supported anti-Saddam oppositionists, while taking steps to isolate and weaken Baghdad. From December 1998, the United States and Britain conducted a sustained, if limited, bombing effort against Iraqi targets.

It is both clear and significant that the United States-Iraqi Crisis started earlier than August 2, 1990—the date that Saddam Hussein invaded Kuwait. Regardless of whether Saddam was misled into conflict with the United States and its allies following his invasion, a deeply rooted crisis between Iraq and the United States already existed, which surfaced with the first real confrontation of conflicting interests. Both sides have strategic interests, goals, and policies to achieve either regionally or globally. For the American administration vision of the Middle East, Philip Gordon (2003: 155) explains that at the heart of the plan is the determination to use America's unprecedented power to reshape the Middle East by supporting America's friends in the region, opposing its enemies and seeking to promote democracy and freedom. This means using force to overthrow the dictatorship in Iraq, promoting gradual political reform among the moderate Arab regimes, and standing by Israel. Saddam Hussein's history of actions in the Gulf region and the Arab world confirms that he was constantly seeking to increase his power. A fundamental principle of his Ba'ath Party is to secure the position of Iraq as a leader in the region. Whatever his particular reasons for seeking this power, he was obviously committed to obtaining it by whatever means possible. This is no different from the leaders of many countries all over the world; however, the difference in Saddam's case was that his ambitions were somewhat unbounded and perhaps unimaginably ambitious. When he called for the short-lived Arab Cooperation Council (ACC) in the period preceding his invasion of Kuwait, he sought to obtain political and military power through regionally strong allies. His invasion itself was an attempt at gaining further economic power. In his speech at the ACC Summit on February 24, 1990, he emphasized the actions necessary for building a strong new league that would be able to face the superpower[2] and solve the region's problems without outside intervention.

The clash of interests, Jervis (2002: 4-6) explains, is a constant in international politics in general. The United States and Iraq are not unique.

Although Saddam may have wanted to dominate the region, he was hardly alone in this ambition. The real conflict of interests between the United States and Iraq can be expressed by the U.S. National Security Advisor Condoleezza Rice's statement that the real problem was with "the ambition and behavior of Saddam Hussein, because sooner or later, the ambitions of Saddam Hussein and the interests of the United States are going to clash" (5).[3] In answering the question regarding whether or not Iraq's WMDs menace American interests, Jervis reminds us of Waltz's argument that the spread of nuclear weapons will bring stability, regardless of the characteristics of the regime and its leader.

Thus, an important question concerning the possession of WMDs needs to be briefly investigated here before moving on to the answer that will clarify much of the ambiguity that surrounds the United States-Iraqi Crisis, and will help us to understand the strategies used: Why does U.S. foreign policy rely on pre-emption for contesting the possession of WMDs in Iraq when in North Korea the strategy is deterrence? Simply put, North Korea was in possession of nuclear weapons while Iraq was only about to be. Thus, as the *San Diego Union-Tribune*'s James Goldsborough stated ironically, "one could laugh if it weren't so serious. President Bush will take the nation to war against a member of his 'axis of evil' nations that isn't building nuclear arms, but give a pass to one that is" (2003, Jan. 6). Similarly, the *Washington Post*'s Mary McGrory wondered "why it is necessary for us to bomb, invade and occupy Iraq while North Korea gets the striped-pants treatment" (Kaplan & Kristol, 2003: 83). Kaplan and Kristol also noted that at that point in time, Iraq obviously did not yet have the bomb. If and when it did, it would, like North Korea, acquire the ability to "blackmail" or deter the United States, and would also get the "striped-pants treatment." For them, Iraq's drive to build a bomb was therefore entirely logical because, armed with nuclear weapons, a rational Saddam could just as easily deter the U.S. from responding to his provocations as an irrational Saddam. However, what really separates America's approach to Iraq (pre-emption) from its approach to North Korea (deterrence), Dunn (2003: 286) explains, is the calculation that Pyong-Yang has the military capability to deter the United States. Thus, America wanted to disarm Iraq before it reached that state. In the eyes of American officials—including Bush, Cheney, and Rice—Saddam wanted nuclear weapons in order to blackmail his neighbors and establish regional dominance. President Bush warned that Saddam intended to "blackmail the world," and Rice believed he would use nuclear weapons to "blackmail the entire international community" (286).

Having a strong understanding of American foreign policy—its real drivers, its primary objectives regarding Iraq, and its instruments to achieve these objectives—will facilitate an investigation into the crisis, by enabling us to avoid misinterpretations, and to recognize the logic behind the U.S.'s decisions, specifically concerning the toppling of Saddam's regime through a preventive war. The foreign policy of the Bush administration, particularly towards Iraq, Dunn (2003: 279) argues, is widely misunderstood, especially in Europe. For example, one of the most commonly held views is that America is motivated by a desire to control or appropriate Iraq's oil wealth. *The Economist*, in January 25, 2003, wrote that one of the most common accusations of the Bush administration is that "it is all about oil: that oil reserves are what makes Iraq differ from North Korea; and that American oil firms are set to grab hold of them" (Threatening Iraq, 2003: 12). And it cannot be denied that the U.S. is concerned, as Vice-President Cheney has warned, that Iraq might "seek domination of the entire Middle East" and "take control of a great portion of the world's energy supplies" (280). Furthermore, as *Business Week* reminded readers a month after the 9/11 attacks, "the U.S. economy was ailing and ... the country was more vulnerable to an 'oil shock' than it had been at the time of the first Gulf War" (Gendzier, 2003: 19). Nonetheless, while no doubt an important consideration, oil is not the only, or even the primary motivation behind U.S. policy; rather, especially in terms of the arguments presented in this book, it would be better considered as a valid but incomplete understanding of the Bush administration's approach.

In essence, as Dunn (2003: 284-295) explains, five key drivers, clearly evident in policy towards Iraq, structure the United States's foreign policy under Bush's administration. These drivers are: 1) Realist anti-appeasement; 2) U.S. providentialism/American exceptionalism; 3) assertive unilateralism; 4) willingness to fight and fighting to win; and 5) threat inflation and conflation. The Bush administration's approach to the world is formed by a concern with traditional security threats—great powers, rogue states, proliferation—rather than "new threats" such as the environment. Linked to this traditional realist approach is the prominence for the Bush administration of the "appeasement analogy"—the desire not to be seen to give in to aggressors. Not only does the U.S. regard itself as the indispensable power in the international system, it also believes that the export of its model of government—liberal democratic market capitalism— is a universal good. American exceptionalism is also imbued with the sense of optimism and progress associated with the Enlightenment project. The Bush administration's willingness to put its national interests ahead of the consideration of international norms and institutions is well documented. Its willingness to exercise American power in this way is also a reflection of its loss of faith in such traditional instruments of diplomacy as deterrence, sanctions, containment and engagement. The United States rejects the idea that the use of force or even war represents the failure of policy. Both the Bush administration and the American people consider themselves at war against terrorism. This colors how they view the current conflict with Iraq. America's history of invulnerability and its fear of surprise attack adds to the tendency towards threat inflation. A related practice is the conflation of disparate potential threats. The application of worst-case thinking to the war on terrorism has lowered Washington's tolerance of Iraq. The potential production and distribution of WMDs to terrorists by Iraq is considered by the U.S. to be grounds for pre-emptive attack.

The U.S. objectives regarding Iraq, according to Byman (2000: 495-496), included preventing any Iraqi regional aggression, stopping Iraq's nuclear, biological, chemical and missile programs, and removing Saddam from power. Another objective—preventing the spread of regional instability—has also guided U.S. actions. To meet these objectives, the United States employed five instruments: economic sanctions, weapons inspections, a strong and large regional military presence, limited and occasional military strikes, and support for the Iraqi opposition.

Thus, after the 9/11 attacks on America, as a strategic policy of the U.S. to fight terrorism and countries or organizations that harbor terrorists was developed and as tensions across the world rose in anticipation of Washington's War on Iraq, the Bush administration "continue[d] to focus on Baghdad's possession of weapons of mass destruction as its prime justification for war." By November 2002, the White House was reported to have "settled on a war plan for Iraq," that "call[ed] for massing 200,000 to 250,000 troops for attack by air, land and sea" (Gendzier, 2003: 18). The White House certainly had many reasons for launching a War on Iraq and considered the Iraqi occupation of Kuwait on August 2, 1990, as the foremost reason. In addition, Iraq posed both a continuing threat to the national security of the United States and international peace and security in the Persian Gulf region, and remained in an unacceptable breach of its international obligations through its continued possession and development of a significant chemical and biological weapons capability; it had an advanced weapons development program that was close to producing a nuclear weapon, and it supported and harbored terrorist organizations, including those that threatened the lives and safety of American citizens. Further, Saddam's regime had demonstrated its capability and willingness to use WMDs against other nations and its own people, and also made no attempt to hide its continuing hostility toward, and willingness to attack, the United States, made evident by the attempt in 1993 to assassinate former President Bush.

Before moving forward to explain the Game-World level and introduce the ideational analogy of a Soccer Game, it is essential here to provide some evidence that supports the whole structure of the game War on Iraq. Bush's fast-moving strategy to take action against Iraq and his seeking an immediate resolution of the problem was his best choice. Despite claims of the significant amount of time that Saddam still needed to produce nuclear weapons as well as fears of the unfortunate outcomes of the war, strategic interests and convincing drivers predominated in precipitating the decision to launch a war. Although some critics of U.S. policy attributed Bush's fast-paced strategy to the U.S. electoral calendar, or to the fact that it takes time to build a coalition, or that only a rapid pace would ensure domestic support, if not the international support that Bush sought, his rational calculations held a great deal of logic. While America was prepared to use a strategy of containment before the 9/11 attacks, its calculations had changed. As Bush observed, "after September 11, the doctrine of containment just doesn't hold any water, as far as I am concerned" (Dunn, 2003: 292). On June 1, 2002 at West Point, Bush made his beliefs clear:

> [A] new world order[4] based on liberalism's cherished values is both necessary and possible. This new liberal order will not construct itself, however. American power will be key in building it . . . more specifically, American military power will be key. . . . Given the goals of rogue states and terrorists, the United States can no longer solely rely on a reactive posture as we have in the past. . . . We cannot let our enemies strike first. . . . The United States has long maintained the option of preemptive actions to counter a sufficient threat to our national security.
>
> (Rhodes, 2002: 2-5)

U.S. policy, Byman (2000: 497) explains, was focused on Saddam himself, as well as the broader threat that a powerful Iraq would pose to the region. U.S. leaders saw Saddam as reckless, vengeful, and bloody—dangerous traits for a leader pursuing WMDs and one whose country strategically houses much of the world's oil supplies. It is clear that there was a great shortage of trust, if indeed any existed at all, between the two adversaries. While Saddam, Jervis (2003: 4) argues, may have believed the threat, he may not have believed the American promise to be restrained in its actions if he did disarm. He then had no reason to comply. Saddam may also have thought that he could inflict such high casualties on the U.S. that it would withdraw from Iraq, or that even if he was defeated, he would go down in history as a great martyr (assuming he preferred this outcome to living with a powerless Iraq).

Bush's choice of the pre-emptive strategy or the preventive war may now be confirmed as the result of rational calculation seeing as other leaders, including those in the same region of Saddam, suggested a similar outcome. For example, the President of the UAE, Sheikh Zayed Bin Sultan Al Nahian, sent a letter to the leaders of the Arab States who participated in the Arab League summit on the Iraq crisis, suggesting that Saddam Hussein, his two sons, and his family should leave Iraq, and that the surrounding Arab States would guarantee, among many other things, a suitable welcome and stay with adequate security, in whatever state Saddam preferred.

Looking back at the 1990/91 Gulf War, Saddam sat quietly for months while the American buildup in the Persian Gulf took place, despite enormous fears in Washington that he would strike before adequate forces were in place, and before the coalition was ready to fight. The significance of his choosing not to do so, it is argued here, is that given his rationality, Saddam must have been benefiting from his lack of action. This is not vague or surprising in the context of the principles of his Ba'ath Party, as well as his stated wishes to confront the superpower in order to unite Arab countries; accordingly, he saw Iraq as becoming a leader in the Middle East region. Consequently, if Saddam's usual defensive strategy (patience and dragging the enemy into the trap), had already succeeded in achieving his principle goals, from his perspective there would be little reason not to repeat it again.

Of the players, Saddam was not the only one thinking of unilaterally and bravely confronting his adversaries; Bush was as well. One of the debatable questions to be raised in the book, is this: if multilateral coercive diplomacy, which the U.S. used in the earlier campaign on Iraq, is the best strategy for dealing with Iraq,[5] why was the Bush administration's strategy one of unilateral preventive war? This unilateral approach has been emphasized repeatedly in Bush's speeches against terrorism in general and Iraq in particular. One possible way to answer this is to relate the benefits of using the unilateral approach to the U.S. objectives and drivers previously mentioned. Again, this confirms that the game has been played rationally and according to the rules.

As long as one crisis can lead to many conflicts and wars, there are always many games to play. Obviously, when structuring a game, defining the start is the first step. In the case under discussion, it is suggested that the game War on Iraq started with the 9/11 attacks on America, after which tensions were raised and U.S. attention was focused against terrorism and the countries that support, such as (according to the U.S.) Iraq. The period that immediately followed 9/11 up to the point that a decision was made to go to War on Iraq was the warm-up for the first move of the game and attack. This game is represented in Chapter 7 as a Chicken Game.

This book adopts Bowen's (1978: 60) classification of games, *Game-World* and *Game-Situation*. For him, a game can be thought of as a deterministic model with two main subsystems: a model of the real world (the Game-World), and a set of *Rules*, describing its behavior as time passes and as the situation develops. The Game-World has one major subsystem, among other lesser ones, i.e., the Game-Situation, which includes everything in the Game-World that is thought to have any relevant effect on the conflict in progress. In the case under discussion here, the Chicken Game represents the major Game-Situation. In addition, Chapter 7 shows various other Game-Situations, or sub-games[6], in the forms of Prisoners' Dilemma Game, Samson and Delilah Game, and the Truth Game. At the same time, this chapter also uses the notion of a Soccer Game to represent the Game-World that combines the previously mentioned Game-Situations. The Game-World structure is presented here as an ideational Soccer Game only to locate players (or countries) around the globe vis-à-vis the crisis.

If the Chicken Game represents the two teams, the Soccer Game represents players of both teams and their audiences (non-players). The former is based on the theory of games while the latter is based on Brams's theory of moves, bringing a dynamic dimension to the classical theory of games. According to Brams (1994: 1-9), players think ahead not just to the immediate consequences of making moves but also to the consequences of countermoves to these moves, counter-countermoves, and so on. The theory of moves[7], by elucidating the rational flow of moves over time, facilitates the dynamic analysis of conflicts in which thoughtful and intelligent players might find themselves engaged. In the theory of games, games are represented either in *normal form*, which is described by payoff matrixes, or in *extensive form*, which is described by game trees. Although one form can translate into another, game trees better capture the sequential nature of a player's choices, which are suppressed in a payoff matrix. The theory of moves benefits from both forms. This theory, Brams explains, begins a game by assuming that players are in a particular state—from which they receive payoffs—where they can, by switching strategy, attempt to move to a better state. The game is dynamic[8] because the players start with a past, defined by their present state, and compare this with future states that they and other players can engender by moving. As they look ahead at their possible moves, the possible countermoves of other players, their own counter-countermoves, and so on, the players try to anticipate where play will terminate, i.e., when they accrue payoffs. The purpose of the theory of moves is not to give a *better outcome*, but rather to provide a more plausible model of a strategic situation that mimics what people might actually think and do.

In order to apply this to War on Iraq on the Game-World level, I attempt to create a representation of a Soccer Game to show the inner policies, strategies, and practices of both adversaries at the Game-Situation level, while remaining under the umbrella of the Game-World level policies. The role of the mass media of the respective players, whether key teams or players, which is illustrated in Chapter 8, rests here. In other words, the Soccer Game here is mainly presented for the sake of locating players (or countries) on the playground (or the soccer field), i.e. determining their position from that of their adversaries. The playground of the Soccer Game represents the United States-Iraqi Crisis in its reactivation stage, i.e. it excludes the time of the 1990/91 Gulf War because it occurs during the 2003 War on Iraq.

Suppose we have two major sides on a playground (i.e., the conflict, in this case the war) —the United States and Iraq. In terms of their roles, countries around the globe are divided into two classifications—players and non-players (audiences). Players belong to one of two teams, and each team consists of five twin groups, i.e., ten single groups. Twin groups are military supporters, non-military supporters, peacekeepers, non-military defenders, and military defenders. Audiences are divided between the two teams. Referees are present in the form of international organizations such as the Security Council, the United Nations, and the General Assembly. The world's mass media are spread around the playground to report on the action. This picture may explain or justify the varying and different perspectives conveyed to audiences due to the various angles and shots their mass media take. Let us assume that the audience is watching the game on television. Cameras and play-by-play commentators convey the game to them. Within the time of playing the game, everyone expects to see deceptive moves, tricks, shuffling, blocking, header kicks, backward kicks, and corner kicks—all under either defensive, offensive, or mixed plans or strategies. Also, the audience expects to see punishments such as offsides, fouls, warnings, and expulsions. At the end of the game, there may be a winner or a loser. However, even in the case where no goals are scored for either team, this still adds overall points to each team's record and is credited in their general history.

STRATEGIC CHOICES:
RATIONALITY OF WAR ON IRAQ DECISION-MAKING

In any game, procedures for the warm-up of teams and players are essential in order to ensure rational performances and obtain favorable outcomes.

These procedures may include players seeking information regarding their opponents, developing plans, examining strategies and tactics, and so on. As shown below, there were also such procedures in the 2003 War on Iraq, which took the form of rationality of decision-making, or selecting among strategic choices.

For instance, both adversaries took diplomatic actions and addressed the global community through the mass media.[9] The United States' major influential diplomatic actions, media speeches, and conferences were orchestrated primarily by President Bush, Vice President Richard Cheney, Secretary of State Colin Powell, and National Security Advisor Condoleezza Rice. Colin Powell's remarks at the United Nations in February 2003, for example, were very strong and effective in presenting new evidence of the Iraqi development of WMDs and its proximity to the possession of nuclear weapons. The Bush administration made a strong case and insisted on the implementation of a pre-emptive strategic plan through a preventive war against Iraq. In doing so, the American administration had its justifications, made its calculations, and reached its judgments. Because he is the head of a democratic country, the President had to also explain his decisions, especially in the face of strong criticism. In this crisis *The Economist* pointed out that Bush's "...charges are preposterous. Yet Mr. Bush [has] some explaining to do. In a democracy, any leader contemplating going to war has a duty to explain, in Mr. Bush's case to Congress and the American people, but also to the wider world—why this needs to be done" (Confronting Iraq, 2002, Sep. 14: 9). For the Bush administration, justification lay in the argument that eliminating Saddam could be done through a cheap, beneficial, and unavoidable war.

The Bush administration developed a vision of the war with Iraq that was more debatable, but still plausible, as Miller (2002: 9-14) describes; this vision suggested that Saddam could be eliminated at a modest cost (in military terms). The Bush administration optimistically anticipated that the war would produce a number of advantageous consequences: 1) eliminate Saddam's regime and bring to an end Iraq's programs to acquire or develop WMDs, thereby removing one of the gravest potential threats to U.S. and regional security; 2) foreclose on the possibility that Saddam might assist Al-Qaeda by providing them with WMD; 3) liberate the Iraqi people from the heavy yoke of Saddam's oppression, which would 4) lead to a wave of democratization throughout the Middle East region. The Bush administration also suggested that war was necessary, even unavoidable, because no acceptable policy alternative existed. The only way to adequately deal with Saddam, according to this view, was to use force. The conclusion that *preventive war* was the only effective option rests on five key assumptions:

1) the containment of Saddam was failing; 2) inspections would never suffice; 3) proliferation was inevitable; 4) Saddam could not be deterred; and, 5) nuclear weapons would facilitate his aggressiveness.

At this point in the discussion of the end-result of the American decision-making process, it might be useful to provide some background. In answering the question "should the United States invade Iraq and depose Saddam Hussein?" John Mearsheimer and Stephen Walt (2002) analyze reasons raised by advocates of war, who saw toppling Saddam Hussein as desirable, and then explain why they consider some of them to be unconvincing and others convincing. Unconvincing reasons include that Saddam was a bloodthirsty tyrant, defied the United Nations on numerous occasions, had backed terrorists in the past, and that removing him would reinforce respect for American power and spark democratic reform in the Middle East. They argue that these reasons may be applicable to leaders of many other nations besides Saddam; there are plenty of other leaders with "bloody hands" who the Americans are not thinking about going after. Several others have defied numerous UN resolutions and this sin is hardly sufficient justification for war. It is also true that a successful war *might* have triggered a wave of democratic reforms in the Arab world, but a bitter anti-American backlash was more likely. However, because of other reasons, they explain, advocates of preventive war did in fact possess a *trump card*. Advocates maintained that Saddam's past behavior proved that he was too reckless, relentless, and aggressive to be allowed to possess WMDs, especially nuclear weapons, and thus Saddam was too dangerous to be deterred or contained if he was left to acquire them. For that reason alone, he had to be removed.

Among the many possible alternatives, strategies, and options available for the American administration to choose from (e.g., deterrence, passive defenses, threat and use of brute force, impose sanctions, negotiation, and appeasement), it selected a somewhat original one. The Bush administration endorsed a policy of *preventive war*. Though this was chosen as the best choice, the American administration was aware of unfortunate expected outcomes and feared[10] a costly war. The administration was uncertain about the duration of the war, a factor that plagued expectations and brought into question expected military scenarios and costs. As Rumsfeld indicated, "the expectation is that the war could last six days, six weeks, I doubt six months" (Dunn, 2003: 293). An assessment of the costs of a war on Iraq, Nordhaus (2002: 55-77) illustrates, is founded on scenarios for the conduct of the war, the aftermath of hostilities, the impacts on oil markets, and the macroeconomic effects. Nordhaus assumed two major scenarios, "quick victory" and a "protracted conflict"[11], and attempted to put price tags on each. The public estimate of the cost of the war by the Bush administration came in an interview by Larry Lindsey, the economist-in-residence in the White House's West Wing. As reported by *The Wall Street Journal*, Lindsey estimated that the *upper bound* cost would be $100 billion to $200 billion. He dismissed the cost as small, stating that these numbers would be only 1 to 2 percent of the U.S. GDP. Nordhaus integrated the different components of the cost of a war on Iraq and concluded that the favorable case indicates that the economic costs over the 2003–2012 period would be $99 billion. This outcome relies on the assumption that the military, diplomatic, and nation-building campaigns are successful. However, the outer limit of the cost would be around $1.9 trillion, most of which would fall outside of the direct military costs.

> [I]f Saddam does succeed in implementing some of his options for making the war painful and messy, if the conflict does produce some of the undesired counterproductive effects feared by opponents of the war—then the cost-benefit calculus associated with this war will be very different from the one offered by the Bush administration. That is what makes this war such a gamble.
>
> (Miller, 2002: 50)

As a further investigation of the U.S. decision of pre-empting him, a great debate was raised regarding whether or not Saddam could be contained, deterred and coerced. As Mearsheimer and Walt (2002) explain, a careful look at the actual history of the 1990/91 Gulf War shows that Saddam was neither mindlessly aggressive nor particularly rash or reckless; indeed, the evidence suggests the opposite. He was not "unintentionally suicidal" (Ibid). More importantly, Saddam Hussein could be deterred.[12] It has been reported that Saddam, before sending his army into Kuwait, approached the United States to find out how it would react. In a now-famous interview with the Iraqi leader, Mearsheimer and Walt confirm, U.S. Ambassador April Glaspie told Saddam that "we have no opinion on the Arab-Arab conflicts, like your border disagreement with Kuwait" (Ibid). The U.S. State Department then reinforced this message by declaring that Washington had "no special defense or security commitments to Kuwait" (Ibid). It is true that the United States may not have intended to give Iraq a green light, but that is effectively what it did. If it is unquestioned that Saddam miscalculated international reaction when he attacked Kuwait, there is no evidence suggesting that he did not weigh his options carefully. History provides significant evidence demonstrating that Saddam could have been deterred. For example, although he did launch SCUD missiles at Saudi Arabia and Israel during the Gulf

War, he did not launch chemical or biological weapons at the coalition forces that were decimating the Iraqi military.

But a key question was raised in this context: should Saddam and his top officials be removed? If so, another more difficult question had to be asked: how? Saddam's regime, Yaphe (2003: 33) argued, had survived the same crises that have destroyed other governments. Internally, it had overcome wars, coup attempts, rebellions and loss of authority over 15 of 18 provinces in 1991. Diplomatic isolation had failed, as more and more countries sent airplanes and emissaries to, and began to trade with, Baghdad. As Byman, Pollack and Waxman (1998: 127) describe, Saddam Hussein's Iraq often appeared immune to coercion. Despite military strikes, political isolation and seven years of the most comprehensive sanctions ever imposed on a country, Saddam refused to abandon his ambitions of regional hegemony, dismantle his WMD programs, or repay Kuwaitis for war atrocities. As a result, in recent years Saddam had become increasingly defiant.

To coerce Saddam's regime, Byman, Pollack, and Waxman (1998: 127-129) suggest that the most effective method was to target its "centre of gravity": the relationship between Saddam and his power base. They explained that the concept of a "center of gravity," identified by Karl von Clausewitz in his monumental nineteenth-century study, *On War*, identifies the center of power and that if destroyed, would cause the enemy's resistance to collapse. The centre of gravity can be material: the enemy's army, its capital city, the army of its strongest ally, or a particular individual. Or it can be intangible: an alliance's "community of interest," public opinion, or morale. Tangible or intangible, for Clausewitz, the surest route to victory was to locate the enemy's centre of gravity and to focus all efforts on destroying it. Therefore, in the present context, in order to coerce Iraq, the U.S. had to first identify and then target its centre of gravity. Byman, Pollack, and Waxman confirm that the most obvious choice was Saddam Hussein himself. Saddam created a totalitarian state in which all power flowed from him. Once removed, the regime would collapse and Iraqi resistance to the international community would dissolve. However, there were five other possible centers of gravity: 1) Iraq's conventional military power; 2) Iraq's WMD and ballistic-missile arsenal; 3) public sentiment; 4) Iraq's economy—particularly its oil wealth; and 5) the relationship Saddam built with his power base that was essential to his control over the Iraqi state.

Things did not go smoothly towards eliminating Saddam's regime, because there were conflicting arguments and debates between advocates of a preventive war and supporters of UN actions. Mearsheimer and Walt (2003: 10) explain that both the hard-line preventive war advocates and the more moderate supporters of inspections accepted the same basic premise: Saddam Hussein could not be deterred, and he could not be allowed to obtain a nuclear arsenal. Advocates of preventive war used many arguments to make their case, but their trump card was the charge that Saddam's past behavior proved that he is too reckless and aggressive to be allowed to possess WMDs. They sometimes admitted that a war against Iraq might be costly, might lead to a lengthy US occupation, and might complicate US relations with other countries, but these concerns were eclipsed because the possibility of Saddam having nuclear weapons was too dangerous to accept. In fact, many opponents of preventive war seemed to agree that deterrence would not work in Iraq; rather than invading Iraq and overthrowing the regime, they preferred to keep Saddam bottled up with bigger and better inspections, a tactic which would both eliminate any hidden WMD and at the same time, ensure that Saddam would not be able to acquire any of these deadly weapons. However, Mearsheimer and Walt argue that this position was almost certainly wrong. They illustrate that the record shows that the US could contain Iraq, even if Saddam had nuclear weapons, just as it contained the Soviet Union during the cold war. The facts tell a different story than that of the advocates of preventive war, who portrayed Saddam as either irrational or prone to serious miscalculation; indeed, some also described him as unintentionally suicidal. Saddam had dominated Iraqi politics for more than 30 years. During that period, he started two wars against his neighbors—Iran in 1980 and Kuwait in 1990. A careful look at Saddam's two wars, Mearsheimer and Walt argue, shows his behavior was far from reckless, as in both instances, he attacked because Iraq was vulnerable and because he believed his targets were weak. In each case, his goal was to rectify a strategic dilemma with a limited military victory. Such reasoning and his willingness to use force on these occasions hardly demonstrates that he could not be deterred.

Ian Williams of *Middle East International* shows that Powell was surely conflicted regarding the war decision. "Powell and the Republican moderates who convinced Bush to go through the UN took the setbacks as a bitter blow." It was conceivable that the standing of Powell and the Republican moderates would fall and the likes of Perle, Wolfowitz and Rumsfeld would emerge ascendant. Powell seemed convinced that Iraq was a serious threat, requiring a military response, yet two of the lessons he took from Vietnam were to avoid both unpopular wars and unnecessary wars. Williams claims that the American public was also conflicted: "According to an opinion poll conducted by the *New York Times* and CBS on 10-12 February 2003, 59% of Americans think the president should give the UN more time. And 63% think the US should hold off from war if it does not have the support of its allies" (2003: 8).

Louis Fisher (2003a:138) argues that there was no evidence that the public, in any broad sense, supported war against Iraq. He shows that available polls revealed no public appetite for immediate military action. A *New York Times* poll published on October 7th, 2002, indicated that 69% of Americans believed that Bush should be paying more attention to the economy. Although support was high (67% approving U.S. military action against Iraq with the goal of removing Hussein from power) for military action, when asked "Should the U.S. take military action against Iraq fairly soon or wait and give the U.N. more time to get weapons inspectors into Iraq?" 63% preferred to wait.

In a 2003 article in *New Politics*, titled "We oppose both Saddam Hussein and the U.S. war on Iraq: A call for a new, democratic U.S. foreign policy", Joanne Landy, Thomas Harrison, and Jennifer Scarlott wrote:

> The Bush administration has already taken advantage of its "War on Terrorism" to intimidate critics, undermine civil liberties and push through a blatantly pro-corporate agenda on a whole range of issues—from trade union rights to the environment. Now it is moving our country ever closer to an illegitimate and dangerous war on Iraq. The administration must not be allowed to get away with its claim that U.S. military aggression has anything to do with bringing freedom to Iraqis or strengthening global security. Instead, the antiwar movement must come forward as the true champion of democracy and peace in the Middle East, and the advocate of a new foreign policy. . . . We do not believe that the goal of . . . war against Iraq is to bring democracy to the Iraqis, nor that it will produce this result. Instead, the Bush Administration's aim is to expand and solidify U.S. predominance in the Middle East, at the cost of tens of thousands of civilian lives if necessary. This war is about U.S. political, military and economic power, about seizing control of oilfields and about strengthening the United States as the enforcer of an inhumane global status quo.
>
>   (2003: 16)

On the Iraqi side, President Saddam Hussein, Prime Minister Ezzat Ibrahim, Foreign Minister Tareq Aziz, Information Minister Said Al-Sahhaf, and Ambassador to the United Nations Mohammed al-Douri were those who acted to counter the U.S. actions. Headed by Ezzat Ibrahim, the Iraqi diplomatic mission to the Arab League summit regarding the United States-Iraqi Crisis was very successful in convincing the Arab States of the Iraqi obligations to the U.N. resolutions, while at the same time successfully defending against accusations of the possession of nuclear weapons, and so received strong support. A day before Baghdad was "expected to hand over a voluminous denial that it harbors any illegal weapons," Mohammed al-Douri said that "his government is tired of repeating 'again and again' that it is not breaking any U.N. resolutions" (Moore, 2002, Dec. 6). However, neither the Iraqi diplomatic actions nor communication with the global community enabled Iraq to obtain any powerful support against U.S. military action.

Robert Bresler of *USA Today* warned that a war with Iraq might be different from any other war previously experienced by the U.S. He claimed that "this [was] high-stakes poker, a war the U.S. [could not] afford to lose" (2002: 13). Bresler, therefore, advised that the Bush Administration must have an operational plan for Iraq that did not require much allied support. Looking at the consequences from both sides—winning or losing the war— he explained that if the campaign was brief and successful, most of the world would be grateful and any significant opposition would fade. In this event, terrorists would have lost an important champion in Saddam, peace between Israel and the Palestinians would be given a boost, other rogue states, such as North Korea, with designs on acquiring weapons of mass destruction, would see the consequences of such actions, and the forces for modernization and democracy in the Middle East could gain serious momentum. But if the campaign bogged down, every jealous, resentful anti-American movement would take to the streets, pressuring their government to oppose American effort actively. Osama bin Laden would find his moment of redemption and perhaps a sympathetic government to harbor his movement. A prolonged struggle would be a losing struggle, with Vietnam as the model.

Investigating Saddam's options and strategic choices, Baram (2002: 214-219) analyzes Saddam's speeches and actions during the 1989-91 period and concludes that the existing evidence showed that the Iraqi President was a high-risk gambler, both in terms of his conventional army and his non-conventional arsenal. Baram argues that Saddam's first goal was to dictate oil prices to the Arab Gulf States and to neutralize the Iranian influence in the Gulf. His next goal was to be recognized as the leader of the Arab world, mainly through assuming a confrontational posture towards Israel and making far-reaching promises to the Palestinians. In April 1990, for example, he promised Arafat that he would liberate Jerusalem with Iraqi missiles and air power alone. In 1990-91, Saddam Hussein also indicated that he saw himself as the potential leader of the whole Islamic world and of the Third World.

An understanding of Saddam's major objectives can illustrate clearly the reasons for his actions and decisions during the United States-Iraqi Crisis in general and the 2003 War on Iraq in particular. For Saddam, it is argued here, confronting the sole superpower was something that was worth, from Saddam's perspective, the many troubles and sacrifices that had already taken place within the whole period of the United States-Iraqi Crisis, because of the advantages to be gained which would satisfy Saddam's needs in terms of his major objectives. His choices in the 2003 War on Iraq are represented in Chapter 7 through the Chicken Game representation.

To conclude, the rationality of actors in the 2003 War on Iraq as a conflict, or political decision-makers, is analyzed here as a fundamental step towards examining the rational performance of mass media decision-makers as key actors in the games structured in Chapter 7. The deeply rooted crisis between Iraq and the United States is mainly based on a confrontation of conflicting interests. Both sides have strategic interests, goals, and policies to achieve either regionally or globally. Bush's choice of the pre-emptive strategy or the preventive war, combined with Saddam's cooperation with the U.N. inspectors, his defensive strategy of patience and luring the enemy into the trap, and finally his refusal to sacrifice his people through a disastrous confrontation, confirm the rational calculations made by both adversaries.

NOTES

1. This term has been selected among others (such as *War in Iraq*, *War with Iraq*, *War against Iraq*, and *War over Iraq*) and adopted here for various reasons. For instance, it was the spontaneous headline that first appeared in mass media that has since been edited and modified. Also, because most terms take the same direction of meaning, i.e. attacking, except for *in* and *with*. Adding 2003 distinguishes this war from those that occurred in the past and those that may likely occur in the future.

2. Although the Soviet Union at that time was also a superpower, Saddam Hussein in that speech focused on America as the stronger challenger.

3. Jervis cites Patrick Tyler's "Chief U.N. Inspector Expects Work on Iraq to Start Nov. 27" of *New York Times* on November 16, 2002.

4. This idea of a "New World Order" was, in fact, an idea borrowed from his father, George H. W. Bush, who also called for such a shift during his presidency in the early 1990s.

5. As Keohane (2002) describes in his article "Multilateral coercive diplomacy: Not 'Myths of Empire'".

6. "A subgame is a segment of an extensive (or dynamic game), i.e. a subset of it. Consider the extensive game's tree diagram: a subset of the diagram qualifies as a subgame provided the following holds: (a) the subgame must start from some node, (b) it must then branch out to the successors of the initial node, (c) it must end up at the pay-offs associated with the end nodes, and finally (d) the initial node (where the subgame commenced) must be a singleton in every player's information partition" (Heap & Varoufakis, 1995: 82).

7. The theory of moves, according to Brams and Mattli (1993: 2), is built around three basic concepts: 1) "nonmyopic equilibria" or the stable outcomes induced when the players think ahead; 2) outcomes induced when one player has "moving power", "order power", or "threat power"; 3) incomplete information, either about player preferences or about the possessor of power in a game.

8. This contributes partly to the dynamic nature of the proposed model in this book.

9. Both President Bush and President Hussein addressed their nations emotionally and rhetorically. They both even used similar words in their speeches such as humanity, religious principles and words, and confronting the evil.

10. Possible negative consequences of the war, as Miller (2002: 14-40) discusses, were potentially expected through scenarios or actions on four levels: 1) Saddam's reactions; 2) harming the war on terrorism; 3) undermining America's global position; and, 4) jeopardizing significant U.S. interests. Expectations regarding Saddam's reactions ranged from disrupting the flow of oil, setting oil fields afire, escalating the war by attacking Israel or threatening others in the region, aggravating the Israeli-Palestinian confrontation, launching an international campaign of terrorism, undertaking a bloodbath in Baghdad for political and propaganda purposes, calling for urban combat in Baghdad, using weapons of mass destruction, or even preempting the preventive war. It was recognized that there were possibilities of harming the war on terrorism by distracting from it, undermining international cooperation on fighting terrorism, or losing hearts and minds and enraging the "Arab street." Also, there were fears of undermining America's global position by provoking resistance toward the United States, damaging America's reputation, undermining U.S. relationships with friends and allies, or undermining America's moral position. Above all, there was some possibility that significant U.S. interests could be jeopardized. For instance, U.S. relations with the Arab world could be damaged, complicating the U.S. presence in Southwest Asia

and the Gulf, provoking proliferation, loose weapons of mass destruction, or economic dislocations.

11.   The "quick victory" scenario involved some combination of strategy and luck in which Saddam Hussein and his top leadership would be captured or killed, the Iraqi ground forces would surrender quickly, and the presence of U.S. forces would prevent civil disorder from breaking out in the South or Kurdish regions. This would mean 30 to 60 days of air war, invasion, and ground combat, followed by 2.5 months of post-victory presence by troops in the theatre. In essence, the quick victory scenario resembled the 1990/91 Gulf War, the Kosovo War, and the Afghanistan War. Alternatively, the outcome might instead be a prolonged conflict if "the dice of war roll unfavorably" (Nordhaus, 2002: 56).

12.   Saddam's decision to invade Kuwait was an attempt to deal with Iraq's continued vulnerability, and not part of a grand design to rule the Persian Gulf. Iraq's economy was badly damaged by its earlier war with Iran (1980-88), and continued to decline in following years. Another important cause of Iraq's economic difficulties was Kuwait's refusal to loan Iraq $10 billion and write off the debts Iraq had incurred during its war with Iran.

CHAPTER 7

The Political Games

of War on Iraq

In this chapter, I discuss and analyze conflictual situations among adversaries and actors involved in the 2003 War on Iraq according to game theory, specifically investigating the United States-Iraqi Crisis as a Chicken Game, and the American accusations to Iraq regarding WMD as a Samson and Delilah Game. These discussions and analyses highlight the relevance of the rationality of game theory to the model that I present in this book.

CHICKEN GAME:
A BROAD STRUCTURE OF WAR ON IRAQ

As the *diplomatic chess game* went on, Baghdad said six civilians were killed and 15 wounded in an overnight raid by US and British planes on the southern port city of Basra.
> Michael Settle, *The Herald* — (March 4th, 2003)

The game's not over: the capture of the deck's biggest card makes it seem as if Washington has won another round in the Iraqi conflict. But Saddam may have another ace up his sleeve: the power to embarrass the West.
> Paul Knox, *Globe and Mail Metro Edition* — (December 15th, 2003: A15)

An ongoing game of wait and see between a force of some 2,500 U.S. military personnel and the heavily armed militia of the young fugitive Shiite cleric Muqtada al-Sadr.
> Wolf Blitzer et al., *CNN* — (April 28th, 2004)

It is essential to stand on the various dimensions or borders of the latest developments of the United States-Iraqi Crisis—the 2003 War on Iraq—in order to structure[1] the game in the terminology of international relations theorists. As noted above, War on Iraq can be investigated as a Chicken Game[2]. The Chicken Game is a simple non-zero sum game, which has played a considerable part in the analysis and classification of conflicts in general. In doing this, I represent the confrontation between the two main adversaries as the major Game-Situation, as indicated earlier, and therefore it has only the two major players—U.S. and Iraq.

Figure 1: **War on Iraq as a Game of Chicken – 2 x 2 Version**

	Iraq	
	Cooperation (Diplomacy) C	Non-cooperation (Military) $\overline{C}$
Cooperation (Diplomacy) C	(3 , 3) *Compromise*	(2 , 4) *Iraq wins*
Non-cooperation (Military) $\overline{C}$	(4 , 2) *U.S. wins*	(1 , 1) *Disaster*

U.S.

Key: (x,y) = (payoff to U.S., payoff to Iraq)

4= best ; 3= next-best ; 2= next-worst ; 1= worst

Both play at the same time

Nash equilibria underscored

In War on Iraq as a Chicken Game[3], the payoff matrix consists of two strategies for each player, cooperation or using diplomacy (C) and non-cooperation or using military ($\overline{C}$), as illustrated in *Figure 1*. The payoff matrix of the Chicken Game is similar to that of the Prisoners' Dilemma Game but differs significantly in that the bottom right hand entry is lower for both parties than any other. The two players can rank the four outcomes from best to worst. It is assumed that the players will be able to choose between the strategies of cooperation/diplomacy (C) and non-cooperation/military ($\bar{C}$). The choices of strategies by each player lead to four possible outcomes, ranked by the players from best (4) to worst (1). The first number in the ordered pair that defines each outcome is assumed to be the ranking of the row player (U.S.); the second number is the ranking of the column player (Iraq). Thus, the outcome (3,3) is considered to be next-best for both players, but no presumption is made about whether this outcome is closer to each player's best (4) or next-worst (2) outcome. Each player obtains his next-best outcome (compromise) by choosing C if the other player does so as well, but both have an incentive to defect from this outcome to obtain their best outcomes (4) by choosing when the other player chooses C. However, if both choose , they bring upon themselves their worst outcome (disaster for both). The fact that neither player has a dominant strategy in chicken means that the better strategy choice (C or $\bar{C}$) for each depends on the strategy choice of the other. This interdependence gives each player an incentive to threaten to choose $\bar{C}$, hoping the other will concede by choosing C, so that the threatener can obtain his preferred Nash equilibrium[4].

Suppose both parties, Iraq (in columns) and U.S. (in rows), are currently at the diplomacy position (3,3). Each player sees that he can make a gain by going to the military position. Both parties are then in a situation where it would be highly beneficial for them to *pre-empt* the other, i.e. to act first in an aggressive manner. If one succeeds, the players arrive at one of the mixed situations: (2,4) or (4,2). However, if they both attempt this simultaneously, they will end up in the mutually harmful scenario (disaster for both) represented by the bottom right hand cell (1,1). The Chicken Game does not have any great measure of stability in the cooperative position. A hypothetical situation meeting the Chicken Game's conditions is when two countries are eyeing an intervening territory in which both see an advantage in having and a disadvantage in the other having. In the 2003 War on Iraq, both countries were eyeing the superior position of controlling nuclear weapons (NW). However, if one country invades (having control over nuclear weapons) before the other, there is little the passive country can do except wage war, which it regards as more harmful even than the other country's possession of the territory, or controlling NW in this case. The solution is for both parties is to move as quickly as possible, but again if they do so simultaneously, war is the result with a loss for everyone (1,1). This may explain why the U.S. preventive war was so fast.

The U.S. military campaign was remarkable in its speed and reach, to the extent that the Iraqi collapse was rapid. As Joffé (2003: 4) explains, Central Command in Doha was claiming that the five Republican Guards divisions before Baghdad had seen their military effectiveness reduced by 50% within days as a result of aerial bombardment and had virtually ceased to exist as organized troop formations. The key to the capture of Baghdad lay in the American dash for its international airport, 14km south west of the centre of the city, which was taken on 4 April. From there it was possible, within two days, to launch massive armored patrols into the heart of the capital and to use their massive superiority in firepower and armor in "thunder runs" to undermine Iraqi morale and military resistance.

The payoffs of War on Iraq have been ranked in this chapter based on the following. For the U.S. side, the best outcome (4), which results from its non-cooperative position while Iraq cooperates, would be constituted by these achievements: 1) destroying Iraq's centre of gravity—Saddam Hussein himself, Iraq's conventional military power, and the relationship Saddam built with his power base; 2) stopping or knowing the truth about Iraq's nuclear program; 3) forbidding Iraq to use, acquire, or develop WMD (biological, chemical, and missile programs); 4) foreclosing on the possibility of providing Al-Qaeda with WMD; 5) protecting U.S. national security; 6) the U.S. reputation for taking bold moves, thereby creating a favorable impact on the behavior of many other leaders; 7) a cheap cost of war—"quick victory" scenario—$100 billion to $200 billion; 8) preventing the spread of instability in the Middle East region; 9) Defeating radicalists and empowering the moderates in the Middle East region; 10) spreading a wave of democratization throughout the Middle East region; and 11) gratifying five key U.S. policy drivers—Realist anti-appeasement, U.S. providentialism/ American exceptionalism, assertive unilateralism, willingness to fight and fighting to win, and threat inflation and conflation.

The U.S. next-best outcome (3), which results from its cooperative position while Iraq also cooperates, would be constituted by these achievements: 1) limiting Iraq's programs to acquire or develop WMD; 2) removing potential threats to U.S. and regional security; 3) a cheap cost of military actions; 4) protecting U.S. national security; and 5) preventing the spread of regional instability. The U.S. next-worst outcome (2), which results from its cooperative position while Iraq does not cooperate, would be constituted by these achievements: 1) a painful and messy war; 2) undermining international cooperation on fighting terrorism; 3) undermining America's global position—provoking resistance toward the United States, and undermining U.S. relationships with friends and allies; and 4) jeopardizing significant U.S. interests—U.S. relations with the Arab world may be damaged, complicating the U.S. presence in Southwest Asia and the Gulf, loose weapons of mass destruction, and economic dislocations.

Finally, the U.S. worst outcome (1), which results from its non-cooperative position while Iraq also does not cooperate, would be constituted by these achievements: 1) a costly war—"protracted conflict" (2003–2012) scenario—$1.9 trillion; 2) Saddam's offensive reactions—disrupting the flow of oil, escalating the war by attacking or threatening countries in the region, aggravating the Israeli-Palestinian confrontation, launching an international campaign of terrorism, calling for urban combat in Baghdad, and using weapons of mass destruction; 3) enraging the Arab street; 4) damaging America's reputation and moral position; and 5) military and humanitarian disaster.

For the Iraqi side, the best outcome (4), which results from its non-cooperative position while the U.S. cooperates, would be constituted by these achievements: 1) enhancing Iraq's centre of gravity—Saddam Hussein and his regime, Iraq's conventional military power, Iraq's WMD (nuclear, biological, chemical weapons and ballistic-missile arsenal), and Iraq's economy; 2) Saddam's offensive reactions and preempting the preventive war; 3) undermining international cooperation with the U.S.; 4) undermining America's global position; 5) jeopardizing significant U.S. interests; 6) threatening U.S. national security; and 7) enhancing Iraq's position in the Middle East region, as a result of confronting the superpower.

The Iraqi next-best outcome (3), which results from its cooperative position while the U.S. also cooperates, would be constituted by these achievements: 1) deterring the U.S.; 2) the continuity of Iraq's centre of gravity; 3) undermining international cooperation with the U.S.; and 4) enhancing Iraq's position in the Middle East region, since threatening the superpower. The Iraqi next-worst outcome (2), which results from its cooperative position while the U.S. does not cooperate, would be constituted by these achievements: 1) weakening Iraq's threats to the U.S.; 2) the decline of Iraq's strong military image; 3) economic losses; 4) social, cultural, and humanitarian problems; 5) damage of Iraq's infrastructure; and 6) keeping strategic principles. Finally, the Iraqi worst outcome (1), which results from its non-cooperative position while the U.S. also does not cooperate would be constituted by these achievements: 1) loss of WMD and incompletion of the nuclear weapons program; 2) an enormous costly war; 3) huge losses in terms of economics, health care, etc.; 4) negative reactions as a result of a state of hopelessness; 5) losing international support; and 6) humanitarian disaster.

Another application of the Chicken Game expands the options for each player, as illustrated in *Figure 2*. Indeed, if deterrence in War on Iraq is viewed as a 2 x 4 version of chicken, in which the U.S. chooses first and Iraq responds to the U.S. strategy choice–Iraq being given four possible strategies, then Iraq's choice of *tat-for-tit* (choose if row chooses C; choose C if row chooses) is dominant. However, the U.S., which does not have a dominant strategy itself but can anticipate Iraq's choice of *tat-for-tit* in a game of *complete information* (that is, one in which the players have full information about the rules of play such as order of choice, payoffs of all players, and so on), should then choose to ensure (4,2), rather than C, which would yield (2,4). In other words, as long as the U.S. chooses , Iraq has to choose C to ensure its best payoffs, although this is worse in comparison with the outcome for the U.S. (4,2), but better than (1,1), the disastrous outcome for both sides.

Figure 2: **War on Iraq as a Game of Chicken – 2 x 4 Version**

Iraq

	C regardless	C̄ regardless	Tit-for-tat	Tat-for-tit
	C / C	C̄ / C̄	C / C̄ *Same*	C̄/ C *Different*
Cooperation (Diplomacy) C	(3 , 3)	(2 , 4)	(3 , 3)	(2 , 4)
Non-cooperation (Military) C̄	(4 , 2)	(1 , 1)	(1 , 1)	(4 , 2)

U.S.

↑
Dominant strategy for Iraq

Key: (*x,y*) = (payoff to U.S., payoff to Iraq)

4= best ; 3= next-best ; 2= next-worst ; 1= worst

U.S. plays first

Nash equilibria underscored

The extensive form of representing War on Iraq, as shown in *Figure 3*, better illustrates the sense that there was a great lack of trust from the U.S. side over Iraq's actions since the U.S. insisted on constantly using its might against Iraq whatever Iraq's position. Michael Settle of *The Herald* wrote on March 4th, 2003, that America insisted that the countdown towards a possible war with Iraq would continue, despite arms concessions by Iraq and more warnings about the consequences of military action.

Figure 3: **War on Iraq as a Game of Chicken – A Game Tree**

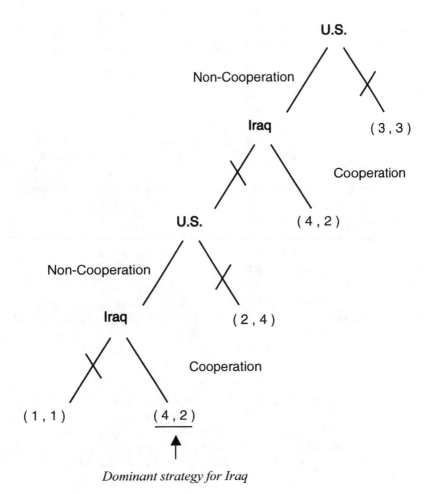

Dominant strategy for Iraq

The cooperative position that Iraqi regime adopts in War on Iraq, i.e., avoiding the use of military confrontation, did not only support the argument that Saddam played the game rationally but also, more importantly, proved that the Iraqi regime did not see its defensive and deescalating strategy in the war as a loss, but instead as a possibility for certain payoffs which may be appear in the future, though some are now known if we consider Saddam's major political objectives. It was an option to choose not to cooperate (or take an offensive rather than defensive position) for Saddam if he reached hopelessness; the consequences of this choice would have resulted in disaster for both parties. However, if Saddam's situation was in fact hopeless, his choice again confirms his rationality, at least in his refusal to sacrifice his people at that stage. As Bassem Mroue of the *Hamilton Spectator* reported on February 24th, 2003, Saddam Hussein was defiant about the U.S. threat of war, and was quoted by the official Iraqi News Agency saying:

> Americans can harm and destroy buildings and installations, but
> will never be able to humiliate Iraq. . . . The people of Iraq are not
> defending only Iraq, but the whole Arab nation and its security.

The final result of any game is the total achievement, or lack thereof, of end-goals. The winner will be the player who reaches his/her desired outcome. Although as of this writing, War on Iraq is not yet over[5] and the winner of the game is still unknown, it is still possible, and important, to investigate the advantages and disadvantages of using specific strategies or tactics for each player or team.

Taking an example of one side—the U.S.—to explain how goals are important for achieving the desired outcome, let us consider the *pre-emptive* plan. Kaplan and Kristol argue that initial U.S. planning saw that one of the advantages of pre-emptive action, as a primarily unilateral tactic, is that it is often less costly than the alternative. Condoleezza Rice stated that "history is littered with cases of inaction that led to very grave consequences for the world. . . . We just have to look back and ask how many dictators who ended up being a tremendous global threat and killing thousands and, indeed, millions of people, should we have stopped in their tracks" (2003: 89).[6] From a different angle, Telhami (2003: 182) suggests that there are three notions that reflect wishful thinking about the desired consequences of War on Iraq. Firstly, the 2003 War on Iraq would turn the country into a shining light of democracy in the Middle East, which would simultaneously put pressure on governments in the region to follow suit and inspire their publics to demand democratic change. Secondly, once the war would be over, the U.S. would be able to turn around and focus its energies on resolving the Arab-Israeli conflict. Thirdly, radicalism in the region would be defeated with the defeat of Iraq and as a result, moderates would then be empowered to take the lead.

However, things might not go exactly as calculated:

> The mounting casualties have made many think that the United States had overestimated its ability in waging a quick, almost bloodless invasion and may be sinking into the quagmire of a protracted war.
>
> (Yanjuan, 2003: 34)

In reviewing the events around April 9, 2003, when Baghdad fell, several political experts argued that Iraqi military was in the process of winning the war. One European strategic analyst emphasized that the Iraqi resistance, largely focused in Sunni-dominated central Iraq, could rapidly be extended nationally, when and if the Shi'ite leadership were to give the order. An Arab strategic specialist in Kuwait explains that Iraq's geographic size, in the heart of the Middle East, presents a situation which the Americans did not envisage; its extensive border is almost impossible to seal to prevent infiltration by pro-resistance forces. As this expert emphasized, American complaints about "foreign terrorists" ignore the fact that not only pro-Saddam Hussein elements are joining the resistance. Furthermore, given the history and character of the Iraqi people, since they would never allow outside elements to dominate or lead any such struggle for liberation, foreign elements must be subordinating themselves to Iraqi leadership. And these foreigners could not function without receiving the support of the population: lodging, food, weapons. This source reported that sentiment in favor of Saddam Hussein was being openly broadcast on Arab TV outlets, which showed jubilant crowds of Iraqis after every major attack. In sum, the Arab perspective is that the Iraqi resistance will grow, and will, in the end, prevail, no matter how long it takes (Mirak-Weissbach, 2003: 53).

On April 16th, 2004 in the *Gulf News*, Saad Al Ajmi, a former Minister of Information in Kuwait and an academic analyst, said that although one might expect Iraqis to be celebrating the demise of Saddam Hussein, one of the most vicious tyrants in history, he noted that it was not the case. For him, while the Iraqi people rejoiced over the capture of Saddam and many in the region hoped Saddam's demise would signal the cessation of wars in the region, the euphoria was short-lived; just one year later, Iraq was in turmoil and sporadic fighting continued. Al Ajmi pointed out that there have been car-bombings and suicide bombings at schools, holy shrines in Najaf, Karbala and Baghdad, UN humanitarian centres and Iraqi police stations. Coalition forces, as well as the insurgents and the Iraqi people have suffered their worst casualties so far as hundreds have been reported killed and many more wounded in Fallujah. Al Ajmi suggested that although the war waged against Saddam a year ago was truly one of liberation and that the outcome should have been continually increasing liberty, not an ugly occupation, the situation may still be salvageable through a transitional period of liberation and occupation; "liberaccupation".

> There were . . . things that the coalition authorities could have done differently to ease the security problem. Two major mistakes were the decision to dissolve immediately all regular Iraqi military forces and the decision to ban all Ba'ath Party members from taking part in public life. . . . By any measure, Saddam's conscript army of almost half a million troops was absurdly bloated and a mainstay of his coercive rule. The Ba'ath Party, too, functioned as an instrument of intimidation designed to dragoon all sectors of society into line behind the "Great Leader." . . . [Coalition Provisional Authority (CPA)] officials seem to have forgotten to ask themselves what it might mean to turn tens of thousands of military officers loose on the streets without at first even the promise of monetary compensation. Similarly, to proscribe all Ba'athists without exception from taking part in reconstruction was to exclude most of the very Iraqi professionals whose services must prove crucial in any scheme to rebuild the country. . . . It is more than likely that Ba'athists and ex-soldiers have been involved in leading concerted attacks against coalition forces. These attacks have not only caused huge disruptions in the CPA's plans to secure and stabilize Iraq, but have led to gravely heightened tensions between Iraqis and coalition forces in some areas. . . . As attacks continued, U.S. soldiers responded with increasing belligerence and less regard for Iraqi cultural norms and sensitivities . . . the CPA failed to do a good job of communicating its plans and policies to the Iraqi people. It was slow to respond to widespread Iraqi fears—stoked relentlessly by the Arab-world media—that the "real" U.S. goal was to dominate Iraq unilaterally and steal its oil.
>
> (Dawisha, 2004: 8-9)

Criticizing the United States and Britain as seeming to be minimally concerned about the post-war situation, preferring instead to concentrate on their achievements, George Joffé (2003: 5) explains that elsewhere, particularly in the Arab world, there has been a sense of stunned disbelief. Many felt that, despite the brutality of Saddam Hussein's regime, at least the

Iraqi dictator had defied the West and, even if defeat was inevitable, Iraqi resistance would salve Arab honor. Cannistraro supports this view:

> Throughout the Arab countries there is certainly a relief at the loss of power of a regional tyrant, but this is joined by feelings of rage and humiliation at the occupation of an Arab capital by a foreign force. ... What the Bush administration seems not to comprehend is that the war against political violence and terrorism is not simply a mechanistic problem whereby you only have to kill or capture members of terrorist groups. The peculiar mixture of American idealism and Old Testament impulses that resulted in the decision to unilaterally invade Iraq to punish "evil doers" and remove a vicious dictatorship may well have had popular support in America, but years of progress in establishing the legitimacy of multilateral actions to protect the common vital interests of the UN members have been undermined.
>
> (2003: 66)

While wondering if the game had ended with the capture of Saddam Hussein and the humiliating display of his televised face, Mitch Potter of *The Toronto Star*, on December 15ᵗʰ, 2003, quoted Sadoun Said, 29, from Iraq: "Saddam is not alone. We have tens of Saddam Husseins. There will be 10 times more resistance. . . . We cry bloody tears for his capture. But this is about oil, this is about Islam, this is about freeing Iraq from the occupiers" (A01). Tim Harper of the same newspaper noted, on December 21ˢᵗ, 2003, that when Saddam Hussein was captured he insisted he was president of Iraq, maintained that neither he nor his military had surrendered to the Americans and blamed Iran for the chemical-weapons attacks on the Kurds. He denied all atrocities, referred to the people he murdered as "traitors and thieves," said he had had nothing to do with insurgent attacks on American troops and insisted he had no weapons of mass destruction, calling that claim a falsified rationale for war cooked up by Bush. The top commander in Iraq Lt.-Gen. Ricardo Sanchez said of the hunt for the ousted Iraqi leader:

> The killing or capturing of Saddam Hussein will have an impact on the level of violence, but it will not end it. ... It won't be the end-all solution. ... It's a needle in a haystack. ... Clearly we haven't found the right haystack. ... We are moving under the assumption that he is still in the country, that he is still operating.
> Jim Krane, *The Chronicle-Herald* — (December 8ᵗʰ, 2003: B11)

Krane also quoted children, in Saddam's hometown of Tikrit:

> We will give our blood, we will give our lives for Saddam. ...
> Saddam is free, he is here, he walks Tikrit in disguise ... U.S.
> soldiers ... are occupiers, they fire on us. Saddam is our father.
>
> (2003: B11)

Not only the Arab publics, but also publics in various regions around
the globe indicated their objections to the use of might against Iraq. For
example, the *Philippine Daily Inquirer*, on March 30th, 2003, conducted
interviews with members of the public asking the question: Is the US right in
using its might against Iraq? and although some agreed or supported the use
of might by the US, the majority of responses did not:

> Legally and morally, the U.S. doesn't have any right to use its
> might and attack Iraq. ... What the U.S. is doing against Iraq is
> plain abuse of its military might . . . The U.S. should respect the
> rights of Iraq as a nation. The U.S. should have waited for U.N.
> inspectors to finish their job and exhausted all efforts and
> diplomatic remedies before invading Iraq. ... From what we
> learned in school, no government has the right to impose its will on
> another sovereign government. That's the essence of the [U.N.].
> So, where does the U.S. get its right to trample on the liberty and
> security of the Iraqi people? ... This will be a precedent. Big and
> powerful nations can now invade small nations. ... The U.S. attack
> on Iraq is inhuman. ... The war in Iraq will only lead to the death of
> and injuries to many innocent civilians . . . It will only encourage
> the people of Iraq to support and defend their leader and their
> country. ... The war is Bush's biggest mistake. ... The game played
> by U.S. President George W. Bush is plain ego-tripping as the U.S.
> has not proven that Iraq is developing weapons of mass
> destruction.

In fact, this leads here to the necessity of investigating the
accusations of Iraq's possession or production of WMDs and its links to
Osama bin Laden's terrorist organization Al-Qaeda, which the United States
has declared as major reasons for launching its pre-emptive War on Iraq.
Consistent with the argument of this chapter that there were *various* Game-
Situations included in War on Iraq, and with the *nature* of their developments
as grounds of War on Iraq, this investigation of the accusations of Iraq's link
to Al-Qaeda and possession of WMDs is undertaken through the use of
Samson and Delilah Game.

SAMSON AND DELILAH GAME:
THE SECRETS OF WMD AND TERRORISM

> On both sides of the Atlantic, the game of "weapons, weapons, where are Iraq's weapons" gathered dangerous political momentum for U.S. President George Bush and British Prime Minister Tony Blair this week.
>
> Pat Reber, *Central European Time* — (January 31st, 2004)

> There is no shortage of Iraqis eager to engage in the blame game. Almost all fingers point to the Bush administration.
>
> Mitch Potter, *The Toronto Star* — (March 20th, 2004: A01)

Before explaining the Samson and Delilah Game, it is first necessary to have a clear understanding of the events and decisions made by both sides in the 2003 War on Iraq. During the early American campaign of launching War on Iraq, despite the strong claims made by the Bush administration that the Saddam regime had links to Al-Qaeda and possessed WMDs, on February 24th, 2003, Bassem Mroue of the *Hamilton Spectator* wrote that Iraq's chief liaison with the UN weapons inspectors insisted that Baghdad was *clean* of weapons of mass destruction and that there should be no new UN resolution on disarming Saddam Hussein, as the United States was demanding. At a packed news conference in Baghdad's Information Ministry Lt.-Gen. Hossam Mohamed Amin gave Iraq's first official comment on an order by chief weapons inspector Hans Blix that it must dismantle its Al Samoud 2 missile program: "We are serious about solving this . . . and we hope it will be resolved peacefully, without the interference of others, particularly the Americans." On September 18th, 2003, *ONASA News Agency* proclaimed:

> Former UN arms inspector Hans Blix said Thursday that the war on Iraq was not justified and that Washington and London "over-interpreted" intelligence data, while a new message attributed to ousted president Saddam Hussein urged Iraqis to fight US occupying forces. In a further sign of their nervousness under almost daily attacks, US troops killed an Iraqi teenager and wounded four others during wedding celebrations in the flashpoint town of Fallujah, witnesses said. Blix, who only a day earlier had said Saddam had not had weapons of mass destruction for 10 years before the war, spoke again after US President George W. Bush said there was no proof tying Baghdad to the September 11 terror attacks in the United States. "No, I don't think so," Blix told BBC

radio when asked if the March 20[, 2003] US-led invasion that led
to the fall of Saddam's regime was justified.

On December 21ˢᵗ, 2003, Tim Harper of *The Toronto Star* showed
how the two major reasons for the Bush administration—Iraq's link to Al-
Qaeda and possession of WMD—were largely discredited and had been
abandoned. Harper noted that Bush's frustration with questions about the
weapons' existence had been on display in an interview with ABC's Diane
Sawyer the week before. Harper wrote that Bush lost patience when
questioned about the gap between his pre-war claim that Saddam had WMD
and his oft-repeated claim that his outgoing weapons inspector David Kay
has found the blueprints for weapons programs. "Bush's leg went up and
down like a jackhammer" as Sawyer pushed: "But stated as a hard fact, that
there were weapons of mass destruction . . . as opposed to the possibility he
could move to acquire those weapons". Harper pointed out that Kay's
planned departure before the search group's work was done was sure to foster
an impression that the search was futile. Kay was said to have decided to
leave for personal and family reasons. Charles Pena of the Cato Institute, a
libertarian think-tank in Washington, said: "The departure of Kay—a former
U.N. weapons inspector who supported the administration's pre-war WMD
claims—would be an indicator that he does not expect to unearth any of the
weapons of mass destruction that had previously been cited by President
Bush as a threat that required U.S. military intervention. Even with Saddam
in custody, nothing changes. This was the wrong war for the wrong reasons"
(F01).

In his 2003 article, titled "Deciding on war against Iraq: Institutional
failures", in the journal *Political Science Quarterly*, Louis Fisher criticizes
the Bush administration and shows how the decision of going into a war
against Iraq was a fundamental failure. Fisher (2003*b*: 389-390) explains that
following the swift U.S. military victory in Iraq, teams of experts conducted
careful searches to discover the weapons of mass destruction that Bush had
offered as the principal justification for war, and claimed that these weapons
represented a direct threat. Much of this rationale was exploded on a regular
basis by the press. The campaign for war was dominated more by fear than
facts, more by assertions of what might be, or could be, or used to be, than by
what actually existed. Months after the president announced victory, no
evidence has been found nor is there much reason to expect anything
significant to emerge and stories began to circulate that perhaps the Bush
administration had deceived allies, Congress, and the American public.
Fisher argues that opposition to the war in Iraq is of the Bush
administration's own making, nourished by statements that lacked

credibility. He contends that the administration and its allies failed a fundamental democratic test because citizens usually stand ready to sacrifice lives and fortunes for national security but at the same time oppose wars that cause needless deaths, and consequently, military force demands solid evidence that a threat is imminent and war is unavoidable. Fisher (410) concludes that the U.S. political institutions failed in their constitutional duties when they authorized war against Iraq because the Bush administration never presented sufficient and credible information to justify statutory action in October 2002 and military operations in March 2003. As a result, the United States finds itself six months after the invasion almost solely responsible for an occupation that has uncertain goals, heavy costs, and open-ended duration.

When analyzing the early announcements by U.S. officials seeking justifications and support for their decision to go to war against Iraq, Fisher (2003*a*) shows that on August 21st, 2002, Bush called himself "a patient man" because of his decision to "look at all options, and consider all technologies available to us and diplomacy and intelligence . . . [and on the same day, Bush noted] there is this kind of intense speculation that seems to be going on, a kind of a—I don't know how you would describe it. It's kind of a churning. . . . Secretary of Defense Donald Rumsfeld supplied the missing word: 'frenzy' . . . Bush agreed with that choice [and said] The country was too preoccupied . . . with military action against Iraq" (135). Five days later, the administration switched to a frenzied mode, Fisher illustrates, as Vice President Dick Cheney delivered a forceful speech that implied that there was only one option: to go to war. Cheney warned that Saddam Hussein would "fairly soon" have nuclear weapons and that it would be useless to seek a Security Council resolution requiring Iraq to submit to weapons inspectors. Wondering *what happened to the options that Bush was carefully weighing?*, Fisher claims that the American administration tried to link Iraq and Al-Qaeda, but the reports could never be substantiated. On September 25th, 2002, Bush claimed that Hussein and Al-Qaeda "work in concert . . . [and on the following day] he claimed that the Iraqi regime has longstanding and continuing ties to terrorist organizations, and there are Al-Qaeda terrorists inside Iraq . . . [but] Ari Fleischer tried to play down Bush's remark, saying that he was talking about what he feared could occur" (137). Secretary Rumsfeld, on September 27, 2002, announced that "the administration had 'bulletproof' evidence of Iraq's links to Al-Qaeda. He said that declassified intelligence reports showing the presence of senior members of Al-Qaeda in Baghdad in 'recent periods' were 'factual' and 'exactly accurate'" (137). However, Fisher explains, when reporters sought to substantiate the claim, officials offered no details to back up the assertions. Despite having claimed bulletproof support, Rumsfeld admitted that the information was not beyond a reasonable doubt. In his speech to the nation on October 7th, 2002, on the eve of the congressional vote over the war, Bush said that Iraq "has trained Al-Qaeda members in bombmaking and poisons and deadly gases . . . Bush claimed that satellite photographs 'reveal that Iraq is rebuilding facilities at sites that have been part of his nuclear program in the past'" (137-138). Fisher illustrates that allies in Europe, active in investigating Al-Qaeda, found no evidence of links between Iraq and Al-Qaeda. Interviews with top investigative magistrates, prosecutors, police, and intelligence officials uncovered no information to support the claims by the Bush administration. Moreover, after dismissing a connection between Iraq and Al-Qaeda, investigative officials in Spain, France, and Germany worried that a war against Iraq would increase the terrorist threat rather than diminish it.

> The U.S. military may have the ability to destroy Saddam Hussein, but the United States cannot promote democracy in the Muslim world and peace in the Middle East, nor can it deal with the threat posed to all of us by terrorist networks such as Al-Qaeda, and by weapons of mass destruction, by pursuing its current policies. Indeed, the U.S. could address these problems only by doing the *opposite* of what it is doing today.
>
> (Landy, Harrison & Scarlott, 2003: 16)

Democratic congressman Robert Wexler of Florida, who voted in October, 2002, to authorize the use of force against Iraq said: "Iraq was not an imminent threat to America. . . . There were no chemical, biological or nuclear weapons. And there was no link between [Al-Qaeda] and Saddam Hussein. The only mushroom cloud resulting from the war in Iraq is that represented by the Bush administration's barrage of deception and lies" (Skorneck, 2004: 705). Also, in an attempt to demonstrate that Bush's policies are unpopular around the world, House Democrats pointed to the Madrid bombings. Jim McDermott said: "We have only to look at what happened in Spain to be reminded the world is no safer. . . . Terrorism threatens America today just as much as terrorism threatened America before we invaded Iraq" (Ibid: 706). On March 15th, 2004, Beth Gorham of *The Telegram* quoted Democrat Howard Dean who blasted Bush's unilateral Iraq invasion as a dangerous diversion and the source of more terror trouble: "For the president of the United States to assert that we are safer because . . . Saddam Hussein is in jail is ludicrous given what happened three days ago in Spain" (A5).

Bogdan Kipling of *The Chronicle-Herald* wrote on April 1ˢᵗ, 2004, that the U.S. political chess game is getting downright ugly. Kipling referred to Richard A. Clarke's book in which the author rearranged all the pieces on Washington's political chess board—including those that may affect the outcome of the November 2004 presidential election. Mr. Clarke, who was the top White House expert on terrorism for three presidents—George H. W. Bush, William J. Clinton, and George W. Bush—testified that Mr. Bush and most Americans see the 9/11 assault as a declaration of war, an attempt to decapitate the United States government and to destroy the country's economic nerve centre. Mr. Clarke told the commissioners investigating the events preceding the 9/11 terrorist attack that he was outraged by Mr. Bush's posturing as the determined leader in the fight against terrorism. In Mr. Clarke's most revealing moment, as Kipling describes, when addressing the nation and the families of those killed in the 9/11 terrorist attack from the commission's witness table, he said: "Those entrusted with protecting you have failed you. And I failed you. . . . And for that . . . I would ask, once all the facts are out, for your understanding and for your forgiveness" (A7). Mr. Clarke blames Bush and Rice for ignoring Osama bin Laden until it was too late. Mr. Clarke's argument is that Clinton fought bin Laden, but all Mr. Bush wanted was to make war in Iraq.

> [However,] the removal of Saddam Hussein's tyranny will do little to increase the domestic security of America, because the Baath regime was not a major influence on global terrorism. But the first American occupation of a Muslim country may substantially increase hostility in the Middle East and South Asia against the United States while providing incentive for new recruits to [Al-Qaeda] and other religiously inspired militant groups waging what they believe is a war against unbelievers: war certainly of cultures and civilizations.
>
> (Cannistraro, 2003: 56-57)

Osama bin Laden, Cannistraro (2003) explains, is the spiritual and political leader of the only terrorist group with a global reach that has been carrying out violence against Americans; he fears that there may well be others in the future as a result of the American policy of preemption. Cannistraro confirms that bin Laden has publicly cited Iraq as the most favorable theatre in which to rally Muslim resistance against America in the Middle East. Bin Laden and his deputy, Ayman Zawahiri, have studied the American involvement in foreign crises and believe that Iraq presents a positive environment in which to wage a war of attrition. In essence, Al-Qaeda and the various Jihadi groups inspired by bin Laden anticipate that a slow, grinding conflict will result in an American withdrawal. Cannistraro considers that what America has succeeded in doing in the war on terrorism is to remove most of the sanctuaries used by the Al-Qaeda leadership, as well as to disrupt the command and control of the group. He shows that many of the senior and experienced leaders of Al-Qaeda have been apprehended and several have been killed. If that is the good news, however, the bad news is the same: the organization may have been diffused and dispersed, but within major societies in the Islamic world there is a benevolent environment for religious fundamentalists. This has forced Al-Qaeda to embrace the concept of resistance without command and control, that of the so-called leaderless resistance.

With this information in hand, and in order to better understand the strategies of choices or decisions used by both adversaries in such a conflictual situation, the Bush administration's accusations of Saddam's regime having links to terrorism and possessing WMDs can be theoretically represented here as the Samson and Delilah Game. But before illustrating how this game has been played by both parties, it is necessary to first give some background about its story and rules.

In the context of interpreting some aspects of his 1994 *Theory of Moves* (TOM), Steven Brams tells the famous story of Samson and Delilah, from the book of Judges in the Hebrew Bible (Old Testament), and represents it as a game. The payoff matrix of this game is shown in *Figure 4*. As Brams (38-40) explains, once Samson's desire has been kindled, Delilah could trade on it either by nagging (N) Samson for the secret of his strength or not nagging (N̄) him and hoping it would come out anyway. Samson, in turn, could either tell (T) the secret of his strength or not tell (T̄) it. The four consequences of each pair of strategy choices in this game are as follows. First, *Delilah unhappy, Samson unforthcoming* (2,4): the next-worst state for Delilah, because Samson withholds his secret, though she is not frustrated in an unsuccessful attempt to obtain it; the best state for Samson, because he keeps his secret and is not harassed. Second, *Delilah happy, Samson forthcoming* (4,2): the best state for Delilah, because she learns Samson's secret without making a pest of herself; the next-worst state for Samson, because he gives away his secret without good reason. Third, *Delilah persuasive, Samson reluctant* (3,3): the next-best state for both players, because though Delilah would prefer not to nag (if Samson tells) and Samson would prefer not to succumb (if Delilah does not nag), Delilah gets her way when Samson tells; and Samson, under duress, has a respectable reason (i.e., Delilah's nagging) to tell. Fourth, *Delilah frustrated, Samson harassed* (1,1): the worst state for both players, because Samson does not get peace of mind, and Delilah is frustrated in her effort to learn Samson's secret.[7]

The game starts at (2,4), when Delilah chooses N̄ and Samson chooses T̄ during their period of acquaintance. These strategy choices are consistent with Delilah's choosing her dominant strategy, and Samson his best response to this strategy, giving the Nash equilibrium of (2,4). Brams explains here that game theory offers no explanation of why the players would ever move to a non-equilibrium outcome, but he claims that this is precisely what they do. Delilah switches to N, putting the players in state (1,1), and Samson responds with T, leading to state (3,3), neither of which is a Nash equilibrium. That is, TOM leads to a unique prediction when the initial state is (2,4), as it predicts from this state that the outcome to be (3,3). Although (2,4) is also a nonmyopic equilibrium[8] (NME), it does not arise unless play starts in state (3,3).

Figure 4: **Samson and Delilah Game**

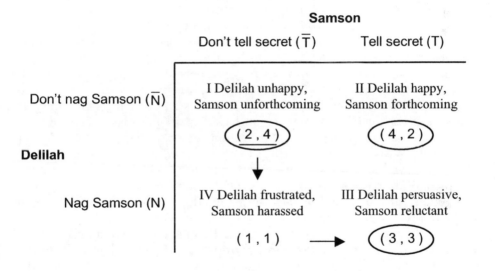

Key: (*x,y*) = (payoff to Delilah, payoff to Samson)

4= best ; 3= next-best ; 2= next-worst ; 1= worst

Nash equilibrium underscored

Nonmyopic equilibria (NMEs) circled

Arrows indicate progression of states to NME of (3,3)

In the United States-Iraqi Crisis, the Bush administration, seeking ways to manage the crisis with Iraq, could either accuse (A) Saddam's regime of possessing WMDs, as a way to know or try to assess his strength, or not accuse (A̱) Saddam's regime, hoping that the reality about Iraq's possession or still-producing of WMDs would come out anyway through the UN inspections. Saddam, in turn, could either reveal (R) this secret and consequently help the Bush administration to assess his strength, or not reveal (Ṟ) any information about his possessing or producing WMDs. The four consequences of each pair of strategy choices in this game between the Bush administration and the Saddam regime, as illustrated in *Figure 5*, are as follows. First, *Bush administration neglected, Saddam uncommunicative* (2,4): this is the next-worst state for the Bush administration, because Saddam's regime withholds its secret. However, the Bush administration is not frustrated in an unsuccessful attempt to obtain the secret. This is also the best state for Saddam, because he keeps his secret and is not stressed. Second, *Bush satisfied, Saddam informative* (4,2): this is the best state for Bush, because he learns Saddam's secret without having to make any painful effort; it is also the next-worst state for Saddam, because he gives away his secret for no good reason. Third, *Bush powerful, Saddam ineffective* (3,3): this is the next-best state for both players, because although Bush would prefer not to accuse (if Saddam reveals) and Saddam would prefer not to inform (if Bush does not accuse), Bush gets his way when Saddam reveals the secret; and Saddam, under threat, has a justifiable reason (i.e., Bush's accusation that could lead to military action) to reveal the secret of whether possessing WMDs or not. Fourth, *Bush frustrated, Saddam stressed* (1,1): this is the worst state for both players, because Saddam does not get the removal of sanctions posed on Iraq and peace of mind regarding UN inspections, and Bush is frustrated in his intelligence investigations to learn Saddam's secret.

The game re: WMDs between the Bush administration and Saddam regime started at (2,4), when Bush chose A̱ and Saddam chose R during their crisis, before, and after the 9/11 attacks, in fact, beginning with the 1990/91 Gulf War. These strategy choices are consistent with Bush's choosing his dominant strategy, and Saddam choosing his best response to this strategy, giving the Nash equilibrium of (2,4). Bush switched to A, putting the players in state (1,1), and Saddam responded with R, leading to state (3,3), neither of which is a Nash equilibrium. The period when the Bush administration was frustrated and the Saddam regime was stressed, i.e. the status (1,1), lasted throughout the 13 years of U.N. inspections, sanctions against Iraq, and diplomatic efforts to manage the United States-Iraqi Crisis.

After 9/11 the Bush administration increased its accusations against Iraq by focusing more on the threat of terrorism to the global world, and also threatened Iraq with using military force in order to find out whether or not Iraq's WMDs actually existed.

Figure 5: **WMD as a Samson and Delilah Game**

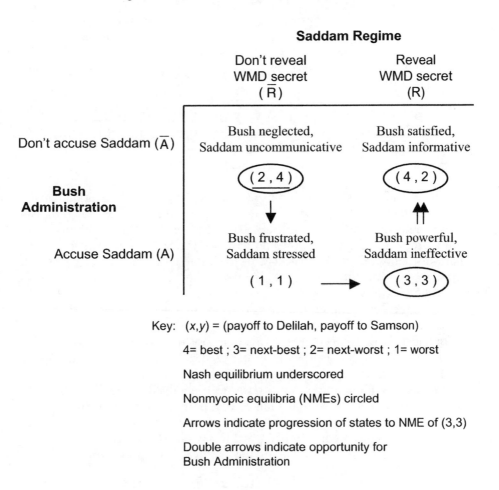

Key: (*x,y*) = (payoff to Delilah, payoff to Samson)

4= best ; 3= next-best ; 2= next-worst ; 1= worst

Nash equilibrium underscored

Nonmyopic equilibria (NMEs) circled

Arrows indicate progression of states to NME of (3,3)

Double arrows indicate opportunity for
Bush Administration

A White House spokeswoman called Iraq's move "part of its game of deception." U.S. Sen. Joseph Biden, the top Democrat on the Senate Foreign Relations Committee, said on "Fox News Sunday" that "destroying all of the missiles is not enough for me."
Kuwait Times — (March 3rd, 2003)

During this period, Iraqi officials, including Saddam himself, were very forthcoming and announced to the whole world that Iraq was clean from any WMDs. They also were more cooperative with UN inspectors trying to uncover the secret than they had been previously.

At this stage of the game, it is argued in this chapter, the Bush administration had a good opportunity to improve its status and simultaneously weaken Iraq's by *moving* from (3,3) to (4,2), as the double arrows indicate in *Figure 5*, that is, by *stopping* their accusations of Iraq, and further, by trying to withdraw from that position and instead claiming that Iraq was about to possess WMDs. The same is for their claims concerning Iraq's link to terrorist groups. On September 19th, 2003, Sridhar Krishnaswami of *The Hindu*, wrote:

> The U.S. President, George W. Bush, said on Wednesday that
> there was no proof tying the former Iraqi leader, Saddam Hussein,
> to the events of 9/11: "We've had no evidence that Saddam
> Hussein was involved with September 11".

This new position would have made the Bush administration capable of confronting the blame campaign against it that destroys their major reason of launching the 2003 War on Iraq. By doing so, the Bush administration would have been satisfied and would have put the Saddam regime in a worse position—being informative (next-worst) with no more secrets for the U.S. to worry about, rather than being ineffective (next-best) with a strong reason, the military invasion.

In the next chapter, the focus of analyzing and discussing conflictual situations (games) of the 2003 War on Iraq is on the role of the communication between players. This does not mean that there was no role for the media during the previously analyzed games, but instead, the media role becomes more apparent in the following game as influential on the developments. Although the media have been involved in the Chicken Game and the Samson and Delilah Game, the political decision-making was superior in influencing the developments. But, in the following Prisoners' Dilemma Game the media decision-making is clearly playing an influential and critical role that even changes the nature of the game (or conflictual situation).

Notes

1. Analysis of the crisis structure is mainly based on, in addition to other sources, quotes from speeches given by Iraqi and American officials. These include President George W. Bush's speeches and news conferences (President Bush's war address, 2003, Mar. 19), President Saddam Hussein's speeches at the ACC Summit on February 24, 1990 and on the withdrawal from Kuwait on February 26, 1991 (Bengio, 1992), and his interview with Dan Rather of CBS on February 26, 2003. In addition, announcements of the Iraqi information minister Said Al-Sahhaf in Al-Jazeera (2003, Mar. 25, 27 and Apr. 5), and the U.S. Secretary of State Colin Powell's remarks at the United Nations from *CBS News* (2003, Feb. 5) are included.

2. The illustration of the Chicken Game is basically drawn from Nicholson (1970: 60-66).

3. Chicken, which derives its name from a "sport" in which two drivers race toward each other on a narrow road, would at first glance seem an appropriate model for this conflict. Brams (1975: 39-40) explains that this game takes its name from the rather gruesome sport that apparently originated among California teenagers in the 1950s. As two teenage drivers approach each other at high speed on a narrow road, each has the choice of either swerving and avoiding a head-on collision, or continuing on the collision course. There are four possible outcomes: 1) The player who does not swerve when the other does gets the highest payoff of 4 for his courage (or recklessness); 2) The player who "chickens out" by swerving is disgraced and receives a payoff of 2; 3) If both players lack the will to continue on the collision course to the bitter end, they both suffer some loss of prestige, obtaining payoffs of 3, but not as much as if only one player had played it safe by swerving; and 4) If both players refuse to compromise, then they hurtle to their mutual destruction and receive the lowest payoffs of 1 each. *Figure 1* illustrates these outcomes.

4. John Nash's concept of equilibrium says that a player considers only the *immediate* advantages and disadvantages of switching his strategy. If neither player in a game can immediately gain by a unilateral switch, the resulting outcome is stable, or a Nash equilibrium. That is, neither player has an incentive to deviate unilaterally from this outcome because he would do worse if he did (Brams, 1985: 67).

5. It is argued here that in order for the War on Iraq to be considered completely finished, the fighting between Iraqi resistance groups and American troops must be stopped. Neither the Iraqi regime's collapse nor Bush's declaration of the end of major military operations in Iraq are

sufficient to confirm the end of the conflict. The harmful consequences for both the Iraqi resistance and the American troops are part of the outcomes of the War on Iraq game and their value should not be underestimated, especially if we think of the possibility of escalating these confrontations into another wave of conflicts that may require another American military campaign. If these circumstances last for a longer period, the outcomes of both parties may need to be recounted in order to recognize the winner. The same can be said of the United States-Iraqi Crisis. If the crisis' latest conflict, the 2003 War on Iraq, has not been completely resolved, this also means that it has not been managed yet, i.e., there still exist a crisis between the United States administration and the Iraqi regime because despite the elimination of Saddam his followers are still there continuing to seek what he originally aimed for.

6. It also appears that, as Jervis said, at least some American leaders "believe that if the U.S. overthrows Saddam it will establish a reputation for taking bold moves, and that this will have a favorable impact on the behavior of many other leaders. This is a form of compellence, and indeed quite a strong one" (2002: 16).

7. The story's background is helpful for understanding Brams' explanation of Samson and Delilah as a game. After abetting the flight of the Israelites from Egypt and delivering them into the promised land of Canaan, God became extremely upset by their recalcitrant ways and punished them severely: "The Israelites again did what was offensive to the Lord, and the Lord delivered them into the hands of the Philistines for forty years (Judges 13:1)" (34). But a new dawn appeared at the birth of Samson, which was attended by God, whose angel predicts: "He shall be the first to deliver Israel from the Philistines (Judges 13:5)" (34). After Samson grew up, he went down to Timnah, and noticed a girl among the Philistine women. On his return, he asked his parents to get her for him as a wife. His father and mother said to him, "Is there no one among the daughters of your own kinsmen and among all our people that you must go and take a wife from the uncircumcised Philistines? (Judges 14:1-3)" (34). The woman whom Samson sought indeed pleased Samson, and he took her as his wife. At a feast, Samson posed a riddle that stumped everybody, and the celebrants appealed to Samson's wife for help: "Coax your husband to provide us with the answer to the riddle; else we shall put you and your father's household to the fire; have you invited us here in order to impoverish us? (Judges 14:15)" (35). Samson's wife was distraught and accused her husband of not loving her, even of hating her. At first Samson refused to tell his wife the answer to the riddle, but because she "continued to harass him with her tears . . . on the seventh day he told her, because she nagged him so (Judges 14:17)" (35). Apparently, Samson's love for Delilah was not requited. Rather, Delilah was more receptive to serving as bait for Samson for appropriate recompense. The lords of the Philistines made her a

proposition: "Coax him and find out what makes him so strong, and how we can overpower him, tie him up, and make him helpless; and we'll each give you eleven hundred shekels of silver (Judges 16:5)" (35). After assenting, Delilah asked Samson: "Tell me, what makes you so strong? And how could you be tied up and be made helpless? (Judges 16:6)" (35). Samson deceived her and said: "If I were to be tied with seven fresh tendons, that had not been dried, I should become as weak as an ordinary man (Judges 16:7)" (35-36). After Delilah bound Samson as he had instructed her, she hid men in the inner room and cried, claiming that the Philistines are upon him, and quickly "Samson's lie became apparent when he pulled the tendons apart, as a strand of tow (flax) comes apart at the touch of fire" (36). So the secret of his strength remained unknown. Therefore, Delilah was angry and accused him of lying and deception. Delilah kept asking Samson how he could be tied up; twice more he gave her erroneous information about the source of his strength, and she became progressively more frustrated by his deception. Finally, and after constant nagging and pressing from Delilah to Samson, he was wearied to death and confided everything to her. The secret, of course, was Samson's long hair. When he told his secret to Delilah, she had his hair shaved off while he slept. (Brams, 1994: 34-36).

8. Nonmyopic equilibria, according to Brams (1985: 67), are long-term stable outcomes, while short-term stable outcomes are *myopic equilibria*. Brams means by *myopic equilibria* those described by John Nash. On the contrary, a nonmyopic equilibrium, defined by Brams, assumes that a player, in deciding whether to depart from an outcome, considers not only the immediate effect of his actions but also the consequences of the other player's probable response, his own counter-response, and so on.

CHAPTER 8

The Media Games

of War on Iraq

My core argument in this chapter is to show the media's involvement in a group of various major games (conflictual situations) of the crisis at stake, to examine their rational performance, and to provide encouragement, using game theory, that may motivate journalistic practices towards ethical conduct during situations where conduct is frequently unethical.

The mass media was a greatly involved in the 2003 War on Iraq on many levels. The strategic choices by political decision-makers on both the U.S. and Iraqi sides have relied to a great extent on the mass media to achieve their goals. The media have been used as tools whether for the initiator of the war, the other adversary, or other players involved. For the United States to achieve their pre-emptive strategy effectively, it had to use the mass media in a different way than in the 1990/91 Gulf War. Also, the Iraqi officials approached the global media to counteract the U.S. strategy against them and to reflect their adopted defensive strategy whether in the Chicken Game, or their clarifying or secret revealing strategy regarding the possession of WMDs and links to Al-Qaeda in the Samson and Delilah Game, as has been illustrated in the previous chapter. Additionally, other players involved in the 2003 War on Iraq such as Canada and the Arab States have used their mass media to represent and enhance their peacekeeping policy and keep and protect their mutual relations away from the dangers of the war.

At many points in this chapter, I examine the importance of communication in general and mass media in particular in the conflictual situations of the 2003 War on Iraq in order to demonstrate their significance in such an international crisis. As the chapter progresses, increased attention is also given to the role of the media in the games.

Because of their involvement in the 2003 War on Iraq, Canada and the Arab League have been put in a situation similar to the Prisoners' Dilemma Game; however, using communication has allowed mutual coordination to convert the game into another— called here the Communication Game—in order to achieve better outcomes. In addition, I also explain how rational thinking can help mass media achieve better outcomes or desired goals. Most importantly, I suggest a rational conduct for the media decision-makers based on their obligation to abide by ethical principles of conduct. Telling the truth as a major principle in the journalistic codes of ethics, as explained in Chapter 5, is highlighted here as a rational form of the Truth Game between the mass media and their audiences.

RATIONALE:

Thirteen years of international economic sanctions and an ongoing game of cat-and-mouse with international inspectors led to the resumption of all-out war last Spring.
                    Saad Al Ajmi, *Gulf News* — (April 16th, 2004)

The past two months have seen the ultimate game of political ping-pong. One week, Mr Bush "takes a hit". The next he strikes back. And this will continue in the months ahead.
                    Alec Russell, *The Daily Telegraph* — (April 8th, 2004: 24)

. . . it is a game that journalists, among others, have to play. It is expected of them. Especially of columnists.
                    Martin Woollacott, *The Guardian* — (April 30th, 2004: 28)

Events during the 2003 War on Iraq are considered rich material for the mass media to cover, or to play with. The mass media of each player participate in the developments of the situation, as well as follow a general policy, whether this policy is their own internal policy or the government's political one, in order to ensure that that policy can achieve positive outcomes for them and their countries. Some examples that one might choose from among numerous others during the mass media coverage of the 2003 War on Iraq, were the announcements by the Iraqi Information Minister Said Al-Sahhaf in reply to American claims and attacks; in the terminology of the soccer analogy of Chapter 6, this might be described as the kicking of the ball against the Iraqi team and its reaction to block the ball. For instance, when Al-Sahhaf asked an American soldier in the first group of prisoners of war, whether the Iraqi public had met him or his colleagues with flowers or guns, the soldier did not understand his question, and the American mass media did not comment on it in the same way as did the Arabic media. Thus, it is evident that both teams of media focused on what was relevant to satisfying their respective strategies. Although the Arabic media explained that Al-Sahhaf was replying to what they described as false claims by President Bush that a) the Iraqi people would welcome Americans if they could feel confident that the Iraqi regime would be removed, and b) that the American troops were coming for the Iraqi people's benefits and prosperity, the American media neglected and ignored this point and shifted attention to the possible mistreatment of hostages. That is, mass media of each side were supporting the general strategy of their teams in the conflict—American military strategy of going to a necessary war and Iraqi diplomatic strategy of objecting illegitimate attack.

It becomes quite clear that media decision-makers, although using the game terminologies in their messages, may not be clearly aware of the rationality required in their coverage, or at least do not study the conflict or crisis situations rationally, in order gain desired outcomes. In some cases, their performance succeeds in achieving strategic goals, if it is connected to political directions that originally arose from the rules of rationality. Therefore, investigating the involvement of the mass media in situations that have been structured according to game theory can help in assessing their rational performance.

PRISONERS' DILEMMA "MODIFIED" GAME: COMMUNICATION IN CHARGE

> Increasingly, the mass media are recognized not simply as observers and reflectors of political life, but as themselves political players and definers of reality.
>
> (Hackett, Gilsdorf & Savage, 1992)

In the 2003 War on Iraq, other Game-Situations stem from the global involvement of a wide range of countries in the United States-Iraqi Crisis. Given the nature of its origination as an *international* crisis (the United States-Iraqi Crisis), the game War on Iraq could have been played by all actors (countries) around the globe had they been interested in playing.

However, the key players in this instance were the United States and Iraq. Other players who participated in the game were playing within teams of the main adversaries, as illustrated in the Soccer Game analogy of Chapter 6. The situations of countries around the world varied significantly regarding the United States-Iraqi Crisis, the 2003 War on Iraq, and the removal of Saddam's regime. The following presents some examples.

Among the major powers, Britain was firmly behind the United States. By taking this position, Britain's Prime Minister Tony Blair subjected himself to continuous internal opposition. "Tony Blair's Iraq campaign is in trouble before it has begun. It has failed to convince either an increasingly sceptical public or MPs of the ruling Labour Party, in spite of the fact that a majority of British newspapers have adopted a pro-war position" (Doyle, 2003*b*: 10). "Blair still has to tread carefully. Anti-Bush feeling remains high in Britain" (2003*a*: 16).

On the other side, France, Germany, Russia, and China harshly criticized U.S. policy many times, claiming that it was both ineffective and unfair. For instance, at the beginning of the American campaign against Iraq, French President Jacques Chirac and German Chancellor Gerhard Schroder, announced their united opposition to a possible American-led war on January 22, 2003. Also, Canada, a U.S. neighbor and major trading partner, stated its position as opposing the attack on Iraq unless clear evidence of Iraqi dangerous actions or UN support was presented. In the Canadian magazine *Maclean's*, Julian Beltrame said,

> It was by most accounts an uncomfortable meeting when Jean Chrétien sat down with George W. Bush for 45 minutes in Detroit's Cobo Hall last week. The Prime Minister had earlier intoned that he was looking forward to hearing from the President why Washington believed that the Baghdad bully Saddam Hussein must be replaced. Canada needed evidence linking him to [Al-Qaeda] or other terrorist organizations...or it would not support a pre-emptive assault on Iraq.
>
> (2002: 16)

Although the Gulf States and Turkey supported a hard line against Iraq in general, they sometimes criticized or opposed principle elements of U.S. policy, such as sanctions or military strikes. Most Arab countries, through the Arab League[1], condemned any military actions against Iraq and refused to participate in the military confrontations, though they did the opposite in the 1990/91 Gulf War. They saw no justification this time for the invasion of Iraq as long as it was willing to cooperate and follow the United Nations resolutions. For example, as with other Arab governments, Jordan "has repeatedly stated its opposition to a U.S. led war against Iraq and insisted that its territory and air space would not be used by U.S. forces" (Kamal, 2003: 17). Even in Kuwait, the country that suffered greatly from Saddam's violations, people on the streets rejected the idea of attacking Iraq but agreed to punish Saddam himself. They who "have seen the worst of Saddam say they hope he can be pushed out of power through measures short of war. Yes, he should be punished . . . but not if it means devastating his whole country" (Wilson, 2003: 812).

However, the countries that had supported the U.S. in its early decisions maintained their position despite the many American causalities resulting from the Iraqi resistance and the refutation of the U.S.'s major reasons for launching the 2003 War on Iraq. For example, the *BBC*, on March 12th, 2004, reported on Singapore's rationale for being supportive to the United States-led War on Iraq, and its argument that the aftermath of the conflict and resulting curbs on the spread of banned weapons has made for a safer regional and international environment. Foreign Affairs Minister S. Jayakumar acknowledged that there were those who questioned the wisdom of Singapore's move especially since Washington was unable to find Iraq's weapons of mass destruction (WMD), which had been a primary reason for the American-led action. However, Jayakumar insisted that, regardless of the outcome, the global threat of WMD proliferation still exists "and must always be of real concern to a small, densely populated country like Singapore. . . . The link between this and terrorism is a greater worry." He claimed that the outcome of the Iraq war had a "salutary effect" as other countries were coming clean about their programs, pointing out that Iran is cooperating with the International Atomic Energy Agency, Libya has dropped its WMD plans, and Pakistan is helping with investigations on the spread of nuclear weapons technology. Also, he argued that support for the US does not come at the expense of ties with other countries as it is not "a zero-sum game".

If, for a minute, we consider the Soccer Game outlined in Chapter 6 as a Game-World, looking at the playground we can see that among the players on the Iraqi team, whatever their role or location in the playground, were the Arab States. Canada was also among the players on the U.S. team. Canada and the Arab countries are examples of players who were interested in joining the game. In fact, they are not just ordinary examples, but unique ones. Their uniqueness stems from their ideological, cultural, and geographical proximity to either adversary. Moreover, Canada and most Arab countries have strong long-term mutual relations that they want to maintain and improve, while managing the crisis. Also, their peacekeeping policies, which they have stressed since the beginning of the U.S.

accusations against Iraq and its call for a pre-emptive war, also need to be protected and maintained in an effective way. Therefore, their interest in participating in this particular game makes sense. To do so, however, they faced two major challenges or roles: 1) protecting the partner from adversarial confrontation while keeping the peace through their intermediary role in the conflict, and 2) protecting their mutual relations and friendship, through selecting better strategic options. This was not an easy mission for either side, and therefore their intervening role needed to be rational and well-calculated.

Canada made its position as opposing the attack on Iraq unless clear evidence of Iraqi dangerous actions or UN support was presented, very clear. Arab countries, through the Arab League, condemned any military actions against Iraq and refused to participate in the military confrontations, though they had done the opposite in the 1990/91 Gulf War. On this occasion, however, rational calculations in the Arab world resulted in reluctance to support an American military effort to topple Iraq's government[2]. They saw no justification this time for the invasion of Iraq, as long as it was willing to cooperate and follow the United Nations resolutions. For example, along with other Arab governments, Jordan "... repeatedly stated its opposition to a U.S.-led war against Iraq and insisted that its territory and air space would not be used by U.S. forces" (Kamal, 2003: 17).

To continue to analyze Arab and Canadian involvement or participation in the 2003 War on Iraq, let us consider the representation of more structured games. Both Canada and the Arab countries (represented in the game through the Arab League position) played the game taking the side of one team, U.S. and Iraq respectively. This does not mean that each should be obligated to its team's action(s), but rather represents its position in the confrontation. Canada has a position in confronting Iraq as a principle adversary, and a position in confronting the Arab League, which Iraq is part of. Also, the Arab League have a position in confronting the U.S. as a principle adversary, and a position in confronting Canada, a major U.S. partner. In the first position for both Canada and the Arab League, each plays an intermediary role between U.S. and Iraq, as illustrated in *Matrix 2* and *Matrix 3* in *Figure 6*. In the second position, they confront each other with a possibility of cooperation or non-cooperation, as illustrated in *Matrix 4* in *Figure 6*.

Figure 6: **Involvement of United States, Iraq, Canada, and Arab League in War on Iraq -- Chicken, Prisoners' Dilemma, and Intermediary Games**

Matrix 1: **Chicken Game**

	Iraq	
	Diplomacy	Military
Diplomacy	(3 , 3)	(<u>2</u> , <u>4</u>)
U.S.		
Military	(<u>4</u> , <u>2</u>)	(1 , 1)

Matrix 2: **Intermediary Game**

	Arab League	
	Support	Opposition
Diplomacy	(3 , 3)	(<u>2</u> , <u>4</u>)
U.S.		
Military	(4 , 1)	(1 , 2)

Matrix 3: **Intermediary Game**

	Iraq	
	Diplomacy	Military
Support	(3 , 3)	(1 , 4)
Canada		
Opposition	(<u>4</u> , <u>2</u>)	(2 , 1)

Matrix 4: **Prisoners' Dilemma**
(No Communication)

	Arab League	
	Cooperation	No
Cooperation	(3 , 3)	(1 , 4)
Canada		
No	(4 , 1)	(<u>2</u> , <u>2</u>)

Key: (*x,y*) = (payoff to U.S. or Canada, payoff to Iraq or Arab League)

4= best ; 3= next-best ; 2= next-worst ; 1= worst

Both adversaries in each game play at the same time

Nash equilibria underscored

The difference between the options of strategies for both Canada and the Arab League and those of the United States and Iraq is that they can take positions of either support or opposition. Their support and opposition can be also reflected in using diplomacy and military respectively, but it can also be reflected in various other ways, hence the selection of such terminations. In addition, the position of Canada and Iraq in what here are called *intermediary games* is another difference between *Matrix 2* and *Matrix 3*. This difference results in a change of the expected outcomes that result from the selection of the available options of strategies.

To compare these outcomes of *Matrix 2* and *Matrix 3*, it is easier to explain by comparing each to *Matrix 1*, the Chicken Game between U.S. and Iraq. In *Matrix 2*, the Arab countries, represented by the Arab League, have two options of strategies: support or oppose the U.S. The outcomes for the Arab League from opposing the U.S. are more significant, whether U.S. chooses to use diplomacy or military actions with the Arab countries. Therefore, the Arab League will stick to the opposition option. Although there is an incentive for the U.S. to choose military action to achieve its best outcome (4), it is deterred by the Arab League' opposition option which will lead to the worst outcome for the U.S. (1). Consequently, the U.S. will remain in the diplomacy position with the Arab League to keep its next-worst outcome (2). The same can be said in the Intermediary Game between Canada and Iraq. In *Matrix 3*, Canada also has two strategic options: support or oppose Iraq. The outcomes for Canada from opposing Iraq are more significant, whether Iraq chooses to use diplomacy or military actions with Canada. Therefore, Canada will stick, as in the Arab League case, to the opposition option. Although there is an incentive for Iraq to choose military action to achieve its best outcome (4), it is deterred by Canada's opposition option, which will lead to the worst outcome for Iraq (1). Consequently, Iraq will remain in the diplomacy position with Canada to keep its next-worst outcome (2). However, there is a significant difference between *Matrix 2* and *Matrix 3*. If we consider that one player can start first, there will be different interactions in the two games, but with the same results. Given that the U.S. started first in the 2x4 version of the Chicken Game, it can also have a step earlier than the Arab League in *Matrix 2*; similarly Canada can have the same in *Matrix 3*. In other words, as a result of the different position of both Canada and the Arab League in the two intermediary games, Canada and the Arab League have unequal status. Canada can start first with Iraq, but the Arab League replies to the U.S. first move. The outcomes will be similar but the interactions are different. In *Matrix 2*, if U.S. starts by taking the military action, as an incentive to get its best outcome (4), the Arab League will oppose in order to improve their outcome from the worst (1) to the next-worst (2). This will threaten the U.S. by getting its worst outcome (1), and consequently will change its strategy to diplomacy, looking for its next-worst (2). Interactions like these are known in studies of game theory as *power moves*. In *Matrix 2*, where Canada can start first by taking the opposition strategy, there will be no *power moves*, as Iraq will stick to diplomacy looking for its next-worst (2) with Canada, as a better option.

Both Canada and the Arab League confront each other, as mediators in the crisis, each representing one side. The outcomes of such confrontation are similar to those of a *Prisoners' Dilemma Game*[3]. The alternatives and outcomes arranged in *Matrix 4* in *Figure 6* illustrate this result. Both Canada and the Arab League have two strategic options: either cooperate with each other during the crisis, or do not cooperate. If both make their decisions spontaneously, without any previous communication and coordination, rational thinking suggests that each should choose not to cooperate for the sake of getting their next-worst in relations to each other (2,2), i.e., a conflictual position, lest getting into the worst outcome in case of cooperating while the adversary is not cooperating. According to the basic story of the Prisoners' Dilemma, the dilemma in the situation is obvious. Clearly both of the participants should *not cooperate* as, no matter what the other one does, each would have done better for itself in this case. However, this results in both of them getting the next-worst outcome whereas, by cooperating, they could both be better off and get their next-best outcome. If they cannot communicate with each other, they end up with a mutually undesirable solution, which could have been improved for both of them.

However, this has never happened during the 2003 War on Iraq between Canada and the Arab League, because although the rules of this game urge both players to choose not to cooperate in order to get each of their next-worst outcome, which occurs as a result of the lack or no communication between the two players, the mutual longstanding relationship between Canada and the Arab League coupled with continuous communication and coordination helped both parties to reach their next-best outcome (3,3).

> If the two participants in a non-zero sum game can agree to co-ordinate their actions, they can normally obtain some outcome which compared with others which might have occurred, is to their mutual benefit.
>
> (Nicholson, 1970: 67)

However, as Nicholson (1970: 67) warns, there are two problems involved here: 1) the question of to what degree they are able to co-ordinate their policies, which is clearly a question of how well they can indicate to each other what actions they will take; and 2) there may be several different outcomes which could be chosen, all of which are better than those occurring without co-ordination, but some of which are relatively better for one party than the other. The activity of two contending parties deciding between themselves what actions to take, when some are better for one than for the other, is called *bargaining*, and if it is done by explicit verbal communication, it is called *negotiation*. Consequently, the two problems inherent in the bargaining process are: 1) that of communication in order to co-ordinate actions appropriately, and 2) that of agreeing on what is the appropriate co-ordination of actions. Communication, Nicholson (69-70) argues, is often a mixture of explicit and implicit messages in cases where it is difficult to know whether to believe the explicit statements. Thus, Nicholson considers the business of communication in such situations to be complex, and therefore claims four categories: 1) no communication; 2) implicit communication; 3) explicit communication where there is doubt about the truth of the negotiators' statements; and 4) explicit communication where there is either adequate policing of the agreement, or faith in the word of the negotiator. In addition, there is the hybrid class of explicit communication reinforced by implicit communication.

As indicated earlier, more attention is paid to the role of the communication between players, through their media, in the explanation of the game between Canada and Arab League. As illustrated in *Figure 7*, the communication between Canada and Arab League converted the *Prisoners' Dilemma Game*, which has no communication between players, into a "modified" version of it, or what might be called a *Communication Game*. Communication[4] was the power that moved their position from a conflictual one to one of better outcomes (3,3). This compromise position of cooperation between both players serves the fundamental policy of both Canada and the Arab League in the 2003 War on Iraq, i.e., *peacekeeping*. They both find in their continuous *peacekeeping* policy the rational path to achieving their goals and obtaining better outcomes, through a hybrid class of explicit communication reinforced by implicit communication, using Nicholson' terms.

The mass media of each side have contributed to the general communication between Canada and the Arab countries during the 2003 War on Iraq. The mass media of both systems qualitatively portrayed and delivered transnational news about the same event that reflected their peacekeeping policies and their strong longstanding mutual relations. Also, while the mass media of both sides played an effective role in directing their audience's attention towards specific areas of interest consistent with the entire policy of their respective political systems, at the same time neither side neglected the nature of their mutual relations. The peacekeeping policy of each side was upheld and their prior relationship was not affected by their geographic and ideological proximity to the adversaries of the crisis.

Figure 7: **Canada and Arab League Involvement in War on Iraq -- A "Modified" Prisoners' Dilemma (Communication Game)**

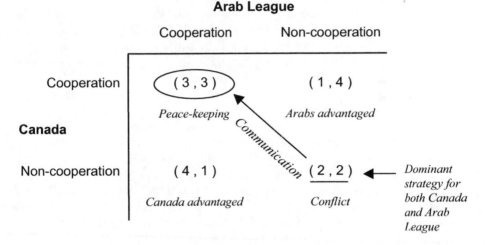

Key: (*x*,*y*) = (payoff to Canada, payoff to Arab League)

4= best ; 3= next-best ; 2= next-worst ; 1= worst

Both play at the same time

Nash equilibrium underscored

Outcomes in circle are results of communication

Peacekeeping has roots in the mutual relationship between Canada and the Arab countries. As retired Canadian Major-General E.L.M. Burns (1985: 37-38) notes, peacekeeping as it is now practiced by the United Nations, had its inception in the Suez War of 1956. Israel, France, and Britain had invaded Egypt in clear violation of their obligations under the United Nations Charter. The Canadian government decided that Canadians should not take the side of their motherlands, France and Britain, in their quarrel with Egypt.

Thus, Canada has a long and proud tradition of involvement in peacekeeping operations. Official Canadian literature, as Allen Sens (1997: 97-99) explains, rarely fails to remind the reader that Canada is the only country to have participated in virtually every U.N. peacekeeping operation since the establishment of the United Nations Truce Supervision Organization (UNTSO) in June 1948. Additionally, Canada claims a special role in the development of the peacekeeping concept; it was Lester B. Pearson who recommended the formation of a multilateral international peace and police force, UNEF, for deployment to the Suez in 1956. Moreover, the force was commanded by a Canadian, Major-General E.L.M. Burns, who was also the serving chief of staff at UNTSO. On the Arab side, Sens explains, the majority of the Arab countries also have a principled position in terms of peacekeeping reflected in their continuous efforts to resolve the Palestinian-Israeli conflict. In many cases, they have suggested that in the resolution of the Iraqi crisis lies the potential resolution to the Palestinian-Israeli conflict.

But neither of these two crises have easy solutions; their roots go deep, and involve a great deal of international "meddling." For instance, Steve Negus (2002: 10) points out that during the United States-Iraqi Crisis, the U.S. has consistently attempted to convince Egypt that Iraq is a serious threat to its national security. For example, in 1999 then Secretary of Defence William Cohen visited Egypt to try and talk Egypt into joining a regional anti-missile warning network. In 2002, the US sent one of its top officials to Egypt to talk up the Iraqi threat, and once again Egypt seems to have been less than convinced. In fact, Jansen (2002: 6) comments that Vice-President Cheney appears to have received no joy from the Arab leaders he met. The heads of state of Jordan, Egypt, Yemen, the United Arab Emirates, Saudi Arabia, Qatar, Bahrain, Kuwait and Turkey expressed firm opposition to the Administration's plans to wage war against Iraqi President Saddam Hussein. The Egyptian foreign minister Ahmad Maher, interviewed by Al-Jazeera TV channel on March 4th, 2003, said

> I think the Arab summit made a great contribution towards clarifying the requirements of peace, and demanding all parties to cooperate with those demands. . . . I feel that regardless of the situation, we should continue to work for peace until the last hour. . . . We have to do our utmost best for the results to spare Iraq and the region the negative consequences of war.

The general Arab policy in the game was to direct the Arab mass media coverage of the 2003 War on Iraq towards the achievement of desired strategic outcomes. This is reflected in the coverage of the Arab media concerning the developments that led to War on Iraq, bolstered by the obvious changes and improvement within the Arab mass media themselves. For years, the Arab world was forced to rely on national presses that were often monitored or controlled by authoritarian regimes, or alternately Western media such as the BBC, CNN, etc. However, in recent years, there has been a proliferation of Arab newspapers and satellite television stations. None of these new sources of information has been more successful nor more controversial than Al-Jazeera.

In *Al-Jazeera: How the Free Arab News Network Scooped the World and Changed the Middle East* (2002), Mohammed el-Nawawy and Adel Iskandar attempt to explain the Arab world's most independent and most controversial media. The Qatar-based satellite station is a testimony to the globalization of communications, marked by the ability of a news organization located in a small Gulf state to attract a global audience and enjoy a global impact. It emphasizes the diversity of its founders and staff as well as the financial support and surprising independence the station has enjoyed from their patron, the emir of Qatar. The most notable evidence of this come from Al-Jazeera's programming, which has included interviews with not only Arabs and Muslims but also with Israeli, American, and European guests. Its hard-hitting journalism has targeted Arab regimes as well as the Israeli and American governments. The station has addressed political, social, and religious issues that would never have been permitted by most Arab and Muslim governments. (Esposito, 2003: 316-317).

In addition to the unique role of Al-Jazeera during the 2003 War on Iraq, there have been a wide range of Arab media which were also very active in reflecting and enhancing the Arab League policy. For instance, Sherine Bahaa of the Egyptian *Al-Ahram Weekly* reported, in the newspaper's March 27th - April 2nd, 2003 issue, that outrage over the US-British War on Iraq had spilled onto Arab streets. She explained that Egypt was the launchpad for the demonstrations that were sweeping the Arab world. Yemen, Sudan, Jordan, Bahrain, Syria and Lebanon witnessed their largest demonstrations in years, which continued round the clock during the first few days of the war. The public was not only frustrated by the U.S.-British alliance against Iraq, but also by the Arabic regimes who were not using their military forces to confront the invasion. The demonstrators considered Saddam Hussein as the only Arab leader who did not cave in under American pressure, an important and vital point to Arabs. Bahaa, in the *Al-Ahram Weekly* issue of April 10th – 16th, 2003, also explained that demonstrations were no longer the only tool for Arabs to demonstrate their anger at the war; the furious public was now resorting to boycotting American and British products. She highlighted the *Agence France Presse* interview with some Saudi Arabian nationals regarding their feelings on the war, quoting one man as saying, "what is happening is breaking my heart and trampling my dignity. The Iraqi people will never forgive us and we will never forgive ourselves for failing to help them," as he watched scenes of death and destruction in Iraq continuously broadcast by Arab satellite TV stations.

Aziza Sami, also of the *Al-Ahram Weekly*, analyzed the Egyptian press[5] coverage of the US-led war against Iraq in the newspaper's April 3rd - 9th, 2003 issue. The Egyptian press highlighted the stiffer than expected resistance of Iraqi troops, and the change this created in Anglo-American military strategy. The rising number of civilian casualties was also given prominence, with many photo-spreads. Several editorials spoke of the political cost the war would entail, notably by promoting terrorism and producing further alienation within the Arab world towards the US and Britain. Lauding the unexpected performance of Iraqi troops during the invasion, the weekly newspaper *Al-Arabi,* mouthpiece of the Arab Nasserist Party, led with a front-page banner in bold red, reading "Baghdad, Fortress of Lions". For its part, the independent weekly *Al-Usbou'* declared, "Confusion", with the paper's editor-in-chief, Mustafa Bakry, writing two articles, "Signs of Victory and Divine Anger" and "Bush is in Shock, and Rumsfeld looks for excuses". In an interview with the *Al-Ahali,* a weekly newspaper issued by the left-wing opposition Tagammu Party, Iraqi Foreign Minister Nagui Sabri was quoted as saying that "the spirit of the Iraqi people remains high." *Al-Ahali*'s front page also featured a photograph of the award-winning American film director Michael Moore, together with his now famous phrase: "Shame on you, Bush!" as the caption.

In addition, the Arab websites have participated intensively. *ArabicNews.Com*, a well-known and active website serving Arab readers, has made a powerful contribution to the anti-war campaign. It announced on March 3rd, 2003, what resolutions had been reached at the 15th Arab Summit held in Sharm El-Sheikh of Egypt on March 1, 2003. Fundamentally, the Arab Summit rejected any military action against Iraq. The Summit rejected any threat to security and territorial integrity of any Arab state, calling for the need to solve the Iraqi crisis by peaceful means in the framework of international legitimacy. Arab League Secretary General Amr Moussa, while declaring the Arab Summit resolutions, indicated that the Arab leaders concurred that a peaceful solution to the Iraq crisis should be found. The final statement of the Summit reiterates outright rejection against striking

Iraq or jeopardizing the security and stability of any Arab state on the grounds that this would be considered a threat against Arab national security. The statement called on all countries of the world to back the Arab efforts aimed at avoiding war, in particular by encouraging Iraq's compliance with UN Security Council resolution 1441/2002. It requested the UN weapons inspectors be given enough time to complete their missions objectively in Iraq, and stressed the UN Security Council's responsibility over keeping Iraq and its people intact, maintaining Iraq's independence and territorial integrity, and asserting guarantees for the security, independence and territorial integrity of Iraq's neighbors.

On March 19th, 2003, *ArabicNews.Com* published a speech by Saudi Arabia's King Fahd Bin Abdul Aziz, which was read by Crown Prince Abdullah and defined four main pillars that can be considered as the broad lines for the Saudi foreign policy regarding Iraq. Fahd said in his speech

> Saudi Arabia at any rate will not take part in the war against sisterly Iraq, and our armed forces, under any condition will not enter one inch of the Iraqi territories ... we expect the war to end as soon as UN resolution 1441 on dismantling mass destruction weapons is implemented. We categorically reject affecting Iraq's unity and territorial integrity, wealth, internal security or (for Iraq) to be militarily occupied. . . . [T]he extraordinary conditions which has been besieging the crisis for 12 years, make it imperative on us not to join an uncalculated adventure that makes the safety of our people and homeland vulnerable. . . . [Regretfully] our efforts and the efforts of our brothers and friends who desire peace did not reach the awaiting results.

The next day, *ArabicNews.Com* highlighted the announcements of Amr Moussa opposing the war. He stressed the importance of the Arab world's complete adherence to the Arab Summit decision to abstain from extending any facilities to the American forces threatening Iraqi unity, safety and lands. Moussa warned against the failure of the world order in case of the declaration of a unilateral American war against Iraq. He also said "it is sad that an Arab nation and people are coming under a military attack that does not take into consideration the civilians . . . we are very sorry and angry." Commenting on the start of military attacks on Iraq, Moussa called on the UN Security Council to shoulder its responsibilities, as a body in charge of keeping international peace and security, and to move fast to halt the war and the aggression on Iraq. Also, he referred to intensive consultations with Arab foreign ministers and their delegates to the Arab

League to take the necessary steps, adding that the league's ministerial meeting will convene within the coming few days.

On the Canadian side, the media also participated in reducing the tense tone in news about Iraq, by reflecting on the importance of keeping the peace in the Middle East region, and emphasizing the strong mutual Arab-Canadian relations. For example, Oliver Moore of *The Globe and Mail*[6], on December 6th, 2002, reported on the Iraqi insistence, through the announcements of the Iraqi Ambassador to the United Nations Mohammed al-Douri, that everything related to the weapons of mass destruction had been destroyed. Moore explained that the Iraqi government was "tired of repeating 'again and again' that it is not breaking any U.N. resolutions". Mohammed al-Douri said

> Everything has been destroyed and we have no intention to do that again . . . Iraq is clean of any kind mass destruction offences. ... We did provide all confirmation they need. ... Inspectors are now in Europe, we are co-operating with them, they have the full access anywhere in Iraq. If Americans have this evidence, they have to tell the inspectors. ... We are saying they will find nothing.

To bring Canadian's attention to a few of the economic consequences of the U.S. invasion to Iraq, particularly on the Middle East, and further, to argue that the reality of the Middle East is more complex than it has been represented in the Western media, Paul Stanway of *The Toronto Sun* wrote on October 14th, 2003:

> We're encouraged to believe that the U.S. invasion of Iraq has been an unmitigated disaster, a horrible mistake by Washington that has made the situation of the world's most politically volatile region worse, rather than better ... [T]he invasion had actually pulled Middle East financial markets out of a multi-year slump ... Year-to-date returns on the Saudi SE index (equivalent to Canada's TSE or New York's Dow Jones) are up a healthy 64%. Jordan's General stock index is up 41%. Qatar's DEM index is up almost 60%, while in the Persian Gulf Emirates the General Index of stock prices is up 26%. But the champs of the Middle East's market rebound are Egypt and Kuwait. The Kuwait stock index is up 78%, while the Egyptian CSE30 is up an astonishing 90%!

Glenn McGillivray of *The Toronto Star* on March 28th, 2003, said that Canada was right to stay out of Iraq because going in would have made a mockery of everything that this country is about, and has been about almost from the beginning. On March 24th, 2003, *The Toronto Star* had conveyed then-Deputy Prime Minister John Manley's announcement that

> Canada has no intention of joining coalition forces in the fight to topple Iraqi dictator Saddam Hussein. . . . I think we've been very clear in our position. . . . We're not participating, but certainly we hope it ends quickly with a minimum number of casualties, if possible, with good results for the coalition.

The Toronto Star on October 5th, 2003, gave considerable attention to Arab League Secretary General Amr Moussa's visit to Canada. The newspaper pointed out that before his current position, which took effect in May, 2001, he was known for his active role as an intermediary between the Israelis and the Palestinians during his 10-year tenure as Egypt's foreign minister. It claimed that he was heading off to face the challenges posed by the uncertain future of Iraq and the deterioration of the Middle East peace process. Moussa, the paper reported, when answering the questions about the purpose of his trip to Canada and his opinions about Canada's role in the United States-Iraqi Crisis, said that the first purpose of his visit was:

> To strengthen the relations between the Arab people and Canada. We have a deep appreciation for Canada and her well-considered positions vis-à-vis so many issues, . . . Canada is the author, or the godfather, if you will, of the peacekeeping policies in the world and these policies rest on the sovereign right of a country to call for them to be brought into that country. Anything short of this is joining the occupation and I do not think any Arab . . . country will do that.

THE TRUTH GAME:
A MEDIA CHALLENGE

> By dropping some of the dispassionate mystique around editorial judgment and by providing viewers with some insightful access to the subjective news-making process, we can open up a space for constructive debate about one of the monumental difficulties journalists do face: just how do you represent a situation in which there is a multiplicity of 'truths'?
>
> (Niblock, 2003: 376)

Sarah Niblock (2003) argues that the 2003 War on Iraq has had a great influence on war reporting. She admits that embedding journalists has enormous implications for accuracy and impartiality. There is plenty of evidence that journalists facing round-the-clock pressures accepted the military line without question, such as a blanket reporting of the easy collapse of opposition in the Iraqi port of Um Qsar. However, she insists that no constraint justifies inaccuracy—the principal moral foundation for journalists is scrupulous adhesion to truth out of respect for the audience. She suggests that much of the coverage of the war was based on speculation, and that we were subjected to many ill-judged turns of phrase in the supposedly balanced broadcast arena. "But if we stand back a little from individual examples and study the overall picture, we have seen considerably less self-aggrandizement by media players after this war, and the beginnings of an acknowledgement that news judgment has to be more than the gut, split-second reaction of the seasoned 'hack'" (377). She quotes Ivor Yorke, the respected trainer of BBC correspondents, who said: "these days broadcast journalists say too much and don't let the pictures tell their own story. Nowhere is this more the case than in wartime when information-hungry rolling news watchers want regular bites of new data to help the story unfold" (377).

In fact, the mass media in the 2003 War on Iraq have played a different role than the one played in the 1990/91 Gulf War, even though both arose from one crisis—the United States-Iraqi Crisis. The United States military not only allowed but also, more significantly, *facilitated* the mass media coverage of the 2003 War on Iraq and the concurrent follow-up of its developments. It also provided access to information about the developments of events. This is curious in contrast with the 1990/91 Gulf War when it imposed a very high degree of censorship on the coverage and access of mass media. This may be attributed to the different strategies the United States used in each war.

> When the United States becomes embroiled in a war, both the press and the military have their jobs to do. The military's job is to fight the battles and defeat the enemy, an undertaking that is— without argument—vital. The press has an important job also: to keep the American people informed about the war and how it is being conducted.
>
> (van Tuyll, 2002: 229)

It became apparent that informing its citizens was not the only function that the U.S. government wanted the media to hold. The *Christian*

Science Monitor's Daniel Schorr, on March 28, 2003, explains that the Iraq war and a revolution in communications technology may have opened the way to reconciliation between the American military and the American news media. He shows that, in planning for the invasion of Iraq, the Pentagon decided to make the news media an offer they would find hard to refuse—a front row seat at the battleground. Some 500 news people were offered the opportunity to be "embedded" in fighting units, witnessing what the warriors witnessed for instantaneous transmission to America. Frequently live on camera, the reporters were given a vivid opportunity to become the hero journalists of the war. However dramatic the pictures, they were still only depicting a small part of the war—"slices of the war," as Secretary of Defense Rumsfeld termed it. But they tended to make the combat reporters true comrades-in-arms. And, if at times these reporters were asked to withhold their location and their movements, it was generally accepted as part of the package. Schorr explains that the new-age-war live coverage presents new problems of professional ethics about how far to accept official dictation. On one occasion, a dozen American soldiers were captured near a Euphrates River bridge. The Arab Al-Jazeera network broadcast some grim scenes showing dead soldiers and other scenes of soldiers being interrogated. The tape was available to American networks, but most of them complied with urgent Pentagon requests to withhold broadcast out of regard for the relatives who were not yet aware of what had happened to their loved ones. Suddenly live coverage had become something more than a video game. Schorr claims that Matt Drudge's obvious question, "If anchormen and others in the media have viewed it, why can't the average citizen?" is one of many professional questions bound to arise in this era of Live from the Battlefront, and most significantly confirms that there is no easy answer for such a question.

> With America and Britain announcing new military deployments almost daily, tension over what looks like a remorseless march to war is also not surprising. That march, and many of the words, are also tactical, however: they are designed to put pressure on Saddam Hussein in the hope either that his nerve will break or that others—Iraqis, or neighbors—will decide that he must be got rid of in order to avert war. That psychological pressure looks well orchestrated and is being well executed.
> *The Economist* — (January 25th, 2003: 12)

Knowing that the Iraqi leader feared a revolt from within more than anything else, U.S. forces, Kitfield (2003: 891) explains, maintained an aggressive psychological-operations campaign of radio broadcasts and leaflet drops to persuade Iraqi forces to abandon a leader who had always reinforced his rule with fear rather than loyalty. Saddam's greatest hope was to make the campaign to unseat him so bloody and destructive, and his propaganda campaign so effective, that world opinion would turn decisively against the United States and force Washington to halt the campaign. However, Kitfield argues, the Pentagon attempted to counter that potential with the unprecedented and somewhat risky strategy of embedding more than 500 reporters with U.S. forces, in essence enlisting the Fourth Estate of the Western world to provide the truth from the ground.

However, questioning such truth is crucial. It is a fundamental function for this chapter as it builds on Chapter 5 to examine one example of the major principles of the journalistic codes of ethics, telling the truth. In essence, I argue here that rational thinking through use of game theory helps to understand and explore the advantage of being obligated by ethical principles of journalism. The problematic of Chapter 5 called for guarantees, or at least, internal motivators for media decision-makers to push their journalistic practices towards ethical conduct during situations where conduct is frequently unethical. It is suggested here that rational performance of journalists, editors, managers, and owners entails them being obligated to adhere to the major principles of codes of ethics, as a key condition for achieving the goal of benefiting all parties in times of international crises. As justification, this chapter explains how truth telling, as one example (the same can be applied to accuracy, and other major principles of codes of ethics), is fundamental in achieving *goodness* and peacefully managing an international crisis or winning a game.

When modeling the verification problem between superpowers in his *Superpower games: Applying game theory to superpower conflict* (1985), Steven Brams introduced a simple two-person, nonconstant-sum (non-zero-sum) game of imperfect information played between a *signaler* (S) and a *detector* (D)—The Truth Game. In this game, Brams (1985: 117-123) explains, the signaler can either tell the truth or lie, and the detector can ascertain the strategy choice of the signaler and choose to believe or not believe the choice s/he detects. If the signaler wants to hide the truth and the detector wants to discover it, sometimes, paradoxically, *both* the detector and the signaler can do better when the detector completely ignores, rather than relies on, her/his detection equipment. However, in general, the detector should pay *selective attention* to the signal s/he detects to maximize her/his expected payoff by either *inducing* the signaler to be truthful or *guaranteeing* herself an expected payoff whatever the signaler does (tells the truth or lies). Whether the detector chooses an optimal *inducement* or *guarantee* strategy, it will always be mixed (randomized) if her/his detection equipment is not perfect. Similarly, the signaler has her/his choice of these two qualitatively different strategies to either *induce* the detector to believe her/his signal or *guarantee* her/himself an expected payoff whatever the detector does (believes or does not believe). The Truth Game is represented by Brams, as shown in *Figure 8*, based on strict ordinal rankings of the outcomes by the two players that satisfy specified primary and secondary goals. Then, assuming particular cardinal utilities/payoffs consistent with these rankings, Brams illustrates a number of propositions about optimal mixed inducement and guarantee strategies on the part of each player that hold for the Truth Game generally.

Figure 8: **The Truth Game**

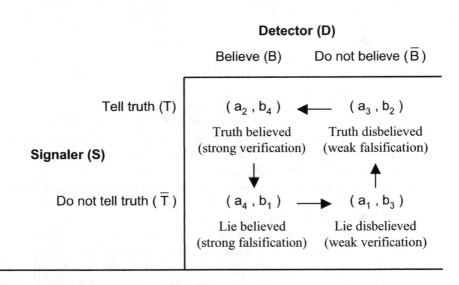

Key: (a_i, b_j) = (payoff to S, payoff to D)

a_4, b_4 = best payoffs; a_3, b_3 = next-best payoffs;

a_2, b_2 = next-worst payoffs; a_1, b_1 = worst payoffs

Arrows indicate cyclical preferences over payoffs

Assume that S must choose between telling the truth (T) and lying (T̄) and, after S has made this choice, D must then decide to believe her/him

(B) or not ($\overline{\text{B}}$), i.e., their choices are not simultaneous. Yet, though S is assumed to choose prior to D, this game cannot be modeled as one of sequential play with perfect information, because Brams assumes that D cannot tell for certain whether S was truthful or not. Thus, D cannot respond to S's strategy by always choosing her/his better strategy (believe or not believe) associated with S's prior strategy choice (be truthful or lie). Since D is unsure which strategy S chose, the Truth Game is technically a *game of imperfect information,* though both players are assumed to have complete information about the payoffs. Assume these payoffs are cardinal utilities, where a_4 and b_4 are the best outcomes for S and D, respectively; a_1 and b_1 are the worst.

Implicit in the rankings of the outcomes by S and D are the following goals. Each has two goals—primary and secondary. S's primary goal: *wants* to *hide* the truth or lack thereof (two best outcomes off main diagonal), while the secondary goal: *prefers* to be believed. D's primary goal: *wants* to *discover* the truth or lack thereof (two best outcomes on main diagonal), while the secondary goal: *prefers* S to be truthful. The primary and secondary goals of each player *completely* specify their ordering of outcomes from best to worst: yes/no answers for each player and each goal automatically rank the four cells of a 2 x 2 game.

In S's case, the primary goal establishes that he/she/it prefers outcomes *off the main diagonal,* where he/she/it lies and is believed (a_4) or tells the truth and is not believed (a_3). In either case, S succeeds in hiding the truth, whereas *on the main diagonal* the truth is discovered, either because S tells the truth and is believed (a_2) or lies and is not believed (a_1). The secondary goal establishes that, between the outcomes *on* and *off the main diagonal,* S prefers those associated with D's believing (first column: a_4, a_2) over not believing (second column: a_3, a_1).

In D's case, the primary goal says that he/she/it prefers outcomes *on the main diagonal* (b_4 and b_3), where he/she/it succeeds in discovering the truth, to those *off the main diagonal* (b_2 and b_1), where D is foiled in his/her/its attempt to uncover the truth. The secondary goal says that, between the outcomes *on* and *off the main diagonal,* D prefers those associated with S's being truthful (first row: b_4, b_2) over those associated with S's lying (second row: b_3, b_1).

It is worth noting that as a hide/discover-the-truth game, with a secondary emphasis on S's desire to be believed and D's desire that S be truthful, the Truth Game enables one not only to distinguish *verification* (main-diagonal outcomes) from *falsification* (off-diagonal outcomes), but also it suggests a *strong* and *weak* distinction in each of these main categories. Thus, Brams considers verification stronger when one believes the truth than when one disbelieves a lie, because *the truth* is still unclear in the latter case. Similarly, falsification seems stronger when a lie is believed than when the truth is disbelieved, because disbelief in the truth indicates that one has missed the truth but not necessarily that one has been hoodwinked into believing a falsehood.

Also, it is worth noting that despite the fact that the primary goals of the two players are diametrically opposed in the Truth Game, the game is not one of total conflict: *both* players do better at (a_2,b_4) than at (a_1,b_3), so what one player *wins* the other does not necessarily *lose*. Because the payoffs to the two players are greater at (a_2,b_4) than at (a_1,b_3) the Truth Game is not constant-sum but variable-sum and, therefore, one of partial conflict. In addition, the fact that (a_2,b_4) is better for both players than (a_1,b_3), and there is not another outcome better for at least one player and not worse for the other than (a_2,b_4), means that (a_2,b_4) is *Pareto-superior*, whereas (a_1,b_3) is *Pareto-inferior*.

In fact, there is no stability in the Truth Game, as the arrows indicating cyclical preferences over the four outcomes in *Figure 8* make evident. S can do immediately better by departing, in the directions shown by the vertical arrows, from (a_2,b_4) to (a_4,b_1) and from (a_1,b_3) to (a_3,b_2). Also, D can do immediately better by departing, in the directions shown by the horizontal arrows, from (a_4,b_1) to (a_1,b_3) and from (a_3,b_2) to (a_2,b_4). Given that one player always has an incentive to depart from every outcome, no outcome is a Nash equilibrium, from which neither player would have an incentive to depart unilaterally. Neither does this game have a nonmyopic equilibrium. However, if D could predict S's strategy choice with certainty and if S knew this, the game would have an equilibrium if it were played sequentially: S would choose T and D would respond with B; each would do worse by departing from these strategies.

If the mass media take the signaler position in the truth game, as illustrated in *Figure 9*, it is a rational choice that they will tell the truth in order to achieve their safer outcome (the next-worst) and avoid the possibility of getting the worst outcome, while they also participate in allowing their audiences to get their best outcome. Adding the social responsibility principle to this game confirms the rationality of that choice if that principle is one of their objectives.

In the truth game between the mass media and their audiences, the mass media face the challenge of telling the truth. They must choose between telling the truth and lying when making decisions regarding their content, and after they have made their choice, their audiences must then decide to believe their content or not.

Each player here has two goals—primary and secondary—when ranking their outcomes. The mass media's primary goal is *wants to hide* the truth or lack thereof (two best outcomes *off main diagonal*), while the secondary goal is *prefers* to be believed. The audiences' primary goal is *wants to discover* the truth or lack thereof (two best outcomes *on main diagonal*), while the secondary goal is *prefers* the mass media to be truthful.

Figure 9: **Mass Media and the Challenge of Telling the Truth to Audiences**

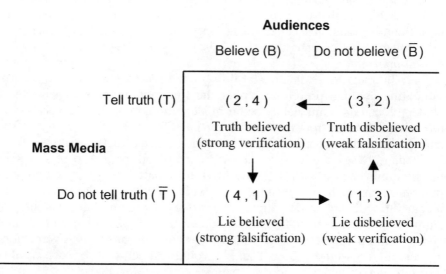

Key: (x,y)= (payoff to Mass Media, payoff to Audiences)

4= best; 3= next-best; 2= next-worst; 1= worst

Arrows indicate cyclical preferences over payoffs

Given the fact that this game is not one of total conflict, *both* players do better at (2,4) than at (1,3), that is, it is better for both the mass media and audiences that the mass media tell the truth and audiences believe it than the mass media not tell the truth nor do the audiences believe it. In other words, truth to be believed is better than lies to be disbelieved because the former is strong verification while the latter is weak verification. In addition, the fact that (2,4) is better for both players than (1,3), and there is not another outcome better for at least one player and not worse for the other than (2,4), i.e., *Pareto-superior*, means that this is the best outcome that the mass media should work for, given that they start first.

Because there is no stability in this game, the mass media can do immediately better by departing, in the directions shown by the vertical arrows in *Figure 9*, from (2,4) to (4,1) and from (1,3) to (3,2). Also, audiences can do immediately better by departing, in the directions shown by the horizontal arrows, from (4,1) to (1,3) and from (3,2) to (2,4). However, if audiences could predict the mass media's strategy choice with certainty and if the mass media knew this, the game would have an equilibrium. If it were played sequentially: the mass media would choose T and audiences would respond with B; but each would do worse by departing from these strategies. In other words, there is a risk for the mass media of not telling the truth as the audiences can disbelieve their lies and consequently the media will get their worst outcome, while if the mass media tell the truth the audiences will seek their best outcome by believing them.

This chapter concludes by providing the media decision-makers with internal motivation to tell the truth, thereby following one of the major journalistic ethical principles, that is based on their recognition that rational thinking will lead to achieving their desired goals and help them to practice their responsible role in society. Therefore, the significance of game theory becomes apparent for media decision-makers. This is not only because of the latest explanation given here of the rationality of adherence to ethical and responsible conduct, but also because throughout this chapter it has been demonstrated that the rationality of game theory in analyzing various conflictual situations during an international political crisis is vital for the media to position themselves in situations, as well as to recognize the available choices and their subsequent outcomes in order to be able to compare these to their goals and consequently work towards more desired outcomes. To this end, game theory, along with its prescriptive nature and its rational thinking, forms a fundamental part of the composition of the suggested theoretical model. The following chapter builds on what we have learned here and in previous chapters, to outline the theoretical basis for the model that I present in this book. As such, Chapter 9 will synthesize a group of roots of theoretical threads that then work as inputs to the structure of the model explained in Chapter 10.

NOTES

1. The situations and decisions of the Arab League rather than individual or group of Arab countries are used here in discussing or analyzing the Arab involvement in the United States-Iraqi Crisis. This is because the individual Arab countries had various differing situations and decisions regarding the crisis and its conflictual situations. Furthermore, the Arab League represents the situations and decisions of the majority of Arab countries, and as a result is more representative and useful for this discussion.

2. Telhami (2002) illustrates some reasons behind the strategic reluctance of states in the Gulf to support an American-led war on Iraq. First, they feared the possible disintegration of Iraq, or continued instability emanating from Iraq, and they did not believe that American assurances to the contrary were credible. They saw the task of maintaining Iraq's territorial integrity and preventing meddling by other states to be potentially overwhelming. Second, even if the United States committed to a sustained presence in Iraq and to the deployment of the necessary military, political, and economic resources to assure Iraq's stability, many of Iraq's neighbors, and others in the region, feared a possible American military/political dominance that would then include Iraq in a way that altered the strategic picture to their disadvantage. Therefore, most Arab states did not see Iraq as posing enough of a serious threat to them to warrant a war that could significantly alter the regional environment and present them with hard choices internally and externally. Third, and most significantly, was their concern over public opinion. Although Arab states remain very powerful in their domestic control, no state can fully ignore the public sentiment in the era of the information revolution. Certainly, they face a public pressure that is sympathetic to Iraq's efforts in general. Thus, they saw Iraq as victim, not as aggressor.

3. The basic story of the Prisoners' Dilemma runs as follows. The police pick up two men in possession of guns. Though they are doing nothing at the time, the police have a strong suspicion they were earlier involved in an armed robbery, but cannot prove it. Therefore, the two prisoners are taken into separate rooms and each is made the following offer, in the knowledge that the other is being made the same offer: If you confess to the armed robbery and your partner does not, then we will speak up for you in court and you will get only one year in prison. The obverse, if you do not confess but your partner does, you will bear the brunt of the punishment and get ten years. If you confess, and your rival also confesses, our plea for leniency will carry less weight and you will get five years. However, if you do not confess and your partner also does not confess, you will not be convicted

for the robbery, but you will both get two years for carrying arms (Nicholson, 1970: 60-66). For more about "Prisoners' Dilemma" see: (Mackie, 1977: 115-118).

4. Littlejohn (2002: 256-257) discusses three advantages of direct communication between the two players in the *Prisoners' Dilemma Game*. First, as communication is symbolic and does not have the actual consequences of the real move, it is, therefore, a way to explore an idea without actually acting on it, which might result in negative consequences. Also, as communication changes the probability of moves, it may reduce competitiveness between the conflicting parties. In addition, communication may help change one of the player's orientations toward the problem or what s/he wants to do.

5. In the area of media production, the Egyptian press is taking the lead among other news agencies in the Middle East and Africa. "Cairo is the largest publishing center in the Arab world and also in Africa. It is home to 17 dailies, 30 weeklies, and more than 30 other publications that publish less frequently. The environment for publishing in Egypt is quite competitive" (Ogan, 1995: 192). The Middle East News Agency (MENA), which is located in Egypt, is defined by Hachten (1996: 38) as one of the most effective second-tier agencies after two great news organizations—DPA in Germany and Kyodo in Japan. "MENA has offices and correspondents in all Arab capitals as well as Paris, London, Belgrade, and Washington. And at home, MENA covers all the provincial capitals of Egypt with its services and correspondents" (Abdel Gawad, 1978: 186).

6. "*The Globe and Mail*, which has been called 'the jewel in the crown of Canadian newspapers,' is the only truly national newspaper in Canada and has long been recognized as one of Canada's leading newspapers of record" (Strentz & Keel, 1995: 365). Soderland, Krause and Price reported that "among those editors who evaluated Canada's newspapers on the dimension of quality of international reporting (N= 42), 71% named *The Globe and Mail* as the best in the country" (1991: 5).

IV.   PROMISE

CHAPTER 9

Interweavement:

A Theoretical Foundation

Because of the need for the rational and responsible conduct of the media in decision-making during times of crises and conflicts, in this chapter I call for the connection of the four elements of the theoretical framework, examined in the previous chapters, into a comprehensive body that can serve as a basis for the model I suggest in this book. The concept of *Interweavement* is a central locus through which the interactions among major theoretical themes are represented in a dynamic ideational architecture, illustrating the possible mutual relationships and creating a foundation for the suggested model.

As a pivotal relationship in the suggested model, the convergence of ethics and rational thinking is investigated in order to show how rational thinking and responsible conduct are two fundamental weights for the effectiveness of the model. An investigation of the philosophical origins of the ethical decision-making process is provided as a useful step in the context of preparing the basis of the model. Also, the use of models in decision-making is discussed before showing the importance of modeling to the process. Then I distinguish between selected models that are relevant to the topic of this book, in order to defend the adoption of the rational choice approach. Finally, the necessary step of recognizing and synthesizing a group of roots of theoretical threads from the major frameworks discussed and analyzed in this book is taken. These roots work as inputs to the structure of the model that are explained in detail in the following chapter.

INTERWEAVEMENT: BUILDING A BASIS FOR A MODEL

At this point, the book arrives at the key stage in the structuring of the model, specifically building its basis. To do this, this chapter will draw on four major fields of the theoretical framework examined in the previous chapters in order to create the theoretical basis for the model, the "Crisis Decision-Making Model for Media Rational Responsibility" (CD-MMM-RR), or what is here called the $CD\_M^3\_R^2$.

Throughout the discussions in the previous chapters, it became quite evident that the topic of the book benefits from the fields of crisis management, decision-making, mathematics, and communication. Reviewing the literature concerning the relationships among the four major theoretical frameworks not only confirms (or at least indicates the investigation of) the existence of the architecturally illustrated bi-lateral and tri-lateral relationships but also proves the absence of reference to such a quadri-lateral relationship. Thus, I present the quadri-lateral relationship, which serves as the theoretical basis of the book's model, here as an introduction to the model itself. This chapter will also show why such a quadri-lateral arrangement is an essential part of the model's framework; in short, because it either benefits, or is fed from: 1) an understanding of the nature of crisis management (C) and its strategies and techniques; 2) the dynamic of the decision-making process (DM) which itself draws from two major decision theories—the mathematical and behavioral; 3) the idea of modeling (M) real situations and the application of game theory, a pure branch of mathematics, to crisis; 4) ethics and the social responsibility theory (R) of the media (M); and finally, 5) the concept of rationality (R) which itself has various applications.

The analysis of this quadri-lateral arrangement is represented here in a dynamic ideational architecture illustrating the possible mutual relationships among the four major theoretical frameworks. The basic idea expressed by this architecture is that friction and interaction between theoretical frameworks happen in a dynamic way. The architecture, as shown in *Figure 10*, consists of four major dynamic, not static, axes: mathematical theories, communication theories, crisis management, and decision-making. Each axis moves to the left and/or to the right. The figure takes the shape of vertical (90-degree angle) relationships between two double axes; that is, each double axis crosses the other at a 45-degree angle.

Figure 10: **Ideational Architectural Relationships in the Interweavement of the Fields in the Crisis Decision-Making Model for Media Rational Responsibility (CD_M^3_R^2)**

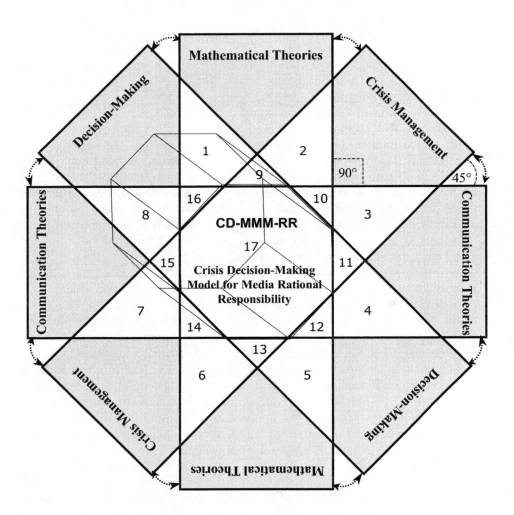

However, it is important to note that this figure does not reflect the actual relationships between axes, since the relationships could take other angles i.e., the four axes could be identical, every double could be identical, three could be identical and one take any angle, and so on; it is shown in a simplified form here for the ease of understanding. The architecture also intertwines the mathematical and communication theories in one double axis, and the crisis management and decision-making theories in another, again for clarification. But the axes are actually free moving and so can intertwine in other relationships. What is not clearly obvious in *Figure 10* is that the combination of any two, three, or four axes results in an interweavement[1] rather than an intertwinement. (To visualize this relationship, it might be helpful to think of a piece of woven cloth.) That is, one part or group of parts from each axis could interlink or intertwine, in various ways, with each other rather than with the whole axis. As such, it is a relationship of interweavement rather than intertwinement.

The motion of the four axes results in 17 areas of meeting or interweaving. Ideationally illustrated in *Figure 10*, every two areas are a result of the interweavement of either two or three axes—bi-lateral or tri-lateral areas. This results in four bi-laterals, four tri-laterals, and one quadri-lateral, combination of areas. The single quadri-lateral area is number 17 where the four axes could be interwoven. The figure takes an *octagonal* shape due to the ideational architecture which defines vertical relationships between the two double axes; this quadri-lateral area could take numerous other shapes, however, as long the axes are moving. The shape of this area when the four axes fully interweave is a square.

The interweavement can be described in more detail as follows. Mathematical and communication theories intertwine in dynamic double axis 1, with crisis management and decision-making in dynamic double axis 2. Areas 1 and 5 constitute possible bi-lateral locations for mathematics and decision-making to meet; similarly, (2 and 6) mathematics and crisis management, (3 and 7) communication and crisis management, and (4 and 8) communication and decision-making. Areas 9 and 13 constitute possible tri-lateral locations for mathematics, decision-making and crisis management to meet; similarly, (11 and 15) communication, crisis management and decision-making; (10 and 14) mathematics, communication and crisis management; and (12 and 16) communication, mathematics and decision-making. The quadri-lateral area number 17, where the four axes interweave, is where the basis of the model, woven by threads from the four theoretical frameworks, is situated.

Before determining the theoretical threads that will feed the model to be discussed in Chapter 10, in this chapter I first describe the interaction of the relationships of the interweavement, i.e., the two basic dynamic axes, the four bi-lateral relationships, and the four tri-lateral relationships, in order to lead the discussion towards its main focus on the quadri-lateral area as the root of the theoretical threads that constitutes the basis of the model. As a subsequent and crucial point of the discussion, I then explain in detail the convergence between two major weights (or forces) that constitute the balance in the model—ethics and rational thinking. This is further developed when the discussion moves to the explanation of rational and responsible models of decision-making.

INTERWEAVEMENT: REPRESENTATION OF INTERACTIONS

The interaction of the relationships of the interweavement is represented as follows: First, there are two basic dynamic double axes—Dynamic Axis 1: Mathematics and Communication, and Dynamic Axis 2: Crisis Management and Decision-Making. Second, there are four bi-lateral relationships—Bi-lateral (1+5): Mathematics and Decision-Making, Bi-lateral (2+6): Mathematics and Crisis Management, Bi-lateral (3+7): Communication and Crisis Management, and Bi-lateral (4+8): Communication and Decision-Making. Third, there are four tri-lateral relationships—Tri-lateral (9+13): Mathematics, Decision-Making and Crisis Management, Tri-lateral (11+15): Communication, Crisis Management and Decision-Making, Tri-lateral (10+14): Mathematics, Communication and Crisis Management, and Tri-lateral (12+16): Communication, Mathematics and Decision-Making. Finally, there is only one quadri-lateral area (17) that receives theoretical threads from the four frameworks. Indeed, I argue here that at the very least the quadri-lateral area and, perhaps even, the whole idea of the interweavement as presented in this book have not been previously studied in academic literature.

In the interaction of the interweavement, the two dynamic double axes are mathematics and communication as one, and crisis management and decision-making as the other (discussed in Chapters 3, 2, and 1 respectively). Indeed, as has been shown in Chapter 3, the field of mathematics has been connected to knowledge and the social sciences in general and communication in particular through the work of major scholars and philosophers. The conditions for connecting the two double axes together arise when the need exists for rational and responsible media decisions in a crisis, i.e., when the media decision-makers are unable to achieve such required performance of balanced decisions and need help. Obviously, during crisis management the process of decision-making is very significant.

However, the purpose of discussing this process here is to remind the reader of a few aspects of each relationship in order to demonstrate their relevance to the topic at hand. Thus, in relation to communication, mathematics can be effectively used as a helpful research tool, and in itself may be considered as a special way of communicating. For instance, as we have seen, game theory, as one pure branch of mathematics, can be intertwined with communication in order to achieve rational thinking.

On the other dynamic double axis, the process of crisis management is essentially based on decision-making, especially when structuring conflicts and crises in the form of games. In return, decision-making is deeply affected by the nature of the crisis situation and strategies of crisis management. Indeed, it may be helpful to remind the reader that the original Greek meaning of the word "crisis" was "to decide", as Bokhari (1997) told us in Chapter 2. This relationship can be better seen through the process of crisis decision-making, and how it is different from, and more significant than, routine decision-making. The influence of crisis on decision-making is an issue of great concern and interest to many theorists. Deterrence theorists, for instance, presuppose rational and predictable decision processes, particularly during intense and protracted international crises. The theory of nuclear deterrence, according to Holsti (1978), assumes that threats not only effectively influence an adversary's behavior, but also that they will enhance calculation, control and caution while inhibiting irresponsibility and risk-taking. Holsti asserts that "these observations appear to confirm the conventional wisdom that in crisis decision-making necessity is indeed the mother of invention" (1978: 39). Williams (1976) suggests that crisis decision-making presents distinct advantages over ordinary or routine foreign policymaking, and discusses how the effects of surprise, shortness of time and elevated threat of the crisis tend to be functional rather than disruptive.

Furthermore, I identify four bi-lateral relationships in the interweavement: 1) Mathematics and Decision-Making (Bi-lateral 1+5); 2) Mathematics and Crisis Management (Bi-lateral 2+6); 3) Communication and Crisis Management (Bi-lateral 3+7); and 4) Communication and Decision-Making (Bi-lateral 4+8).

First, for mathematics and decision-making (Bi-lateral 1+5), given the fact that the game theory approach to decision-making offers a mathematical dimension, and given that decision-makers or game players are human beings, behavioral theory is also involved. So, what I describe here is a relationship between the decision-making process represented by behavioral decision theory and mathematics represented by game theory. To highlight this relationship, the notion of rationality in both theories, as explained in Chapter 3, provides a suitable link. Lee's (1971) notion that behavioral decision theory has been largely concerned with the hypothesis of general rationality, and is particularly concerned with human behavior in relation to decisions, merges normative and descriptive theories into one. That is, as long as the hypothesis of general rationality states that people "do" make the decisions they "should" make, concerns of both normative decision theory, which pertains to the choices that a rational person "should" make in a given situation, regardless of the choices that real people actually make, and descriptive decision theory, which pertains to the choices real people "actually" make, regardless of the choices they should make, are strongly linked together.

Second, for mathematics and crisis management (Bi-lateral 2+6), game theory as a mathematical theory has been applied to the process of crisis management, as explained in Chapter 3. Two points can be examined here to explain this relationship. For the first, mathematics can be applied in the behavioral sciences and, more importantly, in developing theories about the nature of the world around us. As Schellenberg notes, "We can use mathematics as a tool for describing our world, for analyzing data about the world, and for organizing our thinking. In this last activity, we use formal logic and mathematics to assist us in the task of theorizing" (1996: 105). A good example of the use of mathematical models is Lewis Richardson's contribution to theory in the study of social conflict and its resolution, particularly his mathematical formulation of the arms race. Schellenberg (115) explains that Richardson attempted to study social conflict in a thoroughly quantitative manner, and accomplished this through his quantitative analysis of the arms race as a way of introducing formal theory.

For the second point, the relationship between the fields of mathematics and crisis management can be viewed as, for instance, two interlinking lines or dimensions, one representing "rationality" (mathematics) and the other, "management" (crisis management). Looking at 1) management as "control", as defined in Chapter 2 by the Oxford Dictionary, as well as Williams' (1976) view of crisis management as an attempt to maintain "control" over events and not allow them to get out of hand, and at 2) rationality as behavior directed towards more desired outcomes rather than less desired outcomes, it is possible to explore the key role of rationality in achieving the control that leads to desired goals or ends. Management of the crisis situation, in particular, requires that the actors or decision-makers act rationally in their efforts to maintain control over certain aspects of the situation. The vital goal of management is to impose order so as to keep events under control. Looking at the principles of crisis management, for instance, reveals the fact that rationality is important in implementing most of these principles, such as the decision-making process, the limitation of objectives, and the maintaining of flexible options. Rationality is interpreted as an integral part of the attempt to elaborate the precise procedures involved in decision-making. Decision-makers in the management process, exercising prudence, should make rational choices, pick suitable strategies, and maintain control over circumstances and the variables surrounding the situation. A rational person is one who, when a decision is required, makes the optimal choice. As such, rationality is an essential element in the process of management; without it, the latter will be inefficient or, at the very least, incomplete. The strength of the relationship between rationality and management increases when the significance of the consequences of management intensifies, e.g., peaceful settlement or war, depending on the success or the failure, respectively, of managing a political crisis.

Third, for communication and crisis management (Bi-lateral 3+7), it is useful here to remind the reader of Nolan's (1999) definition of communication, mentioned in the beginning of Chapter 1, that suggests the idea that as human beings learn to communicate successfully they begin to achieve "control" over events that affect them. Linking this notion of control to successful communication highlights the relationship between communication and the process of managing crisis. This relationship is based on the fact that the characteristics of crisis information are influenced by, and thus similar to, the characteristics of crisis (see Rosenthal, Hart and Charles' 1989 description of crisis information in Chapter 2). Meisel (1982: 61) maps some of the observable relationships between crises and means of communication. He claims that communications—"the transmission of information by speech, signals, writing, or pictures"—are influenced by crises and, in turn, affect the way that the crises evolve. Also, as Williams (1976: 182) notes, communication can help to define the structure of a crisis so that both sides accurately perceive the relative values of the interests at issue. In addition, communication can help minimize the likelihood of miscalculation, and consequently helps in the de-escalation or managing of the crisis. Finally, the discussions in Chapter 8 are examples of how the mass media of the parties involved in an international political crisis can participate in the crisis management process.

Fourth is communication and decision-making (Bi-lateral 4+8); here there are two areas of decision-making that are related to communication and mass media—governmental decision-making and news-writing by media personnel—both of which have been described in Chapter 1. In addition, there is an interaction model for the relationship between the government policy line and the influence of the mass media; it is called the policy-media interaction model. Piers Robinson (2000) illustrates this model through two principal scenarios. The first involves the occurrence of media influence: "In the absence of a clear and well-articulated policy line, the government is susceptible to critical and extensive media attention. If news reports are critically framed, advocating a particular course of action, the government is forced to do something or face a public relations disaster. Here, media can significantly influence the policy process" (615). In the other scenario there is no media influence because the government policy line is certain, and consequently the news media coverage is indexed to the official agenda. "When the government has clear and well-articulated objectives it tends to set the news agenda. Coverage might become critical if there is elite dissensus. With the executive decided on a particular course of action, media coverage is unlikely to influence policy" (615).

Additionally, I identify four tri-lateral relationships in the interweavement: 1) Mathematics, Decision-Making and Crisis Management (Tri-lateral 9+13); 2) Communication, Crisis Management and Decision-Making (Tri-lateral 11+15); 3) Mathematics, Communication and Crisis Management (Tri-lateral 10+14); and 4) Communication, Mathematics and Decision-Making (Tri-lateral 12+16).

First, for mathematics, decision-making and crisis management (Tri-lateral 9+13), the notion of rationality as a connection in the bi-lateral (1+5) relationship between mathematics and decision-making works to help manage a crisis. Rational decision-making through the application of game theory to a crisis situation is very applicable in crisis management (for instance, see the application of game theory in Chapter 7). Second, communication, crisis management and decision-making (Tri-lateral 11+15) is better understood when thinking of communication during crisis decision-making, which has been discussed in Chapter 2. Third, for mathematics, communication and crisis management (Tri-lateral 10+14), it is clear here that using mathematics as a tool in communication studies and using mathematics, or game theory, in crisis management demonstrates the linkages among the three fields. Mathematics is pivotal for both communication and crisis management as it creates an interwoven relationship that can enhance studying areas of mutual concerns. Fourth, for communication, mathematics and decision-making (Tri-lateral 12+16), it is useful to acknowledge the importance of communication in general and mass media in particular as tools applied to the process of political decision-making using a mathematical theory such as game theory. Using the media as a tool in the game players' hands or as an independent party affects the decision-makers' performance.

Finally, the only quadri-lateral relationship (area 17) is that in which theoretical threads from the four frameworks meet or interweave. The following sequence may help explain the connection(s). First, for social scientists the use of mathematics for analyzing data, investigating social issues, and understanding social behavior is well known. Second, game theory, which originates in the field of mathematics, has been successfully used as a method in conflicts and crises analyses to open new ways, techniques, and strategies for moving towards conflict resolution and crisis management. Third, to understand the connection between the principles of game theory and the field of mass media, it may be useful to think of the mass media as an effective tool in the game between two adversaries. The mass media of one adversary can implement certain functions that help to accomplish its goals during the game against its opponent. Fourth, during times of crisis, certain requirements must be fulfilled in order to shape a crisis decision-making group.

Interweavement, as presented here as a newly created concept, is a starting point in the formalizing of a communication model as one example that could help media or communication personnel understand what must be done in the event of an international political crisis. Here the chapter will clarify some crucial points from the four theoretical backgrounds in order to show their collective interaction in the interweavement. Principally, one field will be explained in terms of its interactions with the other three through an analysis of the definitions, concepts, and processes of each. Here the concept of "communication" is the pivotal point.

> Communication is intertwined with all of human life, and any
> study of human life must touch on this subject. Some scholars treat
> communication as central while others see it as more peripheral,
> but it is always there.
> (Littlejohn, 2002: 2)

Communication, as one field in relation to the other three in the interwoven whole, is regarded in three different forms or shapes that help in the understanding of its many aspects. Communication, it is argued here, is "essentially required" in one field (crisis management), is "in critical need of assistance" from another field (mathematics), and "involves" the third field (decision-making). One of the many possible situations where this idea of interweavement, which entails these particular interactions and relationships, would be applicable is an international political crisis.

To clarify the first relationship of communication, i.e., being "essentially required" within the field of crisis management, it is necessary to understand and distinguish the situation of crisis in addition to recognizing the ultimate goal of the crisis management process. As I argued in Chapter 2, the most important approach to defining a crisis, among the six approaches mentioned therein, is the characteristics approach. In contrast to the other approaches, the characteristics' approach goes directly to the main distinguishing and determining attributes of the situation. The comparative analysis of the distinct characteristics of crisis and similar situations and the connections among them as discussed in Chapter 2 shows the similarities and differences of crisis and similar stress situations in order to help avoid misinterpretation in dealing with them. The proposed definition of crisis proposed in Chapter 2 takes into account only the unique characteristics of the crisis situation and relies solely on successful crisis management.

Communication, among other factors, is a basic principle of crisis management as previously illustrated. The maintenance of communication among adversaries through open, direct, and clear channels is one dimension of management. The idea of the "management of messages" in defining communication, as referred to in Chapter 1, achieves a similar goal to that of the concept of "control" as in the original meaning of the word "management" in the context of rational behavior. Management in relation to rational behavior aims at achieving the desired outcome, whatever it is, in terms of the situation. In relation to communication, the purpose of management is "creating meaning". Here again there is an underlying desired output or goal. Ironically, communication itself, in Peters' (1999) perspective, entails "uncertainty",[2] and is a "risky adventure without guarantees". The other dimension is the work of mass communication as a representative system, including that of the political, among others, of each adversarial entity. Again, as discussed in Chapter 2, the work of mass communication can play an effective part in containing or de-escalating the crisis situation and overcoming the states of uncertainty, misunderstanding, and miscalculation that prevail at that time, if, and only if, specific rules and tools are used. Rules take us to the ethics and social responsibility recommended for the work of communication, explained in Chapter 4, while tools direct our attention, as explained in Chapter 3, to a field in the social sciences used effectively for the betterment of performance and achievement of desired outcomes—mathematics.

I link ethics and mathematics through the concept of rationality, which is essential to both areas. It will be pointed out that "rational" is a central distinguishing characteristic of thinking about ethics. In addition, one more point can be introduced here. I see a clear connection between ethics and mathematics through the idea of *enquiry for social betterment or goodness*. This is supported by 1) Wittgenstein's (1918) definition of ethics as the enquiry into what is valuable, really important, makes life worth living, and the right way of living—generally what is good; 2) Rugina's (1998) suggestion that ethics as a science can be concerned only with social values (therefore its proper name is "social ethics"); and 3) Lazarsfeld and his colleagues' ultimate goal of using mathematics in the social sciences, particularly communication research, for the betterment of living standards.[3] Both Wittgenstein's enquiry and Lazarsfeld's research are consistent and connected to the "social" dimension of goodness that in turn is interrelated to Rugina's suggestion of the "social" dimension of ethics.

As for mathematics, which as mentioned above forms the second relationship with communication, i.e., "in critical need for assistance from", it has been more frequently regarded as a unique and necessary tool in social science in general and communication in particular as explained in Chapter 3. It is not a normal tool, but it is sometimes the only tool for achieving specific purposes. Moreover, it is active and participatory, not passive. Mathematics as "creation" or an "act of will" is an active determinant. In game theory, as an example of a branch of mathematics where it is used as prescription but not description since it recommends a rational course of action and then describes the consequences of such conduct, it is clear that mathematics is active, not passive. It creates (uses methods of reasoning) rather than just deals with being created (numbers, symbols, etc.). That is, it follows the concept of "employing mathematics" rather than only "doing mathematics". Wittgenstein's 1953 *Philosophical Investigations* and his philosophy of mathematics as a collection of "techniques or methods" for inferring one proposition from another, rather than as a body of knowledge about mathematical objects or a set of mathematical facts strongly supports this view. Scholars from various disciplines discuss important functions of mathematics that are related to the topic at stake. For example, Boudon (1974) sees an essential function of mathematics in sociology, i.e., clarification of particular problems, concepts, and research procedures. The group of scholars including Shannon who rely on processes for both the coding and decoding of messages in defining the communication process, use mathematics as an essential tool. Significantly, Collins' (1998) assertion that mathematics and intellectual operations are internalized in communication is another connecting dimension. The need for mathematical theories such as game theory to explain how individual decisions are interrelated and how those decisions result in outcomes is one more function. However, another dimension of the relationship between mathematics and communication should be taken into account; that is, mathematics itself, or some branches of it such as game theory, has an internalized need for communication. For example, Littlejohn (2002) explains the importance of direct communication between the two players (prisoners) in the Prisoner's Dilemma Game. He argues that if they can communicate and consequently agree to cooperate, both will receive lesser punishments.

The third relationship of communication, which "involves" the process of decision-making, is regarded here mostly in terms of Ofstad's idea of making a judgment regarding what one ought to do in a certain situation after having deliberated on some alternative courses of action. Rationality is a basic element in this process to the extent that failure of the decision process to achieve what is expected or desired from it is regarded as irrationality. A prevailing concept that I present in this book is found in the definition of the process of decision-making—getting to the best, optimal, or desired choice, outcome, or end. The connection between rationality and ethics, and the conception that rationality is a fundamental element in the decision-making process, allow us to conclude that there is a consequent link between ethics and decision-making.

THE CONVERGENCE OF ETHICS AND RATIONAL THINKING

> *Ethical rationalism* is the doctrine that reason is the road to right action. . . . According to ethical rationalism, right moral action results from knowledge and reason. If one wishes to find out what action is good, one must reason . . . furthermore, moral action will result in happiness and the good life.
>
> (Lee, 1971: 2)

This section will highlight the significance of one of the relationships included in the interweavement in relation to the structure of the model I present in this book. The tri-lateral relationship (12+16) represents interactions among lines that may come from three fields: communication, mathematics, and decision-making. Rational thinking and responsible conduct are two weights or forces fundamentally necessary for creating the balance in the model. That is, *rational* and *responsible* aspects of the model are crucial to achieving its main purpose and to making it *effective*. Therefore, an investigation of this relationship between both rational thinking and ethics as well as an investigation of the philosophical origins of the ethical decision-making process are essentially useful here in the context of preparing the basis of the model.

Following the argument that "logic is the study of correct reasoning . . . If it works in logic, it can also work in any other study about nature and human societies where scientific method is applicable", Anghel Rugina

(1998: 834) selected the 1961 English edition of Wittgenstein's *Tractatus Logico-Philosophicus* (1918) as a testing ground. He claims that Wittgenstein was an original and powerful thinker, whose influence in leading a revolution in logic was similar to that of Einstein in physics, Freud in psychology, Weber in methodology, and Keynes in economics. Historically, there are two kinds of logic: the logic of truth-content and the logic of truth-form. Wittgenstein attempted to free logic from any concern about content. He eliminated the quest for "meaning" or content of propositions[4] and in this way he moved logic into a field of enquiry where only pure signs and symbols are assumed to exist. Thus the door was open to permitting a wide use of mathematics in logic. The result was a new type of logic called modern, mathematical, formal, nominalistic logic. And so the expression of "formal logic" or "logic of truth-form" is appropriate. As to the problem of values, for Weber they existed but could not be accepted in science because they were subjective, while for Wittgenstein, there are no values at all:

> All propositions are of equal value. The sense of the world must lie outside the world. In the world everything is as it is, and everything happens as it does happen: in it no values exist—and if it did exist, it would have no value.
>   (Wittgenstein, *Tractatus*, quoted in Rugina, 1998: 835)

Ethics is an important issue that is connected to the problem of values. Rugina explains that whereas Weber could not accept ethics as a part of science because he did not have a logical solution to the problem of "value-judgments", Wittgenstein goes much further and negates the possibility of developing ethical propositions at all. Rugina points out that after the statement that values "must lie outside the world", Wittgenstein drew this conclusion: "And so it is impossible for there to be propositions of ethics" since "propositions can express nothing that is higher". For Wittgenstein "ethics cannot be put into words. Ethics is transcendental" (836). Rugina suggests that the first step to be taken to liberate ethics from false arguments is to separate clearly personal, subjective, individual values from social, impersonal, objective values. Ethics as a science can be concerned only with social values; therefore, its proper name is "social ethics" (844).

Redpath (1986: 119) explains that Wittgenstein, when defining "ethics", starts by adopting Moore's definition of ethics as "the general enquiry into what is good". However, Wittgenstein widens the term slightly by enumerating a "row of synonyms" intended to enable the audience to see "the characteristic features of ethics":

> Ethics is the enquiry into what is valuable.
> Ethics is the enquiry into what is really important.
> Ethics is the enquiry into the meaning of life.
> Ethics is the enquiry into what makes life worth living.
> Ethics is the enquiry into the right way of living.

According to Wittgenstein, there is yet another dimension to ethics, the "supernatural":

> [I]f a man could write a book on Ethics which really was a book on Ethics, this book would, with an explosion, destroy all other books in the world. . . . Our use of words in science and ordinary discourse is confined to natural meanings and to expressing facts. That is all they are capable of containing. To attempt to use them to express ethical thoughts is like trying to pour a gallon of water into a teacup. Our words only express facts. Ethics, if it is anything, is supernatural, that is, it does not have to do with "natural" meaning and sense.
>
> (quoted in Barrett, 1991: 45)

Since Wittgenstein's view of ethics differs quite significantly from the discussion of codes of ethics governing journalistic performance in Chapter 5, the reader may well ask, "so do ethics exist or not?" The point of presenting Wittgenstein's view of ethics here, i.e., as the enquiry into what can be considered generally good, is to emphasize how difficult it is to adhere to or understand ethics in social practices, as well as to consider ethics from a mathematical point of view. However, Rugina's suggestions for separating individual values from social values, i.e., his call for social ethics, may help solve the confusion. In addition, it may be helpful to point out again that the social dimension of ethics and the idea of the enquiry towards social betterment or goodness are consistent with the analysis found in Chapter 5: ethics can be put into words or the codes of a profession, in this case journalism, *as long as* they are separated from personal, subjective, and individual values, and ultimately work towards the ultimate social betterment.

Of central importance to Wittgenstein's philosophy of mathematics, Klenk (1976: 49-50) explains, is the emphasis on the inferential nature of mathematics. For Wittgenstein, there is no such thing as a mathematical object, or a mathematical reality corresponding to our mathematical assertions. Wittgenstein considers the mathematician as a creator rather than an explorer, and most importantly, mathematics not as a descriptive science, not "the natural history of numbers", but rather, a "practice", an activity of transforming patterns or shapes according to paradigms or "rules of inference". That is, Wittgenstein puts the emphasis on the process itself rather than the end result. Therefore, mathematics is seen generally as a collection of "techniques or methods" for inferring one proposition from another, rather than as a body of knowledge about mathematical objects or a set of mathematical facts. Klenk (69) quotes from Wittgenstein: "Mathematics—I want to say—teaches you, not just the answer to a question, but a whole language-game[5] with questions and answers".

Heap and Varoufakis (1995) present a view inspired by Wittgenstein that "what is instrumentally rational is not well defined unless one appeals to the prevailing norms of behavior" (162). Although they acknowledge that this may seem a little strange in the context of the Prisoners' Dilemma Game "where the demands of instrumental rationality seem plain for all to see . . . [as a] defect", they argue that "the norms have already been at work in the definition of the matrix and its pay-offs because it is rare for any social setting to throw up unvarnished pay-offs. A social setting requires interpretation before the pay-offs can be assigned and norms are implicated in those interpretations" (162). In other words, a norm such as "truth telling" or "promise keeping" in the Prisoners' Dilemma leads each prisoner to keep an agreement "not to confess". Heap and Varoufakis explain that when "individuals make decisions in a context of norms and these norms are capable of overriding considerations of what is instrumentally rational", this may be seen as a "departure from the strict instrumental model of rational action" (157). However, they argue that the Prisoners' Dilemma Game itself "is transformed by the presence of the norms and the model of instrumental rational action does not seem to require modification in order to explain cooperation" (159), a view that is inspired by Wittgenstein's *Philosophical Investigations* which would deny that "the meaning of something like a person's interests or desires can be divorced from a social setting" (160).

Further, this point becomes more crucial here if rationality is compared to intuition which is based on experience. The significance of rationality in events of conflict or crisis, when rational choices should be made, appears superior to intuition. The Prisoners' Dilemma again shows how intuition is unreliable in conflict situations and simultaneously proves Wittgenstein's assertion that a person's interests cannot be separated from his/her social setting:

The reason for regarding . . . [the Prisoners' game] as a dilemma, or even a paradox, is obvious. Both players act in a rational manner, but they end up in a position which could be improved on for both of them. Both could have been better off if they had selected the other strategy. Individual rationality in this case does not lead to social rationality, which is a disturbing conclusion and violates many intuitive preconceptions of the consequences of individual rational conduct. Intuitively one feels that, if everyone is motivated only by his individual self-interest and acts according to some precepts of rational conduct, then either all, or at least some, of the actors should be better off. However, this case shows that this is not true. Two people acting according to rules of individual self-interest *both* fail to achieve as much according to this criterion as if they had violated such rules.

(Nicholson, 1970: 61)

There is a relationship between moral (i.e., social context of ethical) reasoning and ethical decision-making. Moral reasoning, according to Day (2000: 53), is "a *systematic* approach to making ethical decisions". He explains that moral reasoning as a form of intellectual activity, takes the form of logical argument and persuasion. As long as ethical judgments involve the rights and interests of others, ethical decisions must be made with care and be justifiable through a reasoned analysis of the situation.

McKercher and Cumming, in their *Canadian Reporter* (1998), explain that systems of moral reasoning contain some process of identifying issues and balancing values and principles. They consider the "Potter Box", formulated by Dr. Ralph Potter of the Harvard Divinity School, as "by no means the only system of evaluation, of course" (376). They explain that some scholars in media ethics, led by Clifford Christians and his associates' study of 1983, use this model of moral reasoning. The box contains four stages of analysis: Defining facts, defining values[6], applying principles, and defining loyalties. Christians and his associates (2001: 3-25) illustrate that moving from one quadrant to the next in analyzing an issue in terms of this box leads to the construction of action guides. They emphasize that the matter of choosing loyalties usually needs the closest examination since the Potter Box is a model for social ethics and, therefore, forces us to articulate where our loyalties lie when making a final judgment or adopting a particular policy. They consider choosing loyalties as an extremely significant step in the process of making moral decisions. For example, choices for media personnel who are sincere about serving society must be made among various segments of that society: audiences, sources of information, politicians, ethnic minorities, children, judges and lawyers, and so on.

Given the previously illustrated connection between rationality and ethics, and the conception that rationality is a fundamental element in the decision-making process, there is a consequent link between ethics and decision-making. In fact, it would be worthwhile here to analyze the philosophical origins of the ethical decision-making process to illustrate its logical connection to the three other elements in the theoretical framework of this book. Larry Leslie (2000) has selected a number of philosophers, who in general represent various historical periods and in particular emphasize important decision-making concepts and processes, to discuss and illustrate their ethical philosophies. For this chapter, the decision-making tools contained in ethical philosophies of historical/cultural periods from ancient Greece to the Postmodern have been grouped and described in *Table 3*.

Leslie, using these ethical decision-making tools, establishes a decision-making model. He claims that getting to successful ethical decision-making requires resistance to post-modern tendencies and engagement in a rational, systematic examination of an ethical problem and its possible solutions. He warns of the difficulty of doing so because post-modern thinking has essentially rejected the "reasoned approach" to the solving of problems as it considers that individuals have moved away from the absolutes, the rules, and the structures that reason often produces. He explains that reason, or rational thinking, is essentially a product of the Enlightenment, which began in the eighteenth century. Introducing a decision-making model in the form of a flowchart, he explains that it is a pictorial plan to show what a decision-maker wants to do and in what order. The purpose of using a flowchart is to improve the ethical decision-making process by making it both systematic and rational (2000: 145-147).

This chapter analyzes Leslie's discussion (2000: 22-160) in order to trace the mutual concepts and processes found in the philosophers' ethical decision-making tools, and consequently to formulate a preliminary understanding of the general philosophical perspectives of ethical decision-making. This analysis explores eight groups of recommended actions and concepts common to all the philosophers' teachings: 1) seeking real knowledge of the situation; 2) reasonable/rational thinking; 3) prudence and self-control; 4) social justice; 5) responsibility; 6) morality; 7) selection of choices; and 8) doing what is just-right/good.

Table 3: **Philosophers' Decision-Making Tools throughout Historical Cultural Periods**[7]

Culture Period (App. Dates)	Philosopher	Decision-Making Tool
A Greek View (1200 B.C. - 320 B.C.)	Plato 427 B.C. - 347 B.C.	Refrain from wrongdoing regardless of the consequences. Set aside the views of society, acquire the knowledge necessary to make a good decision, then act in such a way that you are pleased and others are served by the action. The action must meet the tests of courage, moderation, respect, wisdom, and justice. (28)
	Aristotle 384 B.C. - 322 B.C.	When faced with an ethical problem, avoid extremes by determining the mean, the just-right, and act by doing what is appropriate after considering all relevant factors. (32)
Transition Figures	Peter Abelard 1079 - 1142	Actions can be considered good or evil, that is, ethical or unethical, depending solely on one's intentions. (40)
Middle Ages A.D. 400 - A.D. 1300	Thomas Aquinas 1225 - 1274	Ethical behavior stems from appropriate human action, action guided by the four cardinal virtues: prudence, justice, temperance, and courage. (42)
Renaissance & Reformation A.D. 1300 - A.D. 1650	Francis Bacon 1561 - 1626	Apply the powers of reason, understanding, and will to control the appetites that life subjects each individual to. Seek constantly for new knowledge and truth. (45)
Rebels Renaissance & Reformation A.D. 1300 - A.D. 1650	Niccolo Machiavelli 1469 - 1527	Examine a problem situationally and flex the ethical absolutes only to the degree necessary to gain the desired ends. (52)
Enlightenment A.D. 1650 - A.D. 1850	Thomas Hobbes 1588 - 1679	Rise above self-interest; promote justice and strive for mutual accommodation; fulfill your obligations. (55)

	Francois Marie Voltaire 1694 - 1778	Use reason to balance the passions; act for the greater good of society. (59)
	Jean Jacques Rousseau 1712 - 1778	Use conscience, compassion, and reason to make ethical decisions that promote harmony among all those involved. (62)

Traditionalists

Enlightenment A.D. 1650 - A.D. 1850	Benedict Spinoza 1632 - 1677	Use reason to determine the proper course of action. First, determine the good, that is, the ideal or standard against which the action may be judged. Then set aside emotion; think through the problem and reach a just, faithful, and honorable conclusion. Be prepared to provide a rational answer to the question, Why did you do what you did? (72)
	Immanuel Kant 1724 - 1804	Considering your responsibility to self and others, act only on those principles that you would have generalized to all. Ask these questions: What is the rule authorizing this act I am about to perform? Can it become a universal law for all human beings to follow? (77)
Modern age A.D. 1850 - A.D. 1945	John Stuart Mill 1806 - 1873	Act by following the moral rule that will bring about the greatest good (or happiness) for the greatest number. (82)

The Continental Connection

Enlightenment A.D. 1650 - A.D. 1850	Arthur Schopenhauer 1788 - 1860	Think carefully about any action you may be inclined to take. Acknowledge the influence of the will, but use experience to achieve a balance & act with compassion so that you respect yourself and others. (93)
Modern age A.D. 1850 - A.D. 1945	Emile Durkheim 1858-1917	Determine the moral ideal or moral fact that governs a planned action. Explain how society benefits from the action, that is, how does the proposed action contribute to and reflect the existing social and moral fabric of life? (97)

Modern Influences

Modern Age A.D. 1850 - A.D. 1945	Jean-Paul Sartre 1905 - 1980	Get a clear and accurate picture of a situation by examining the choices of action available. Select an option for which you can provide a justification and for which you accept total responsibility. (109)
	Ayn Rand 1905 - 1982	Examine the reality of a situation in as objective a manner as possible. Determine the standards to be followed and the goals to be met by a decision. Submit these observations to a reasoning process yielding a solution that meets your needs as an individual. (114)
Postmodern Age A.D. 1945 - Present	Lawrence Kohlberg 1927 - 1987	Before attempting to find a solution to an ethical dilemma, determine on which moral level you are presently functioning. As you approach a new ethical problem, make a decision that is backed by logical reasoning and sound moral judgment, always moving toward the more mature postconventional level of decision-making. (118)
Continued in the modern period and is not time-bound	Judeo-Christian Tradition	Remembering that an individual's primary responsibility is to serve and be faithful to God, resolve an ethical dilemma by acting in accordance with the principles set forth by the Jewish or Christian religious traditions. (122)

Postmodernist Approaches

Modern Age A.D. 1850 - A.D. 1945	Jean Baudrillard 1929-	Examine possible responses to an ethical dilemma and select the one that is least manipulative and intrusive, the one that most closely represents true reality. (137)
Postmodern Age A.D. 1945-Present	Michel Foucault 1926 - 1984	Recalling the set of truth obligations, examine an ethical problem and determine a desired course of action. Ask two questions: Is the proposed solution a reflection of my personal ethical standards? What power relationships influenced the solution? If you are comfortable with the answers to each of these questions, implement the desired action. (132)

1) *Seeking real knowledge of the situation* is drawn from the following statements: "acquire the knowledge", "act ... considering all relevant factors", "Seek constantly for new knowledge and truth", "avoid stagnation", "Get ... accurate picture of the situation", and "Examine the reality of a situation". 2) *Reasonable/Rational thinking* is drawn from the following statements: "Apply the powers of reason", "Use reason", "provide a rational ...", "Think carefully", "Select an option for which you can provide a justification", "... a reasoning process yielding a solution that meets your needs", and "make a decision that is backed by logical reasoning". 3) *Prudence and self-control* is drawn from the following statements: "The action must meet the tests of ... moderation ... wisdom", "avoid extremes by determining the mean", "action guided by ... prudence ... temperance", "control the appetites", "to balance the passions", "set aside emotion", and "use experience to achieve a balance". 4) *Social justice* is drawn from the following statements: "act in ... a way that you are pleased and others are served by the action", "Rise above self-interest", "strive for mutual accommodation", "act for the greater good of society", "promote harmony among all those involved", "Considering your responsibility to self and others", "... for the greatest number", "so that you respect yourself and others", "The action must meet the tests of ... respect", "The action must meet the tests of ... justice", "action guided by ... justice", and "promote justice". 5) *Responsibility* is drawn from the following statements: "fulfill your obligations", "Considering your responsibility", and "Select an option ... for which you accept total responsibility". 6) *Morality* is drawn from the following statements: "Act by following the moral rule", "Determine the moral ideal or moral fact", "Determine the standards to be followed", "Use conscience" and "make a decision that ... sound moral judgment". 7) *Selection of choices* is drawn from the following statements: "examining the choices of action available", "Examine possible responses", "reach a just ... conclusion", "to gain the desired ends", "determine a desired course of action", and "... the goals to be met by a decision". And 8) *Doing the just-right/good* is drawn from the following statements: "Refrain from wrongdoing", "determining ... the just-right", "doing what is appropriate", "good or evil, that is, ethical or unethical", "determine the proper course of action", "determine the good", "reach [an] ... honorable conclusion", and "bring about the greatest good".

The above eight groups of recommended actions and concepts pertain to, or suggest the need for, their application and adoption in the theories of communication research and social responsibility, mathematics, and the behavioral theories of decision-making. This implication supports the core theme of this chapter, especially if it is acknowledged that the significance of the above-mentioned three groups of theories increases in the presence of the fourth one—crisis management. Furthermore, seeking a decision-making tool relevant to the topic of the book becomes a logical step. At this point, it is useful to bring attention to the importance of modeling the process of decision-making and to distinguish between selected models relevant to the topic of this book in order to defend the adoption of the rational choice approach.

MODELING DECISION-MAKING

Thierauf (1970: 14-19) defines a model as a representation or abstraction of an actual object or situation, which shows the relationships (direct and indirect) and interrelationships of action and reaction in terms of cause and effect. He classifies models into three types: iconic, analogic, and symbolic (mathematical). Formal modeling,[8] according to Morrow (1994: 6-7), is a research strategy. Given the complexity of the social world, Morrow sees the simplification of formal models as a way of providing insights into that world. He considers simplification a virtue, since modeling tries to capture the essence of a social situation.

In addition, Harrison (1993: 27-33) explains, models represent a particular segment of the real world at a given time and place under varying conditions, and reduce the almost infinite number of complex variables in decision-making to a small number of causal factors, which are significant and understandable. Therefore, a decision-making model that includes some optimum number of variables that will explain the real-world phenomenon being modeled, should enable the decision-maker to predict real-world phenomena with valuable consistency and accuracy. In today's increasingly complex and changeable world, there is a new movement, Harrison explains, which has moved away from the traditional approaches to decision-making that relied solely and heavily on the disciplines of economics, mathematics, and statistics, to the imperative of taking into account the relevant aspects of many other disciplines. He explains that decision-making is considered a meeting ground for psychologists, economists, sociologists, organizational theorists, statisticians, philosophers and others, and it is from here that its complexity originates. Specifically a decision-making model should include some optimum number of variables, which would explain the real-world phenomenon being modeled. Harrison introduces four models[9] of decision-making—the rational model, the organizational model, the political model, and the process model—emphasizing their importance in helping us to better understand the complex nature of decision-making. The process model of decision-making, he suggests, may be the ideal choice for decisions that have long-term consequences since it has strong managerial emphasis and objectives-oriented outcomes, for decisions with apparent levels of uncertainty attendant on the outcome. It is oriented towards innovation and organizational change with a particular emphasis on long-term results. Also, although it relies mainly on the judgment of the decision-maker, it does not exclude computation or compromise that fits special decision-making situations.

Geller and Singer (1998) distinguish decision-making models according to the assumption of rationality, and therefore divide models into rational and non-rational. Claiming that "nonrational models, whether focusing on psychological variables or organizational interests and routines, maintain that decisions are frequently distorted by systematic perceptual, cognitive, or bureaucratic biases" (31), they argue that in the philosophical and conceptual debate around rationality, "minimal criteria for an instrumentally rational decision would include the logical requirements of consistency and coherence in goal-directed behavior" (31). They summarize their advocate view towards the rational model by saying:

> Nonrational models focus on psychological or bureaucratic factors associated with individuals or organizations and often require detailed information on specific people or bureaucratic structures and processes, whereas rational models offer the simplifying assumption that psychological or bureaucratic biases have little impact and that decision makers (or decision-making units) all calculate in more or less the same way.
>
> (1998: 31)

In their explanation of rational decision-making, Geller and Singer discuss three models: *procedural rationality*, *instrumental rationality*, and *rational choice* or expected-utility theory. They explain that *procedural rationality* "suggests that decision makers follow a series of steps for determining the selection of options in the pursuit of goals" (40). The factors impinging on procedural rationality include "misperceptions, psychological mechanisms which bias information reception and option selection, emotional responses, and so on. . . . [As well,] organizational processes, bureaucratic politics, and domestic political pressures [are] among the elements constraining procedurally rational decision-making" (41). *Instrumental rationality* for them is a more limited conception than the image of procedural rationality. They (41-42) demonstrate that decision-makers are rational in the instrumentalist sense if they have "connected" and "transitive" preferences across a series of outcomes. "Connectivity is defined as the ability to compare outcomes and evaluate them coherently" (41). If a decision-maker is presented with two outcomes, A or B, connectivity implies that s/he will either prefer A to B, B to A, or be indifferent toward them, that is, A > B, B > A, or A = B. As such, a decision-maker whose preferences do not conform to this rule of connectivity is not rational in the instrumentalist sense. Transitivity, the second rule, implies that if a decision-maker prefers outcome A to outcome B, and prefers outcome B to outcome C, s/he will prefer outcome A to outcome C, that is, if A > B, and B > C, then A > C. If preferences do not conform to the rule of transitivity, then they are logically incoherent and the decision-maker is not rational in the instrumentalist sense. Finally, *rational choice* models of international politics and foreign policy based on game theory and expected-utility theory are grounded in the concept of instrumental rationality. The foundation of this model "is located in microeconomic theory which assumes that decision-makers will attempt to secure through probability calculus the largest net gain available to them, based on a cost/benefit comparison of options, given the levels of risk associated with each outcome" (42). Geller and Singer claim that expected-utility theory remains one of the most important constructs in the analysis of war decisions.

THEORETICAL THREADS FOR FEEDING THE MODEL

A consequent step here is to synthesize the theoretical threads from the major fields discussed and analyzed in this book. These will work as inputs to the structure of the model that will be explained in the following chapter. If the main criterion in discussing and analyzing the theoretical frameworks up to this point was their relevance and applicability to the topic of this book, then the criterion for synthesizing theoretical threads is greatly similar, although with perhaps more concentration on the specifics of the topic. In other words, a discussion and analysis, for example, of the nature of crisis and other similar stress situations, as well as of the relevant literature concerning the management of international political crisis, is relevant to the topic of the book, given the nature of the United States-Iraqi Crisis. Thus, in synthesizing threads from this area, this chapter concentrates on what is relevant to the 2003 War on Iraq and its developments. The same logic of synthesizing can be used regarding the other three areas—communication, mathematics, and decision-making.

It is seen here that the various threads grow from seven main roots: 1) the understanding of international political crisis and its successful management; 2) the structure and functioning of decision-making; 3) the knowledge and comprehension of game theory; 4) the significance of rationality; 5) the communication process and fundamentals of news-writing; 6) the ethical principles for mass communication; and 7) the role of the media within international political crisis, with application to the United States-Iraqi Crisis and its latest consequence, the 2003 War on Iraq.

The formation of these roots constitutes what can be called here "the entire-exterior degree of interweavement". That is, depending on the volume and value of information, concepts, theories, and so on, that are drawn from the major four theoretical frameworks, according to their relevance to the general or the situational structures of the crisis, the interaction of interweavement takes specific shape. In other words, it can happen that in either the general or situational structure of the crisis the model relies extensively on some threads while relying less on others. This not only leads to the numerous shapes of the interweavement, but also indicates that the dynamic nature of the model is reflected in the volume and value of its inputs which vary according to the change in the general or situational structure of the crisis. Another dimension of the dynamicity of the model stems from the possibility of updating and correcting these threads, which consequently will affect the decision-making functioning in the model. Nevertheless, the entire-exterior degree of interweavement is a composition of a group of "fractional-interior degrees of intertwinements". That is, the various theoretical threads are interwoven together again in various ways to give numerous shapes, depending on how they are related to each other in the explanations of events and developments throughout the general or situational structure of the crisis.

If we consider this in light of the case study for this book—the United States-Iraqi Crisis and the 2003 War on Iraq—the first root, "the understanding of international political crisis and its successful management", may contain the following threads:

> A strong understanding of American foreign policy, real drivers, and primary objectives regarding Iraq, as well as of its instruments to achieve these objectives.

> Acknowledgment that the argument that the two wars, the 1990/91 Gulf War and the 2003 War on Iraq, were launched as a result of an original crisis between the United States and Iraq. This crisis, which can be classified under the category of international political crises, has not yet been resolved, which in turn has resulted in the on-going nature of conflicts and wars between the parties.

➤ The deeply rooted crisis between Iraq and the United States is mainly based on a confrontation of conflicting interests. Both sides have strategic interests, goals, and policies to achieve either regionally or globally.

➤ The necessity of understanding and distinguishing the crisis from other similar stress situations in order to deal with it effectively.

➤ The purpose of crisis management is to resolve a dangerous confrontation without fighting, and with vital interests preserved. It attempts to maintain control over events, not allowing them to get out of hand.

➤ It is necessary to have an understanding of the principles of crisis management, including Richardson's (1988) and Neuhold's (1978), requirements for successful crisis management, including George's (1991a) and Cimbala's (1999), strategies of crisis management, including George's (1991c), and finally levels of strategies, including Grattan's (2004). Principles of crisis management include: the decision-making process, the implementation of policy, the limitation of objectives, maintaining flexible options, time pressure, perception of the adversary, communication, and consideration of the precedent effect of crisis behavior. Requirements for successful crisis management include: the slowing down of military movements to enhance diplomatic communications in assessing the situation; coordination between military movements and diplomatic actions; consistency between military threats and limited diplomatic objectives; avoidance of the military threats to give the impression of resorting to war; the diplomatic-military tendency to negotiation rather than military solution; communications transparency; and the reduction of time pressure on policymakers. For crisis management strategies, there is no single dominant strategy that is equally suitable for managing every crisis, but instead, strategy needs to be carefully formulated and sometimes carefully adapted to meet the distinctive configuration of the crisis. Strategies can be offensive or defensive. Also, there is a parallel between the crisis discussions and strategic management thought.

The second root, i.e., "the structure and functioning of decision-making", may contain the following threads:

➤ An understanding of Eilon's (1979) description of the decision process and his model that consists of eight stages: information input, analysis, performance measure, model, strategies, prediction of outcomes, choice criteria, and resolution.

➤ Obstacles related to the decision-making process that face crisis management during international crises include: misperception, insufficient information or simple errors of judgment, which can lead to decisions that diminish rather than enhance the possibilities for containing and defusing a crisis.

➤ Recognition of Kahn's (1991) assumption that the decision-making process becomes more complicated when organizations are large and consist of numerous semiautonomous sub-units.

➤ The argument that "bureaucratic decision theory", which drops the assumption that the decision-maker is a unitary actor, can be applied to the mass media as a communication system. Each department and sub-department in a communication system develops its own preferred mode of functioning through an interpretation of its responsibilities. Also, the rational component of the bureaucratic theory on mass is applicable to the mass media as they have a rational component that stems from their unique and influential power.

➤ The significance of the decision-making process increases in times and situations of high stress. Crisis and its consequent conflicts, including wars, are situations that place the highest level of stress on decision-makers.

➤ Use of the results of this chapter's analysis of Leslie's (2000) discussion of philosophers' decision-making tools throughout historical cultural periods that led to the formulation of a preliminary understanding of the general philosophical perspectives on ethical decision-making. The eight groups of recommended actions and concepts common to the philosophers' teachings are: seeking real knowledge of the situation; reasonable/rational thinking; prudence and self-control; social justice; responsibility; morality; selection of choices; and doing what is just-right/good.

The third root, i.e., "the knowledge and comprehension of game theory", may contain the following threads:

➤ Significant acknowledgment of Shubik's (1954) pioneering argument that without mathematics, researchers analyzing a social phenomenon or problem, which involves multiple factors, could not carry out the analysis without facing substantial difficulty because verbal discussion of the phenomenon would become so complex as to be almost unmanageable.

➤ An understanding of Senn's (2000) distinction of two basic concepts: "doing mathematics" and "employing mathematical methods". Doing mathematics means performing a mathematical operation, while employing mathematical methods refers to how problems are formulated and handled. Therefore, more understanding of how to employ mathematical methods is required as it is very applicable to game theory.

➤ The indispensability of game theory in analyzing the United States-Iraqi Crisis and the 2003 War on Iraq, as it is most used in analyzing crisis and conflict situations. Therefore, it is useful to understand Morrow's (1994) explanation that game theory helps to explain how individuals' decisions are interrelated and how those decisions result in outcomes. In addition, it is crucial to understand Nicholson's (1970) explanation that game theory is prescriptive and not descriptive. It recommends a rational course of action and then describes the consequences of such conduct. It tells us what would happen if the recommended rules of behavior are followed. Therefore, knowing the basic assumptions of game theory is important. For example, Schellenberg's (1996) explanation of its assumptions regarding the way the interests of different individuals may be related to each other, which is able to be analyzed mathematically, demonstrates that: 1) games always involve two or more players, each with an opportunity to choose between alternatives; 2) each available alternative is fully known to each player; 3) all possible outcomes occurring to any player may be expressed in terms of numerical measures of utility; and 4) each player will make those choices that will provide the maximum expected utility.

➤ Game theory has various types and classifications. It is, therefore, very important to understand the characteristics of games, rules, terms, forms of representation, and so on.

➤ Understanding Bowen's (1978) classification of games, and accordingly, the Game-World level of structure of the United States-Iraqi Crisis and the Game-Situation structures of the 2003 War on Iraq.

The fourth root, i.e., "the significance of rationality", may contain the following threads:

➤ Acknowledgment of Nicholson's (1970) assertion that conflict decisions should be made on the basis of tested knowledge rather than of intuitive guesses.

➤ A concentration on the rational-choice approach to crisis research. The rational-choice approach shares the common assumption that decision-makers are rational.

➤ An understanding of Nicholson's (1997) argument for comparing rational people to feeling people and his favoring of rational people for the sake of more effectiveness.

➤ The study of the theories about the process of decision-making, including the "rational actor" theory, the bounded rationality, and the bureaucratic politics.

➤ The discussion of the decision-making process is confined to rational decisions. The decision-maker has several options from which to choose, and that choice includes a comparison between those options and the evaluation of their outcomes. This explanation provides a sense of the process (including resolution and selection criteria) that the decision-maker goes through to reach a decision.

➤ An understanding of the game theory scholars' view of rational behavior, rather than the more common meanings of the term rationality. For example, Morrow's (1994) definition asserts that rational behavior means choosing the best means to gain a predetermined set of ends. It is an evaluation of the consistency of choices and not of the thought process, of implementation of fixed goals and not of the morality of those goals. That is, rational behavior is goal directed; actors are trying to create more desired outcomes rather than less desired outcomes. Also, Nicholson's (1996) explanation to rationality calls for the efficient pursuit of consistent goals.

> ➤ The linking of the view of game theory scholars' to Hybel's (1993) claim that realization of rationality in decision-making does not guarantee success, proves the need for some sort of balance.

The fifth root, i.e., "the communication process and fundamentals of news-writing", may contain the following threads:

> ➤ A consideration of communication in general and international mass communication practices in particular as decision-making processes.

> ➤ Communication is a complex process that is influenced by the context in which it occurs. In addition, there must be a recognition of the complexity of mass communication processes such as what is reflected in definitions by Wilson and Wilson (2001) and Hiebert, Ungurait and Bohn's (1974). This acknowledges the existence of professional communicators who are sorting, selecting, sharing, shaping, and transmitting information, ideas, messages, social values, experiences, and attitudes that influence large audiences. These processes are series of actions or operations, always in motion, directed toward particular goals.

> ➤ An assumption that Mowlana's (1984a) four approaches—idealistic-humanistic, political proselytization, information as economic power, and information as political power—which have characterized international communication, may be involved when talking about crisis. In the idealistic sense, communication tries to promote understanding among nations, governments, or individuals in order to manage the crisis. Also, each adversary may use one-way communication as propaganda during a crisis to manipulate and ideologically confront the other side's claims. In addition, using information as economic power sometimes helps to exert pressure on the weak party or parties in a crisis to implement the desired action or decision. After all, using information as political power through forms of mass media is an indispensable way of communicating among participants in a crisis.

> ➤ An understanding of three of Frey et al.'s (1991) five basic levels of human communication—group, organizational, and

societal communication. Media decision-makers have a group communication among themselves to achieve commonly recognized goals. They also have organizational communication that occurs within a particular social system, which includes formal and informal channels of communication, and is also concerned with both internal (within an organization) and external (among members of various organizations) communication. Their societal communication occurs within and between social systems, focuses on communication within a particular culture as well as different cultures, and has two forms: public and mass communication.

➢ International communication is communication that occurs across international borders, encompasses political, economic, social, cultural and military concerns, and becomes more widespread and multi-layered.

➢ A recognition of Nolan's (1999) notion of successful communication through achieving control over events, which affect communicators and others.

➢ An investigation of decisions that are made under stress or tension can help to evaluate the performance of media institutions.

➢ The importance of the argument presented by Dennis and Ismach (1981) that news-writing has seven distinct stages, which include many decisions that must be made: 1) choosing a subject; 2) planning; 3) news gathering; 4) prewriting; 5) writing; 6) rewriting and polishing; and 7) getting feedback. With more consideration in times of crisis, there will be numerous decisions that should be made in the context of news-writing.

➢ Significant attention must be paid to Zinsser's (1998) emphasis on thinking before writing, and his explanation of the countless successive decisions that go into every act of writing, some of which are big while some are as small as the smallest word.

➢ An understanding of Lorenz and Vivian's (1996) and Garrison's (1990) explanation of the organizational structure of mass media where decisions are made, as well as the nature of duties assigned to media personnel in various levels of management.

The sixth root, i.e., "the ethical principles for mass communication", may contain the following threads:

➤ Acknowledgment that social responsibility theory is relevant and significant in the development of recommendations and directions for the functioning of mass media in society. It imposes a burden on media practitioners and increases the need for testing the mass media as responsible instruments of a diverse society.

➤ An understanding of Day's (2000) three branches of ethics— metaethics, normative ethics, and applied ethics. While metaethics is concerned with the study of the nature or characteristics of ethics, examines the meaning of abstract terms such as "good", "right", "justice", and "fairness", and provides the broad foundation for ethical decision-making, normative ethics is concerned with developing general theories, rules, and principles of moral conduct. A logical next step is the task of applied ethics, which is the use of the insights derived from metaethics and the general principles and rules of normative ethics in addressing specific ethical issues and concrete cases.

➤ An understanding of Leslie's (2000) explanation of ethics as moral principles for living and making decisions. Morality, a term closely related to ethics, often involves issues reaching beyond the individual to the larger social group. In addition, it is significant to realize that ethics, which is a broad scholarly discipline that falls under the study of philosophy and contains many perspectives, subcategories, and approaches, refers to the principles of "right conduct" or doing "the right thing" rather than just anything at all.

➤ Media codes of ethics are useful, necessary, and greatly benefit the common good of society. Journalistic codes of ethics attempt to balance in a moral way the interests of the journalist, the public, and media organizations. However, media personnel's obligation to these codes and responsibility to the common good of society have proven largely inadequate and deficient.

➤ An acknowledgment of Gordon's (1999a) and Wheeler's (2002) arguments that media codes of ethics are useful and necessary to the mass media and to society, because they serve an important purpose by setting standards against which conduct can be measured and evaluated. Also, understanding that they attempt to balance in a moral way the interests of the journalist, the public, and media organizations.

➤ Use of the results of the analysis of the existing journalistic codes of ethics, introduced in Chapter 5, which leads to the exploration of the wide umbrella of responsibility, and which contains a wide range of principles, many values, and a tremendous number of rules. ASNE, for example, sets responsibility at the head of its Statement of Principles. The analyzed codes suggest a wide range of general principles and a tremendous number of detailed practices that can guide the work of either the whole profession (journalism), a specific medium or kind of media, or journalists. The six prevalent principles are: independence, truth, accuracy, fairness, integrity, and serving the public interest. However, within these general principles there are others which intervene in relation to these such as objectivity, balance, and maintaining context.

➤ Linked to the theme of media responsibility is the concept of media accountability. Bertrand's (2002) and others' explanations of media accountability are useful in showing how media professionals are accountable for themselves, their employers, their peers, their sources, the people involved in the news, and the media users. Codes acknowledge that the journalist's responsibility towards the public exceeds any other responsibility, particularly towards employers and authorities.

➤ An understanding of Kieran's (1998) explanation that good journalism aims at discovering and promoting the audience's understanding of an event via truth-promoting methods. This increases the significance of impartiality, and therefore considers a failure of impartiality in journalism as a failure to respect one of the methods required in order to fulfill the goal of journalism, i.e., getting to the truth of the matter. On the other hand, bad journalism is truth-indifferent and fails to respect truth-promoting practices.

➤ Gordon's (1999b) suggestion to consider truth telling as a first principle in journalism, to the point where if choices must be made, truth must be given primacy over any other ethical concerns.

The seventh root, i.e., "the role of the media within international political crisis, with application to the United States-Iraqi Crisis and its latest consequence, the 2003 War on Iraq", may contain the following threads:

> ➤ When a crisis, the most extreme of the stress situations, occurs on a transnational level it is known as an international crisis. The international political crisis and the international protracted conflict deserve the highest degree of attention from media decision-makers because they are the worst kind of conflict with the potential of leading to internal conflict on the national level or to a war or wars, on the international level.
>
> ➤ The interaction on the global level through their mass media between countries with different backgrounds, ideologies, cultures, and so on, is connected to the process of decision-making, similar to their interaction on the political level.
>
> ➤ An understanding of communication as a decision-making process will let communication meet with theories of crisis management and mathematics on the central ground of decision-making.
>
> ➤ An understanding of the relationship between the mass media and the government, especially during situations of stress, and the use of transnational media in support of peace.
>
> ➤ The crisis political decision-making process, which occurs under conditions of high tension and extreme pressure, may negatively affect the functioning of the media.
>
> ➤ On many levels, there was a great involvement of the mass media in the 2003 War on Iraq. The strategic choices by political decision-makers on both the U.S. and Iraqi sides have relied to a great extent on the mass media to achieve their goals. The media have been used as tools whether by the initiator of the war, the other adversary, or other players involved.
>
> ➤ The intervention of the media in times and situations of the highest level of stress on decision-makers, such as crisis and its consequent conflicts, including wars, has the nature of double-edged sword that can either help de-escalate the crisis or exacerbate it.

➤   A proposed argument that the media decision-making process must be effective, through being rational and responsible, in order to effect de-escalation of a crisis and become key players in helping the opponents to manage it.

➤   The analysis of the rationality of the political decision-makers in the United States-Iraqi Crisis and the 2003 War on Iraq is useful in examining the rational behavior of media decision-makers.

➤   The need for media ethics is greater during war, given the great effects of the consequences. Examples of the media coverage during the 2003 War on Iraq demonstrate the use of unethical journalistic practices.

➤   The significant role of the media during wars requires that they act with a sense of responsibility; when the coverage of the United States-Iraqi Crisis and its latest development, the 2003 War on Iraq, is examined in this light, it can be seen that the media failed to act responsibly.

To conclude, this chapter covers an essential stage towards the structuring of the model I put forward in this book. It uncovers the need for a quadrilateral area, according to the concept of interweavement, as an essential basis for the model. This quadrilateral area benefits from: 1) an understanding of the nature of crisis management and its strategies and techniques; 2) the dynamic of the decision-making process that feeds from two major theories—the mathematical and behavioral; 3) the idea of modeling real situations and the application of game theory, a pure branch of mathematics, to crisis; 4) ethics and the social responsibility theory of mass media; and 5) the concept of rationality that has various applications. The argument that I make here is that rational thinking and responsible conduct are two fundamental weights or forces for making the balance of the model, which means that *rational* and *responsible* aspects of the model are crucial for achieving its main purpose, thus making it *effective*. Therefore, it is necessary to synthesize a group of roots of theoretical threads from the major fields discussed and analyzed in this book, in order to use them as inputs for feeding and structuring the model. In the following chapter, I will explain the structure of the model and how its components work.

NOTES

1. The word "interweavement" has been looked up in a number of English dictionaries in order to ensure that it is the most relevant term to use here. Although it sometimes appears in the English language, it does not exist in the dictionaries searched, including: *The Oxford American Dictionary and Thesaurus* (2003); *Merriam-Webster's Collegiate Dictionary* (10th ed., 2001); *Canadian Dictionary of the English Language* (1997); and *Chambers English Dictionary* (1989). However, when tracing its origin in the English language, it is obviously evident that it comes from the verb "to interweave". This verb has been defined as "to weave together" (Oxford, 786; Merriam-Webster, 612; Canadian, 713; and Chambers, 748). Also, it has been defined as to "blend intimately" (Oxford, 786); "mix or blend together" (Merriam-Webster, 612); "blend together; intermix" (Canadian, 713); "to intermingle" (Chambers, 748). It is the equivalent of the verb "to intertwine" (Merriam-Webster, 612; and Canadian, 713). The verb "to intertwine" has been defined as "become entwined" (Oxford, 786); "to unite by twining one with another" (Merriam-Webster, 612); "to join or become joined by twining together" (Canadian, 712); and "to twine or twist together" (Chambers, 748). The verb "to intertwine" is the equivalent of the verb "to entwine" (Oxford, 786). The verb "to entwine" has been defined as "to interlace, braid, weave, intertwine, twine, plait, wreathe, twist, wind, splice, . . . tie, knit, crisscross . . . [and] interweave" (Oxford, 482); "to twine together or around . . . to become twisted or twined" (Merriam-Webster, 387); "to twine around or together . . . to twine or twist together" (Canadian, 459); and "to interlace . . . to weave" (Chambers, 477). Here, the meanings come back to the verb "to weave" which has been used, as mentioned above, in defining the verb "to interweave"—"to weave together"—following the explanations of the interrelated verbs. The verb "to weave" has been defined as "to form (cloth) by interlacing strands (as of yarn) . . . to make (cloth) on a loom by interlacing wrap and filling threads . . . to interlace (as threads) into cloth . . . to interlace esp. to form a texture, fabric, or design . . . to produce by elaborately combining elements . . . to unite in a coherent whole . . . to introduce as an appropriate element" (Merriam-Webster, 1335). A noun of the verb "to intertwine" is "intertwinement" (Oxford, 786; Merriam-Webster, 612; Canadian, 712; and Chambers, 748), and a noun of the verb "to entwine" is "entwinement" (Oxford, 482; and Canadian, 459). Therefore, it is similarly suggested here to use "interweavement" as a noun to the verb "to interweave". The adjective of the verb "to intertwine" is "intertwining" (Chambers, 748), and therefore, "interweaving" can be also used here as an adjective. However, using a noun is more relevant to the process at hand.

2. Dennis and Ismach (1981) explain that "uncertainty" has been considered as a principal cause of pressure in newsrooms and a factor in reporters' professional lives. They confirm that "uncertainty" has been described as a "bargaining game between and among newsroom personnel (such as reporters bargaining with editors) and with news sources (for example, reporters convincing sources to give them information)" (284). They claim, "What makes journalism a particularly vital field, though, is the fact that there are continuing battles about what constitutes proper and professional behavior in various news situations and in relationships between reporters and news sources. There is obviously much uncertainty in this continuing search for certainty and definite answers to particular questions" (285).

3. Lazarsfeld's main interest in developing his understanding of mass society was to improve the standards of people living under the conditions of industrialization.

4. Similarly, Whitehead and Russell, in the preface of their 1968 *Principia Mathematica*, assert that the importance of a proposition originates from its hypothesis, which, in turn, is more widely applicable. "We have sought always the most general reasonably simple hypothesis from which any given conclusion could be reached. For this reason, . . . the importance of a proposition usually lies in its hypothesis. The conclusion will often be something which, in a certain class of cases, is familiar, but the hypothesis will, whenever possible, be wide enough to admit many cases besides those in which the conclusion is familiar" (vi).

5. In his *Philosophical Investigations*, 1953, Wittgenstein says our language is like an old town, "a maze of little streets and squares, of old and new houses, and of houses with additions from various periods; and this surrounded by a multitude of new boroughs with straight regular streets and uniform houses" (quoted in Specht, 1986: 131-132). In this picture, language is a structural growth, not a construction drawn up according to a uniform plan. The stock of words and grammatical forms, transmitted down the centuries, Specht (132-133) illustrates, is like "the maze of little streets and squares" of the old town. New technical languages and technical terminologies are like new annexes and street systems. Finally, the artificial languages of mathematics and logic can be compared with the modern parts of the town, built on a uniform plan, sometimes still closely connected, at other times only quite loosely connected to the centre of the town. Wittgenstein calls the whole of language and all the activities woven into it "the language-game", and certain partial systems or individual ways of using fully developed everyday language are called "language-games."

6. Examples of the values which are often considered to be important in media practice are: professional, moral, sociocultural, logical, and aesthetic. Professional values include: proximity, firstness, impact, recency, conflict, human interest, entertainment, novelty, toughness, thoroughness,

immediacy, independence, watch-dog, public's right to know, no prior restraint, and independence. Moral values include: truth-telling, humanness, fairness, honesty, stewardship, nonviolence, commitment, and self-control. Sociocultural values include: thrift, hard work, energy, restraint, and heterosexuality. Logical values include: consistency, competence, and knowledge. Aesthetic values include: the harmonious, the pleasant, and the imaginative (Christians et al., 2001: 25).

7. This table has been created based on Larry Leslie's (2000: 22-160) discussion.

8. James Morrow (1994: 311-312) explains how to build a model by considering three requirements: designing a game tree, assigning payoffs to the outcomes, and solving the resulting game. He stresses a single and most important principle in modeling, that of simplifying, since simple models are easier to solve and follow. The beginning of the building process consists of writing down in a specific order a sequence of choices that actors have; next, defining the information they have when making choices, which lead to outcomes; and finally, considering plausible preferences over these outcomes that the actors might hold. Thierauf (1970: 20-23) further explains the process of constructing the model as well as its evaluation. For more, see Saaty and Alexander (1989: 5-11).

9. These models, which reflect uni-dimensional and multi-dimensional perspectives of decision-making, Harrison considers as constituting an ideal medium for illustrating the interdisciplinary character and diverse nature of decision-making. The rational model, the classical approach in the field of decision theory that provides the foundation for the quantitative discipline of economics, mathematics, and statistics, is essentially normative in that it takes a prescriptive rather than a descriptive approach to decision-making. Its primary decision-making criterion is maximized outcome. The organizational model combines the behavioral disciplines with quantitative analysis. Thus the decision-maker's choice takes note of constraints caused by the external environment. Its primary decision-making criterion is satisfying outcome. The political model, which is based primarily on the disciplines of political science, philosophy, and sociology (behavioral foundation), employs a compromise or bargaining decision-making strategy and aims towards an outcome that is acceptable to many external constituencies. Its primary decision-making criterion is acceptable outcome. The process model, whose usage is increasing, draws selectively on the quantitative disciplines of economics, mathematics, and statistics. It recognizes the behavioral disciplines of philosophy, psychology, and sociology and is open to the external environment. Its primary decision-making criterion is objectives-oriented outcome.

CHAPTER 10

The Crisis Decision-Making Model

for Media Rational Responsibility

In this final chapter, I suggest a media decision-making model that contributes to rendering the performance of the media decision-makers *effective*, as a consequent result of being *rational* and *responsible*. The Crisis Decision-Making Model for Media Rational Responsibility (CD_M^3_R^2) is *theoretical*, *prescriptive* and *dynamic* in nature. Through this model, I provide recommended actions that may be required of media practitioners during their news-writing process in times of international political crisis with specific applications to the crisis in question.

Introducing the Simple Form of the CD_M^3_R^2

Wars follow from decisions. Therefore, any explanation of war must incorporate, explicitly or implicitly, a model of decision-making.

(Geller & Singer, 1998: 31)

Although scholars have provided a number of models of rational decision making, I know of no theory of "effective" decision making that seeks to improve the ad hoc judgments top policymakers often feel obliged to make. This remains an important problem that requires additional research and reflection.

(George, 2003: 266)

[D]istinctions [are made] between models of decision making that simply *describe* what it is that people do when they engage in a cognitive task and those that *prescribe*, or mandate, what people ought to do to be effective decision makers.

(Galotti, 2002: 9)[1]

The CD_M^3_R^2 is best introduced at the beginning of this chapter in a simple form that consists of its main four components; this is followed by separate explanations of the tasks of each component, which lead into an illustration of the extensive form that demonstrates the whole structure, including all components and their tasks together. The four main components of the model are the media's: rational thinking, responsible conduct, crisis decision-making and final acts. As *Figure 11* illustrates, these components of the model feed from the roots of the theoretical base, built in and explained in the previous chapter, in an entire-exterior degree of interweavement.

The selection of the word "component" rather than others such as "phase", "stage", "step", and so on, has been done in keeping with the nature of how the model functions. For instance, while the word "phase" gives an impression that the tasks of the model operate in a cyclical manner, the word "stage" gives the impression that the tasks should be implemented in a sequential order, one stage before or after the other; finally, the word "step" gives a third impression of broken tasks, i.e. moving towards a next step does not allow for returning to the previous. However, the nature of how the model functions and the tasks that should be implemented therein reflect that there is a cyclical nature of a group of tasks, a sequential nature of another group, and a flexible nature in moving among the tasks. Therefore, the word "component" has been adopted here to combine various natures of the model's tasks, in addition to reflecting the collective coherence of the model. That is, the model has four components whose tasks work together, sometimes in a cyclical, or sequential, or flexible way, depending on the nature of each group of tasks.

Basically, the components "rational thinking" and "responsible conduct" of the media work as the two balancing sides of a weighing scale, i.e., two forces or strengths whose influences are directed towards a third component—that of crisis decision-making; hence the direction of arrows. As I have argued in the previous chapter, *rational* and *responsible* aspects of the model are crucial to achieving what is being proposed in this book, that is the ultimate goal of making the model *effective*. The rectangular shapes are used to portray the suggested understanding of being weighing scales. The component of "crisis decision-making", while receiving the inputs of the theoretical threads from below, also receives the output of the functioning of both the previous two components, then carries out its functioning process, and finally feeds the fourth component—hence the circular shape.[2]

Figure 11: **The Simple Form of the CD_M^3_R^2**

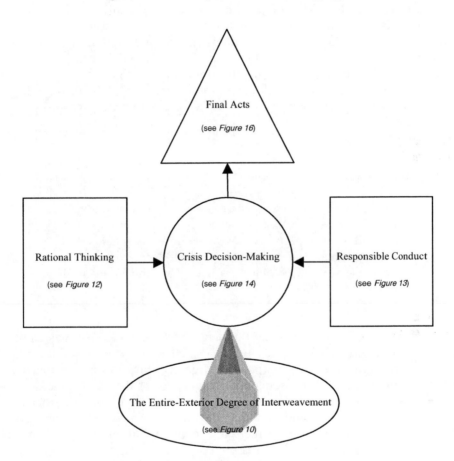

The component "final acts" of media, harvests the information from the three other components through the component "crisis decision-making", (it is for this reason that the three components are shown on the same level), in order to finalize the tasks. The triangular shape is used to reflect the synthesizing and conclusive nature of the tasks in this component. Needless to say, the bottom-to-up direction of functioning, which also appears in the tasks involved, is a result of structuring the model in a way that allow roots of theoretical threads to feed the components of the model. In total, the components of the model work together, in a coherent way, to help the media decision-makers during a given international political crisis achieve a *rational* and *responsible*, i.e., *effective* performance. How these components work and how their tasks should be implemented are the themes of the following discussion, in which each component is explained individually, prior to reaching the book's concluding vision—the extensive form of the whole model.

THE MEDIA'S RATIONAL THINKING

> We think when we are in doubt about how to act, what to believe, or what to desire. In these situations, thinking helps us to resolve our doubts: It is purposive. We have to think when we *make decisions,* when we *form beliefs,* and when we *choose our personal goals,* and we will be better off later if we think well in these situations.
>
> (Baron, 2000: 6)

The component "rational thinking", as *Figure 12* illustrates, consists of six consecutive and successive tasks, each of which again contains consecutive and successive actions. Consecutive and successive mean that they are implemented in a sequential nature, but at the same time are also subject to reimplementation as many times as is necessary in order to achieve the component of rational thinking during the crisis. Also, the actions involved in each task are of the same nature. Although actions have a predetermined order, each action is *not always* a prerequisite for the next, as it can happen that after completing some actions decision-makers go back and re-work earlier actions; needless to say, they can all be in the process of implementation simultaneously.

However, the arrows indicate the logical sequence for conducting these actions in order to help find starting points. The six tasks are: 1) distinguishing crisis situation; 2) studying the crisis; 3) recognizing actors; 4)

Figure 12: **The Media's Rational Thinking**

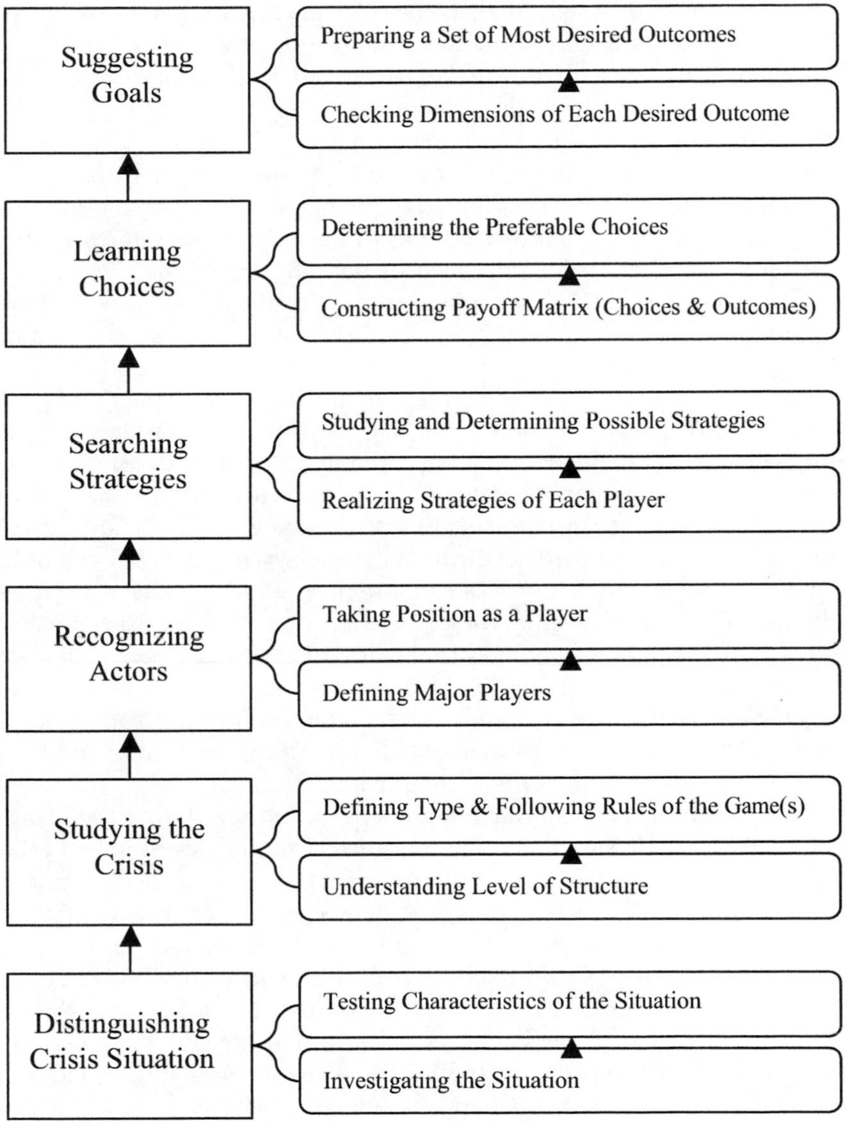

Suggesting Goals	Preparing a Set of Most Desired Outcomes
	Checking Dimensions of Each Desired Outcome
Learning Choices	Determining the Preferable Choices
	Constructing Payoff Matrix (Choices & Outcomes)
Searching Strategies	Studying and Determining Possible Strategies
	Realizing Strategies of Each Player
Recognizing Actors	Taking Position as a Player
	Defining Major Players
Studying the Crisis	Defining Type & Following Rules of the Game(s)
	Understanding Level of Structure
Distinguishing Crisis Situation	Testing Characteristics of the Situation
	Investigating the Situation

searching strategies; 5) learning outcomes; and 6) suggesting goals. There are certain actions that need to be taken in order to fulfill each of these tasks.

To distinguish a crisis from other similar stress situations, the situation should be investigated, and its characteristics tested. In so doing, media decision-makers need to clearly understand the political policies of their adversaries in the crisis, the adversaries' real drivers, primary objectives, and the instruments needed to achieve these objectives. This investigative effort enables media decision-makers to avoid misinterpretations, and to recognize the logic behind the adversaries' decisions.[3] Then, testing the characteristics of the situation in order to make sure that it is a crisis, not a similar stress situation, helps in knowing how to deal with the situation according to the rules of crisis management. The analysis conducted in Chapter 2 is a helpful guideline for media decision-makers in this context. Based on the characteristics approach of defining crisis, the United States-Iraqi Crisis and the 2003 War on Iraq, the case study used in this book, is confirmed as a real international political crisis. As we have seen, the crisis originated suddenly in 1990 between the George H. W. Bush administration of the United States and the Saddam regime of Iraq. It contained within it the serious threat of the destruction of the basics of the two nations' respective political systems, combined with an uncertainty as to the unfolding of events. Its life cycle began instantly and grew quickly towards maturity which, unfortunately, was in turn unsuccessfully managed; the result was the 1990/91 Gulf War. The life cycle reached decreasing points of conflicts between the adversaries until the emergence of new causes (claims of producing WMD and links to Al-Qaeda's acts of terrorism, especially 9/11) which reactivated the crisis again, and for the second time unsuccessful management resulted in the failure of diplomatic activities and the launch of the 2003 War on Iraq. As such, any intervention in this situation should rely on crisis management to de-escalate its circumstances, as well as to maintain control over events, not allowing them to get out of hand.

To study the crisis effectively, the different levels of structuring the crisis should be understood, and the crisis itself and its developments should be defined mathematically as specific types of games with specific rules that should be followed. To recognize actors included in the crisis according to its game structure, major players in the game should be defined and the media organization should position itself as a player. The Game-World structure presented in Chapter 6 as an ideational Soccer Game was presented specifically to locate players (or countries) around the globe vis-à-vis the crisis. The 2003 War on Iraq, as the latest development of the United States-Iraqi Crisis, was analyzed in Chapter 7 and presented as a Chicken Game.

Therefore, if the goals of the media systems of each of the main adversaries' countries, as well as those of the other countries involved, are identical to those of their respective political systems, they should logically follow the same strategies and choices available to their political systems. For example, although Canada and the Arab world media were generally successful in coping up with their political systems' choices for achieving their goals, practices and policies were randomly implemented.

To search for strategies for playing the game, or for participating in the crisis or its consequent conflict, the strategy of each player participating in the game should be realized, and possible strategies should be studied carefully and fully understood. For example, after the War on Iraq was launched, if a U.S. media organization chose to deal with the political system, rational thinking assumes that it should have adopted the same choices available to the political system, i.e. to continue in a non-cooperation position against Iraq, and therefore, any shifting from this general policy would work against the media organization and its political system. On the other hand, Iraqi media given their governmental nature before and during the early military actions, in order to be better off, should have followed the cooperation strategy. However, to a great extent the actual practices on both sides ran counter to this rationality. The Iraqi media before and at the beginning of the war, concentrated on adopting an anti-American tone in their coverage rather than providing factual evidence of not having WMD and links to terrorism. Also, although there was general U.S. media support for decisions made by the Bush administration against Iraq, some of those media, when trying to balance their news, discredited the administration's decisions and consequently ended up working against achieving the planned goals.

To learn about the possible choices for each player in the crisis, the payoff matrix of each game should be constructed to include outcomes of each choice, and consequently the preferable choice should be determined. Examples of that were presented in Chapters 7 and 8 in the context of explaining various conflict situations as games during the 2003 War on Iraq. For example, after Saddam's revealing of the secrets regarding WMD in a Samson and Delilah Game played between the Bush administration and the Saddam regime, the Bush administration had a good opportunity to improve its status (payoffs) while simultaneously weakening Iraq's by stopping their accusations of Iraq, and further, by trying to withdraw from that position, instead claiming that Iraq was about to possess WMD. This new position would have made the Bush administration capable of confronting the blame campaign against it that discredited their major reason for launching the 2003 War on Iraq. Although the U.S. media conveyed this politically-played-right position (change position and claim Iraq's status near to possess WMD), illogically, they were not supportive enough and sometimes conveyed more of a tone of blame.

> [I]n a goal-directed model [there] are *actors* who have *preferences* over the possible consequences of conditions which might arise. . . . These preferences can be referred to as the *goals* of the actors . . . where it is assumed that they seek to achieve these goals as effectively as possible. There is an *environment,* which might be inanimate or consist of other actors. . . . The environment and the goals indicate which *acts* must be carried out in order to achieve the *consequences.* There are also *rules,* which are derived from the goals that dictate the choice of the act under certain conditions; that is, specified states of the environment.
>
> (Nicholson, 1996: 152-153)

To suggest rational goals, the dimensions of each desired outcome should be checked, and consequently a set of the most desired outcomes should be prepared. For example, Galotti (2002) argues that goals differ in a number of ways, which she calls "dimensions of goals". She (12-14) lists nine dimensions: content, time frame, complexity, difficulty, specificity, controllability, degree of realism, importance/centrality, and autonomy of the goal.

In sum, the outcomes of this "rational thinking" component to be incorporated in the functioning of the "crisis decision-making" and the "final acts" components are: 1) suggested strategies; 2) preferable choices; and 3) most desired outcomes (or goals).

THE MEDIA'S RESPONSIBLE CONDUCT

The component "responsible conduct", as *Figure 13* illustrates, consists of four cyclical tasks, each of which contains actions; two of these tasks maintain their cyclical nature while the other two have a consecutive and successive nature. Cyclical means that they have no specific order in which they must be implemented and that they continue until achieving the responsible conduct during the crisis. Also, the actions involved in each of the four tasks have the same nature as the tasks themselves. The two tasks of a cyclical nature are: 1) balancing various responsibilities; and 2) emphasizing ethical principles; while the two tasks of the consecutive and successive nature are: 1) confronting major effects on decision-makers; and

Figure 13: **The Media's Responsible Conduct**

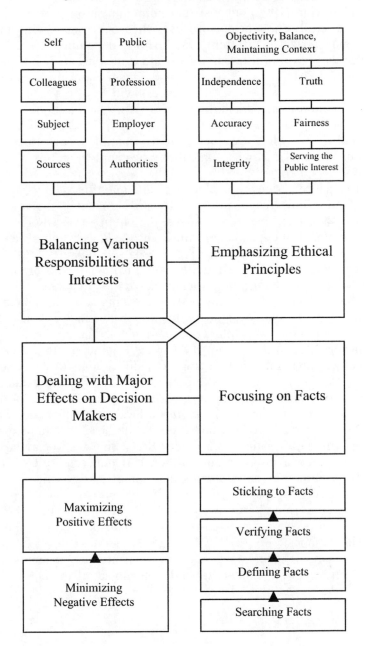

2) focusing on facts. In order to fulfill each of these tasks, there are actions that need to be taken.

In the context of investigating how ethical decisions are made, Lorenz and Vivian (1996) suggest that communication professionals who "follow a carefully thought-out process when confronted with an ethical dilemma may arrive at different conclusions, depending on the relative importance they give to different values and principles" (572); significantly they follow a six-step process. Lorenz and Vivian claim that answering the six main questions asked during this process will lead to reasonable ethical decisions "in almost any ethical dilemma" (572). The questions are: 1) what happened or what are the facts of the situation?; 2) what communication values apply?; 3) what are the ethical principles?; 4) to whom are responsibilities owed?; 5) what ethical theories apply?; and 6) what are the alternatives?

To balance various responsibilities and interests, the media decision-makers should show responsibilities towards, or serve the interests of, themselves, colleagues, subjects, sources, the public(s), the profession, their employer or organization, and authorities. The media decision-makers should make sure that their news satisfies journalists' self interests, shows respect among themselves and to their colleagues in other media organizations, protects the subject's humanitarian and other rights, maintains the rights of sources, serves the public's interest, represents a good image of the profession, helps the employer or the institution to achieve their goals, and finally, maintains a mutual helpful coordination with authorities.

In the 2003 War on Iraq, there were a number of cases in which imbalance was evident when trying to achieve one or more of these responsibilities. For example, although they were reporting facts, some journalists used ironic statements in reporting officials involved in the 2003 War on Iraq. In *The Economist*, there was a heading "Mohammed Saeed al-Sahaf: The Scheherazade of Baghdad" and a sub-heading "Iraq's marvelous minister of (mis)information" on a story describing the vocabulary of the then-Iraqi minister of information. Further, it is unnecessary to remind the reader of the numerous news stories that sarcastically criticized Saddam Hussein and George W. Bush. However, it is worth mentioning, especially in the reporting concerning lower level of officials involved in the 2003 War on Iraq, in order to explain that even though journalists were presenting facts and showing responsibility such as keeping the publics informed and so on, nonetheless some of them exaggerated by using ironic statements in a way that shows irresponsible conduct towards the subject of the news story. For example:

> If NO-ONE will miss Saddam Hussein, his information minister will be recalled with a certain affection. Mohammed Saeed al-Sahaf's memorable, often surreal, daily press briefings were all that proved to the world that the regime was still there. Mr Sahaf's English statements, while smooth and fluent, always seemed a little ludicrous. But it was in Arabic that his true demented genius shone through. His vocabulary was salty and, at times, archaic. Terms such as "animals", "thugs", "cowards" and "criminals" were sprinkled in every sentence. His most enduring legacy may be the reintroduction of the word *ulug* (roughly, "louts") into the Arabic lexicon. The London-based Arabic daily *al Sharq al-Awsat* even devoted an article to exploring the linguistic and cultural roots of his unique vocabulary. Mr Sahaf's apotheosis came on Monday April 7th[, 2003]. With American tanks occupying the Baghdad parade ground, he stood calmly a couple of hundred yards away, on the roof of the Palestine Hotel, to tell reporters that none of this was really happening. Smiling extra-wide, he said: "Don't repeat the lies of the liars." For many Arab viewers, he became a star. Their hope is that he will re-emerge in time, unscathed and unconvicted of war crimes, to be given his own talk-show on [Al-Jazeera].
>
> *The Economist* — (April 12th, 2003)

As well, the concentration of media coverage on a given specific aspect or aspects of the developments during War on Iraq may have resulted in harmful effects for the authorities in charge. For example, in the United States:

> The impact of media coverage on American public opinion, and subsequently on decision-making in foreign policy, cannot be underestimated, particularly in . . . [the 2004] presidential elections, where foreign policy is expected to play a major role. . . . [T]he impact of graphic images of Americans being mutilated in Fallujah could, indeed, shake US public support for the military occupation and may play into the presidential campaign. . . . Media coverage is important for shaping the environment within which foreign policy decisions are made in the U.S.
>
> Marwan Al Kabalan, *Gulf News* — (April 14th, 2004)

In order to emphasize ethical principles, media decision-makers should adhere to six major ethical principles (independence, truth, accuracy, fairness, integrity, and serving the public interest), as well as three others (objectivity, balance, and maintaining context) which intervene with the six principles, as explained in Chapter 5. Media decision-makers, in order to make sure that they carefully consider the ethics of their actions, may want to adopt a checklist, from which they ask themselves a list of questions that will confirm the use of ethical principles. It may be true that such a list will not ensure that an ethical decision will always be made, but it will at least improve the chances of doing so because it will help to ensure that the decision is made thoughtfully.

Telling the truth is a key principle and it has been explained and understood by media scholars and practitioners in connection to some of the other previously mentioned ethical principles. For example, Day (2000) considers that three concepts underlie the notion of truth in reporting. Day argues that reporting should be "accurate," "promote understanding", and be "fair and balanced." To be accurate, the facts of the situation "should be verified; that is, they should be based on solid evidence" and if there is still any doubt about the facts, "it should be revealed to the audience" (81). For accuracy, Day emphasizes that quotes should be checked and research results should be "examined with exacting scrutiny when it comes from a public advocacy group or an organization with a commercial or political ax to grind" (83). Certainly, the publics in the case of both quotes and research results have the right to know the sources to better assess credibility. To promote understanding, the goal of reporting "should be to provide an account that is *essentially* complete. A story should contain as much relevant information as is available and essential to afford the average reader or viewer at least an understanding of the facts and the context of the facts" (83). To be fair and balanced, not only is it necessary to avoid bias, but also journalists "should attempt to accord recognition to those views that enhance the understanding of the issue. Every effort should be made to represent them fairly and not to use quotes out of context" (83-84).

In the 2003 War on Iraq, Sarah Niblock (2003) shows that "on an unprecedented level, senior journalists have been candid about their difficulties in establishing what was true, in a war that was being fought as much in the media as it was in the so-called 'theatre'. At each stage during the rolling stream of text and images in real time from the war zone, it was easy to hit upon some running commentary—in print, online or on air—from senior editors justifying their precarious judgments." She argues that with each new reported incident, executives were simultaneously capitulating to accusations of inaccuracy and bias. Niblock claims that it was one of the most surreal moments when Mark Damazer, deputy of the BBC's director of news Richard Sambrook, "publicly admitted that the BBC had been making mistakes 'on a daily basis' during the first week of the war". Niblock witnessed "BBC director general Greg Dyke expressing grave concerns about the integrity of reports from embedded journalists within his own organization, and calling for academic research into this" (375).

In order to deal with any major effects on decision-makers, media decision-makers should minimize negative effects, and maximize positive effects. For example, Wallace (1999: 15) explains that there are positive and negative effects on the decision-making process in crisis. The negative effects include: narrowing of options, over-reliance on experts, taking refuge in value judgments, poor mental performance, overloaded communications, meddling in lower levels, reduced team performance, and lack of a long term view. The positive effects include: increased responsiveness, enhanced innovation, and improved flexibility.

I argue that to focus on facts, media decision-makers should carefully go through the processes of searching, defining, verifying, and sticking to facts. For example, in searching for facts the media decision-makers should investigate the origins of the facts and collect them from various sources before defining them because once they verify the facts and are confident of their reliability they will stick to them. Michael Parenti (2003) calls for not accepting the claims of Washington policymakers uncritically, because human motives are impossible to observe in a direct empirical way. Although they claim that the purpose of U.S. global interventionism is "propelled by an intent to bring democracy to other peoples, maintain peace and stability in various regions, protect weaker nations from aggressors, defend U.S. national security, fight terrorism, protect human rights, oppose tyranny, prevent genocide, and the like", Parenti argues that some observers see that the overriding purpose of U.S. global interventionism is "to promote the interests of transnational corporations and make the world safe for free-market capitalism and imperialism". Parenti considers that the problem of recognizing the actual motives becomes crucial when attempting to discover the intent of political leaders, "many of whom make a regular practice of lying about their actions" (19).

> Are the news media giving Americans an accurate picture of what's really going on in Iraq? . . . A CBS News poll released on May 24 [2004] revealed that 61 percent of those polled believe the news media are spending too much time on the Abu Ghraib story. This jibes with what some of us on the editorial board have been hearing more and more: that average Americans believe the news media are obsessed with bad news from Iraq and aren't paying enough attention to the good things going on there. We decided to search photo wire service archives for the past month, looking for images of U.S. soldiers engaged in helping Iraqis instead of

shooting at them . . . [only one photo was moved on the wires in recent weeks.] . . . This newspaper's photo department told me that if news photographers aren't shooting those pictures, it's because media back home aren't interested in those stories. . . . This is not necessarily an issue of media bias. It's extremely dangerous for journalists to be in Iraq now, which limits the number of photojournalists in the field . . . but this means that Americans are not getting the complete story from their media . . . there are other positive developments to report. . . . We in the media owe you, the reader, a more complete picture.

Rod Dreher, *The Dallas Morning News* — (June 1st, 2004)

When emphasizing the importance of covering a news story the same way it happens, Dary (1973) compares nonfiction writing to fiction writing. He explains that "the writer of fiction may decide what his story is going to be, who his characters are, and whether there will be a happy or sad ending"; quite differently, the news writer does not have this choice as he/she "must tell the story as it happened." He explains that many people never read any fiction and many more "may read it only a few years out of their lifetime," but he claims that "everybody writes nonfiction and everybody reads it. The news writer and his audience have one common bond-interest in nonfiction" (64).

Harris and Spark suggest that news writers should stick to facts and be accurate[4]. They advise reporters that

Whatever you decide to leave out of your opening sentence, always retain its clarity and accuracy. The sentence must be readily comprehensible at first reading. It must also be accurate, not just approximate. Much criticism of newspapers stems from opening sentences which, for the sake of sharpness or impact or simplicity, go further than the established facts.

(1997: 58)

The outcomes of this "responsible conduct" component that will be incorporated in the functioning of the "crisis decision-making" and the "final acts" components are: 1) most significant ethical principles; 2) verified and reliable facts; 3) helpful circumstances in decision-making environment; and 4) attention towards most significant responsibilities and interests.

THE MEDIA'S CRISIS DECISION-MAKING

The component "crisis decision-making", as *Figure 14* illustrates, consists of five consecutive and successive tasks, each of which again contains consecutive and successive actions. Also, the involved actions in each task have the same nature as the tasks themselves. The five tasks are: 1) analysis of information; 2) setting goals; 3) selecting strategies; 4) making choices; and 5) taking decisions. To fulfill each of these tasks, there are actions that need to be taken.

To analyze the information of the crisis, media decision-makers should go through the processes of gathering and updating, verifying and checking, and preparing and adopting information. To set goals, the rational goals coming from the "rational thinking" component should be examined by the measures of the "responsible conduct" component, new goals other than those rationally suggested should be generated, final goals should be decided, and then the final goals should be revised and refined. To select strategies, the strategies suggested in the "rational thinking" component should be tested by the measures of the "responsible conduct" component; new strategies should be generated, final strategies should be confirmed, levels of strategies should be set, strategies of each level should be defined, and strategies should be distributed to media decision-makers.

There should be a careful analysis of the information that is to be incorporated into the news in order to avoid being guilty in cases of unethical practices by journalists. The process of gathering information should be accompanied by constant updating to include the latest information. Measures of verifying the collected information should be followed by checking, that is, if verification requires relying on various sources to have agreed-upon information that has been verified by many sources, there should be also supervision of those who gathered and verified the information. Once the information has gone through these processes it can be prepared for dissemination and placed in news stories. Otherwise, the performance can be expected to be badly interrupted:

> Though experts say the news media generally do a good job of policing themselves, a reporter determined to deceive his bosses can get away with it. And if editors at the nation's "paper of record"—*The New York Times*—can be duped, reporters elsewhere may also be getting away with the highest of journalistic sins: faking quotes and concocting interviews. Sunday [May 11, 2003], in a 7,500-word account that filled two pages, the *Times* detailed how Jayson Blair, 27, "committed frequent acts of journalistic

Figure 14: **The Media's Crisis Decision-Making**

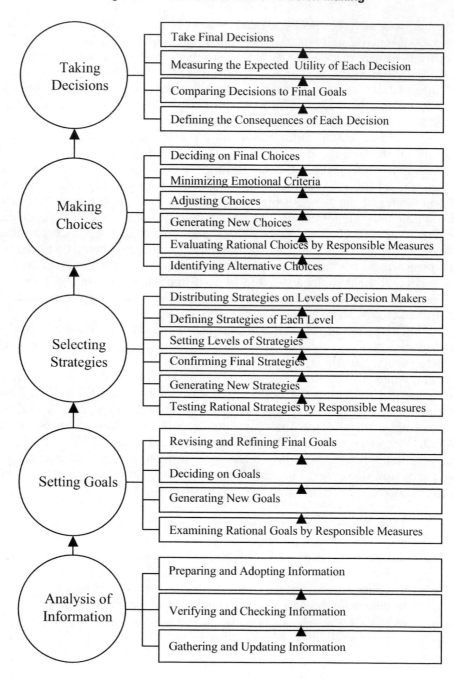

fraud" covering the Washington, D.C., sniper case and the war with Iraq. . . . The *Times* found problems in at least 36 of the 73 articles written by Blair from late October to his resignation May 1. The article called it "a low point in the 152-year history of the newspaper," while publisher Arthur Sulzberger Jr. called it a "huge black eye." Harvard media analyst Alex Jones, a former *Times* reporter, is troubled that many of the people Blair identified and quoted in his articles didn't contact the paper—even after knowing that he fabricated quotes because they had never talked to him. . . . A few recent publicized journalistic lapses may give the impression of a trend: A *Los Angeles Times* photographer faked a photo during the war; two *Salt Lake Tribune* staffers sold information about the Elizabeth Smart case to the *National Enquirer*.

> Peter Johnson, *USA Today* — (May 12th, 2003)

When making choices, alternative choices should be identified, choices coming from the "rational thinking" component should be evaluated by measures of the "responsible conduct" component, new choices should be generated, choices should be adjusted, emotional criteria in making choices should be minimized, and final choices should be decided. The argument that I make in this book about the balance this model tries to accomplish can be seen here in the evaluation of rational choices by responsible conduct measures. The evaluation of rational choices by ethical principles will lead to the selection of a better choice. The Truth Game presented in Chapter 8 is a good example.

Rapidly changing circumstances . . . suggest that professional communicators and society in general are best served by developing their own moral reasoning mechanisms and accepting responsibility for their own actions . . . [ethical decisions can be made] . . . [o]n the basis of rules-prescribed by tradition or authority. . . . [and] . . . [o]n the basis of the thoughtful application of principles and through reason.

> (Englehardt & Barney, 2002: 3)

Also, it is suggested here that during this task, media decision-makers can generate new choices based on that evaluation if the news choices will better serve to achieve their goals. The action of minimizing the emotional criteria that should be taken before deciding on final choices is significant in times of crises when emotions are hardly avoidable. Some journalists described images depicting the torture of Iraqi detainees under emotional stress, using these violations to illustrate what they consider to be one aspect of the occupation forces' daily war crimes and also to criticize Western democracy.

> Photographs of US military personnel torturing and sexually abusing Iraqi prisoners in Abu Ghraib prison, south of Baghdad, have been scrutinised by millions across the world as they filled TV screens and newspapers. These pictures of American soldiers gloating at the sight of hooded and naked Iraqi male prisoners constitute a complete violation of the Fourth Geneva Convention. . . . Human rights groups were keen to remind the United States of these provisions following CBS's release of the photos on [March 28, 2004]. Apparently "some" members of the 800th Military Police Brigade involved in Abu Ghraib pictures "did not see a copy of the Geneva Convention rules for handling prisoners of war" until after they were charged for abuse last month. In other words, these American soldiers didn't know that torture of Iraqi prisoners—that also involved sodomy, electrocution, forcing detainees to remove their clothing and keeping them naked for several days at a time and placing a dog chain around a naked detainee's neck among other creative American torture methods— is a serious breach of international law. . . . According to Alaa Shalabi, a spokesperson for the Arab Organisation for Human Rights who was part of a fact-finding committee that visited Iraq last month, "Torture, which is deliberately racist in nature, is the policy of the occupation forces in dealing with the Iraqis with the aim of humiliating them," he told *Al-Ahram Weekly*. . . . "We are not surprised by the Abu Ghraib pictures," commented Shalabi. "Reality is much worse and what the media is debating now is only a sliver of what's going on in Iraq."
>
> Amira Howeidy, *Al-Ahram Weekly* — (May 6-12th, 2004)

To take decisions, the consequences of each decision should be defined, decisions should be compared to final goals, the expected utility of each decision should be measured, and then final decisions should be taken. There many ways of measuring the expected utility of each decision in order to be better able to take the decision that can help achieve goals. A simple form is the decision tree, while a more challenging form is the expected utility equation, used when decisions have more influence on the strategic policies. In *Figure 15*, Stephen Slade (1994) provides a simple example of a decision tree, which is a schematic representation of choices. The box at the left stands for a choice point with two alternatives I and II. Choice I will result in either outcome A or outcome B, with equal likelihood of either. The payoffs for A and B are 40 and 0, respectively. Similarly, choice II results in outcome C or D, which have payoffs of 100 and -10, respectively.

Figure 15: **Decision Tree: A Schematic Representation of Choices**[5]

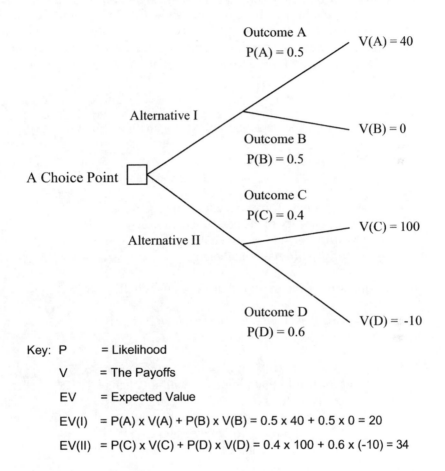

Key: P   = Likelihood

V   = The Payoffs

EV   = Expected Value

EV(I)   = P(A) x V(A) + P(B) x V(B) = 0.5 x 40 + 0.5 x 0 = 20

EV(II) = P(C) x V(C) + P(D) x V(D) = 0.4 x 100 + 0.6 x (-10) = 34

In this case, outcome D is slightly more likely than outcome C. The method of deciding between choice I and choice II is straightforward according to *Figure 15* where the expected value of each alternative can be calculated, according to the equation, and then the choice with the higher expected value can be selected.

The rational choice or expected utility model, as Geller and Singer (1998) explain, "can be placed in the context of a general decision problem of whether or not to challenge an existing policy" (43). The overall expected-utility equation demonstrates that "it is rational to challenge an existing policy when the expected gains from the challenge exceed the expected value of inaction" (43). The overall expected-utility equation is summarized as:

$$E(U) = E(U)_c - E(U)_{nc}$$

The equation for the expected utility of a challenge is:

$$E(U)_c = P_s(U_s) + (1 - P_s)(U_f)$$

where

$E(U)_c$	= expected utility of challenging the policy
P_s	= probability of successful challenge
U_s	= utility of successful challenge
U_f	= utility of failed challenge

The equation for the expected utility of not challenging is:

$$E(U)_{nc} = P_q(U_q) + (1 - P_q)[P_b(U_b) + (1 - P_b)(U_w)]$$

where

$E(U)_{nc}$	= expected utility of not challenging the policy
P_q	= probability that the policy will not change
U_q	= utility of the policy
P_b	= probability that the policy will change with positive utility
U_b	= utility of a positive policy change
U_w	= utility of a negative policy change

The outcomes of this "crisis decision-making" component that will be incorporated in the functioning of the "final acts" component are: 1) strategies of various levels of media decision-makers; 2) revised final goals; and 3) final decisions for directing news-writing.

THE MEDIA'S FINAL ACTS

The component "final acts", as I illustrate in *Figure 16*, consists of three consecutive and successive tasks, each of which again contains consecutive and successive actions. As well, the involved actions in each task have the same nature. The three tasks are: 1) transferring strategies into policies and plans; 2) directing news-writing; and 3) finalizing news form and content. To fulfill each of these tasks, there are actions that need to be taken.

To turn strategies into policies and plans, the various levels of the crisis strategy will be transferred into the media levels of management. That is, if the crisis strategies are distributed, for example, on three levels—grand, situational, and functional—the policies and plans of the media levels of management should be general, specific, and daily policies and plans respectively. Grattan's (2004) suggestion, in the context of studying strategy during the 1962 Cuban Missile Crisis, as explained in Chapter 2, is to distribute strategy in crisis discussions into three levels parallel to strategic management thought. In this respect, it is suggested at this point in the model that there are three levels of strategy resulting from the model's crisis decision-making process, i.e., grand, situational, and functional strategies. These levels of strategy will be transferred into media policies and plans in the media final acts stage, preserving similar levels of media management. That is, the grand strategy of the crisis decision-making will be transferred into a general policy and plan for the media organization during the crisis. The same situational strategy will be transferred into specific policies and plans that deal with the various events involved in the crisis according to the nature of the developments. Also, functional strategies will be transferred into daily policies and plans that deal with daily developments.

For example, the general policy of a U.S. media organization should be consistent with the grand strategy of the crisis if the media organization chooses to cope with the political system position in the United States-Iraqi Crisis, i.e., by taking a pre-emptive strategy, the specific policies and plans (consistent with the situational strategy) should be non-cooperation in War on Iraq played as a Chicken Game. Furthermore, they should stop making accusations against Saddam's regime; in investigating WMDs played as a Samson and Delilah Game, the daily policies and plans (consistent with the functional strategies) should maintain the continuity of taking the non-

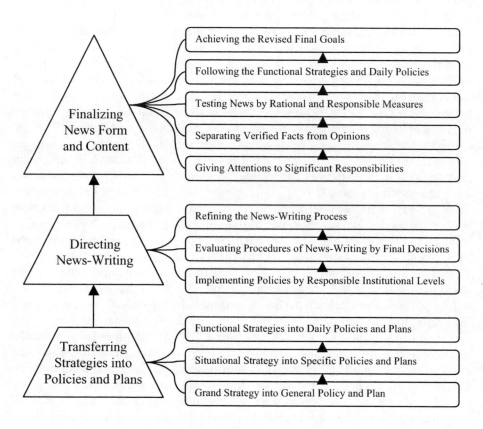

Figure 16: **The Media's Final Acts**

cooperative position in the Chicken Game whatever the responses from Iraq, and finally, they should move between practicing and stopping their accusations according to Saddam's reactions.

To direct news-writing, policies and plans should be implemented by each institutional level held responsible, procedures of news-writing should be evaluated by the final decisions made, and the process of news-writing should be refined. It is therefore a suitable distribution of responsibilities in the managerial or institutional structure in media organizations to have the general policies defined by the publishers and the specific policies by managers and directors, while the daily policies and plans are defined by editors.

When it comes to daily policies and plans, there will be a wide range of actions during the news-writing process for editors to make decisions about. Therefore, good explanations of general and specific policies are important for reaching reliable daily policies. The many areas of making decisions that editors face during news-writing become more problematic in times of crisis. For example, it is argued here that although "spot news writing is almost always done with inverted pyramid organization" (Garrison, 1990: 76), while chronologies "work well for crime, accidents, or other disaster stories" (Ibid: 81), in crisis situation most approaches of structuring news stories can be used. However, there are risks attached to the choice of structure especially under circumstances of crisis. For example, the inverted pyramid can be used given that the information is provided to readers and listeners in descending value of importance, facts of the story will be revealed, and the story utilizes summary leads. On the other hand, the chronological approach may be a better choice for events that have a sequence of steps to explain. However, readers and audiences who like the inverted pyramid approach because they do not have to read the whole story for the facts may not like it during the crisis if they want to know about the sequence of the events. As well, those who like the chronological approach may not have enough time to follow the explanatory steps if they are searching out facts from many sources. Therefore, it is anticipated that carefully considering in order to select the most appropriate story structure may not only serve the audiences better and lead to creating new forms of more relevant and appropriate story structure (even if these are a combination of existing ones), but may also help in avoiding making mistakes or picking the wrong approach. The same can be said regarding various ways and techniques in news stories such as the use of transitions, itemization, etc.

To finalize the news form and content, attention should be given to significant responsibilities, verified facts should be separated from opinions, news should be tested by measures of the "rational thinking" and "responsible conduct" components, functional strategies and daily policies should be followed, and the revised final goals should be achieved. In sum, it is an essential task of revisions, whose main purpose is to make sure that the functioning of the other tasks of various components is present in the produced news.

> One of the most overlooked parts of the news-writing process is revising—self-editing, rewriting, and updating. Some media writing books skip past revising as if the step was not necessary. It is, in fact, *very necessary*.
>
> (Garrison, 1990: 97)

For example the action of separating verified facts from opinions is very crucial as the task of this component is to protect the credibility of the media organization.

> The attempted separation of fact and opinion that is at the core of objective journalism undoubtedly reinforces the credibility of news. Such credibility depends upon the appearance that the "facts" reported in news are straightforward, indisputably concrete, value-free translations of the real.
>
> (Hackett, 1991: 84)

The final acts can therefore vary greatly from one media organization to another, according to the difference in the way they implement their crisis decision-making processes. On May 31, 2004, Paul Cochrane of *The Daily Star* wrote that the profusion of graphic televised footage of dead bodies "has raised difficult ethical and journalistic decisions for news editors, whether at CNN or the Hizbullah-backed Lebanese channel Al-Manar." In a series of interviews, *The Daily Star* talked with editors about their decision-making policies on screening disturbing images. Cochrane, as an example, shows the different approaches taken by the channels regarding the coverage of the four U.S. civilian contractors whose bodies were mutilated after a roadside attack in the Iraqi town of Fallujah in late March. Chris Cramer, managing director of CNN International, said the images that came into the news room from Fallujah varied from long shots to close-ups. Cramer said: "We made a judgment that this was a bit of a watershed in violence against Westerners in Iraq . . . and therefore it was acceptable to include images which I think, if they had occurred in other stories in other parts of the world, we might not have included." In contrast to CNN, the BBC only aired the event once, with a three-second long shot on the 10 p.m.

evening news, and a BBC spokesperson said "this was heavily prefaced with a warning." Jihad Ballout, media relations spokesperson for Al-Jazeera, said the editorial committee took a different route "by not showing the mutilated corpses being dragged by kids or hung from bridges. . . . We showed footage indicative and reflective enough . . . the burning and stoning of the car and a long shot of a charred corpse. We described what happened and felt that the description was strong enough. . . . The jubilation of the crowd was more reflective of the mood than the hanging on the bridge." Hassan Fadlallah, news editor at Al-Manar, said they did not use all the images available of the dead contractors. "We only showed a little bit, because it is against the ethics and morals of our religion, and of Al-Manar's policy. We believe there is a certain sanctity of the human body. . . . We try not to show dead soldiers' bodies in detail, using long shots rather than in close focus, so as to not hurt the feelings of the soldier's family."

There are some cases in which the irrational and irresponsible performance of media decision-makers result in ugly images of the media in general.

> During this time of war, the news is the most important show of the day. But the major networks seem to confuse news with entertainment. People all over the nation and the world want to know what is happening in Iraq. . . . When news shows excitedly promote the latest war footage as if it's entertainment, they have lost their sense of responsibility. No pictures from the war zone are exciting. They are heartbreaking and terrible. . . . I admit that in the beginning I was like most Americans. . . . I found myself mesmerized by the war coverage. But as the war progressed, I began to wonder if it was necessary for us to see the same building blown up several times, and how many different ways a team of reporters could explain the same attack. This is not a video or PlayStation game. This is not a made-for-TV movie. But more and more often it began to feel that way. . . . I think some of the journalists who are in Iraq need to ask themselves why they are really there. Is it for the sole purpose of providing the American public with information in a responsible, meaningful way? Do they really feel that this type of coverage is responsible journalism?
>
> Ian Schwab, *The Post-Standard* — (April 29th, 2003)

The three tasks of this component "final acts" are highly dependent, as we have seen, on tasks of the three components of the model. While this was evident in the previous discussions, it is more obvious when we look at the extensive form of the model.

THE EXTENSIVE FORM OF THE CD_M³_R²:
LIMITATIONS AND IMPLICATIONS

In order to better visualize the whole structure of the model it is useful to look at all its components along with their tasks and actions involved. *Figure 17* illustrates the extensive form of the model. Accordingly, nothing can be more timely here than putting the model into words, i.e., briefly defining it.

The Crisis Decision-Making Model for Media Rational Responsibility, $CD\_M^3\_R^2$, is a *theoretical*, *prescriptive*, and *dynamic* model designed for media decision-makers to use to help them achieve *effective* performance in the event of international political crisis. The model feeds from a theoretical basis—a group of synthesized roots of theoretical threads from four major fields, communication, mathematics, crisis management, and decision-making—in an entire-exterior degree of interweavement, an ideational architecture of mutual theoretical interactions. The recommended tasks and actions of the model, that are included in its composition of four components—"rational thinking", "responsible conduct", "crisis decision-making", and "final acts", and which are required of media practitioners during their news-writing process, can be practically examined in a dynamic way sensitive to specific features and conditions of application.

The $CD\_M^3\_R^2$ is a *theoretical* rather than a *practical* model which can be practically tested or examined in terms of specific conditions of application. One significant reason for the theoretical nature of the model is that no such model has previously existed. That is, at this time, it will be a cursory step to compare what ought to be done (the model) and what has already been done (the practical testing of the model) only within specific contexts. Rather, theorizing a contingent model and leaving the door open for practical application is more useful than limiting it to a description of mere existing practices. This leads also to the issue of applying this model to a specific country or region. It is true that the $CD\_M^3\_R^2$ is contingent to specific features of a specific type of crisis under specific conditions, but there is no limitation for future application to a specific country. This helps avoid the exclusion of many players from the conflicts (or games) included in a political international crisis and allow for the possibility of its application in various contexts after the specific necessary adjustments are made. It goes without saying that the cultural differences, national goals during a crisis, the role played, relations to adversaries, media capabilities, and ideologies of players such as the United States, Australia, United Kingdom, France, Germany, Japan, China, India, and the Arab world, vary to

Figure 17: **The Extensive Form of the CD_M³_R²**

Finalizing News Form and Content
- Achieving the Revised Final Goals
- Following the Functional Str. & Daily Polic.
- Testing News by Rational & Responsible M.
- Separating Verified Facts from Opinions
- Giving Attentions to Sign. Responsibilities

Directing News-Writing
- Refining the News-Writing Process
- Eval. Proced. of News-Writing by Final Dec.
- Implementing Policies by Responsible Inst. L.

Transferring Strategies into Policies and Plans
- Functional Strategies into Daily P. & P.
- Situational Strategy into Specific P. & P.
- Grand Strategy into General Policy & Plan

Final Acts

Rational Thinking

Suggesting Goals
- Preparing a Set of M. Des. O.
- Checking D. of each Des. O.

Learning Choices
- Determining the Pref. Chs.
- Constructing Payoff Matrix

Searching Strategies
- Studying & Det. Poss. Str.
- Realizing Str. of each Player

Recognizing Actors
- Taking Position as a Player
- Defining Major Players

Studying the Crisis
- Def. T. & R. of the Game(s)
- Understanding L. of Struct.

Distinguishing Crisis Situation
- Testing Charact. of the S.
- Investigating the Situation

Crisis Decision-Making

Taking Decisions
- Take Final Decisions
- Measuring Exp. Ut. of each Dec.
- Comparing Decs. to Final Goals
- Defining the Conseq. of each Dec.

Making Choices
- Deciding on Final Choices
- Minimizing Emotional Criteria
- Adjusting Choice
- Generating New Choices
- Evaluating Rat. Chs. by Resp. M
- Identifying Alternative Choices

Selecting Strategies
- Distributing Str. on L. of Dec. M.
- Defining Strategies of Each Level
- Setting Levels of Strategies
- Confirming Final Strategies
- Generating New Strategies
- Testing Rational Str. by Resp. M.

Setting Goals
- Revising and Refining Final Goals
- Deciding on Goals
- Generating New Goals
- Examining Rat. Goals by Resp. M.

Analysis of Info
- Preparing and Adopting Info
- Verifying and Checking Info
- Gathering and Updating Info

Responsible Conduct

Self	Public	Objectivity, Balance, Maintaining Context
Colleagues	Profess.	Independ.	Truth
Subject	Employer	Accuracy	Fairness
Sources	Authorities	Integrity	Serv. the Public In.

Balancing Various Responsibilities and Interests

Emphasizing Ethical Principles

Dealing with Major Effects on Decision Makers

Focusing on Facts

Maximizing Positive Effects
- Sticking to Facts
- Verifying Facts

Minimizing Negative Effects
- Defining Facts
- Searching Facts

The Entire-Exterior Degree of Interweavement

some extent and these differences affect the structure of a decision-making model. However, the CD_M^3_R^2 does not neglect the fact that there exists a group of variables that are either commonly rooted in, or applicable to, many cultures or that can at the least, be generally applied. Therefore, these variables were represented in the theoretical threads which fed the model, i.e., which provided the basis on which the model has been built. Also, the model acknowledges the fact that it neither offers a one-size-fits-all solution, nor contains *all* potential variables from *all* possible theoretical approaches in its structure. For example, although the model takes into account some of the variables that stem from the political economy of communication approach (e.g., the institutional structure, the influence of ownership on setting goals, and so on), it still does not rely intensively on that approach. This is because relying on such variables is a flexible and changeable process conditioned to specific features or circumstances for individual decision-makers in specific media organizations whose objectives greatly vary.

The CD_M^3_R^2 is *prescriptive* in nature, not descriptive, because it provides recommended actions that may be required of media practitioners during their news-writing process in times of international political crisis, with specific applications to the crisis in question, rather than just describing what used to be done. This prescriptive nature of the model is reflected in its structure and the composition of four components—"rational thinking", "responsible conduct", "crisis decision-making", and "final acts"—each of which has specific tasks which call for specific actions that should be done in order to achieve *effective* performance of media decision-makers.

The CD_M^3_R^2 is one example of a model that could help media decision-makers understand what ought to be done in the event of an international political crisis to achieve the goals sought. These can be those of the media organization, the national media system, or the government if they are identical to those of the media and are in place for the benefit of the whole society. The CD_M^3_R^2 is *dynamic*, not static, i.e., it is contingent on the specific features of a specific type of crisis (international political crisis) under specific conditions (circumstances, nature, developments, including conflicts and wars of the crisis in question, i.e., the United States-Iraqi Crisis), given that 1) crisis management tends to be highly context-dependent; 2) the precise configuration of each crisis varies in ways that have different implications for the selection of an appropriate strategy and therefore there is no single dominant strategy that is equally suitable for managing every crisis; and 3) models are used for representation of an actual specific situation in the real world at a given time and place under varying conditions.

The dynamic nature of the model that makes it contingent to the features of the situation and the conditions under which it works can be considered here as a way of responding to one kind of potential criticism of the $CD\_M^3\_R^2$ that calls for the required "parsimonious" nature of its variables (i.e., its actions) when it comes to its potential practical application. This criticism may see a dissemination of variables that can be unusable by decision-makers in media organizations under the pressure of the conditions of international political crisis. There may be resistance to some of these required actions as a result of ideological, ownership, deadlines, and other concerns. Therefore, what should be included and/or excluded to make this model parsimonious?

Briefly, the answer to this question can be presented here in the following way: it depends! However, the more variables that are included in the application, the greater the potential for media decision-makers to achieve an *effective* performance. The dynamic nature of the model is not only contingent upon the features of the international political crisis but also upon the conditions under which the decision-makers work. These conditions include their own media organization's ideology, structure, type of ownership, goals, circumstances of work, etc. So, it is evident that the application of such recommended actions such as these depends on the conditions and circumstances that vary widely from one media organization to another. However, as a key point in the suggested model, every single recommended component, task, and action is generally fundamental. In specific cases, it therefore becomes the choice of media decision-makers to apply these variables according to their own conditions, keeping in mind that the more they apply recommended actions the more their performance becomes effective. However, it is very crucial to note here that the components of the model and their internal tasks cannot be discarded. That is, they must be present when the model is applied. In other words, if the media decision-makers choose not to include some actions for whatever reasons, they should not do the same regarding the components and their internal tasks. The components and their internal tasks are key for having rational and responsible, i.e., effective conduct. As well, there are also what may be considered as fundamental actions in each task, which, depending on the features of the international political crisis and the individual media organization conditions, should not be excluded in application.

To better clarify the previous point, suppose that various media organizations were about to apply the $CD\_M^3\_R^2$ to the United States-Iraqi Crisis, and its latest consequence, the 2003 War on Iraq. What variables would they include and/or exclude? As indicated earlier, the main structure of the model, i.e. its basis, four components, and their internal tasks must be present in order to achieve the most effective outcome. Optimally, all of the recommended actions would also be included. However, as noted above, because the various media organizations vary in terms of their capabilities, conditions of work, ideologies, types of ownership, internal policies, and so on, they may configure their usage of the actions differently, i.e., include some and/or exclude others. And so it is important to note that the dynamic nature of $CD\_M^3\_R^2$ allows for compensating the absence of some actions by concentrating more on others, where necessary to stay consistent with the media organization conditions and features of the situation. For example, in the internal task "dealing with major effects on decision makers" of the component "responsible conduct", if a media organization cannot implement the action of maximizing positive effects, for reasons such as the small size of the organization, shortage of finances and so on, it can compensate for that by concentrating more on the action of minimizing negative effects. That is, if it cannot increase its capabilities of responsiveness to developments of the situation, enhance innovations in newsroom work, nor improve flexibility of the procedures of work, it can pay more attention to finding reliable experts, look for ways to think more deeply about the situation, or spend time planning the long term view. Or as another example, if, for reasons such as: governmental ownership and anti-American ideology, if media decision-makers in an Arabic media organization, engaged in the internal task "balancing various responsibilities and interests" of the component "responsible conduct", cannot balance responsibilities towards themselves, their colleagues, the subject of their news stories, their news sources, their publics, and the whole profession equally as it can towards the employer (the government) and authorities, they may compensate by concentrating more on responsibilities towards those that serve others. That is, by behaving responsibly towards their own profession, they will avoid being guilty of not behaving responsibly towards their audience, their news sources, and so on

Also, the dynamic nature allows for merging a group of actions into one. For example, in the internal task "focusing on facts" of the component "responsible conduct", if, for financial reasons, a media organization cannot implement the action "searching facts" separately from the action "verifying facts", it can merge both actions together with a third action "defining facts" by relying on only those facts that have been verified through various sources in the process of searching facts. As another example, if, for a reason of coordinating with officials to protect national security, media decision-makers in an American media organization, in the internal task "recognizing actors" of the component "rational thinking", cannot understand or determine major actors in the 2003 War on Iraq, they may merge this action to the next "taking position as a player" and take the American administration position in the conflictual situations as long as their responsible conduct component does not object to goals of the American administration.

However, again all components should be present in the application of the model, i.e., there is no acceptable way for the model to reach its ultimate goal—effective performance of media decision-maker—without having the four components working properly. As well, the internal tasks of the components should be present and used in the advised order. That is, the absence of any task of each component will lead to failure to complete the component. Even the implementation of one task in a way inconsistent with the nature of each component, for instance in a different order, will result in an unstable and hence ineffective component. For example, if the task "selecting strategies" has been implemented before the task "setting goals" or "analysis of information", and given that the nature of the tasks in the component "crisis decision-making" is consecutive and successive, the resulting end performance of the whole component will be unstable and, hence, ineffective. The same can be said regarding the involved actions in each task that have the same nature as the tasks themselves.

For instance, it would be expected that such an ineffective crisis decision-making performance would result in a Canadian media organization if it had selected a strategy of coordinating and cooperating with Arabic news sources in order to enhance mutual national relations, if the media organizations did not set as one of its goals "to help the government achieving its peacekeeping policy in the War on Iraq," and if in turn this goal had not been set based on a good analysis of the information at hand.

Thus, it is evident that there are many examples that might be drawn from the case study in question to demonstrate how the dynamic nature of the model can respond to potential criticism regarding application.

To conclude, the *theoretical*, *prescriptive*, and *dynamic* model that I suggest has drawn from the body of theories most relevant to the book's topic of investigating the media decision-making process during times of international political crisis, specifically the United States-Iraqi Crisis and its latest development the 2003 War on Iraq. It analyzes them based on a newly created concept, that of interweavement, in order to help to render the performance of the media decision-makers *effective*. The structure of this model consists of four components—"rational thinking", "responsible conduct", "crisis decision-making", and "final acts"—each of which has specific tasks requiring specific actions, which in turn strongly rely on the assumption that the consequence of being *rational* and *responsible* is the *effective* performance of media decision-makers.

NOTES

1. Similarly, Slade (1994) explains that there is a basic dichotomy in the decision-making literature between prescriptive and descriptive models. "Prescriptive or normative models focus on how people *should* make decisions, while descriptive theories explore how people *do* make decisions" (194).

2. There are many scholars who have tried to formulate the stages or phases of the decision-making process. For example, Galotti (2002) suggests five phases of the decision-making process, which are: setting goals, gathering information, decision structuring, making a final choice, and evaluating. She preferred to use the word "phases" to reflect the cycling nature of stages including in the process rather than the ranking.

3. An example of such an investigation of the crisis was presented in Chapter 6.

4. Accuracy is an important issue. In the previous chapter, the analysis of philosophical decision-making tools included a call for getting an "accurate picture of the situation" (listed under the category *seeking real knowledge of the situation*). Although "accuracy" is included in the codes of ethics analyzed in Chapter 5, and used to refer to "thoroughness," it is still criticized in terms of the possibility of application. Karim, talking about "an informed and conscientious journalism," says, "I have deliberately avoided using the terms . . . 'accuracy'—an ideal more suited to mathematics, not journalism" (2000: 179). Indeed, this may explain the inadequacy of accuracy guidelines for media workers. However, the argument of Chapter 3 about the interlinking between mathematics and communication, and the assumption made in the $CD\_M^3\_R^2$ of relying on rational and responsible components to achieve effective performance may help clarify the tricky nature of accuracy.

5. This figure has been created based on Stephen Slade's (1994: 195-196) discussion.

Conclusion

While there are certainly numerous ways of understanding communication, I have chosen to look at communication from the angle of decision-making. This does not mean that other perspectives have been ignored; rather, I focused on this angle because of its relevance to the various themes that are investigated in this book. Specifically, it is evident that the type of communication studied here is conducted between or among countries with different histories, ideologies, cultures, and so on. The interaction on the global level between such countries, which often occurs through the transnational media, is connected here to the process of decision-making, which is similar to their interaction on the political level. Thus, from the many vantage points of researching international communication, the main concern of this book is the involvement of international news media of the implicated countries during times of international political crisis.

The interactive relationship between the media decision-makers and political decision-makers, along with the complexity of the decision-making process in media newsrooms, highlights the importance of investigating and evaluating the quality of the media's performance in making decisions, which is, of course, vital in international crises because of the potential ramifications of their consequences. I argue that investigating and challenging the decision-making process for decisions that are made under stress, can result in a better evaluation of the performance of media personnel and institutions. Introducing communication in this book as consisting of, or at least involving, a process of decision-making, highlights how the nature of news-writing in media organizations is full of decisions with consequences that significantly shape the content of their communication. A consideration of the wide range of choices in each stage of the news-writing process, specifically the media's decision-making choices, also shows not only the reasons behind specific choices, but also provides some options for making better choices.

As a result of the fact that communication is a main component in the management process of international crises, understanding and distinguishing the crisis situation from other similar stress situations better helps media of communication to deal with it and achieve positive outcomes. The analysis conducted here to distinguish crisis from other similar stress situations and the definition of crisis presented, demonstrates the necessity for successful management because the opposite will result in negative developments. The argument raised here is that the indicator of good or bad usage of communication is the degree to which it affects the escalation or de-escalation of the international political crisis. In order to avoid escalating the situation that may erupt into a war, the media should decrease tension and violence and should work effectively towards managing the crisis. The requirements for successful crisis management and its strategies discussed in this book reflect a major fact—mediators in the management of crises, including the media practitioners and theorists, should analyze the media decision-making process, especially when it is under stress, very seriously. For this reason, I introduce the major theories of, and approaches to, decision-making focusing specifically on its relevance to crisis and conflict situations.

I, therefore, argue in this book that the media decision-making process must be *effective*. The way I present effectiveness relies on two major dimensions—*rationality* and *responsibility*. When the media are used rationally and responsibly as an important means to effect de-escalation of a crisis, they become key players in helping the opponents to manage the crisis. Because of the shortage of comprehensive, dynamic, and contingent models, it has been difficult for the participants in a complex conflict or crisis situation to structure the problem systematically and to access the possible means for management. To work towards this end, the discussions here cover those dimensions—rationality and responsibility—and then apply them to the example of the United States-Iraqi Crisis and the 2003 War on Iraq in order to provide the required background for the construction of the book's model. Together with the rationality of mathematics and decision-making, ethics and social responsibility are included in the construction of the model in order to keep a balance and to function as safety valves in the process of managing the crisis, that is, the actors involved should work not only towards individual desired utilities but also for the social good.

I also examine the responsible side of the required *effective* performance of media decision-makers in times of crises and conflicts. I bring to the reader's attention the importance of ethical and responsible communication in a general sense, and particularly in the face of the most dangerous circumstances of our world: international political crises and conflicts. Therefore, it is fundamental to draw a delineated picture of ethical conduct in terms of its principles, values, and rules. Through an analysis of a group of major codes of ethics of media, and research into the principles and fundamentals of journalistic practices, I address important issues regarding media ethics and responsibility and explored major ethical principles. The analysis provides a categorization that lists a selection of major and prevalent principles and then points out individual major statements of guidance under each principle. The six prevalent principles are: independence, truth, accuracy, fairness, integrity, and serving the public interest. In addition, within these general principles there are others, which intervene in relation to the general principles, such as objectivity, balance, and maintaining context.

Based on an investigation of the ethical/unethical paths that journalistic coverage or practice takes, especially when applied to the circumstances of the subject under discussion, I suggest a solution, i.e., a motivator towards ethical conduct. It has been assumed that journalists, editors, managers, and owners are likely to agree to the solution if it can be proven to them that being obligated by ethical principles will benefit the journalist, which in turn benefits the medium, and which ultimately contributes to the common good of society. That is, the solution calls for them to be obligated to follow the majority of the key principles of codes of ethics, as a condition for achieving the goal of benefiting all parties. This is especially crucial in times of international crises, when the stakes are much higher. The proof of this claim has been presented mathematically through one version of game theory—the Truth Game. It is demonstrated that telling the truth, as one key example of the major ethical principles explored from the analysis, is fundamental in achieving *goodness* and managing peacefully an international crisis—or winning a game, in the terminology of international relations theorists. Therefore, motivation towards ethical conduct, where otherwise the tendency may be to opt for another path, would stem from a desire to achieve beneficial consequences. Furthermore, this contributes to clarifying the debate surrounding the ambiguity of "ethical and unethical, but from whose perspective", as journalists recognize that in telling the truth, whose veracity has been checked and verified by them, regardless of what it is, or who is favored by its content, will benefit them, and ultimately result in favorable outcomes. However, in relation to the previous notion of a good usage of communication to de-escalate an international political crisis, there may be a potential related tension when the media's focus would be on the objective truth. This tension may result from the possibility of escalating the situation by adhering to the objective truth. Therefore, the suggested model in this book recommends tasks and actions that enable the decision-maker to overcome this tension through actions which are based upon the rational and responsible investigation of the outcomes of decisions and an evaluation of them in terms of the media goals.

It is demonstrated here that advocates of mathematics worked hard to prove that the social sciences are highly dependent on mathematics. This was done by highlighting some historical uses of mathematics in the social sciences and its contribution to knowledge which proved that mathematics is a process of creation that has been a required tool for social theorists to apply towards social problems. In sociology, for instance, one of the key functions of mathematics is to clarify problems, concepts, and research procedures. It is also one of my objectives for the book to argue that just as mathematics has been associated with the arts, religions, technology, sociology, sciences, economics, and politics, it can also be associated to communication. Thus, in terms of communication, I argue here that mathematics can be effectively used in communication as a helpful research tool; moreover, I assert that mathematics is a special way of communicating. Following from this, it is demonstrated that there is a fruitful relationship between communication and game theory.

What truly increases the importance of the relationship between mathematics and communication within the processes of decision-making in crisis situations is the inability of decision-makers to react or make rational decisions because of the circumstances posed by the crisis. In such cases, mathematics and accessible, well-designed, and contingent models are strong options. The effective contribution mathematics can provide to decision-makers in general, and media decision-makers in particular, is to implement what they either cannot, or find very difficult to, under the stressful conditions inherent in crisis situations. This holds true even under non-crisis conditions if the aim is to conduct a sophisticated process of decision-making, which includes inputs and outputs that are varied, numerous, and interconnected.

In discussing the rational side, I explain how the suggested model can effectively draw from mathematical theory to theorize the performance required by media decision-makers in times of conflicts and crises. From among the many angles that define and formulate the concept of rationality, I explain which particular version has been adopted, specifically that of game theory scholars, whose perspective particularly looks at the more focused meaning of rational behavior rather than the wide meanings inherent in the term "rationality". This requires choosing the best means to gain a predetermined set of ends. Thus, it is goal-directed since actors are trying to create more desired outcomes rather than less desired ones. The focus is on how individuals' attempts to achieve their goals are constrained by one another's actions and the structure of the game. In decision theory, it is also suggested that a rational person is one who, when confronted with a decision situation, makes the choice or decision that is best for him/her; thus, this best decision is called a rational, or optimal decision. Combining the two visions of rationality together was important here in order to focus more on rational decision-making under conflict or crisis situation rather than under normal circumstances. That is, strategic rather than non-strategic decision-making is the focus.

Game theory, as a pure branch of mathematics, is adopted as a result of its great relevance to the topic in hand. Since it can model conflict situations, an exploration of game theory is useful in explaining both how individuals' decisions are interrelated and how those decisions result in outcomes, in this case using the example of communication as decision-making processes as well as studying media decision-makers in times of conflicts and crises. A fundamental characteristic of game theory is that it is prescriptive and not descriptive. It recommends a rational course of action and then describes the consequences of such conduct, and tells us what would happen if the recommended behavior rules are followed. It studies the behavior of rational players in interaction with other rational players. When applied to the on-going developments of the United States-Iraqi Crisis and its latest major conflict, the 2003 War on Iraq, there continues to exist various games able to be represented in the terminology of international relations theorists. The rationality of the actors in the war—the political decision-makers—is analyzed here to discuss gaming situations and to examine the rational performance of media decision-makers as key actors in the structured games.

For the sake of better locating countries around the globe involved in the crisis at hand, I propose an ideational analogy of a Soccer Game in order to look at the crisis from the Game-World structure. I then investigate the 2003 War on Iraq, a major Game-Situation structure, as a Chicken Game, while investigating a key situation in the war such as U.S. accusations of Iraq having WMDs and links to terrorism, as a Samson and Delilah Game. I also present the involvement of other major players in the war in various forms of games; for instance, Canada and the Arab League in their mutual game that resulted in a form of Prisoner's Dilemma. This is in order to lead the discussion towards the importance of communication in times of crises and conflicts. It is shown how they both were able to use communication to achieve better results and convert the original game to a new, modified one, that I call a *Communication Game*. Therefore, I investigate the media's rational performance, and importantly, demonstrate, through an explanation of the Truth Game, how rational involvement is connected to adhering to major principles of ethics. As such, I suggest a rational conduct for the media decision-makers based on their obligation to abide by ethical principles of conduct. Telling the truth as a major journalistic ethical principle is highlighted at this point as a rational form of the Truth Game between the media and their audiences.

Because of the need for the rational and responsible conduct of media decision-makers during times of crises and conflicts, I call for the connection of four major theoretical frameworks—communication, mathematics, crisis management and decision-making—into a comprehensive body, creating a basis that eventually provides the foundation for the suggested model. I create the concept of *Interweavement* as a central locus in representing interactions among the frameworks in a dynamic ideational architecture, illustrating the possible mutual relationships among them. The discussions clarify basic relationships and answer important related questions, as well as present an analysis of each of the theoretical frameworks that together result in a broad interactive relationship between communication and the other three components of the interweavement. Furthermore, it clarifies how communication is intertwined in various mutual relationships with the other three fields—mathematics, crisis management, and decision-making.

As a pivotal relationship in the suggested model, the convergence of ethics and rational thinking is investigated in order to show how rational thinking and responsible conduct are two fundamental weights for the effectiveness of the model. When structuring the basis of the model, I uncover the need for a quadrilateral area, according to the concept of interweavement, as an essential framework for the model. This quadrilateral area benefits from: 1) an understanding of the nature of crisis management and its strategies and techniques; 2) the dynamic of the decision-making process that feeds from two major theories—the mathematical and behavioral; 3) the idea of modeling real situations and the application of game theory, a pure branch of mathematics, to crisis; 4) ethics and the social responsibility theory of mass media; and 5) the concept of rationality that has various applications.

The analysis is represented in a dynamic ideational architecture illustrating the possible mutual relationships among the four major theoretical frameworks; the basic idea expressed by this architecture is that friction and interaction between theoretical frameworks happen in a dynamic way. The interaction of the relationships of the interweavement, specifically the two basic dynamic axes, the four bi-lateral relationships, and the four tri-lateral relationships led the discussion to focus on the quadrilateral area as a root of theoretical threads that constitutes the basis of the model. The argument made here that rational thinking and responsible conduct are two fundamental weights or forces for creating balance within the model means that *rational* and *responsible* aspects of the model are crucial for achieving its main purpose, thus rendering it *effective*. Therefore, an investigation of this relationship between both rational thinking and ethics, as well as an investigation of the philosophical origins of the ethical decision-making process, are essentially useful here in the context of preparing the basis of the model.

I also demonstrate that there is a linkage between rationality and ethics, and that rationality is a fundamental element in the decision-making process; as a result, there is a consequent link between ethics and decision-making. When analyzing the philosophical origins of the ethical decision-making process to formulate a preliminary understanding of the general philosophical perspectives on ethical decision-making, I explain that there are eight groups of recommended actions and concepts common to all the philosophers' teachings: 1) seeking real knowledge of the situation; 2) reasonable/rational thinking; 3) prudence and self-control; 4) social justice; 5) responsibility; 6) morality; 7) selection of choices; and 8) doing what is just-right/good. As discovered in this book, these eight groups of recommended actions and concepts suggest the need for their application and adoption in the theories of communication research and social responsibility, mathematics, and the behavioral theories of decision-making. This approach not only further supports the book's theme of connecting these frameworks together to form a comprehensive body but also acknowledges the significance of these three groups of theories in the presence of the fourth one—crisis management. The distinction made between the various models of decision-making reveals how relevant rational models are to the topic of the book, as well as the significance of the expected-utility theory in the analysis of decisions in time of war. It is also necessary to synthesize a group of roots of theoretical threads from the major frameworks discussed and analyzed in this book, in order to use them as inputs for feeding and structuring the model. I develop seven main roots: 1) the understanding of international political crisis and its successful management; 2) the structure and functioning of decision-making; 3) the knowledge and comprehension of game theory; 4) the significance of rationality; 5) the communication process and fundamentals of news-writing; 6) the ethical principles for mass communication; and 7) the role of the media within international political crisis, with application to the United States-Iraqi Crisis and its latest consequence, the 2003 War on Iraq.

Finally, I suggest a media decision-making model—called here, the Crisis Decision-Making Model for Media Rational Responsibility ($CD\_M^3\_R^2$)—that contributes to making the performance of the media decision-makers *effective*, as a consequent result of being *rational* and *responsible*. The $CD\_M^3\_R^2$ is *theoretical, prescriptive*, and *dynamic* in nature. It is a *theoretical* rather than a *practical* model that can be tested practically or examined in terms of specific conditions of application. The $CD\_M^3\_R^2$ is *prescriptive* in nature and provides recommended actions required of media practitioners during their news-writing process in times of international political crises. The case study for specific applications in this book has been to the United States-Iraqi Crisis and the 2003 War on Iraq. The $CD\_M^3\_R^2$ consists of four main components: rational thinking, responsible conduct, crisis decision-making and final acts. These components of the model feed from roots of the theoretical basis in an entire-exterior degree of interweavement. The $CD\_M^3\_R^2$ is one example of a model that could help media decision-makers understand what ought to be done in the event of an international political crisis to achieve the sought-after goals. It is *dynamic*, not static: it is contingent on the specific features of a specific type of crisis (international political crisis) under specific conditions (circumstances, nature, developments, included conflicts and wars, most recently, the 2003 War on Iraq, of the crisis at stake, the United States-Iraqi Crisis). This dynamic nature of the model also makes it contingent on the circumstances and the conditions under which it will work when it is tested in practical situations. Although the recommended actions built into the model work best if applied exactly as designed, the model still has built-in-flexibility to adjust to different contextual circumstances such as newsroom policy, ideology, ownership, finances, and other concerns.

References

Abdel Gawad, Mohamed. (1978). "Attempts of the Arab world to participate in balancing the flow of information". In Philip C. Horton (Ed.), *The third world and press freedom* (pp. 173-186). New York: Prager Publishers.

Abunimah, Ali & Masri, Rania. (2002). "The media's deadly spin on Iraq." In Anthony Arnove (Ed.), *Iraq under siege: The deadly impact of sanctions and war* (pp. 101-119). Cambridge: South End Press.

Abu-Nimer, Mohammed. (1999). *Dialogue, conflict resolution, and change: Arab-Jewish encounters in Israel.* New York: State University of New York Press.

Ackerman, Seth. (2003*a*). The great WMD hunt: The media knew they were there—but where are they? *Extra*, July/August. Available at: http://www.fair.org/extra/0307/wmdhunt.html.

Ackerman, Seth. (2003*b*). Where did all the weapons go? Before the war, media overlooked a key story. *Extra*, May/June. Available at: http://www.fair.org/extra/0305/kamel.html.

Agor, Weston H. (1986). *The logic of intuitive decision making: A research-based approach for top management.* New York: Quorum Books.

Ahmad Maher, Al-Jazeera. (2003, March 4). *Al-Jazeera.* Retrieved March 21, 2003, from Lexus-Nexus.

Al Ajmi, Saad. (2004, April 16). Iraq must pass through 'liberaccupation' phase. *Gulf News.* Retrieved April 30, 2004, from Lexus-Nexus.

Al Kabalan, Marwan. (2004, April 14). Fallujah is not like Mogadishu. *Gulf News.* Retrieved April 30, 2004, from Lexus-Nexus.

Alexander, Yonah & Latter, Richard. (Eds.). (1990). *Terrorism and the media: Dilemmas for government, journalists and the public.* Washington: Brassey's (US), Inc.

Alger, Dean E. (1989). *The media and politics.* New Jersey: Prentice Hall.

Arab League stresses opposition to the war. (2003, March 20). *ArabicNews.Com.* Retrieved March 25, 2003, from: http://www .arabicnews.com/ansub/Daily/Day/030320/2003032011.html.

Arab Summit rejects any military action. (2003, March 3). *ArabicNews.Com.* Retrieved March 25, 2003, from: http://www.arabicnews.com/ ansub/Daily/Day/030303/2003030324.html.

Arno, Andrew. (1984*a*). "Communication, conflict, and storylines: The news media as actors in a cultural context." In Andrew Arno & Wimal Dissanayake (Eds.), *The news media in national and international conflict* (pp. 1-15). Boulder: Westview Press.

Arno, Andrew. (1984*b*). "The news media as third parties in national and international conflict: Duobus litigantibus tertius gaudet." In Andrew Arno & Wimal Dissanayake (Eds.), *The news media in national and international conflict* (pp. 229-238). Boulder: Westview Press.

Australian radio admits to sarcasm but denies bias in Iraq war coverage. (2003, July 21). *Agence France Presse.* Retrieved July 21, 2003, from Lexus-Nexus.

Azar, Edward E. (1999). "Protracted international conflict: Ten propositions." In Harvey Starr (Ed.), *The understanding and management of global violence: New approaches to theory and research on protracted conflict* (pp. 23-33). New York: St. Martin's Press.

Bahaa, Sherine. (2003, April 10 - 16). Arab anger. *Al-Ahram Weekly.* Retrieved April 20, 2003, from: http://weekly.ahram.org.eg/2003/633/sc8.htm.

Bahaa, Sherine. (2003, March 27 - April 2). Arabs show their rage: Outrage over the US-British war on Iraq has spilled onto Arab streets. *Al-Ahram Weekly.* Retrieved April 20, 2003, from: http://weekly .ahram.org.eg/2003/631/sc12.htm.

Baram, Amatzia. (2002). "Saddam's state, Iraq's politics and foreign policy." In Barry Rubin (Ed.), *Crises in the contemporary Persian Gulf* (pp. 199-221). London: Frank Cass Publishers.

Baran, Stanley J. & Davis, Dennis K. (2000). *Mass communication theory: Foundations, ferment, and future*. Australia: Wadsworth, Thomson Learning.

Baron, Jonathan. (2000). *Thinking and deciding*. Cambridge: Cambridge University Press.

Barrett, Cyril. (1991). *Wittgenstein on ethics and religious belief*. UK: Basil Blackwell Ltd.

Barthes, Roland. (1991). *The responsibility of forms: Critical essays on music, art, and representation* (Richard Howard, Trans.). Berkeley and Los Angeles, California: University of California Press.

Barton, Allen H. (2001). Paul Lazarsfeld as institutional inventor. *International Journal of Public Opinion Research, 13*(3), 245-269.

Baylor, Amy L. (2001). A U-shaped model for the development of intuition by level of expertise. *New Ideas in Psychology, 19*(3), 237-244.

Beltrame, Julian. (2002, Sep. 23). No way out: George W. Bush wants war, and in the end Canada may have to follow. *Maclean's*, 16-18.

Bengio, Ofra. (1992). *Saddam speaks on the Gulf Crisis: A collection of documents*. Tel Aviv: Tel Aviv University.

Berkman, Robert I. & Shumway, Christopher A. (2003). *Digital dilemmas: Ethical issues for online media professionals*. Iowa: Iowa State Press, A Blackwell Publishing Company.

Bertrand, Claude-Jean. (2002). *Media ethics and accountability systems*. New Jersey: Transaction Publishers.

Blitzer, Wolf, Wedeman, Ben, Arraf, Jane, Neisloss, Liz & Franken, Bob. (2004, April 28). Very intense fighting in Fallujah. *CNN*. Retrieved April 30, 2004, from Lexus-Nexus.

Blix says Iraq war unjustified. (2003, September 18). *ONASA News Agency*. Retrieved April 15, 2004, from Lexus-Nexus.

Bokhari, Imtiaz H. (1997). *Management of third world crises in adverse partnership: Theory and practice*. Karachi: Oxford University Press.

Bouchard, Joseph F. (1991). *Command in crisis: Four case studies.* New York: Columbia University Press.

Boudon, Raymond. (1974). *The logic of sociological explanation* (Tom Burns, Trans.). England: Penguin Education.

Bowen, K. C. (1978). *Research games: An approach to the study of decision processes.* London: Taylor & Francis.

Brams, Steven J. & Mattli, Walter. (1993). Theory of moves: Overview and examples. *Conflict Management and Peace Science, 12*(2), 1-39.

Brams, Steven J. (1975). *Game theory and politics.* New York: The Free Press.

Brams, Steven J. (1985). *Superpower games: Applying game theory to superpower conflict.* New Haven: Yale University Press.

Brams, Steven J. (1994). *Theory of moves.* Cambridge: Cambridge University Press.

Bresler, Robert J. (2002). Bush, war, and Iraq. *USA Today, 131*(2690), 13.

Burns, E. L. M. (1985). "Canada's peacekeeping role in the Middle East." In Tareq Y. Ismael (Ed.), *Canada and the Arab World* (pp. 37-43). Alberta: The University of Alberta Press.

Burton, John W. (1993). "Conflict resolution as a political philosophy." In Dennis J. D. Sandole & Hugo van der Merwe (Eds.), *Conflict resolution theory and practice: Integration and application* (pp. 55-64). Manchester: Manchester University Press.

Byman, Daniel, Pollack, Kenneth & Waxman, Matthew. (1998). Coercing Saddam Hussein: Lessons from the past. *Survival, 40*(3), 127-152.

Byman, Daniel. (2000). After the storm: U.S. policy toward Iraq since 1991. *Political Science Quarterly, 115*(4), 493–516.

Callahan, Sidney. (2003). New challenges of globalization for journalism. *Journal of Mass Media Ethics, 18*(1), 3-15.

Canada to remain out of Iraq: Manley. (2003, March 24). *The Toronto Star*, p. A14. Retrieved October 15, 2003, from Lexus-Nexus.

Canadian dictionary of the English language: An encyclopedic reference. (1997). Scarborough, Ontario: ITP Nelson, a division of Thomson Canada Limited.

Cannistraro, Vincent M. (2003). The emerging security environment: Preemptive war and international terrorism after Iraq. *Mediterranean Quarterly, 14*(4), 56-67.

Cassata, Mary B. & Asante, Molefi K. (1979). *Mass communication: Principles and practices*. New York: Macmillan Publishing Co., Inc.

Chaffee, Steven H. & Rogers, Everett M. (1997). *The beginnings of communication study in America: A personal memoir by Wilbur Schramm*. California: Sage Publications.

Chambers English dictionary. (1989). Cambridge: W & R Chambers Ltd and Cambridge University Press.

Chittick, William O. (1970). *State department, press, and pressure groups: A role analysis*. New York: John Wiley & Sons, Inc.

Christians, Clifford G., Fackler, Mark, Rotzoll, Kim B. & McKee, Kathy Brittain. (2001). *Media ethics: Cases and moral reasoning*. New York: Longman.

Cimbala, Stephen J. (1999). Nuclear crisis management and information warfare. *Parameters, 29*(2), 117-128.

Clutterbuck, Richard L. (1993). *International crisis and conflict*. New York: St. Martin's Press.

Cochrane, Paul. (2004, May 31). To show or not to show? Stations face dilemma over graphic news footage. *The Daily Star*. Retrieved June 5, 2004, from Factiva.

Cohen-Almagor, Raphael. (2002). Responsibility and ethics in the Canadian media: Some basic concerns. *Journal of Mass Media Ethics, 17*(1), 35-52.

Collins, Randall. (1998). *The sociology of philosophies: A global theory of intellectual change*. Massachusetts: The Belknap Press of Harvard University Press.

Colman, Andrew M. (1995). *Game theory and its applications in the social and biological sciences*. Oxford: Butterworth-Heinemann Ltd.

Colosi, Thomas. (1987). "A model for negotiation and mediation." In Dennis J. D. Sandole & Ingrid Sandole-Staroste (Eds.), *Conflict management and problem solving: Interpersonal to international applications* (pp. 86-99). London: Frances Pinter Publishers.

Condon, John C. (1975). *Semantics and communication*. New York: Macmillan Publishing Co., Inc.

Confronting Iraq. (2002, September 14). *The Economist*, p. 9.

Coser, Lewis A. (1984). "Salvation through communication?" In Andrew Arno & Wimal Dissanayake (Eds.), *The news media in national and international conflict* (pp. 17-26). Boulder: Westview Press.

Crabb, Annabel. (2003, May 28). Alston accuses ABC of bias over War in Iraq. *The Age*, p. 3. Retrieved May 28, 2003, from Lexus-Nexus.

Cramér, Harald. (1955). *The elements of probability theory: And some of its applications*. New York: John Wiley & Sons, Inc.

Crelinsten, Ronald D. (1989). Terrorism and the media: Problems, solutions, and counterproblems. *Political Communication and Persuasion, 6*(4), 311-339.

Crozier, Ray & Ranyard, Rob. (1997). "Cognitive process models and explanations of decision making." In Rob Ranyard, W. Ray Crozier & Ola Svenson (Eds.), *Decision making: Cognitive models and explanations* (pp. 5-20). London: Routledge.

Curran, James & Seaton, Jean. (1997). *Power without responsibility: The press and broadcasting in Britain*. London: Routledge.

D'Ambrosio, Ubiratan. (2001). Mathematics and peace: A reflection on the basis of western civilization. *Leonardo, 34*(4), 327-332.

Dary, David. (1973). *How to write news for broadcast and print media*. USA: TAB Books.

Davis, Richard. (2001). *The press and American politics: The new mediator*. New Jersey: Prentice Hall.

Davison, W. Phillips. (1974). *Mass communication and conflict resolution: The role of the information media in the advancement of international understanding*. New York: Praeger.

Dawisha, Adeed. (2004). Iraq: Setbacks, advances, prospects. *Journal of Democracy, 15*(1), 5-20.

Day, Louis Alvin. (1997). *Ethics in media communications: Cases and controversies*. California: Wadsworth Publishing Company.

Day, Louis Alvin. (2000). *Ethics in media communications: Cases and controversies*. Australia: Wadsworth, Thomson Learning.

Dean, Jonathan. (1987). "The pragmatic view." In Dennis J. D. Sandole & Ingrid Sandole-Staroste (Eds.), *Conflict management and problem solving: Interpersonal to international applications* (pp. 215-217). London: Frances Pinter Publishers.

Dennis, Everette E. & Ismach, Arnold H. (1981). *Reporting processes and practices: Newswriting for today's readers*. California: Wadsworth Publishing Company.

Deutsch, Karl W. (1982). "Crisis decision-making: The information approach." In Daniel Frei (Ed.), *Managing international crises* (pp. 15-28). Beverly Hills: Sage Publications.

Dordick, Herbert S. (1984). "New communications technology and media power." In Andrew Arno & Wimal Dissanayake (Eds.), *The news media in national and international conflict* (pp. 37-42). Boulder: Westview Press.

Dotson, Bruce. (1987). "Issues from the practice of environmental mediation." In Dennis J. D. Sandole & Ingrid Sandole-Staroste (Eds.), *Conflict management and problem solving: Interpersonal to international applications* (pp. 158-161). London: Frances Pinter Publishers.

Doyle, Chris. (2003*a*). Blair at large. *Middle East International, 701*, 16.

Doyle, Chris. (2003*b*). Blair on his own. *Middle East International, 694*, 10.

Dreher, Rod. (2004, June 1). Q: What's wrong with this picture? A: It's the only one like it we could find. *The Dallas Morning News*, p. 11A. Retrieved June 5, 2004, from Factiva.

Dummett, Michael. (2002). "What is mathematics about?" In Dale Jacquette (Ed.), *Philosophy of mathematics: An anthology* (pp. 19-29). Massachusetts: Blackwell Publishers.

Dunn, David Hastings. (2003). Myths, motivations and 'misunderestimations': The Bush administration and Iraq. *International Affairs, 79*(2), 279-297.

Dupont, Christopher & Guy-Olivier, Faure. (1991). "The negotiation process." In Jeffrey Z. Rubin (Ed.), *International negotiation: Analysis, approaches, issues* (pp. 40-57). San Francisco: Jossey-Bass Publishers.

Edwards, Ward. (1967). "The theory of decision making." In Ward Edwards & Amos Tversky (Eds.), *Decision making: Selected readings* (pp. 13-64). England: Penguin Books.

Eichberger, Jürgen. (1993). *Game theory for economists.* San Diego: Academic Press, Inc.

Eilon, Samuel. (1979). *Management control.* Oxford: Pergamon Press.

Elliott, Deni. (2003). Balance and context: Maintaining media ethics. *Phi Kappa Phi Forum, 83*(2), 16-21.

Elmquist, Søren. (1990). "The scope and limits of cooperation between the media and the authorities." In Yonah Alexander & Richard Latter (Eds.), *Terrorism and the media: Dilemmas for government, journalists and the public* (pp. 74-80). Washington: Brassey's (US), Inc.

Englehardt, Elaine E. & Barney, Ralph D. (2002). *Media and ethics: Principles for moral decisions.* Australia: Wadsworth, Thomson Learning.

Epstein, Edward Jay. (1973). *News from nowhere: Television and the news.* New York: Random House.

Erlich, Reese. (2003). "Media coverage: A view from the ground." In Norman Solomon & Reese Erlich (Eds.), *Target Iraq: What the news media didn't tell you* (pp. 11-20). New York: Context Books.

Esposito, John L. (2003). [Review of the book *Al-Jazeera: How the free Arab news network scooped the world and changed the Middle East* by Mohammed el-Nawawy and Adel Iskandar]. *Political Science Quarterly, 118*(2), 316-318.

Fabun, Don. (1976). "The silent languages." In Joseph A. DeVito (Ed.), *Communication: Concepts and processes* (pp. 118-123). New Jersey: Prentice-Hall, Inc.

Finn, John E. (1990). "Media coverage of political terrorism and the first amendment: Reconciling the public's right to know with public order." In Yonah Alexander & Richard Latter (Eds.), *Terrorism and the media: Dilemmas for government, journalists and the public* (pp. 47-56). Washington: Brassey's (US), Inc.

Fisher, Louis. (2003*a*). Deciding on war against Iraq. *Perspectives on Political Science, 32*(3), 135-142.

Fisher, Louis. (2003*b*). Deciding on war against Iraq: Institutional failures. *Political Science Quarterly, 118*(3), 389-410.

Fisher, Ronald J. (1990). *The social psychology of intergroup and international conflict resolution.* New York: Springer-Verlag.

Flanagan, Thomas. (1998). *Game theory and Canadian politics.* Toronto: University of Toronto Press.

Foucault, Michel. (1994). *The order of things: An archaeology of the human sciences.* New York: Vintage Books.

Fraser, Niall M. & Hipel, Keith W. (1984). *Conflict analysis: Models and resolutions.* New York: Elsevier Science Publishing Co., Inc.

Frey, Lawrence R., Botan, Carl H., Friedman, Paul G. & Kreps, Gary L. (1991). *Investigating communication: An introduction to research methods.* New Jersey: Prentice-Hall, Inc.

Friedman, Gil. (1999). "Conceptualizing protracted conflict and protracted conflict management." In Harvey Starr (Ed.), *The understanding and management of global violence: New approaches to theory and research on protracted conflict* (pp. 35-67). New York: St. Martin's Press.

Galotti, Kathleen M. (2002). *Making decisions that matter: How people face important life choices.* Mahwah, New Jersey: Lawrence Erlbaum Associates, Publishers.

Garrison, Bruce. (1990). *Professional news writing.* Hillsdale, New Jersey: Lawrence Erlbaum Associates, Publishers.

Garthoff, Raymond L. (1989). *Reflections on the Cuban Missile Crisis.* Washington: The Brookings Institution.

Gaughan, Lawrence D. (1987). "Divorce and family mediation." In Dennis J. D. Sandole & Ingrid Sandole-Staroste (Eds.), *Conflict management and problem solving: Interpersonal to international applications* (pp. 107-118). London: Frances Pinter Publishers.

Geller, Daniel S. & Singer, J. David. (1998). *Nations at war: A scientific study of international conflict.* Cambridge: Cambridge University Press.

Gendzier, Irene. (2003). Oil, Iraq and US foreign policy in the Middle East. *Situation Analysis*, (2), 18-28.

George, Alexander L. (1988). "U.S.-Soviet global rivalry: Norms of competition." In Gilbert R. Winham (Ed.), *News issues in international crisis management* (pp. 67-89). Boulder: Westview Press.

George, Alexander L. (1991*a*). "A provisional theory of crisis management." In Alexander L. George (Ed.), *Avoiding war: Problems of crisis management* (pp. 22-27). Boulder: Westview Press.

George, Alexander L. (1991*b*). "Is research on crisis management needed?" In Alexander L. George (Ed.), *Avoiding war: Problems of crisis management* (pp. 3-6). Boulder: Westview Press.

George, Alexander L. (1991*c*). "Strategies for crisis management." In Alexander L. George (Ed.), *Avoiding war: Problems of crisis management* (pp. 377-394). Boulder: Westview Press.

George, Alexander L. (1991*d*). "The Cuban Missile Crisis." In Alexander L. George (Ed.), *Avoiding war: Problems of crisis management* (pp. 222-268). Boulder: Westview Press.

George, Alexander L. (2003). "Analysis and judgment in policymaking." In Stanley A. Renshon & Deborah Welch Larson (Eds.), *Good judgment in foreign policy: Theory and application* (pp. 259-268). Lanham, Maryland: Rowman & Littlefield Publishers, Inc.

Goldsborough, James O. (2003, January 6). Bush finds N. Korea one crisis too many. *San Diego Union-Tribune*.

Gordon, A. David. (1999*a*). "Media codes of ethics are useful and necessary to the mass media and to society." In A. David Gordon & John Michael Kittross (Eds.), *Controversies in media ethics* (pp. 61-68). New York: Longman.

Gordon, A. David. (1999*b*). "Truth precludes any need for further ethical concerns in journalism and public relations." In A. David Gordon and John Michael Kittross (Eds.), *Controversies in media ethics* (pp. 73-80). New York: Longman.

Gordon, Philip H. (2003). Bush's Middle East vision. *Survival, 45*(1), 155-165.

Gorham, Beth. (2004, March 15). U.S. side-stepping the blame game: Officials muster offensive on Madrid bombing. *The Telegram*, p. A5. Retrieved April 20, 2004, from Virtual News Library.

Grattan, Robert F. (2004). The Cuban Missile Crisis: Strategy formulation in action. *Management Decision, 42*(1), 55-68.

Gross, Gerald. (Ed.). (1966). *The responsibility of the press.* New York: Simon and Schuster.

Haas, Tanni. (2003). "Reporters or peeping toms?: Journalism codes of ethics and news coverage of the Clinton-Lewinsky Scandal." In Howard Good (Ed.), *Desperately seeking ethics: A guide to media conduct* (pp. 21-43). Lanham: The Scarecrow Press, Inc.

Hachten, William A. (1996). *The world news prism: Changing media of international communication.* Ames: Iowa State University Press.

Hackett, Robert A. (1991). *News and dissent: The press and the politics of peace in Canada.* Norwood, New Jersey: Ablex Publishing Corporation.

Hackett, Robert A., Gilsdorf, William O. & Savage, Philip. (1992). News balance rhetoric: The Fraser Institute's political appropriation of content analysis. *Canadian Journal of Communication* [Online], *17*(1). Available: http://www.cjc-online.ca/viewarticle.php?id=69.

Hafez, Kai. (2002). Journalism ethics revisited: A comparison of ethics codes in Europe, North Africa, the Middle East, and Muslim Asia. *Political Communication, 19,* 225-250.

Harcup, Tony. (2002). Journalists and ethics: The quest for a collective voice. *Journalism Studies, 3*(1), 101-114.

Hardt, Hanno. (1992). *Critical communication studies: Communication, history and theory in America.* New York: Routledge.

Hardt, Hanno. (2001). *Social theories of the press: Constituents of communication research, 1840s to 1920s.* Lanham: Rowman & Littlefield Publishers, Inc.

Harper, Tim. (2003, December 21). 'We got him' glow could backfire Saddam standoff. *The Toronto Star,* p. F01. Retrieved April 30, 2004, from Lexus-Nexus.

Harris, Geoffrey & Spark, David. (1997). *Practical newspaper reporting.* Oxford: Focal Press.

Harrison, E. Frank. (1993). Interdisciplinary models of decision-making. *Management Decision, 31*(8), 27-33.

Head, Richard G., Short, Frisco W. & McFarlane, Robert C. (1978). *Crisis resolution: Presidential decision making in the Mayaguez and Korean confrontations*. Boulder: Westview Press.

Heap, Shaun P. Hargreaves & Varoufakis, Yanis. (1995). *Game theory: A critical introduction*. New York: Routledge.

Hermon, Sir John. (1990). "The police, the media, and the reporting of terrorism." In Yonah Alexander & Richard Latter (Eds.), *Terrorism and the media: Dilemmas for government, journalists and the public* (pp. 37-41). Washington: Brassey's (US), Inc.

Herrscher, Roberto. (2002). A universal code of journalism ethics: Problems, limitations, and proposals. *Journal of Mass Media Ethics, 17*(4), 277-289.

Hiebert, Ray Eldon, Ungurait, Donald F. & Bohn, Thomas W. (1974). *Mass media: An introduction to modern communication*. New York: David McKay Company, Inc.

Hindman, Elizabeth Blanks. (1997). *Rights vs. responsibilities: The Supreme Court and the media*. Westport, Connecticut: Greenwood Press.

Hoffmann, Gregg. (2004). Seeking unmediated truths. *Etc, 61*(1), 75-79.

Holsti, Ole R. (1978). "Limitations of cognitive abilities in the face of crisis." In C. F. Smart & W. T. Stanbury (Eds.), *Studies on crisis management* (pp. 39-55). Canada: Institute for Research on Public Policy.

Howeidy, Amira. (2004, May 6-12). The bigger picture: Images depicting the torture of Iraqi detainees are just one aspect of the occupation forces' daily war crimes. *Al-Ahram Weekly*. Retrieved May 8, 2004, from http://weekly.ahram.org.eg/2004/689/re7.htm.

Hybel, Alex Roberto. (1993). *Power over rationality: The Bush administration and the Gulf Crisis*. New York: State University of New York Press.

Iraq War: Political scholar on media ethics. (2003, April 2). *Hungarian News Agency*. Retrieved April 4, 2003, from Lexus-Nexus.

Iraq's recovery key: Moussa. (2003, October 5). *The Toronto Star*, p. F03. Retrieved January 20, 2004, from Lexus-Nexus.

Is the US right in using its might against Iraq? (2003, March 30). *Philippine Daily Inquirer*. Retrieved April 7, 2003, from Lexus-Nexus.

Jansen, Michael. (2002, Mach 22). Cheney pre-empted? *Middle East International*, *671*, 6-8.

Jervis, Robert. (2002). The confrontation between Iraq and the U.S.: Implications for the theory and practice of deterrence. Special Section on U.S. Policy and Iraq, *Ciao: Columbia International Affairs Online*.

Jervis, Robert. (2003). Random thoughts on the credibility of US threats against Iraq. Special Section on U.S. Policy and Iraq, *Ciao: Columbia International Affairs Online*.

Joffé, George. (2003). Iraq: The endgame begins. *Middle East International*, (698), 4-8.

Johnson, Paul E. (1989). Formal theories of politics: The scope of mathematical modelling in political science. *Mathematical and Computer Modelling*, *12*(4/5), 397-404.

Johnson, Peter. (2003, May 12). Media weigh in on 'journalistic fraud'. *USA Today*, p. 3D. Retrieved May 12, 2003, from Lexus-Nexus.

Jones, Mary Lynn. (2003, May). No news is good news; How Bush gets a free ride—again and again and again. *The American Prospect*, p. 39. Retrieved June 15, 2003, from Lexus-Nexus.

Jönsson, Christer. (1991). "The Suez war of 1956: Communication in crisis management." In Alexander L. George (Ed.), *Avoiding war: Problems of crisis management* (pp. 160-190). Boulder: Westview Press.

Kahn, Robert L. (1991). "Organizational theory." In Jeffrey Z. Rubin (Ed.), *International negotiation: Analysis, approaches, issues* (pp. 148-163). San Francisco: Jossey-Bass Publishers.

Kamal, Sana. (2003). On the eve of war. *Middle East International*, *696*, 17.

Kaplan, Lawrence F. & Kristol, William. (2003). *The war over Iraq: Saddam's tyranny and America's mission*. California: Encounter Books.

Karim, Karim H. (2000). *Islamic peril: Media and global violence*. Montréal: Black Rose Books.

Keeble, Richard. (2001). *Ethics for journalists*. London: Routledge.

Keeler, John D., Brown, William & Tarpley, Douglas. (2002). "Ethics." In W. David Sloan & Lisa Mullikin Parcell (Eds.), *American journalism: History, principles, practices* (pp. 44-54). Jefferson, North Carolina: McFarland & Company, Inc., Publishers.

Kelly, Micheal J. (1989). "The seizure of the Turkish embassy in Ottawa: Managing terrorism and the media." In Uriel Rosenthal, Michael T. Charles & Paul 'T Hart (Eds.), *Coping with crises: The management of disasters, riots and terrorism* (pp. 117-138). Illinois: Charles C. Thomas Publisher.

Keohane, Robert O. (2002). Multilateral coercive diplomacy: Not "Myths of Empire." Special Section on U.S. Policy and Iraq, *Ciao: Columbia International Affairs Online*.

Kieran, Matthew. (1997). *Media ethics: A philosophical approach*. Westport, Connecticut: Praeger.

Kieran, Matthew. (1998). "Objectivity, impartiality and good journalism." In Matthew Kieran (Ed.), *Media ethics* (pp. 23-36). London: Routledge.

King Fahd: We will not take part in war nor enter Iraq. (2003, March 19). *ArabicNews.Com*. Retrieved March 25, 2003, from: http://www .arabicnews.com/ansub/Daily/Day/030319/2003031917.html.

Kipling, Bogdan. (2004, April 1). U.S. political chess game gets downright ugly. *The Chronicle-Herald*, p. A7. Retrieved April 20, 2004, from Virtual News Library.

Kitfield, James. (2003). Peering into Saddam's mind. *National Journal*, *35*(12), 890-891.

Kittross, John Michael. (1999). "The social value of journalism and public relations requires high-quality practices reflecting ethical considerations that go beyond truth and objectivity to accuracy and fairness." In A. David Gordon and John Michael Kittross (Eds.), *Controversies in media ethics* (pp. 80-89). New York: Longman.

Klenk, V. H. (1976). *Wittgenstein's philosophy of mathematics*. Netherlands: Martinus Nijhoff.

Knox, Paul. (2003, December 15). The game's not over. *Globe and Mail Metro Edition*, p. A15. Retrieved April 28, 2004, from Lexus-Nexus.

Kovach, Bill & Rosenstiel, Tom. (2001). *The elements of journalism: What newspeople should know and the public should expect*. New York: Crown Publishers.

Krane, Jim. (2003, December 8). Saddam's capture wouldn't halt attacks, American general warns. *The Chronicle-Herald*, p. B11. Retrieved April 20, 2004, from Virtual News Library.

Krishnaswami, Sridhar. (2003, September 19). Saddam not linked to 9/11, says Bush. *The Hindu*. Retrieved April 30, 2004, from Lexus-Nexus.

Kruckeberg, Dean. (1995). "International journalism ethics." In John C. Merrill (Ed.), *Global journalism: Survey of international communication* (pp. 77-87). New York: Longman.

LA Times sacks photographer for manipulating war photo. (2003, April 2). *Agence France Presse*. Retrieved April 3, 2003, from Lexus-Nexus.

Landy, Joanne, Harrison, Thomas & Scarlott, Jennifer. (2003). We oppose both Saddam Hussein and the U.S. war on Iraq: A call for a new, democratic U.S. foreign policy. *New Politics*, *9*(2), 16-18.

Laue, James. (1987). "The emergence and institutionalization of third party roles in conflict." In Dennis J. D. Sandole & Ingrid Sandole-Staroste (Eds.), *Conflict management and problem solving: Interpersonal to international applications* (pp. 17-29). London: Frances Pinter Publishers.

Lazarsfeld, Paul F. & Henry, Neil W. (1966). "Mathematics and the social sciences." In Paul F. Lazarsfeld & Neil W. Henry (Eds.), *Readings in the mathematical social science* (pp. 3-18). Chicago: Science Research Associates, Inc.

Lazarsfeld, Paul F. (1954*a*). "A conceptual introduction to latent structure analysis." In Paul F. Lazarsfeld (Ed.), *Mathematical thinking in the social sciences* (pp. 349-387). New York: Russell & Russell.

Lazarsfeld, Paul F. (1954*b*). "Introduction: Mathematical thinking in the social sciences." In Paul F. Lazarsfeld (Ed.), *Mathematical thinking in the social sciences* (pp. 3-16). New York: Russell & Russell.

Lebow, Richard Ned. (1983). The Cuban Missile Crisis: Reading the lessons correctly. *Political Science Quarterly*, *98*(3), 431-458.

Lebow, Richard Ned. (1987*a*). Is crisis management always possible? *Political Science Quarterly*, *102*(2), 181-192.

Lebow, Richard Ned. (1987*b*). *Nuclear crisis management: A dangerous illusion*. New York: Cornell University Press.

Lee, Wayne. (1971). *Decision theory and human behavior.* New York: John Wiley & Sons, Inc.

Leslie, Larry Z. (2000). *Mass communication ethics: Decision making in postmodern culture.* Boston: Houghton Mifflin Company.

Levine, Andrew. (1981). *Liberal democracy: A critique of its theory.* New York: Columbia University Press.

Littlejohn, Stephen W. (2002). *Theories of human communication.* Australia: Wadsworth, Thomson Learning.

Lorenz, Alfred Lawrence & Vivian, John. (1996). *News: Reporting and writing.* Boston: Allyn and Bacon.

Lupia, Arthur, Mccubbins, Mathew D. & Popkin, Samuel L. (2000). "Beyond rationality: Reason and the study of politics." In Arthur Lupia, Mathew D. Mccubbins & Samuel L. Popkin (Eds.), *Elements of reason: Cognition, choice, and the bounds of rationality* (pp. 1-20). Cambridge: Cambridge University Press.

MacGillivray, Karen Patrick & Winham, Gilbert R. (1988). "Arms control negotiations and the stability of crisis management." In Gilbert R. Winham (Ed.), *News issues in international crisis management* (pp. 90-117). Boulder: Westview Press.

Mackie, J. L. (1977). *Ethics: Inventing right and wrong.* England: Penguin Books Ltd.

Maher, F. Marshall. (2003, May/June). When journalists attack: The Boston Herald's loose cannon. *Extra.* Available at: http://www.fair .org/extra/0305/journalists.html.

Maher, Mike & Chiasson, Lloyd. (1995). "The press and crisis: What have we learned?" In Lloyd Chiasson (Ed.), *The press in times of crisis* (pp. 219-223). Connecticut: Greenwood Press.

Markel, Mike. (2001). *Ethics in technical communication: A critique and synthesis.* Westport, Connecticut: Ablex Publishing.

Marriner, Cosima. (2003, July 22). ABC review rubbishes claims of Iraq War bias. *Sydney Morning Herald*, p. 4. Retrieved July 22, 2003, from Lexus-Nexus.

McDowell, Stephen D. (2002). "Theory and research in international communication: A historical and institutional account." In William B. Gudykunst & Bella Mody (Eds.), *Handbook of international and intercultural communication* (pp. 295-308). Thousand Oaks, California: Sage Publications.

McGillivray, Glenn. (2003, March 28). Staying the course. *The Toronto Star*, p. A29. Retrieved June 4, 2003, from Lexus-Nexus.

McKercher, Catherine & Cumming, Carman. (1998). *The Canadian reporter: News writing and reporting*. Toronto: Harcourt Brace & Company Canada, Ltd.

Mearsheimer, John J. & Walt, Stephen M. (2002). Can Saddam be contained? History says yes. Special Section on U.S. Policy and Iraq, *Ciao: Columbia International Affairs Online*.

Mearsheimer, John J. & Walt, Stephen M. (2003). An unnecessary war. *Prospect*, (84), 10-13.

Mehrabian, Albert. (1976). "Communication without words." In Joseph A. DeVito (Ed.), *Communication: Concepts and processes* (pp. 99-106). New Jersey: Prentice-Hall, Inc.

Meisel, John. (1982). "Communications and crisis: A preliminary mapping." In Daniel Frei (Ed.), *Managing international crises* (pp. 61-75). Beverly Hills: Sage Publications.

Meissner, W. W. (2003). *The ethical dimension of psychoanalysis: A dialogue*. New York: State University of New York Press.

Merriam-Webster's collegiate dictionary (10th ed.). (2001). Massachusetts: Merriam-Webster, Incorporated.

Miller, Steven E. (2002). "Gambling on War: Force, order, and the implications of attacking Iraq." In Carl Kaysen et al. (Eds.), *War with Iraq: Costs, consequences, and alternatives* (pp. 7-50). Cambridge: American Academy of Arts and Sciences.

Mirak-Weissbach, Muriel. (2003). The United States is losing the Iraq war. *Executive Intelligence Review*, 30(44), 53.

Mody, Bella & Lee, Anselm. (2002). "Differing traditions of research on international media influence." In William B. Gudykunst & Bella Mody (Eds.), *Handbook of international and intercultural communication* (pp. 381-398). Thousand Oaks, California: Sage Publications.

Mohammad Said Al-Sahhaf. (2003, March 25). *Al-Jazeera*. Retrieved March 26, 2003, from Lexus-Nexus.

Mohammad Said Al-Sahhaf. (2003, March 27). *Al-Jazeera*. Retrieved March 31, 2003, from Lexus-Nexus.

Mohammed Saeed al-Sahaf: The Scheherazade of Baghdad. (2003, April 12). *The Economist*, p. 25.

Moore, Oliver. (2002, December 6). 'Everything has been destroyed,' Iraq insists. *The Globe and Mail*. Retrieved February 15, 2004, from http://www.globeandmail.com/servlet/ArticleNews/front/RTGAM/20 021206/wiraq1206/Front/homeBN/breakingnews.

Mor, Ben D. (1993). *Decision and interaction in crisis: A model of international crisis behavior*. Connecticut: Praeger.

Morrison, David E. & Tumber, Howard. (1988). *Journalists at war: The dynamics of news reporting during the Falklands conflict*. London: Sage.

Morrow, James D. (1994). *Game theory for political scientists*. New Jersey: Princeton University Press.

Moskowitz, Herbert & Wright, Gordon P. (1979). *Operations research techniques for management*. New Jersey: Prentice-Hall, Inc.

Moussa: Sad day for all Arabs. (2003, March 20). *ArabicNews.Com*. Retrieved March 25, 2003, from: http://www.arabicnews .com/ansub/Daily/Day/030320/2003032027.html.

Mowlana, Hamid. (1984*a*). "Communication, world order, and the human potential: Toward an ethical framework." In Andrew Arno & Wimal Dissanayake (Eds.), *The news media in national and international conflict* (pp. 27-35). Boulder: Westview Press.

Mowlana, Hamid. (1984*b*). "The role of the media in the U.S.-Iranian conflict." In Andrew Arno & Wimal Dissanayake (Eds.), *The news media in national and international conflict* (pp. 71-99). Boulder: Westview Press.

Mroue, Bassem. (2003, February 24). Iraq plays the waiting game. *Hamilton Spectator*, p. C01. Retrieved February 28, 2003, from Lexus-Nexus.

Muhammed Saeed Al-Sahhaf, delivering address on behalf of Saddam Hussein. (2003, April 5). *Al-Jazeera*. Retrieved April 7, 2003, from Lexus-Nexus.

Nathanson, Stephen. (1991). Kennedy and the Cuban Missile Crisis: On the role of moral reasons in explaining and evaluating political decision-making. *Journal of Social Philosophy, 22*(2), 94-108.

Negus, Steve. (2002, Mach 22). Egypt unconvinced. *Middle East International, 671*, 10.

Netanyahu, Benjamin. (1986). "Terrorism: How the West can win?" In Benjamin Netanyahu (Ed.), *Terrorism: How the West can win* (pp. 199-226). New York: The Jonathan Institute.

Neuhold, Hanspeter. (1978). " Principles and implementation of crisis management: Lessons from the past." In Daniel Frei (Ed.), *International crises and crisis management: An East-West symposium* (pp. 4-18). England: Saxon House.

News outlets have declared war on Iraq. (2003, March 31). *Daily Trojan.* Retrieved March 31, 2003, from Lexus-Nexus.

Niblock, Sarah. (2003). Television's reporting of the Iraq war: Reflexivity or ratings? *Visual Communication, 2*(3), 375-377.

Nicholson, Michael. (1970). *Conflict analysis.* London: The English Universities Press Limited.

Nicholson, Michael. (1996). *Causes and consequences in international relations: A conceptual study.* London: Pinter.

Nicholson, Michael. (1997). *Rationality and the analysis of international conflict.* Cambridge: Cambridge University Press.

Nolan, Riall W. (1999). *Communicating and adapting across cultures: Living and working in the global village.* Westport, Connecticut: Bergin & Garvey.

Nordenstreng, Kaarle & Topuz, Hifzi. (Eds.). (1989). *Journalist: Status, rights and responsibilities.* Prague: International Organization of Journalists.

Nordhaus, William D. (2002). "The economic consequences of a war with Iraq." In Carl Kaysen et al. (Eds.), *War with Iraq: Costs, consequences, and alternatives* (pp. 51-85). Cambridge: American Academy of Arts and Sciences.

Ogan, Christine. (1995). "The Middle East and North Africa". In John C. Merrill (Ed.), *Global journalism: Survey of international communication* (pp. 189-207). White Plains, New York: Longman.

Parenti, Michael. (2003). "The logic of U.S. intervention." In Carl Boggs (Ed.), *Masters of war: Militarism and blowback in the era of American empire* (pp. 19-36). New York: Routledge.

Pein, Corey. (2003, May/June). The victories that weren't: In the "war on terror," media slight facts for spin. *Extra*. Available at: http://www.fair.org/extra/0305/war-on-terror.html.

Peters, John Durham. (1999). *Speaking into the air: A history of the idea of communication*. Chicago: The University of Chicago Press.

Peterson, Theodore. (1956). "Introduction." In Fred S. Siebert, Theodore Peterson & Wilbur Schramm (Eds.), *Four theories of the press: The authoritarian, libertarian, social responsibility and Soviet communist concepts of what the press should be and do* (pp. 73-103). Illinois: University of Illinois.

Philippine daily cites press freedom, media ethics as casualties of Iraq War. (2003, April 8). *World News Connection*. Retrieved April 10, 2003, from Lexus-Nexus.

Phillips, Luke. (2003, March 31). Front-line journalists in Iraq face tough time reporting war. *Agence France Presse*. Retrieved April 1, 2003, from Lexus-Nexus.

Picard, Robert. (1990). "News coverage as the contagion of terrorism: Dangerous charges backed by dubious science." In Yonah Alexander & Richard Latter (Eds.), *Terrorism and the media: Dilemmas for government, journalists and the public* (pp. 100-110). Washington: Brassey's (US), Inc.

Pious, Richard M. (2001). The Cuban Missile Crisis and the limits of crisis management. *Political Science Quarterly*, *116*(1), 81-105.

Plaisance, Patrick Lee. (2000). The concept of media accountability reconsidered. *Journal of Mass Media Ethics*, *15*(4), 257-268.

Pocklington, T. C. (1985). *Liberal democracy in Canada and the United States: An introduction to politics and government*. Toronto: Holt, Rinehart and Winston of Canada, Limited.

Porter, William. (1996). The responsibility of the media for their impact on society. *Dialogue and Universalism*, *6*(3), 13-19.

Potter, Mitch. (2003, December 15). Humiliation hits yesterday's men. *The Toronto Star*, p. A01. Retrieved April 15, 2004, from Lexus-Nexus.

Potter, Mitch. (2004, March 20). Iraq today: Better and worse and. *The Toronto Star*, p. A01. Retrieved April 30, 2004, from Lexus-Nexus.

President Bush's war address. (2003, March 19). *CBS News*. Retrieved March 25, 2003, from: http://www.cbsnews.com/stories/2003/03/19/iraq/main544714.shtml.

Pritchard, David. (1991). The role of press councils in a system of media accountability: The case of Quebec. *Canadian Journal of Communication*, *16*(1). Available: http://cjc-online.ca/title.php3?page=6&journal_id=5&document=1.

Pritchard, David. (2000*a*). "Introduction: The process of media accountability." In David Pritchard (Ed.), *Holding the media accountable: Citizens, ethics, and the law* (pp. 1-10). Bloomington: Indiana University Press.

Pritchard, David. (2000*b*). "Structural flaws in press council decision-making." In David Pritchard (Ed.), *Holding the media accountable: Citizens, ethics, and the law* (pp. 90-108). Bloomington: Indiana University Press.

Pritchard, David. (2000*c*). "The future of media accountability." In David Pritchard (Ed.), *Holding the media accountable: Citizens, ethics, and the law* (pp. 186-193). Bloomington: Indiana University Press.

Protheroe, Alan H. (1990). "Terrorism, journalism, and democracy." In Yonah Alexander & Richard Latter (Eds.), *Terrorism and the media: Dilemmas for government, journalists and the public* (pp. 64-69). Washington: Brassey's (US), Inc.

Pruitt, Dean G. (1987). "Creative approaches to negotiation." In Dennis J. D. Sandole & Ingrid Sandole-Staroste (Eds.), *Conflict management and problem solving: Interpersonal to international applications* (pp. 62-76). London: Frances Pinter Publishers.

Raju, Sripada K. S., Jagadeswari, S. K. & Dissanayake, Wimal. (1984). "Treating the Indo-Pakistan conflict: The role of Indian newspapers and magazines." In Andrew Arno & Wimal Dissanayake (Eds.), *The news media in national and international conflict* (pp. 101-131). Boulder: Westview Press.

Rather, Dan. (2003, February 26). Saddam Hussein interview. *CBS News*. Retrieved March 25, 2003, from: http://www.cbsnews.com/stories/2003/02/26/60II/main542151.shtml.

Reber, Pat. (2004, January 31). Iraq weapons controversy gathers political momentum. *Central European Time*. Retrieved April 15, 2004, from Lexus-Nexus.

Redpath, Theodore. (1986). "Wittgenstein and ethics." In John V. Canfield (Ed.), The philosophy of Wittgenstein: *Aesthetics, ethics and religion*, Vol. 14 (pp. 117-141). New York: Garland Publishing, Inc.

Reilly, Bernard J. & DiAngelo, Joseph A. (1990). Communication: A cultural system of meaning and value. *Human Relations, 43*(2), 129-140.

Rhodes, Edward. (2002). Onward, liberal soldiers? The crusading logic of Bush's grand strategy and what is wrong with it. Special Section on U.S. Policy and Iraq, *Ciao: Columbia International Affairs Online*.

Richardson, James L. (1988). "Crisis management: A critical appraisal." In Gilbert R. Winham (Ed.), *News issues in international crisis management* (pp. 13-36). Boulder: Westview Press.

Rivers, William L. & Schramm, Wilbur. (1969). *Responsibility in mass communication*. New York: Harper & Row, Publishers.

Robinson, Piers. (2000). The policy-media interaction model: Measuring media power during humanitarian crisis. *Journal of Peace Research, 37*(5), 613-633.

Rogers, Don. (1976). "How do I communicate with you." In Joseph A. DeVito (Ed.), *Communication: Concepts and processes* (pp. 255-259). New Jersey: Prentice-Hall, Inc.

Rogers, Everett M. & Hart, William B. (2002). "The histories of intercultural, international, and development communication." In William B. Gudykunst & Bella Mody (Eds.), *Handbook of international and intercultural communication* (pp. 1-18). Thousand Oaks, California: Sage Publications.

Rogers, Everett M. (1994). *A history of communication study: A biographical approach*. New York: The Free Press.

Roidt, Joe. (2003, February 11). Preventive war media leaves public misinformed on war with Iraq. *Charleston Gazette*, p. P5A. Retrieved February 11, 2003, from Lexus-Nexus.

Rosenthal, Uriel, et al. (1989). "From case studies to theory and recommendations: A concluding analysis." In Uriel Rosenthal, Michael T. Charles & Paul 'T Hart (Eds.), *Coping with crises: The management of disasters, riots and terrorism* (pp. 436-472). Illinois: Charles C. Thomas Publisher.

Rosenthal, Uriel, Hart, Paul 'T & Bezuyen, Michel. (1998). "Flood response and disaster management: A comparative perspective." In Uriel Rosenthal & Paul 'T Hart (Eds.), *Flood response and crisis management in Western Europe: A comparative analysis* (pp. 1-13). Germany: Springer-Verlag.

Rosenthal, Uriel, Hart, Paul 'T & Charles, Michael T. (1989). "The world of crises and crisis management." In Uriel Rosenthal, Michael T. Charles & Paul 'T Hart (Eds.), *Coping with crises: The management of disasters, riots and terrorism* (pp. 3-33). Illinois: Charles C. Thomas Publisher.

Rubin, Barry. (2002). "The Persian Gulf amid global and regional crises." In Barry Rubin (Ed.), *Crises in the contemporary Persian Gulf* (pp. 5-20). London: Frank Cass Publishers.

Rugina, Anghel N. (1998). The problem of values and value-judgments in science and a positive solution: Max Weber and Ludwig Wittgenstein revisited. *International Journal of Social Economics*, *25*(5), 805-854.

Russell, Alec. (2004, April 8). Bush is still favourite to be in the White House. *The Daily Telegraph*, p. 24. Retrieved April 15, 2004, from Lexus-Nexus.

Russell, Bertrand. (1963). *Unarmed victory*. London: Allen and Unwin.

Sami, Aziza. (2003, April 3 - 9). The war in the Egyptian press. *Al-Ahram Weekly*. Retrieved April 20, 2003, from: http://weekly.ahram.org.eg/2003/632/sc10.htm.

Sawant, P. B. (2003). Accountability in journalism. *Journal of Mass Media Ethics*, *18*(1), 16-28.

Scanlon, Joseph. (1999). Emergent groups in established frameworks: Ottawa Carleton's response to the 1998 Ice Disaster. *Journal of Contingencies and Crisis Management*, *7*(1), 30-37.

Schellenberg, James A. (1996). *Conflict resolution: Theory, research, and practice*. Albany, NY: State University of New York Press.

Schiller, Dan. (1986). "Transformations of news in the US information market." In Peter Golding, Graham Murdock & Philip Schlesinger (Eds.), *Communicating politics: Mass communications and the political process* (pp. 19-36). New York: Leicester University Press.

Schorr, Daniel. (2003, March 28). Uneasy evolution of war coverage. *Christian Science Monitor*, p. 10. Retrieved March 28, 2003, from Lexus-Nexus.

Schramm, Wilbur. (1966). "Who is responsible for the quality of mass communications?" In Gerald Gross (Ed.), *The responsibility of the press* (pp. 348-361). New York: Simon and Schuster.

Schramm, Wilbur. (1976). "How communication works." In Joseph A. DeVito (Ed.), *Communication: Concepts and processes* (pp. 11-19). New Jersey: Prentice-Hall, Inc.

Schramm, Wilbur. (1996). "The master teachers." In Everette E. Dennis & Ellen Wartella (Eds.), *American communication research: The remembered history* (pp. 123-133). New Jersey: Lawrence Erlbaum Associates, Publishers.

Schwab, Ian. (2003, April 29). War coverage more like video games than news. *The Post-Standard*, p. B6. Retrieved April 30, 2003, from Lexus-Nexus.

Scimecca, Joseph A. (1991). "Conflict resolution in the United States: The emergence of a profession?" In Kevin Avruch, Peter W. Black & Joseph A. Scimecca (Eds.), *Conflict resolution: Cross-cultural perspectives* (pp. 19-39). Connecticut: Greenwood Press.

Scimecca, Joseph A. (1993). "Theory and alternative dispute resolution: A contradiction in terms?" In Dennis J. D. Sandole & Hugo van der Merwe (Eds.), *Conflict resolution theory and practice: Integration and application* (pp. 211-221). Manchester: Manchester University Press.

Seaton, Jean. (1999). "The new 'ethnic' wars and the media." In Tim Allen & Jean Seaton (Eds.), *The media of conflict: War reporting and representations of ethnic violence* (pp. 43-63). London: Zed Books Ltd.

Seeks no-war pledge: Change of regime not on. (2003, March 3). *Kuwait Times*. Retrieved April 20, 2003, from Lexus-Nexus.

Self, Charles C. (1996). "Credibility." In Michael B. Salwen & Don W. Stacks (Eds.), *An integrated approach to communication theory and research* (pp. 421-441). New Jersey: Lawrence Erlbaum Associates, Publishers.

Senn, Peter. (2000). Mathematics and the social sciences at the time of the modern beginnings of the social sciences. *Journal of Economic Studies*, *27*(4/5), 271-291.

Sens, Allen G. (1997). *Somalia and the changing nature of peacekeeping: The implications for Canada*. Ottawa: Public Works and Government Services.

Settle, Michael. (2003, March 4). Countdown continues as US dismisses Iraq's pledge. *The Herald*, p. 1. Retrieved April 28, 2003, from Lexus-Nexus.

Severin, Werner J. & Tankard, James W. (1988). *Communication theories: Origins, methods, uses*. New York: Longman.

Sfard, Anna. (2002). Mathematics as a form of communication. *PME Conference 26, 1*, 1/145-1/149.

Shannon, Claude Elwood & Weaver, Warren. (1949). *The mathematical theory of communication*. Urbana: University of Illinois Press.

Shiels, Frederick L. (1991). *Preventable disasters: Why governments fail*. Maryland: Rowman & Littlefield Publishers, Inc.

Shrivastava, Paul. (1989). "Managing the crisis at Bhopal." In Uriel Rosenthal, Michael T. Charles & Paul 'T Hart (Eds.), *Coping with crises: The management of disasters, riots and terrorism* (pp. 92-116). Illinois: Charles C. Thomas Publisher.

Shubik, Martin. (1954). "Introduction to the nature of game theory." In Martin Shubik (Ed.), *Readings in Game theory and political behavior* (pp. 1-11). New York: Doubleday & Company, Inc.

Siebe, Wilfried. (1991). "Game theory." In Jeffrey Z. Rubin (Ed.), *International negotiation: Analysis, approaches, issues* (pp. 180-202). San Francisco: Jossey-Bass Publishers.

Siebert, Fred S., Peterson, Theodore & Schramm, Wilbur. (1956). "Introduction." In Fred S. Siebert, Theodore Peterson & Wilbur Schramm (Eds.), *Four theories of the press: The authoritarian, libertarian, social responsibility and Soviet communist concepts of what the press should be and do* (pp. 1-7). Illinois: University of Illinois.

Simmons, Charles A. (1998). *The African American press: A history of news coverage during national crises, with special reference to four black newspapers, 1827-1965.* North Carolina: McFarland & Company, Inc.

Singapore FM defends support for US-led war on Iraq, says world becoming safer. (2004, March 12). *BBC.* Retrieved April 30, 2004, from Lexus-Nexus.

Skorneck, Carolyn. (2004). Debate on Iraq war resolution: A test of campaign potshots. *Congressional Quarterly Weekly, 62*(12), 705-707.

Slade, Stephen. (1994). *Goal-based decision-making: An interpersonal model.* Hillsdale, New Jersey: Lawrence Erlbaum Associates, Publishers.

Snyder, Glenn H. & Diesing, Paul. (1977). *Conflict among nations: Bargaining, decision making, and system structure in international crises.* New Jersey: Princeton University Press.

Soderlund, Walter C. & Lee, Martha F. (1999). International reporting in Canadian newspapers: Results of a survey of daily newspaper editors. *Canadian Journal of Communication, 24*(2). Available: http://cjc-online.ca/title.php3?page=6&journal_id=31&document=1.

Soderlund, Walter C., Krause, Robert M. & Price, Richard G. (1991). Canadian daily newspaper editors' evaluation of international reporting. *Canadian Journal of Communication, 16*(1), 1-13.

Solomon, Norman & Erlich, Reese. (Eds.). (2003). *Target Iraq: What the news media didn't tell you.* New York: Context Books.

Solomon, Norman. (2001). The narrow separation of press and state. *The Humanist, 61*(2), 3-4.

Sontag, Susan. (Ed.). (1982). *A Barthes reader.* New York: Hill and Wang, a division of Farrar, Straus and Giroux.

Specht, Ernst Konrad. (1986). "The language-game as model-concept in Wittgenstein's theory of language." In John V. Canfield (Ed.), The philosophy of Wittgenstein: *Meaning,* Vol. 6 (pp. 131-154). New York: Garland Publishing, Inc.

Stanway, Paul. (2003, October 14). Good news in the Mideast; 'Arab Street' puts its money where its mouth isn't. *The Toronto Sun*, p. 15. Retrieved February 15, 2004, from Lexus-Nexus.

Starr, Harvey. (1999). "Introduction: A protracted conflict approach to the study of social conflict." In Harvey Starr (Ed.), *The understanding and management of global violence: New approaches to theory and research on protracted conflict* (pp. 1-20). New York: St. Martin's Press.

Stein, M. L. (1985). *Getting and writing the news: A guide to reporting*. New York: Longman.

Steuter, Erin. (1990). Understanding the media/terrorism relationship: An analysis of ideology and the news in Time Magazine. *Political Communication and Persuasion*, 7(4), 257-278.

Stevenson, Robert L. (1996). "International communication." In Michael B. Salwen & Don W. Stacks (Eds.), *An integrated approach to communication theory and research* (pp. 181-193). New Jersey: Lawrence Erlbaum Associates, Publishers.

Strentz, Herb. (2002). Universal ethical standards? *Journal of Mass Media Ethics*, 17(4), 263-276.

Strentz, Herbert & Keel, Vernon. (1995). "North America". In John C. Merrill (Ed.), *Global journalism: Survey of international communication* (pp. 355-394). White Plains, New York: Longman.

Sussman, Leonard R. (1995). Media ethics and its relationship to peace education. *The International Journal of Humanities and Peace*, 11(1), 76-77.

Svenson, Ola & Verplanken, Bas. (1997). "Personal involvement in human decision making: Conceptualisations and effects on decision processes." In Rob Ranyard, W. Ray Crozier & Ola Svenson (Eds.), *Decision making: Cognitive models and explanations* (pp. 40-57). London: Routledge.

Tasic, Vladimir. (2001). *Mathematics and the roots of postmodern thought*. New York: Oxford University Press.

Tehranian, Majid. (2002). Peace journalism: Negotiating global media ethics. *The Harvard International Journal of Press/Politics*, 7(2), 58-83.

Telhami, Shibley. (2002). US policy toward Iraq: The calculations of governments in the Middle East. Special Section on U.S. Policy and Iraq, *Ciao: Columbia International Affairs Online.*

Telhami, Shibley. (2003). After a war with Iraq: Democracy, militancy, and peacemaking? *International Studies Perspectives, 4*(2), 182–185.

Text of Powell speech to U.N. (2003, February 5). *CBS News.* Retrieved March 25, 2003, from: http://www.cbsnews.com//stories/2003/02/05/iraq/main539459.shtml.

The Oxford American dictionary and thesaurus: With language guide. (2003). New York: Oxford University Press.

Thierauf, Robert J. (1970). *Decision making through operations research.* Richard A. Grosse (Ed.). New York: John Wiley & Sons, Inc.

Thomassen, Niels. (1992). *Communicative ethics in theory and practice* (John Irons, Trans.). New York: St. Martin's Press.

Thrall, A. Trevor. (2000). *War in the media age.* New Jersey: Hampton Press, Inc.

Threatening Iraq: A psychological war, on many fronts. (2003, January 25). *The Economist*, p. 12.

Thussu, Daya Kishan. (2000). *International communication: Continuity and change.* London: Arnold.

Torres, Manuel O. (2002). "War coverage." In W. David Sloan & Lisa Mullikin Parcell (Eds.), *American journalism: History, principles, practices* (pp. 236-247). Jefferson, North Carolina: McFarland & Company, Inc., Publishers.

Trenholm, Sarah. (1995). *Thinking through communication: An introduction to the study of human communication.* Boston: Allyn and Bacon.

Tyler, Patrick. (2002, November 16). Chief U.N. inspector expects work on Iraq to start Nov. 27. *New York Times.*

van Tuyll, Debra Reddin. (2002). "The press and war." In W. David Sloan & Lisa Mullikin Parcell (Eds.), *American journalism: History, principles, practices* (pp. 229-235). Jefferson: McFarland & Company, Inc., Publishers.

Voakes, Paul S. (2000). Rights, wrongs, and responsibilities: Law and ethics in the newsroom. *Journal of Mass Media Ethics, 15*(1), 29-42.

Wald, Abraham. (1954). "The theory of games." In Martin Shubik (Ed.), *Readings in Game theory and political behavior* (pp. 33-42). New York: Doubleday & Company, Inc.

Wallace, Jim. (1999). Strategy and crisis. *Defence Force Journal, 136*, 13-21.

Warburton, Nigel. (1998). "Ethical photojournalism in the age of the electronic darkroom." In Matthew Kieran (Ed.), *Media ethics* (pp. 123-134). London: Routledge.

Wedge, Bryant. (1987). "Conflict management: The state of the art." In Dennis J. D. Sandole & Ingrid Sandole-Staroste (Eds.), *Conflict management and problem solving: Interpersonal to international applications* (pp. 279-288). London: Frances Pinter Publishers.

Weintraub, E. Roy. (1985). *General equilibrium analysis: Studies in appraisal.* Cambridge: Cambridge University Press.

Wheeler, Thomas H. (2002). *Phototruth or photofiction? Ethics and media imagery in the digital age.* New Jersey: Lawrence Erlbaum Associates, Publishers.

Whitehead, Alfred North & Russell, Bertrand. (1968). *Principia mathematica.* London: The Cambridge University Press.

Whittaker, David J. (1999). *Conflict and reconciliation in the contemporary world.* London: Routledge.

Wilkinson, Paul. (1990). "Terrorism and propaganda." In Yonah Alexander & Richard Latter (Eds.), *Terrorism and the media: Dilemmas for government, journalists and the public* (pp. 26-33). Washington: Brassey's (US), Inc.

Williams, Ian. (2003). The UN puts war on hold. *Middle East International,* (694), 4-9.

Williams, Phil. (1976). *Crisis management: Confrontation and diplomacy in the nuclear age.* London: Martin Robertson & Co. Ltd.

Wilson, George C. (2003). Kuwaitis want Saddam gone, but without war. *National Journal, 35*(11), 812-813.

Wilson, James R. & Wilson, Stan Le Roy. (2001). *Mass media mass culture: An introduction.* Boston: McGraw-Hill.

Wittebols, James H. (1992). Media and the institutional perspective: U.S. and Canadian coverage of terrorism. *Political Communication, 9*(4), 267-278.

Woollacott, Martin. (2004, April 30). From Vietnam to Iraq in search of the big picture. *The Guardian*, p. 28. Retrieved April 30, 2004, from Lexus-Nexus.

Wright, Donald K. (1996). "Communication ethics." In Michael B. Salwen & Don W. Stacks (Eds.), *An integrated approach to communication theory and research* (pp. 519-535). New Jersey: Lawrence Erlbaum Associates, Publishers.

Yanjuan, Wang. (2003). Analyzing the war. *Beijing Review, 46*(14), 34-36.

Yaphe, Judith S. (2003). America's war on Iraq: Myths and opportunities. *Adelphi Papers, 354*, 23-44.

Zimbabwe: Official terms "barbaric" coverage of Iraq war by international media. (2003, March 25). *BBC*. Retrieved March 25, 2003, from Lexus-Nexus.

Zinsser, William. (1998). *On writing well: The classic guide to writing nonfiction.* New York: HarperPerennial, A Division of HarperCollins Publishers.

Author Index

335

Subject Index

A

Abdul Aziz, Fahd Bin, 209
Abelard, Peter, 243
Abu Ghraib prison, 281–282
Accident, 27, 45, 287
Accountability, 102–103, 127–128,
    130–131, 258
Accuracy, 113–114, 134–135, 258,
    265, 296
Accurate, 43, 86, 112–113, 129,
    183, 245, 276, 278
Accusation, 3, 104, 169, 180, 186,
    188–190, 200, 271, 276,
    285, 287
Action-reaction sequence, 28
Activation, 3
Adversaries, 5, 6, 49, 51, 53–54, 61,
    158–159, 169–170, 234,
    270–271
Afghanistan War, 168
Agence France Presse, 208
Agenda, 35
Al Nahian, Zayed Bin Sultan, 156
Al-Ahali, 208
Al-Ahram Weekly, 207–208, 282
Al-Arabi, 208
al-Douri, Mohammed, 164, 165, 210
Al-Jazeera, 105, 191, 206–207, 213
Allawi, Iyad, 3

Al-Manar, 288–289
Al-Qaeda, 116, 180–190, 270
Al-Sahhaf, Said, 164, 191, 196–197
Al-Usbou', 208
American administration, 3, 151,
    159, 160, 183, 294–295
American Society of Newspaper
    Editors, 129–130, 144,
    146, 258
Amin, Hossam Mohamed, 181
Analogic, 247
Analysis, 127–128, 130, 132
Analytic rationality, 31
Announcement, 2, 3, 46, 96, 183,
    191, 196, 209–211
Aquinas, Thomas, 243
Arab Cooperation Council (ACC),
    151, 191
Arab League, 156, 164–165, 196,
    198–199, 220
Arab World, 93, 151, 160, 173, 178,
    207–209, 290
ArabicNews.Com, 208, 209
Architecture, 226–229, 302–303
Aristotle, 243
Ascriptive, 102–104
Associated Press Managing Editors,
    129, 144
Assumption, 71